# THE CITY OF LIGHT

'Wrapped in a piece of "seventeenth-century silk", [the manu-script] was written in mediaeval Italian vernacular and was the account of a journey from Italy to China by one Jacob d'Ancona – a Jewish scholar-merchant who preceded Marco Polo by a few years. He puts Marco's prose in the shade . . .

'The journal moves from vivid descriptions of the places he visits, to philosophical contemplations of the Maimonidean type, to references to "Torah truth", to momentary crises of faith, to explorations of inner states (giving us, along the way, an under-standing of how mediaeval trade actually worked, insights into Jewish commercial activity and into the relationships between Jews, Muslims and Christians). One moment pious, orthodox and moralistic, the next all intelligent scepticism and rational curiosity about the world, Jacob d'Ancona was a complex man.

'There are storms, near shipwrecks, days of "twice-baked" heat in the deserts of Syria, until, at last, he reaches the City of Light – Zaitun, in southern China. It is his account of his months in this city that elevates the journal to a masterpiece . . .

'This vast and vigorous metropolis is in a ferment of social, political and cultural change. There is a new elite forming within the entrepreneurial nouveau riche, at loggerheads with the old Manderinate – a time not unlike our own. Jacob is greatly con-cerned with these conflicts and seeks out individuals and groups with whom to discuss them . . . [And] Jacob's intellectual curiosity takes him as far as the back streets of the underworld . . .

'This is too grand a book to do justice to in a short review. But its charm, for me, lies in the affection one cannot help but feel for the author – whoever he may be – and in the intimate quality of his narrative, so that the country of the past he described is not peopled by incomprehensible Others, but by ourselves'

Robyn Davidson, *The Times*

D1050521

'Seven hundred and twenty-six years ago, a learned Jewish merchant called Jacob set out from the Adriatic port of Ancona on a journey that would take him from Italy through Syria, the Persian Gulf, and India. He reached China before Marco Polo, and like the Venetian who followed him, resolved to write an account of his travels. Some time after his return to Italy in 1273, Jacob wrote a magisterial memoir, more than 400 pages long, called *The City of Light* . . .

'[It] describes an epic adventure across the deserts and on the high seas. It is far better literature than the book that Polo wrote with his cellmate Rustichello of Pisa. Although Christopher Columbus read *The Travels* for inspiration, he might have learned more from *The City of Light* . . .

'Jacob's book is the intensely personal recollection of a scholar who also happened to be a wealthy merchant, a man who knew as much about the wisdom of the rabbinical sages as he did about the value of the velvet, wool, gold, wire, mercury, linen, soap, wine and corn which he took with him to the Orient. At [the book's] heart is an unparalleled account of medieval Chinese society and manners seen through the eyes of a Western intellectual'

Matthew d'Ancona, *Sunday Telegraph*

*David Selbourne* is one of the few scholars who could have done justice to the translation and annotation of Jacob d'Ancona's many-faceted manuscript. He was born in London, the son of a doctor and the grandson of one of the greatest of modern rabbinical philosophers, Moshe Avigdor Amiel (1882–1945). He studied Latin and Greek at Manchester Grammar School and Jurisprudence at Balliol College, Oxford, where he was Winter Williams Law Scholar and Honorary Exhibitioner, also gaining the Jenkins Prize and Paton Studentship. He has been a British Commonwealth Fellow at the University of Chicago, Aneurin Bevan Memorial Fellow, Senior Research Fellow at the Centre for the Study of Developing Societies in New Delhi, and for two decades taught the history of ideas at Ruskin College, Oxford. He is the author of, among other books, a distinguished work of political philosophy, *The Principle of Duty* (1994), which was influenced by his study of Jacob d'Ancona's manuscript. He lives in Urbino in the Marche region of Italy.

## ALSO BY DAVID SELBOURNE

An Eye to India

An Eye to China

Through the Indian Looking-Glass

The Making of A Midsummer Night's Dream

Against Socialist Illusion: A Radical Argument

Left Behind: Journeys into British Politics

In Theory and in Practice:
Essays on the Politics of Jayaprakash Narayan (ed.)

A Doctor's Life:
The Diaries of Hugh Selbourne M.D., 1960–63 (ed.)

Death of the Dark Hero: Eastern Europe, 1987–90

The Spirit of the Age

Not an Englishman: Conversations with Lord Goodman

The Principle of Duty:
An Essay on the Foundations of the Civic Order

# THE
# CITY OF LIGHT

### JACOB D'ANCONA

TRANSLATED AND EDITED BY
## DAVID SELBOURNE

An *Abacus* Book

First published in Great Britain by
Little, Brown and Company 1997
Published by Abacus 1998

Copyright © David Selbourne 1997

The moral right of David Selbourne has been asserted.

All rights reserved.
No part of this publication may be reproduced, stored in a
retrieval system, or transmitted, in any form or by any
means, without the prior permission in writing of the
publisher, nor be otherwise circulated in any form of
binding or cover other than that in which it is published
and without a similar condition including this condition
being imposed on the subsequent purchaser.

Map by Alec Herzer

A CIP catalogue record for this book is
available from the British Library.

ISBN: 0 349 10895 1

Typeset in Adobe Garamond by M Rules
Printed and bound in Great Britain by
Clays Ltd, St Ives plc

Abacus
A Division of
Little, Brown and Company (UK)
Brettenham House
Lancaster Place
London WC2E 7EN

*Habent sua fata libelli*
Terence

# Acknowledgments

I should like to thank the owner of the manuscript of Jacob d'Ancona for giving me access to it for extended periods between September 1991 and June 1996, for permitting the publication of this translation, and for generously vesting the rights over the translation in me. I must also express my gratitude for many varieties of help and moral support during the course of my travails in particular to the late Eliezer Amiel, Dr Domenico Cossi, Matthew d'Ancona, Joseph Hassan, Boris Kaz, Maria Luisa Moscati Benigni, Dr Luigi Paci, Dr Gustavo Pesarin, Meir Posen, Carol Thomas and Professor Donald Thomas, as well as to many others too numerous to mention for their responses to my queries upon a hundred and one different matters. I owe great debts of gratitude, too, to my wife for her collaboration, intellectual and practical, in carrying this work forward, to Christopher Sinclair-Stevenson, to Philippa Harrison of Little, Brown and to Andrew Wille, whose skills and judgment informed many editorial decisions taken during the production of this book.

*David Selbourne, Urbino, 1997*

# Contents

BOHEMIA

Bruggia
(Bruges)

Paris

Marsiglia
(Marseilles)

Genoa

Firenze
Rome

Barcelona
in Arigone

Same
scale

Sea
of Azov

Continued above

Vinegia
Sinigaglia  Zara
(Senigallia)
Jesi  Ancona
(Iesi)
Rome
Brindisi

Ragusa
(Dubrovnik)

Corcyra

Ithaca

Zante

Kytheria

Creta

Patara

Rodi (Rhodes)

Famagusta

Mediterranean Sea

Tauris
(Tabris)

Cascara
(Kashgar)

BADASCIAN
(BADAKHSHAN)

San
Geovanni

Damascus

Jerusalem

Baudas
(Baghdad)

Isfahan

Through Abilene
by River Abania

R.
Euphrates

Damascus

Mt Hermon
R. Jordan

R. Aurano
(Wadi Hauran)

To
Bastra

Desert
of
Syria

CH
(KA

San
Giovanni d'Acri
(Acre)

Jerusalem

100 mls
140 kms

Alexandria

Fustat
(Cairo)

Bastra
(Basra)

Saraggi

Cormosa
(Bandar Abbas)

MAKRAN

Cius (Qus)

Ciusi (Quseir)

Medina

I.ef Cusam

Cambaett
(Cumbay)

GUJARAT

Ceneda

Mestre

Vinegia
(Venice)

Ferrara

Firenze
(Florence)

Lucca

Pisa

S. Angelo
in Vado

Arezzo

Siena

Camerino

Foligno

Zara

DALMATIA

Fano

Lor Campo

Fonte
Avellana

Ancona

Fiastra

Ascoli

Curzola (Korcula)

Zede (Jeddah)

Dahlak
I. Arch.

Cambaett
(Cumbay)

Mangial
(Mangalo)

Rome

200 mls
300 kms

Edente
(Aden)

HABESCIA
(ABYSSINIA)

Route
uncertain

Outward journey      Inward journey

(Suzhou)   Place names in brackets refer to modern names

'Towards.' Quotation from Jacob d'Ancona

Miles
100        250        500        750        1000

600        1200
Kilometres

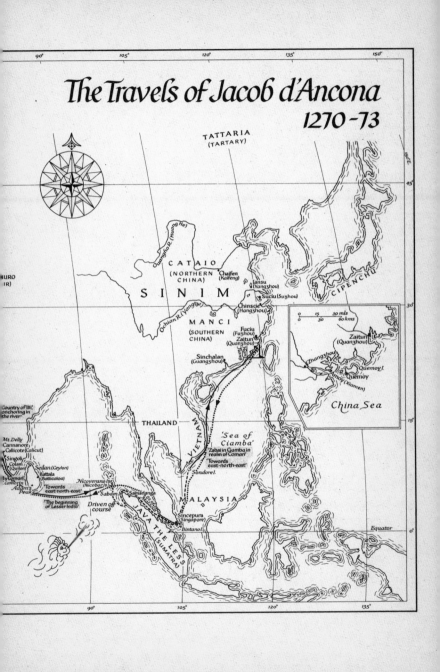

# The Travels of Jacob d'Ancona
## 1270-73

TATTARIA
(TARTARY)

CATAIO
(NORTHERN CHINA)

Quanho R. (Huang He)

Chaifen (Kaifeng)

Iansu (Yangzhou)

Suciu (Suzhou)

S I N I M

Ochian R. (Yangtze)

MANCI
(SOUTHERN CHINA)

Chinscie (Hangshou)

Fuciu (Fushou)

Zaitun (Quanzhou)

Sinchalan (Guangshou)

CIPENCHU

China Sea

Zaitun (Quanzhou)

0   15   30 mls
0   30   60 kms

Zhangshou

Quemoy I.
Quemoy
Emoy (Xiamen)

THAILAND

VIETNAM

'Sea of Ciamba'

Zabai in Ciamba in realm of Coman

'Towards east-north-east'

Sondore I.

Country of 'Illi', anchoring in the river'

Mt. Delly
Cannanore
Callicote (Calicut)

Singoli
Colam (Quilon)

Battala (Batticaloa)

Seilan (Ceylon)

Syloman
Comorin

Adam's Peak

'Towards east north-east'

'The beginning of Lesser India'

Nicoversano Isa (Nicobar Is)

Sabim

Saitarlanga

MALAYSIA

Driven off course

Sincepura (Singapore)

Bintan I.

JAVA THE LESS (SUMATRA)

Equator

MURO

90°    105°    120°    135°    150°

45°

30°

15°

0°

# Introduction

THE EXISTENCE AND POSSESSION, IN private hands, of the manuscript I have translated were first made known to me early in
1990 by a visitor to my home in Urbino. He was aware of my
interest in Judaica and declared that he had 'no trust' in disclosing to an Italian what he was prepared to disclose to me. I
was eventually (in December 1990) shown the work, which
was wrapped in a piece of seventeenth-century silk delicately
embroidered with chaplets of blue and pink flowers, similar in
design to one of the vestments of the Scrolls of the Law which
are kept in a cupboard of the town's synagogue, now disused
since fewer than half a dozen Jews remain.

Nevertheless, several months elapsed before I prevailed upon
the owner, who lives in the Italian Marche region and is not
himself a Jew, to let me examine and attempt to read the text in
his presence. But it was not until September 1991, after lengthy
discussions of the problems that would be involved in disclosing the manuscript's existence – for both its provenance and
rights of ownership over it are unclear – that I was able to begin
studying it closely (always at the owner's home), with a view to
its translation and publication.

Although I am fluent in modern Italian, I was unfamiliar
with mediaeval Italian vernacular, apart from having read Dante
with the aid of a crib years before, and I also had the task of

mastering the handwriting of the author, or scribe, of the work. Moreover, the owner changed his mind several times about the wisdom of permitting the book's existence to become known, while I, having been made aware that he would probably not permit the book's exact whereabouts to be identified during his lifetime, and that his heirs might do likewise, wrestled with my own doubts about translating a manuscript to which others would not have easy access, and even no access at all.

It was a difficult choice to make. But my overarching interest was in the content of the manuscript, and I eventually took the view that everyone else's interests would be best served by a faithful interim translation of the text into English, and by my keeping my word to the manuscript's owner. Although I have naturally come under pressure to reveal more, I do not intend to do so. It is both a matter of honour and of gratitude for an act of faith.

As I worked intermittently on the manuscript, first when I was cogitating the book which became *The Spirit of the Age* and later when I was planning *The Principle of Duty*, I became increasingly aware that I had an extraordinary find – a gift – in my hands, and a responsibility to make its content known whatever difficulties it might cause me. The fact that a Jewish scholar-merchant, Iacobbe (Jacob) d'Ancona, had preceded Marco Polo by a handful of years to the furthest Orient, leaving a brilliant account of his travels and experiences, was of course enough to drive my translation on; in particular, the astonishing description which he gives of the tribulations of the southern Chinese city of Zaitun, as Mongol conquest drew near, was an inspiration to me to continue.

But equally intriguing was the fact, or tradition, that the manuscript, so I was told, had 'remained hidden' within a local Jewish family 'for generations' long before it came into the hands of the present owner. Once I had succeeded in reading it through, I came to the clear conclusion that the principal ground for this was the manuscript's dangerous observations upon religious questions.

In inquisitorial times Jacob would have had good reason for his caution, a caution which, it seems, had been transmitted through the generations, so that even the manuscript's present non-Jewish owner was aware of it. (Local Jews were reminded of the need for such caution in 1553 when there was a public burning in Urbino of books owned by them.) Moreover, when the manuscript was written – probably during the last years of the thirteenth century or the first years of the fourteenth – theological debates in Italy between Christians and Jews had become more hostile and intimidatory towards the latter. A century later, in 1409, the faculty of arts at the University of Padua admitted Jews; Elijah del Medigo gave public lessons in philosophy there, and Pico della Mirandola (1463–94), the great Italian humanist, was among his pupils, Jewish thinkers playing a significant part in the Quattrocento Renaissance.

But in the previous century the aspersions against Christianity that Jacob's text contains, revealing a strong animus outspokenly expressed, would, if discovered, have caused him and his family great harm. It was as if a family taboo had remained attached to the object which I now held in my hands, and which related directly across the ages to ancient Jewish fears of Christian accusation of blasphemy and irreligion. Indeed, Jacob d'Ancona himself writes at the end of the manuscript, 'I fear that if all I have seen and written were to be made known, no faith would be put in me because of the marvellous things I have observed and recounted, and other parts would be considered a serious wrong.' It is thus likely that the book was well hidden, and if the manuscript is an early copy from Jacob's original, copied only by the most trusted of familiars.

Just as there were many travellers from Europe, and in particular from Italy, to the Near and Far East in the middle ages, so there are significant numbers of manuscripts, known and unknown, in Italian libraries – above all in the Vatican – recounting their tales. Their veracity as historians and geographers is often suspect; 'mediaeval' exaggerations are a commonplace, and there has even been doubt expressed as to whether Marco Polo, the most famous of the adventurers in the Orient, went to China at all.[1] Certainly Jacob d'Ancona, for all his own scepticism, cannot be wholly trusted in the matter of volumes and numbers, but in general he does not appear to be a victim of the Munchausen syndrome – the propensity in old travellers to gild every lily and multiply every total, and to invest himself with inordinate courage.

How he wrote the manuscript – that is how the record of his journey was kept, and how and in what circumstances he wrote it up – we can only guess. Marco Polo is said to have dictated the account of his journey to a cell-mate in Genoa, and not even in his own language, which stretches credulity for all the authenticity of its content. In the case of Jacob d'Ancona's manuscript, so much of which is given over to a detailed account of dialogues and debates in which he claims to have participated, it is clear from what he says of the role in Zaitun of his guide and interpreter Lifenli, for example, that some at least of the material on which the manuscript is based was derived from notes taken at the time and prepared for him by his faithful servant, to whom he gave a handsome reward on parting. Jacob declares that he understands the words of those who speak to him, 'through the mouth of a third'; he himself speaks 'through the tongue of another'. He orders Lifenli to 'make ready all, page by page, of the things which we had written', thus suggesting that they also worked *together* on materials Jacob would take with him from China on his return journey.

Yet it is plain, from first principles as well as from a detailed scrutiny of the content of the manuscript, that much of the text must have been elaborated at leisure in Italy, perhaps when Jacob had ceased his merchant activity and returned to his studies. (Indeed, at one point in the manuscript he declares, in Hebrew, 'May blessings be upon Him who guides my hand', the encomium of someone writing up his account after the event.) Jacob certainly must have kept something akin to a journal during his outward journey as well as in China, so meticulous (and accurate) are the dates of the Julian and Jewish calendars that he gives, and of the correspondences between them. But the lengthy reports of his exchanges on philosophical and other matters in China, although Lifenli appears always to be present, cannot be verbatim, not least because passages *in Hebrew* appear among his reported words which would not have been spoken at the time.

As to the hitherto unknown (or unrecorded) existence of Jacob d'Ancona's manuscript, for those who know Italy and the condition of its patrimony well, there can be little surprise. I myself do not doubt that, along with so many other Italian works of art, this is merely one 'lost' rarity among the rest; works stolen, 'diverted', traded or, as I believe in this case, merely held in private hands without the slightest knowledge of it divulged beyond the immediate circle of the owner. Moreover, that an owner – from fear of its confiscation, theft or loss – should be coy about disclosing a possession is also reasonable in Italian circumstances.

In the last few years, and choosing at random, I have seen a signed presentation copy of Baldassare Castiglione's *Il Cortegiano* (1528) – written at the Renaissance court of Urbino – mouldering at risk in an out-of-the-way corner of the Marche; have examined part of a synagogue's ancient archive, kept in cardboard boxes at the home of one of its congregants; and have found rare old letters discarded inside the prayer-stalls of another synagogue in the Marche. In December 1996 I attended a 'world première' of 'lost' lute music of the court of the Dukes of Urbino which had been 'discovered' in a manuscript on the shelves of the Biblioteca Oliveriana in the Adriatic coastal town of Pesaro; the concert included works by the Montefeltro (and Medici) court-musician and dancing-master, Giuglielmo Ebreo, or William the Jew (1497–1543).

The errant work of Jacob d'Ancona has its own context.

The manuscript, bound in creased and discoloured vellum, is 25.5 cm tall and 19.5 cm wide, and contains 280 leaves, written for the most part on both sides of each page. It is written on clean, fine paper in a small but careful and usually clear running italic hand, although with quite a large number of deletions, emendations and marginal comments, some in a different hand from that of the main text. There is an average of forty-seven lines of writing per page. The many words and phrases in the text that are in Hebrew are in a practised hand, and are almost certainly in the same hand as that of the main body of the work. The text is undecorated throughout, has no title, and has no divisions into books or chapters. No name of a scribe is given. At the foot of its last page, in a different hand and differently coloured ink from that of the main body of the text, the name 'Gaio Bonaiuti' is written.

The fact that the manuscript is written on paper (although bound in parchment) arguably points to a fourteenth-century date, and therefore after the lifetime of its author, who tells us that he was born in 1221. Paper was already in use among merchants for their letters in the early thirteenth century, and was imported into Europe from China and Muslim countries even earlier. But it was only towards the end of the thirteenth century that it began to be manufactured in Italy (including by Jews). Indeed, the paper of the manuscript may have come from Fabriano, which is a short distance from Ancona and where paper began to be manufactured between 1268 and 1279; it would be somewhat fanciful to assert, without evidence, that it was written by Jacob on paper he had himself brought from China, although it remains a possibility, since the paper is without distinctive watermark.

That the work is in the vernacular Italian, or *volgare*, rather than in Latin, may raise a presumption – but no more – that the text was not written by Jacob d'Ancona in his own hand, but was a translation (perhaps from a Hebrew original) into the more accessible vernacular, in order to meet a secret demand. However, it should be pointed out that Latin was in any case generally eschewed by learnèd Jews – although there are also passages in Latin in the manuscript – it being considered the alien language of the Church. Moreover, the oldest example of the written vernacular in Italy dates back to AD 960; and as early as the eleventh and twelfth centuries was gradually coming into usage.

Hence, I retain an open mind about whether the manuscript was written in Jacob's own lifetime, but am inclined, perhaps from wishful thinking, to believe that it was, and is in his own hand, from the egregious mixture of languages (Italian, Hebrew and Latin, with some Arabic and Greek words in their original scripts) employed, and which point away from a later copyist or translator. If the manuscript was written by Jacob himself, it is unlikely to be of much later date than 1290, when he would have been nearly seventy years old.

There are other possible clues in the text itself which suggest an early date for the first writing of the manuscript. One is a reference to 'the late earthquake which fell upon us', which occurs in an undoubtedly re-worked and elaborated account given by Jacob of what he claims to have said in Zaitun when addressing its elders. There were damaging earthquakes in Ancona in 1269 and 1279, the first in the year preceding Jacob's departure and the second when he had been back in Italy for six years.

A second, more obscure, clue to a date for the writing of the manuscript relates to the word *arguni*, which Jacob uses for mixed-race offspring of Chinese and Europeans in Zaitun. An Italianised version of a word of Tartar origin, it is unlikely to have been current in Zaitun when Jacob was there; the city fell to the Tartars after his departure in 1277. I would surmise that he came to know this word through subsequent merchant-contact with Mongol China, and that this too points to a date in the early 1280s for the writing of the manuscript.

The signature, 'Gaio Bonaiuti', is most certainly of later date, and suggests an important clue to the vicissitudes of the manuscript. For a 'Gaio Bonaiuti' (the surname is Jewish) is recorded as conducting a bank in Ancona with his partners until 1430, and is subsequently known to have been involved, with other Jews, in setting up a bank in Urbino in 1433. I surmise that

Bonaiuti was a lineal descendant of Jacob's wife, whose name is given in the manuscript as Sara Bonaiuta of Jesi; Jacob also refers in the manuscript to his brother-in-law Isaac de Bonaiuta, and to a cousin Eliezer Bonaiuto whom he visits in Acre. The surnames Bonaiuta, Bonaiuto and Bonaiuti are known among the Jews of Ancona and the region of the Marche to this day, and variant spellings and slight modifications of names (as in singular and plural forms) are common in the histories of Italian families.[2]

It is thus possible that the book originally found its way from Ancona to Urbino – a distance of about fifty miles – through the Bonaiuta family. The signature was, of course, a further hostage to fortune, and if of mid-fifteenth-century date would have furnished additional ground for the continued hiding of the manuscript within the family which possessed it.

For in this dark period, as we have already seen, books owned by Jews might always be put in jeopardy. Thus a decree of 11 November 1593, issued by Duke Guidobaldo II of Urbino, ordered the confiscation and destruction of Talmudic texts in the city, whether in the possession of Christians or Jews. They were given eight days in which to produce these works to the Lieutenant of Urbino so that they might be 'immediately burned publicly in the piazza'. The sanctions for failure to obey were severe for a Jew, to be 'hanged by the neck' and to lose all his possessions; for a Christian, to be 'perpetually banned from all the territory of the Duke and his goods to be confiscated'. In both cases, an accuser who disclosed the presence of such books to the authorities was to receive one-quarter of the victim's confiscated possessions.[3]

As I have indicated, the language of the manuscript is predominantly that of the vernacular Italian of the thirteenth and perhaps fourteenth centuries: it is basically educated Tuscan – Jacob tells us that his grandfather was a Florentine rabbi – but with some Venetian words and spellings, and occasional phrases which can be identified as the mediaeval Jewish dialect of Ancona. Apart from phrases, words and a few extended passages in Latin, there are many passages and words in Hebrew script, mostly of Biblical and Talmudic provenance. In addition, the work contains many pious invocations and turns of phrase, as well as peculiarities of language and sentiment, which, whether written in Italian or Hebrew, can clearly be recognised to be Jewish or Hebraic.

Nearly all the direct quotations made by Jacob from the Old Testament and the Talmud are in Hebrew in the manuscript. I refer in more detail to these matters in an appendix, pp. 462–70.

It is not impossible that the manuscript might once have been in the famous Renaissance library of the dukedom of Urbino, and in particular in the collection formed by Duke Federico of Montefeltro (1422–82), whose court was one of the most brilliant of the age. It was a library – most of which is now in the Vatican – which contained a fabulous treasury of manuscript works in Aramaic, Syriac, Greek, Latin, Italian and Hebrew; its librarian, from about 1477, was a Jew 'greatly learnèd in Latin', Lorenzo Abstemio. Among the Hebrew texts were bibles, works of Talmudic scholarship, rabbinical commentaries on Averroes,[4] Avicenna[5] and Aristotle, and such works as those of the Jewish philosopher Maimonides (1135–1204) on medicine, on science and on love. (There was also a folio manuscript on vellum, bound in red leather, described as 'Against the Jews'; this may have been Augustine's *Tractatio Adversus Iudaeos.*)

There were mediaeval manuscript versions of Artistotle and Dante, of Homer and the Koran, of dictionaries and psalteries; and works on horse-breeding, on gardening, on lions, on the removal of stains, on chess-playing, on the habits of adolescents and on the immortality of the soul. There were also manuscript books of travels, including that of the Friulian friar Odorigo to India and China, a journey made fifty years after that of Jacob d'Ancona.

On the death in April 1631 of the sixth and last Duke of Urbino, Francesco Maria II, the ducal territories passed to the Papal State, but the library itself had been specifically willed to the *comune* of Urbino. An inventory of its contents was therefore drawn up in 1632 by Flaminio Catelano, Urbino's librarian, and attested by the town's public notary, Francesco Scudacchi. It contains tantalising references to anonymous 'bundles of diverse writings' and even 'various secrets' (*secreti varii*, item no. 1418). Moreover, it is known that after the 1632 inventory had been made books began to disappear from the collection, hastening the transfer to Rome in 1657, during the papacy of Alexander VII, of what remained.[6]

The transfer of the library is resented to this day in Urbino, not least because of the grounds then adduced to justify it, which are still considered spurious. 'The people of Urbino,' declares Pallavicini Sforza, maintaining the tradition of papal contempt for the local thievery, 'were without culture and neglectful custodians'[7] of the ducal library.

Whether the manuscript copy of *The City of Light* was one of the books that disappeared from the ducal collection between 1631 and 1657, or whether it remained concealed within the Jewish community of Urbino – which was sealed into its own ghetto in the town from 1633 – cannot be known. But it is certain that the eclectic tastes and humanist sympathies of Duke Federico were broad enough, in principle, to have admitted Jacob d'Ancona's book to his shelves some two centuries before.

Apart from the scale, interest and general accuracy of Jacob d'Ancona's observations of the world, and his extraordinary involvement in the affairs of a Chinese city during the Southern Sung dynasty, the text is of importance as a rare work of mediaeval Jewish autobiographical writing. Mediaeval Jewish historiography – as distinct from philosophical and religious writings – is thin indeed. Even thinner is that of personal testimony of the kind found in this manuscript.

We have, for example, the twelfth-century *Travels* of Rabbi Benjamin of Tudela, twelfth-century merchants' letters discovered in a Cairo synagogue, and the *Kitab al-Mu'tabar* (or 'The Book of what has been established by Personal Reflection') by the Jewish philosopher-physician Abu al-Barakat of Baghdad, who flourished between 1160 and 1170, and who became a convert to Islam late in his life.

But a scholarly Jewish Marco Polo of the late thirteenth century, who may have been both a rabbi and a physician as well as a merchant, and with a secular interest in political disputation, is another matter.

Thirteenth-century China was not known only to missionary friars, the Polos, and Muslim traders from the Levant. I have already referred to the Spanish rabbi, Benjamin of Tudela, who preceded Jacob d'Ancona to the Orient by one hundred years, leaving a diary of his journey, written in Hebrew, which was apparently completed in Castile in 1173, and first published in Constantinople in 1543. It is assumed that, like Jacob, he travelled as a merchant, reaching 'Khuzistan' – identified variously in south-western Iran, on the Indian Ocean, or on the frontiers of China – in a journey which seems to have taken thirteen years. Later, in the fifteenth century, there were the Italian Jews Elijah of Ferrara, a Talmudist and traveller, and at the end of the century Meshullam of Volterra, both of them rabbi-merchants.

The list of non-Jewish Italians who knew the Orient in mediaeval times, and wrote of it, is of course much longer. Plano Carpini was in Karakorum in about 1246. The Venetian Marco Polo set out for China in 1271, the year following Jacob d'Ancona's departure, reaching the Mongol (or 'Tartar') court of Kublai Khan at Shangdu – the fabled Xanadu – in mid-1275, two years after Jacob's safe return to Italy; in 1292, after serving the Mongol conquerors of Sung China as an administrator and envoy, he embarked upon his return journey to Italy from the Zaitun that Jacob knew.

The Franciscan Giovanni di Monte Corvino (1247–1328) sailed from Hormuz to Zaitun in 1291, later being appointed archbishop of Khanbalik (Beijing) by Pope Clement V; the already mentioned friar of Friuli, Odorigo, or Odoric, was in China from 1324 to 1327 and visited Zaitun also; while another renowned Italian friar who left a record of his travels, Giovanni di Marignolli, visited China in the 1340s.

Of Muslim traveller-writers in the mediaeval period who knew India and China there were many, including Rashid al-Dīn (1247–1317), a Jew by birth who converted to Islam and who was a contemporary of Jacob d'Ancona, Wassaf, who was in China in about 1300, Abulfeda (1273–1331), and perhaps best known Ibn Battuta (1304–77), who again disembarked at, and later set sail from, the port of Zaitun more than half a century after Jacob d'Ancona had found himself caught up in its affairs.[8]

Although I at times found the manuscript-hand, superscriptions and marginal additions difficult to follow, and may have made some errors – there were occasions when alternative readings were possible – I believe I have rendered the text accurately.

It is not subdivided in the manuscript into parts or chapters, and the divisions here are mine, as is the title of the work itself.

I have called the author *Jacob* d'Ancona; he refers to himself as 'Iacobbe', 'Giacobbe' and 'Iacob'. In other instances I have followed his spellings of personal names and place-names and his transliterations of the Chinese names he heard. Where they can be identified, or an informed guess can be made as to what they were, they turn out to be rather accurately reported, albeit in transcriptions into the nearest Italian sounds.

Indeed, where there is corroborative evidence of Jacob's account, as of known historical facts, names, places and dates, the accuracy of his record is on the whole impressive. However, from the editor's (and reader's) point of view there are also some excesses in the text, as in his religious vindications of Jewish belief and philosophical disquisitions which require too much knowledge of the mediaeval context. Here I have made cuts. I have also cut some of his pious exclamations and epithets where they unduly burdened the translation.

Where Jacob quotes a passage or phrase from the Bible, and I (or my helpers) have recognised it as such, I have generally not translated it literally from the Hebrew (or Italian), but have adopted the authorised translation of the King James Bible.

Where he cites opinions of the rabbinical sages, as from the Mishnah, I have been wholly reliant upon others in tracing their sources and making the translations, since they are invariably written in Hebrew.

I also do not conceal that I was so often taken up by the spirit and language of the original Italian text that (as often happens in translating from the Greek and Latin classics), I fell into certain archaisms in my translation also. Some of these translations may irritate, but I have in general retained them on revision as being my own response to the text, and because I did not wish to violate its rhythms, colours and word-orders with modern usages remote in spirit from those of the original. I have also annotated the text wherever I thought it helpful.

## CHAPTER TWO

# It was in the year 1270…

AGED FORTY-NINE IN APRIL 1270, 'Giacobbe ben [son of] Salomone d'Ancona, grandson of rabbi Israel di Firenze' tells us little of himself, but that little is revealing. Thus he describes himself more than once as being of a 'noble rabbinical lineage', a proud self-description which lends some strength to my belief that he was a rabbi himself, although he nowhere says so in terms. He merely refers to himself as 'pious and learnèd' (*'om pio e dotto*'), but his knowledge of rabbinics was profound.

Moreover, there are three moments in the text when the presumption of his being a rabbi gains ground, without its being certain. First, he remarks on the consequences 'if a rabbi should counsel them [sc. idolaters] to pray to God'; has he had experience of this as a rabbi himself, or is it second-hand? Next, and more persuasive, when he is among Jews in a southern Indian port, he reports that 'the young men, knowing of my lineage' – not, however, his status as a rabbi himself – 'addressed many questions to me concerning the Torah and the opinion of the sages'; an unlikely event if he were not a rabbi, or, at least, had not had some rabbinical training, as I suspect. Thirdly, at another point, he declares roundly (to a rabbi) that certain prohibitions 'need not be followed in our synagogues', a declaration unfitting for anyone who had no rabbinical authority himself.

Was he also a doctor? Here the evidence that he was,

although inconclusive, is equally strong, or stronger. Certainly not in doubt is that he had medical knowledge. He eats fruit 'so that my kidneys be kept healthy and my water clean'; he seeks to arrest a female servant's 'flux'; he inspects his excrement for signs of his own illness; more significant still, he examines 'the eyes, tongue and pulses' of another sick servant, and gives instructions to an apothecary for a particular 'salve' to be made up for his own 'sores'. He also remarks that in China he had 'much discourse' with local sages 'upon medicine, philosophy and other things'.

It was in the year 1270 ...

It is not impossible that he was both a rabbi and a doctor of medicine; there are many precedents for it among Jewish scholars of the time, and to be simultaneously a merchant is also known. Of himself he justly says that he was 'no simple merchant', and plainly has the intellectual and moral confidence of a man of parts, God 'having opened my mind at an early age', as he puts it.

As to his appearance, there are stray references. More than once he refers to his 'grey beard'; he is described by another, in a dispute, as having 'dark eyes and the nose of a hawk'. We also observe him, tantalisingly, in a self-description, as wearing some kind of striking hat and robe which cause the Chinese to stand aside at his approach.

Of his place of birth and childhood education we know nothing. Of this, all that is certain is that he was the son, perhaps the eldest son, of a Jewish merchant of Ancona who was himself most likely of Florentine origin; indeed there were close mercantile ties between Florence and Ancona in the twelfth and thirteenth centuries, Ancona serving as the Adriatic outlet for Tuscan wares.

The fact that the language of the manuscript is largely Tuscan (see appendix on Jacob's Language) cannot in itself confirm that Jacob was educated as a child in Florence – perhaps with a view to a rabbinical career and under his grandfather's aegis – since it is not finally clear whether the language of the manuscript is Jacob's original work. Jacob himself spoke Hebrew, Arabic (as he tells us) and Italian, was sufficiently learnèd in Latin to use it intermittently in his manuscript in a scholarly way, and plainly had some knowledge of Greek. He may, judging by a remark he makes in passing, have also spoken Persian.

Of the few facts bearing upon the identity of Jacob d'Ancona that we have, one other is of the greatest significance: his passing reference to 'Jacob ben Abba Mari Anatoli' as 'my teacher in Naples'. Here, a world of identification opens up as to Jacob d'Ancona's intellectual background. For there can be no doubt at all that this is Jacob Anatoli (or Anatolio) (1194–1256), who was a follower of Maimonides (Mose ben Maimon, 1135–1204), the renowned rabbi, humanist and doctor of medicine, and author of *Guide to the Perplexed* (1190).

Anatoli – like his master a physician, Aristotelian philosopher and rabbi, as well as a mathematician – played a large part in disseminating Maimonidean teachings in Provence and Italy; translated works of logic and astronomy from Arabic into Hebrew; had close contact with the Christian intellectual world; and is known to have been present, with other Jewish savants, at the court and university of Frederick II in Naples in the 1240s, when Jacob would have been in his early twenties.

Described by some modern scholars as a 'rationalist' and even more fancifully as a 'thirteenth-century liberal', Anatoli's influence on Jacob's own philosophical views – which he gives us at length – can perhaps be discerned. For there is in Jacob an unusual combination of piety and intelligent scepticism, rational curiosity about the world and conventional moral orthodoxy, which he may have got from his master in Naples. Thus, there is a strong recoil in him from astrology, a recoil rare among both Christians and Jews at the time, but which marks out Jacob as himself a follower of the Maimonidean school. His frequently expressed hostility to superstition and idolatry is of related stamp.

Jacob cannot however be described as a 'free-thinker', a sceptic, though he often seems to be; his proofs for the existence of God are typical of the 'advanced' scholasticism of his time, and were shared by Jewish, Muslim and Christian Aristotelians. Yet, It was in the year 1270 ... despite his pietistic observations and continuous deference to 'Torah truth', in his discussson of the natural world he often adopts a 'more modern' materialistic, or pre-scientific, position against the cabbalists, neo-Platonists and others who 'speak too arcanely of the created world', as he puts it in one memorable passage. 'A man,' he declares, 'must swim in the great sea of being whether the Light of God shine upon him or not, and whether he be Christian, Saracen or Jew.'

This kind of stance, which would have been regarded as extremely radical by orthodox Talmudists – although perhaps more acceptable to Maimonideans – must surely have been developed in Jacob during his time in Naples. Frederick II of Hohenstaufen (1194–1250), Holy Roman Emperor from 1220 until his deposition in 1245 at the Council of Lyons, had established an academy, or university, in Naples in 1224. He showed a deep interest in Jewish learning, inviting to Naples many of the leading scholars of the day, Jews among them, some of whom lectured in Hebrew. Eventually to fall out with the Papacy, to be condemned as a heretic and to be defeated in battle, Frederick, himself a man of sceptical spirit, made of his Neapolitan court in its heyday a great centre of learning. Among the sages whom he gathered around him, and befriended, was Michael Scott (Scotus), scientist, philosopher and astrologer, translator of Aristotle from Arabic into Latin, and famous in his day as a soothsayer and prophet. Frederick II died at the age of fifty-six, but the academy he founded lived on; Aquinas (1227–74) taught theology there after 1259. In addition to Anatoli, Moses ibn Tibbon, one of the most formidable Jewish translators of classical Greek and Arabic philosophical and scientific works into Hebrew, was present at Naples in 1244–5. The grandson of the 'noble' Florentine rabbi, so it would seem, was among the circle of students who sat at the feet of these scholars.

More generally, throughout Provence, Italy and Spain, this was a period of intense questioning about the nature of God

and the created world – reflected in Jacob's manuscript specu-
lations – in which Jewish, Muslim and Christian scholars and
divines took part, at best together as when an enlightened ruler
such as Frederick II invited discourse between them. For Jewish
scholars the principal contemporary subjects of intellectual
debate concerned proofs of the existence of God; the unity and
non-corporeality of God; the nature of the universe and its creation and composition; the nature of the soul, its faculties, and
its relation with the body; the nature of miracles; and the rec-
onciliation of scriptural truth with the then new forms of
understanding of the world being provided by speculation
(including mathematical speculation) and early scientific experiment in astronomy and physics.

There are obvious traces – even if sometimes no more than as
asides – in Jacob d'Ancona's manuscript of his interest, occa-
sionally a profound interest, in such questions. Philosophical
speculation and intellectual exchange among the learnèd Jews of
southern Europe, who might be men of affairs and merchants as
well as rabbinical scholars, were intense and widespread in his
day. Translations (especially of Aristotle and other classics of
Greek philosophy and science) into Hebrew and Arabic, and of
Hebrew and Arabic texts into Latin, Provençal and probably
vernacular Italian too, circulated widely. In particular, transmis-
sion of such learning, as in the teaching of rabbinics, was most
commonly from a master to a circle of pupils.

In addition, it is not surprising, as I have suggested, that the
young man who had studied in Naples in early manhood
should be the Jewish merchant of Ancona in his adult years.
The great Maimonides himself had been a gem merchant who
traded with India, although he left his younger brother, David,
to do the travelling on his behalf. Indeed, Maimonides' moving
lament – dating from about 1170 and found in the Cairo
Genizah synagogue-hoard of manuscripts – upon the drowning
of his brother reveals the extent to which the merchant life and
the scholarly life were interwoven in mediaeval Jewry. 'He
drowned in the Indian Sea,' Maimonides mourns, 'carrying

much money belonging to me, to him and to others ... He grew up on my knees, he was my brother, he was my student; he traded on the markets and earned, and I could safely stay at home ... Now, all joy has gone ... whenever I see his handwriting or one of his letters, my heart turns upside down.'[1]

It was in the year 1270 ...

Hence, when Jacob himself regrets, on his departure from Ancona for the Orient, that he must leave his studies as well as his family, his is a recognisable (albeit rather extraordinary by other standards) mediaeval Jewish persona: that of the scholar-merchant, at home equally in the spice trade as in discussion upon the nature of the soul.[2]

However, there are also more than a few traces in Jacob's manuscript of the somewhat naive autodidact, even allowing for the limited nature of mediaeval knowledge upon many subjects. Not all of his observations are those of the finished scholar. This leads me to surmise that his studies may have been interrupted and that he was claimed by the merchant life in Ancona – perhaps in dutiful rescue of his father's unsuccessful enterprises – with his scholarly ambitions unfulfilled.

Finally, his tantalisingly brief reference to 'my friend Hillel ben Samuel' suggests significant acquaintance with leading Italian Jewish scholars of his day. For this 'friend', given the context of the reference to him, may well have been Rabbi Hillel ben Samuel of Verona (1220–c.1295), a notable follower of Maimonides who studied rabbinics at Barcelona and medicine at Montpellier, and who was in Naples himself in 1254, doubtless after Jacob's own student days were past.

The historian of mediaeval Ancona is handicapped by an almost complete lack of the early archival sources.[3] Municipal acts and laws are extant only from 1378, as are documents relating to the granting of commercial licences to merchants, and in which one might have found traces of the activities of Salomone and Jacob d'Ancona. The harbour authorities' statutes and rules are also available only from the end of the fourteenth century. It is certain, too, that the mediaeval Jewish community had its own rules for merchants, religious court decisions on trading and other questions, synagogue papers and so on, but nothing survives for the thirteenth century.

But known from many other sources is the substantial growth, from the first half of the twelfth century, of Ancona's economic prosperity, mostly derived from foreign trade. In the middle ages it was, with Venice – whose fame and splendour have overshadowed it – the most important Adriatic port of Italy, with a scale of overseas mercantile activity and a degree of freedom in its external relations which have been neglected by historians. Like Venice, it lacked a rich agricultural hinterland, and, like Venice, it was therefore dependent on its port for imports of food, for example cereals from Apulia, which were brought in by sea.

The name of Ancona is taken from the Greek work for an elbow, *ankon*, describing the shape of its natural harbour. Founded in 390 BC by Dionysius of Siracusa, it was the port of disembarkation for Trajan's legions in his campaigns against the Dacians. It was sacked twice by the Saracens, in AD 840 and 850 – to which Jacob makes passing reference – and as early as AD 996 it was called a *civitas*, or city. Long under Byzantine influence, it was a thorn in the side of Venice, both as a rival port and centre of political and commercial relations with the Byzantine empire. By 1135, it is known to have been a thriving port with its own communal administration,[4] successfully resisting sieges – including by Emperor Frederick Barbarossa[5] – which aimed to destroy its political independence.

As its prosperity and strength grew, it minted its own coinage (the *agontano*), and in 1220, the year before Jacob's birth, extended the city walls. But at the same time rivalry with Venice increased for the domination of the Adriatic, while the efforts of the Church to bring Ancona under papal dominion also became more intense. Between 1228 and 1231, when Jacob was a boy, there were several unsuccessful attempts by the Venetian fleet to blockade the port, as Venice sought to turn the whole Adriatic into its fiefdom. Despite such pressures, the thirteenth century was a period of influence and prosperity for the city.

It was in the year 1270 ...

Steering its own course in the further struggles between Frederick II – patron of Jacob's teacher in Naples – and Pope Innocent IV, it was sedulously courted by the Church for its crucial strategic position, much more favourable than that of Venice, and for its thriving commercial relations with the Greek and Muslim worlds. In such relations, the Jews of Ancona (Jacob's father among them) must have played a significant role; we know, for instance, that Salomone traded with the ports of the Black Sea, for Jacob tells us so.

In the course of the thirteenth century, the Church's influence over the often recalcitrant city grew. There are bitter references in the manuscript, which probably reflect a wider hostility in Ancona as a whole, to the pope's grasping legates in the city. (At one stage, Ancona refused to pay an annual tribute to the Curia.) The complex struggle of the city to preserve its political independence from the Church, even while being allied with it, and its flourishing commerce, also go some way towards explaining the relatively favourable position of the Jews in Ancona, at least as judged by Jacob's account. There was leverage, as well as an attractive commercial prospect, in the city's status. It might also be surmised that the pride of his city in the face of superior powers influenced Jacob in his own views on the tribulations of the city of Zaitun, helping to make him such a bold interlocutor in the affairs of another independent port city on the far side of the world.

At the time of Jacob's journey, Ancona had succeeded in maintaining and defending most of its independent commercial rights and had retained its powers over the operations of the port. With unusual skill it had refused to cede such rights to the Church, while continuing throughout the century to insist upon its political autonomy in other respects.

In Cyprus, on the island of Chios, in Constantinople, in Trebizond, in Acre (as Jacob confirms), in Romania and in other places it had its own colonies, or trading settlements of

Ancona citizens, and its consuls.[6] Pilgrims flowed through the port to the Holy Land; it was the principal trading port of central Italy, shipping out goods – including wine, grain and olive oil – from Arezzo, Florence, Perugia and Siena to southern Italy, Dalmatia, the Levant and beyond; into the port came the foodstuffs the city required, as well as wool and animal skins from Dalmatia, copper, silver and lead from Bosnia, and oriental spices and cloths. It was thus a centre both of local and long-distance trade, its volumes of business less than those of Venice, Genoa or Pisa but nevertheless substantial. There seems also to have been a trade in slaves, to which Jacob makes a brief (and slighting) reference of great interest.

Finally, the population in Ancona in 1270, when Jacob set sail, I estimate to have been between 15,000 and 20,000. In the *Liber de Obsidione Ancone*, whose writing can be dated between 1198 and 1201, the mediaeval historian Magister Boncompagno da Signa (1170–1240) gives a figure of '10,000' for Ancona's population in 1173, 'a large part of which,' he says, 'lived by trade and navigation'.[7] Whatever the true figure, it would have increased significantly thereafter, in a period of prosperity and expansion. By 1354, a half-century after Jacob's time, the *Descriptio Marchie* gives a figure of '7,000 hearths' for Ancona, which at five persons per hearth, the ratio generally in use among historians of mediaeval Europe, produces a total of 35,000 persons.

The Inquisition, with its purposes of discovering and prosecuting 'heretics' and instituted at the beginning of the thirteenth century – some twenty years before Jacob's birth – bore with great and long-lasting, but variable, severity upon the Jews of Europe. They were seen by the promoters of the Inquisition not only as 'perfidious' heretics themselves, guilty of deliberate unbelief in the divinity of Christ, but as seducers of others to heresy, especially in their capacity as intimates of the Devil. They were even called *filii diaboli*, Sons of the Devil.[8]

At the Fourth Lateran Council in 1215 – attended by more than 1,200 delegates from the Christian world (six years before Jacob's birth) – a militant policy towards the Jews was inaugurated, under Pope Innocent III, in the name of strengthening the papacy and striking against 'Jewish perfidy'. New Church taxes were to be imposed on the Jews and they were henceforth to be excluded from public office, 'since it is absurd that anyone who blasphemes against Christ should exercise power over a Christian'. In addition, paragraph 68 of the decree of 11 November 1215 declares that 'whereas in certain provinces of the Church the difference in their clothes sets the Jews apart from the Christians, in certain other lands there has arisen such confusion that no differences are noticeable ... therefore we decree that these people ... shall be easily distinguishable.'

The Church ordinance that the Jew (and Muslim) should wear a conspicuous badge was not always enforced, or its intent was evaded, as by wearing it on the inside of a cloak or jacket where it could not be seen; this was the case in Ancona, as Jacob tells us. Bribes might also be paid to avoid the incubus of it, or, in some places, Jews might be permitted to discard it on long journeys. In Italy, sympathetic local rulers, and even prelates, might waive the rule entirely. Hence, in 1257, when Jacob was in his mid-thirties, the Lateran decree was repeated in a papal bull of Alexander IV which, it seems, led to greater stringency in the application of the rule.

The sign – Jacob calls it the 'sign of Cain' – imposed upon the Jews varied from Christian country to country, and even from Italian city to city. In Rome, after the papal bull of 1257, it was a yellow circle fixed to a man's hat or a woman's veil; after 1310, a more prominent red cloak, while Jewish women were obliged to wear two blue bands, or *strisce*, on their veils. Or again, elsewhere, the entire hat would have to be distinct, and generally either red or yellow.

But the wearing of a badge or outward sign – whose effect, intended or otherwise, successful or not, was to shame and to make vulnerable as well as to distinguish the wearer – was one thing. For a man of devotion and learning such as Jacob d'Ancona, the anathemas pronounced during his lifetime against the Talmud were another. Thus in 1232 – when Jacob was eleven and approaching the age of his formal introduction into the Jewish community as an adult – the Dominican order of mendicant preachers was entrusted by Pope Gregory IX with the task not only of conducting 'inquisitions' in Italy, Spain and Portugal but of seeking out, censoring and burning books written in Hebrew. Four years later, when Jacob was fifteen and doubtless a fully participant member of his faith, the Dominicans persuaded the pope to condemn the Talmud itself as a work of 'blasphemy and sacrilege'.

To judge the actual effect of such decrees, and of the spirit which they expressed, upon particular communities and individuals in thirteenth-century Italy is difficult; Jacob's exceptional testimony on this is as valuable as it is rare. Nor was there consistency in the impact of such anathemas, not least because of Italy's anomalous position within mediaeval Christendom. The heart of the papacy, it was also a land of increasingly independent communes and of warring noble fiefdoms – whose conflicts might aid as well as imperil the Jews – and a land in which Jewish settlement predated the Christian era itself.

The Jews of Italy, and especially of Rome, were indigenous inhabitants, not migrants. In some cities, and under some local rulers, they would have been seen by their neighbours in Jacob's time to have a presumptive right to be where they were after more than 1,500 years of uninterrupted settlement.[9] In some cities, there are grounds to believe, they were treated as citizens *de facto*, if not *de jure*.[10] Indeed, the Fourth Lateran Council's prohibition upon the holding of public office by Jews suggests that in some places they did hold such office; and, as Jacob's manuscript indicates, a Jew might, for all the papal bulls, and especially in Italy, be a prominent and established figure.[11]

I doubt, however, that an Italian Jew in the mediaeval period could have been a fully entitled city burgess, since he was unable to swear to Christian oaths. But that the Jewish communities of mediaeval Italy were a settled and significant presence, whatever odium might be shown towards them, is clear from the evidence that many mediaeval Italian cities in addition to Rome and particularly in the north – Lucca, Pavia, Padua and others – were centres of Talmudic learning.

The truth appears to be, in fact, that mediaeval popes and prelates, notwithstanding their often cruel and discriminatory decrees *urbi et orbi*, generally opposed the committing of excesses against 'their' Jews in Italy. Moreover, Italian Jews in Jacob's time, although they were predominantly urban, could own land and were to be found in agriculture and viniculture, as in the region (or 'march') of Ancona. They lived in small towns and even in hamlets, as well as in the larger cities. But, above all, they were engaged in commerce – including large-scale foreign trading ventures, as Jacob d'Ancona's manuscript reveals – and artisanal activity, especially in cloth-work, dyeing and silk manufacture. Nevertheless, special local taxes and prohibitions (quite apart from the perennial Jewish fear of a drastic change in their fortunes) always dogged their steps, in Italy as elsewhere; in Venice, for example, an old regulation forbade – at least on paper – the carrying of 'Jewish merchandise' in vessels belonging to Venetian Christian owners.

To be set against this familiar form of discrimination is what we can see of the position of Jacob d'Ancona. He himself complains that he is 'without title of fame in his own land' yet has contacts with the prior of the monastery of Fonte Avellana, with the abbot of the monastery of San Lorenzo in Campo and with the bishop of Fano, for the purpose of furnishing them with precious incense. Jacob's father, Salomone, appears to have lent money to, and have been deceived by, the pope's legate in Ancona, Cardinal Rainer. Jacob himself sets sail 'with the knowledge and protection of *rettore* Simone' – who must be Cardinal Simone, a succeeding papal legate in Ancona from 1266 – 'who in bad conscience had undertaken to make recompense for the misdeeds of Ser Raniero' (see p. 34). He also leaves Italy with let-ters of presentation, although he does not say from whom, at Cyprus; and the *podestà,* or mayor, of Ancona, named as Giovanni Confalonieri, whom Jacob calls 'our neighbour', says farewell to him on his departure, while Jacob 'prays to him … that my family might be kept safe from harm'. These appear to be intimate relations.

Arguably more striking still is that Jacob's partners in the risks of the voyage included 'Benvenuto and Alberto de' Tarabotti'. The Tarabotti were the leading family of Ancona in the thirteenth and early fourteenth centuries; and Benvenuto was a magistrate of the nearby town of Arcevia in the year of Jacob's departure, while Alberto was *podestà* of the same town in the following year.

Yet from 1265, under Pope Clement IV and during the imperial rule of Charles of Anjou – conqueror of Frederick II – there is also countervailing evidence of increasing hostility towards the Jews. In 1268, two years before Jacob's departure for the Orient, the Inquisition was being introduced into south-ern Italy; the preaching of the Dominicans in Italy against the Jews was becoming everywhere more strident; there was increas-ing pressure upon the Jews to convert, including under the inducement of special tax concessions.

Thus Jacob must have left his family in the early summer of 1270 with little emotional certitude as to his or their prospects, anxious for his wasting fortunes, and fearful (as he makes plain) of the hazards of the journey. But, as we also see, he was unaf-fected in his energies. He was a man with a place in the community of Ancona, both Jewish and Christian, but without assurance that his world would not be overthrown and lost in a turn of fortune's wheel against the Jews. Whether he was also wearing his 'badge of shame' he does not say.

Despite the poverty of the mediaeval archival sources, it is known that there were landholders with Jewish names near Ancona in AD 967; there is also a brief local documentary reference dating from AD 949 to 'David, the Jew'. We know, too, that Jews elsewhere in the Marche region in Jacob's time were engaged in banking, in the flax and wool trades, in tanning, in wine and oil production, and as physicians and scholars. There are also extant thirteenth-century documents from Rimini showing that Jews were involved there, under contract, in collecting harbour dues from 1230 onwards.[12] Jacob himself asserts in his manuscript that (by 1270) Jews had been in Ancona 'for a thousand years', but there is no surviving local tradition of it, and no record.

But what was the relation between Jacob and his family and the city of Ancona? The surname 'd'Ancona',[13] which Jacob attaches both to himself and to his father as a name of provenance according to Italian Jewish custom, suggests that his grandfather, Rabbi Israel of Florence, had himself left Florence and settled in Ancona by the time of the birth of Jacob's father. To the support of this surmise that the family had been locally settled for some time is Jacob's marriage to Sara, the daughter of a family from Jesi, a town to the south-west of Ancona with a small Jewish population in the middle ages. But it is obviously not conclusive. Such a Jewish marriage could have been as readily arranged, at a young age and by brokers, between a girl in Jesi and a youth in Florence as between a pair who lived at a few miles distance from one another.

Jacob himself calls Ancona his *patria*, literally his 'father's place'. But this term does not necessarily signify that it was either Jacob's *birthplace* or his father's birthplace – he might have used the term *loco natio* for that. Rather, it means 'place of belonging', or, as we would say, 'home', and where his father Salomone was to be found.

It is accepted by historians of Italian Jewry that in the middle ages Ancona's was the largest Jewish community in central Italy outside Rome. They assert, too, that a significant part of its number – Jacob d'Ancona's father, and perhaps his grandfather, might be included – had been attracted there by the opportunities offered by its profitable port. The only relevant documents found so far relate to permissions to stay in the city and to engage in commercial activity given to certain Jews of Rome in the second half of the fourteenth century, some eighty years after Jacob's voyage. It is also known that in the same period there were large numbers of 'foreign merchants' in Ancona, including Greeks, Dalmatians, Spaniards and Germans.

As I indicated earlier, it is doubtful that indigenous Italian Jews came under this designation. It is more likely that the Jewish merchants of Ancona possessed a corporate charter specifically allowing them to conduct foreign trade, with rules governing their activities, the taxes and dues to which they were subject, the numbers of merchants permitted to take part, the resolution of disputes, and so on. Such charters concerning the Jews (and others) are extant from other European cities; the earliest dates back to the Carolingian period.

It also seems probable that the Jews of Ancona in the thirteenth century possessed special privileges and formally granted exemptions – as Jewish communities had elsewhere under tolerant, if precarious, local rule – such as to own land and to employ Christian and domestic servants, as Jacob and his family did according to his own testimony.

There are two other clues, one oblique, to the nature of Jewish commercial activities in Ancona in Jacob's time. Early fourteenth-century papal letters to the city[14] seek to forbid Ancona's trade with the Saracen world in materials and means – such as arms, horses and iron[15] – which could aid the latter's bellicose purposes. It may be inferred that in the preceding period, the time of Jacob, Ancona merchants were profiting from this trade to the irritation of Rome; and I think it can also be inferred that Jewish merchants, whose knowledge of the Levant (and of Arabic) gave them particular access to such trade, were among them. Indeed, if, as is generally asserted, the fortunes of Jewish merchants waned in Italy after Jacob's lifetime, the papal communications with Ancona may be evidence of the kinds of restrictive pressure that bore most heavily upon them.

It is also known that, in the early fourteenth century, Jews from Ancona and Rimini were involved in banking and money-lending in Padua: possibly a sign that long-distance Jewish merchant-traders from the Adriatic ports had been driven to seek other livelihoods elsewhere.

Jacob d'Ancona's trading enterprise to the Orient, a venture which (as the manuscript amply shows) was part of a family business – perhaps first established by his father Salomone – was one in which partners invested risk capital in return for a share of the profits, and in which each voyage might be separately financed, as was his. Jacob tells us that, apart from his father and his brother-in-law Baruch, his partners were the two members of the Tarabotti family, Samuele di Nathan of Lucca, and Levi di Abramo of Camerino[16] – both plainly Jews and who might have been relatives – and Domenico Gualdi[17] of Florence: eight in all. (In such partnerships, the travelling partner was usually called, in the formal contracts which survive from mediaeval times, the *tractor*; the investor, or sleeping partner, the *stans*; the shares were called *sortes*; the loan-investment each shareholder made was called a *commenda*.)

The Jewish merchant-trader is an archetypal figure both in the cultural history of the Jews and in the history of world trade itself. Thus 'The Jews alone,' Henri Pirenne declares, 'from the beginning of the Carolingian era [sc. eighth century AD] carried on a regular commerce, so much so that the word *Judaeus* [Jew] and *mercator* [merchant] appear almost synonymous.'[18] For how long Jacob's forebears, perhaps even including his rabbinical grandfather, had been thus engaged it is impossible to say. But the fact that he had relatives involved in foreign trade in Acre and Alexandria, married his son to a Jewish merchant's daughter in Basra, and had familiar acquaintances among the Jewish trading communities of western India, plainly suggests that his family and its traditions were wedded to this trading world.

In it the Jews were adepts, polyglot, always literate – the Jew who could not read the scriptures was, in effect, not a member of the community – risk-taking and, historically, often pioneers, drawing the remotest parts of the globe together. For example, the antiquity of Jewish participation in the Chinese silk trade and of contact with the furthest Orient is shrouded in mystery, but ninth-century Arab sources allude to the Jews having been in China 'from time immemorial'; a subject which was of great interest to Jacob also, for reference is made to it in the manuscript. A date as early as that of the Han dynasty (200 BC–AD 226) occurs in some traditions, and it is most interesting to discover from the manuscript that the Chinese knew of this tradition also.

The Jewish travelling merchants of the ninth to the fourteenth centuries AD, who are often described in Arabic sources as 'Radanites' – derived from a Persian word signifying that they 'knew the way' – moved freely between Europe and the Far East, with particular commercial success in periods when the principal routes were barred to Christian traders by Saracen power. Hailing originally from Iraq east of the Tigris, the Radanites are said to have been the first to bring to the West oranges, sugar and rice, sandalwood and senna, cinnamon and camphor, musk, jasmine and lilac.

Indeed, in the early mediaeval period, according to Robert Lopez, it was 'the Jews alone', generally journeying in groups, 'who maintained the trading and cultural links between Catholic Europe, the Islamic world, the Byzantine Empire, and even India and China'.[19] The Jewish trader of this tradition was himself the traveller; Jacob d'Ancona's journey is, among other things, one more of such odysseys in the Radanite fashion.

Large fortunes could be made and, says Pirenne, the 'rise to wealth' could be 'very rapid'. 'The longer the journey and the greater the rarity of the imported goods,' he declares, shedding light for us on Jacob's impulse and referring specifically to spices and silks, 'the greater the prospect of profit', a profit sufficient to 'counterbalance the hardships and risks'.[20] Above all, Pirenne states, 'the power of capital reigned supreme, dominating both … navigation and land transport, both the import and the export trade.'[21] Risk capital, such as was provided by the investors (Jewish and Gentile) in Jacob's venture, was the driving force in such activity. Both the Church – often secretly – and the landed gentry were involved.

It was in the year 1270 …

Moreover, in the middle ages it was Italy, especially northern Italy, which set the pace in the expansion of long-distance mercantile trade. It is therefore the less surprising that there is such a high proportion of Italians in the list of those who have left accounts of their oriental travels in this period, and that missionaries followed in the merchants' paths. The important innovations in commercial practices and accounting methods, in modes of payment and systems of representation through a network of local factors and agents, were largely Italian in origin. The Crusades, from the first in 1096 to the fifth in 1217, additionally boosted the fortunes of the Italian maritime cities – the ship-owners of Venice, Genoa, Pisa and Ancona greatly benefited from the carrying of Crusaders and pilgrims to the Levant. In all these activities we may be sure that the Jews, Europe's first internationalists, participated, including doubtless in the Crusader traffic.

For these mercantile developments, 'revolutionary' as they may have been in their scale for the emergent populations of feudal Europe, were not revolutionary to the Jews. They were habituated to free trading activity, of which they were the leading practitioners of the age. Their specialities were in threads and fabrics; in dyeing and dyeing materials; as well as in medicinal plants, spices, aromatics, perfumes and incenses; in gold and silver; and in pearls and corals. In the trade in spices, which were the most valuable (as Jacob's purchases confirm) of the long-distance cargoes brought from India and the Far East, the Jews had long been expert. In the trade with India, in particular, Jewish merchants 'formed a kind of closed club, known to each other',[22] upon which Jacob's manuscript sheds new light. Thus, in the southern Indian trading post of Singoli (or

31

Cranganore, as it is now known), 'so frequented is the port by
Jewish merchants,' writes Jacob, 'and so much the trade that we
bring, that our merchandise is free of toll.' Similarly, for the
mediaeval economy of Aden, visited by Jacob in September
1272, we know that Jewish traders to India were of considerable
importance.

It has long been the conventional view, however, that during
the twelfth and thirteenth centuries the ascendancy of Jewish
traders in Europe was lost to others (including to other Jewish
traders in the Levant and Maghreb), and that the odium of the
Church, together with restrictive guild regulations and jealous
competition, had successfully squeezed the Jewish merchant
and banker out of international commerce and into the humil-
iations of petty money-lending and small-scale, itinerant local
trade.[23] The manuscript of Jacob d'Ancona shows that, even if
this was broadly true, such pressures must have been slower to
take effect in Italy (and Provence) than elsewhere in Europe,
and that his own family's business in Ancona continued according to pattern.

But whether it survived the end of the century may be
doubted.

Jacob's journey, which lasted three years and one month from
April 1270 to May 1273, took him to southern China and
back. The outward journey, via Acre, Basra, Hormuz, the western coast of India, Ceylon, the Nicobar islands, Sumatra, the
Malacca straits and ports in what are now Malaysia and
Cambodia, took sixteen months. This included a two-month
stay in Basra and a period of shelter from the weather of nearly
three months in Sumatra. He was in Zaitun, the great mediaeval port city of southern China, for six months.

He set sail for Ancona in late February 1272, again via Java
and western India, but thereafter via Aden, Fustat (Cairo) and
Alexandria. His homeward voyage took just over fifteen
months, including a period of shelter in Sumatra from the
south-west monsoon, and a three-month stay during the winter

of 1272–3 in Alexandria, where he had family members and business partners.

It was in the year 1270 …

These routes, which also involved arduous overland caravan journeys in the Levant, were broadly similar to those taken by other thirteenth-century merchant travellers from Europe to the Orient, some of whom journeyed by the Nile and the Red Sea, and others by way of the Euphrates and the Persian Gulf. (Marco Polo, however, chose to go by land through Persia to India, rather than hazarding himself to a sea journey down the Persian Gulf in the frail vessels at his disposal; our traveller was better provided for by his co-religionists in Basra, as the manuscript tells.)

Before Jacob d'Ancona's time, the camel caravans from Acre or Aleppo to the Persian Gulf would normally pass through Baghdad. But in 1270, twelve years after its seizure by the Mongols under Khan Hulagu, it was no longer the trading centre it had been; Jacob makes only the briefest references to it, saying that 'it is in the hands of the Tartars'. There was also 'danger in tarrying long' in Damascus, as he reports. The region was unsettled, and in October 1271, sixteen months after he had passed through it, northern Syria also suffered Mongol invasion.

Otherwise, his outward and homeward journeys followed a familiar pattern. They were governed in their sea-borne passages by fears of piracy, the mariners' huge exertions, and the prevailing winds; in favourable conditions a mediaeval ship equipped with both sails and oars seems to have been able to make some seventy miles a day. Nor need the length and daring of a journey through Indian and Chinese seas with oars and under sail surprise us. As Jacques Gernet points out, 'in the first few centuries of our era, the coasts of southern India and Ceylon were already connected to Sumatra by non-stop voyages and the long trip between Palembang (in Sumatra) and Canton [Guangzhou] seems to have been made regularly as early as the seventh century.'[24]

The length of Jacob's absence from Ancona was also what

one would have expected. A trading voyage to India and China from Europe necessitated an absence of two years at least in the middle ages, and often longer.

 t was in the year 1270, which is to say 5030 years from the creation of the world,[25] blessèd be He, upon the sixteenth day of April and the twenty-third day of Nisan[26] when Giovanni Confaloniere was *podestà* and Matteo Angeli and Giacomo Bladioni were captains of the people, that I, Jacob, son of Salomone of Ancona and grandson of the great Rabbi Israel of Florence, may his memory be recorded, merchant of Ancona, embarked on board ship for my departure to Greater India and the farthest shores of the earth.

I was in my forty-ninth year, may God be praised, in good health but of weak constitution and with many travails, but strengthened in my courage by the love of my family and my noble rabbinical lineage,[27] may the Creator be magnified and exalted. I was also much sustained that Ser Giovanni bade me farewell, I in turn praying to him that my family might be kept from harm.

Since I have determined to give here a true account of all that befell me between the time of my departure and the time of my return, may God be honoured, and in this book of my journeys shall set down even such things as may not always be fitting to be made known, I declare that I set sail with the knowledge and protection of *rettore* Simone, who in bad conscience had undertaken to make recompense for the misdeeds of Ser Raniero and Ser Capocci.[28] For the said Simone had secured for my profit that the abbot of Avellana[29] near Mount Catria, as also the priests of San Tommaso in Foglia and San Lorenzo in Campo, should receive from me precious incenses by which to make fragrant their orations to their idols, and had done other things besides.

Yet I felt immeasurable grief that thus I should be voyaging in dangers to the ends of the earth, and that for so many years I should be a traveller far from my native place, even to Manci, which some call Cin, and among us is named Sinim.[30] Indeed, so great was my grief that I began to weep, fearing misadventure, praying to God, may the Unnameable One be praised, that I should complete the voyage without shipwreck. Many fears assailed me of bandits and pirates, or lest it chance that my ship broke up, or that it might run aground in shallow water, or that it should be damaged on some rock and the water come in through the breach.

It was in the year 1270 …

For if by such mischance my ship should founder, since the ships which sail the Indian sea and the sea of Sinim are often shipwrecked, so stormy and perilous are their waters, what should I do who cannot stand water as high up as the ankles? Did not David, the brother of our blessèd Rabbi Mose ben Maimon, may his soul be quickened at the end of days, not drown in the sea, causing his brother to grieve deeply for him? Hence, I prayed to the Holy One, blessèd be He, that if my ship should touch ground or break asunder, or when sailing

---

'RABBI MOSE BEN MAIMON'

*Maimonides, or Moses ben Maimon, who has been called the 'Jewish Aristotle', was a philosopher, Talmudist and physician. He was born in Cordoba in 1135 and died in Palestine in 1204, his greatest work being* Guide to the Perplexed *(1190), called in Hebrew* Moreh Nevukhim. *In it he sought to reconcile the demands of reason and the claims of faith; in discussing the themes of providence, the creation of the world and man's free will he shows himself to be both a rabbinical and an Aristotelian thinker. His skill as a doctor of medicine was renowned and he wrote several medical treatises – Richard the Lionheart offered him the position of court physician at London, an offer he refused. During his lifetime he was consulted for his religious opinions by Jews throughout the mediaeval world, and was the author of a learnèd compendium of rabbinical law. His influence upon the thinking of Aquinas has also been noted.*

at night should lose its way, or if I should find any other manner of harm close at hand, that He should spare me. For all who embark on such ships must give themselves into the hands of God, may His name be revered.

But I feared also the avarice and desire of others, and the danger of being robbed before my profits could be made. For so bitter is life and so many the disasters which threaten even the most pious of Jews that only before the Divine Presence may we find justice according to our merits.

I also had fear that some harm or accident could befall a member of my household, as that the sickness and infirmity of my father, may he be inscribed in the book of forgiveness, might grow worse in my absence, for so it befell, and that the fortunes of our house might go from bad to worse and to ruin.

With such thoughts, praying also to God, blessèd be He, that I might keep the Sabbath and that I be not driven to eat abomination,[31] I besought Him to preserve my household in peace and health, and my own self in safety. Thus in my purse, which I kept hidden about me, I placed the golden besant which had been given to me by our sage Rabbi Menahem,[32] and which I had undertaken to restore to him upon my safe return, God willing.

With much sadness I then sought forgiveness from my wife Sara and from my sons for my father's misfortunes, which had brought me to my venture. I declared to my sons that in the bitter world he who takes upon himself to correct harm may be counted a just man, and that by necessity he may be constrained to enter into danger in order that his ends be gained. And, knowing well that from no fault of mine the wealth which my father had made in trade with Ragusa and the other parts of Dalmatia, but without recourse to the base trade in slaves,[33] he had permitted to be scattered in his ventures in the Black Sea and Tana,[34] they prayed for my safety, also shedding tears lest all might come to ruin in the troubles of the way.

But they took much pleasure that in Basra I should encounter our beloved son Isaac, God preserve him in health and wealth, who, having been one year in Aden as factor[35] for me and for Gershon ben Judah of Venice and Haim ben Abraam Ha-Levi of Sinigaglia, would come there to take the daughter of Isaia of Ascoli in marriage. To them, since they began again to weep, I said that we must always place ourselves in the palm of God, honoured be He, and that all blessing proceeds and comes from Him.

It was in the year 1270 …

Hence, I declared, they should keep in their thoughts that, if God were willing, I should return to them with rich cloths, silk, pepper, incense, jewels and other rare things of great value and that they should therefore not despair. Moreover to me fell the task, for so I told them while the sailors made ready, to instruct others in their neglected duties and to get the better of all the thieves who by their frauds and tricks have sought to deceive our house and to steal from us, as by sending false goods, or goods of bad quality, or by other wicked means.

Thus I spoke of my burdens, so that I might be able to quell their fears, saying that it fell to me to repair our fortunes by seeking out in one place that which a man sells for its weight in gold in another, to collect all that which has been owing to us for merchandise sent from our country and also to dismiss the thieves and choose others from among the Jews of each place as agents,[36] as well as to reward those who had been faithful in our service.

Yet as the time drew nearer for my departure, the vessel being set in order at prow and stern, and the wind blowing towards the east-north-east, I again became seized with grief and my wife Sara also, who sought to comfort me without avail. Alas, I was the unhappiest man who had ever been in the world. I thought that I was ready to die of grief, seeing that I had been compelled, according to the law, to grant my spouse, Sara Bonaiuta of Jesi, a divorce, to which Sabbato ben Menahem and Lazzaro Ha-Coen, elders, made witness. Thus I, Jacob of Ancona, fearing the accidents which might befall me, granted

*37*

her the right to marry again in case I perished in my travels, as by acts of God, blessèd be He, or was unable to return to her in less than three years, in the meantime entrusting her and my sons to the care of my brothers Dattalo Porat of Fano and Isaia Sullam Hagiz, should necessity demand.

But now, the pilot fearing a contrary wind and anxious to make our way to Zara[37] as fast as we could with oar and sail, they were instructed to disembark from the ship. Thus with many tears and last embraces we parted, I counselling my wife Sara to temper her spending lest our affairs went from bad to worse, each giving over the other into the hand of God, magnified and exalted be He.

So we set sail, I in my heart reciting the Shema, seeing that the ropes on the right and the left were cast off. I carried with me in this vessel much cargo of cloth of velvet and wool, our gold wire[38] for which they pay dear in Sinim, mercury, linen, soap of Ancona in wooden cases, as well as wine and corn in a great quantity for Ragusa, and many other valuable things besides.

---

'ACCORDING TO THE LAW . . . GRANTED HER THE
RIGHT TO MARRY AGAIN'

*'According to the law' plainly means 'according to the Jewish marriage law', under which a bill of separation could be given in the circumstances described. (The formality of this description in the manuscript suggests that Jacob is quoting from the original document or has it before him while he writes.) Separation for three years gives rise, under Talmudic regulation, to a presumption of divorce, since it represents a failure on the husband's part to fulfil his obligations to his spouse for so long a period as to make her free. In fact, Jacob was away for three years and one month, after which they were reunited, the 'divorce', or get, remaining a dead letter. The entrusting of his wife and children to two fellow-Jews – called 'brothers' in the manuscript – seems to have been a form of extra-familial emergency guardianship, and was probably organised by the elders of the Ancona synagogue, just as the document itself would have been drawn up and attested by them.*

I also bore hidden upon me jewels to carry and to serve in Basra, as also against such hire of ships as I should need. But of money I had little, neither of Venetian groats nor of gold besants, so that the wicked might be less tempted to take my life, which God forbid.

Thus I departed with my Christian servants about me, taken from Ancona, among whom were my two honest clerks, Pietro Armentuzio and Simone Pizzecolli. There were also the cooks Pecte and Rustici, and young Berletto, their servitor. Of the others I had two servants for the washing of my clothes, the woman Bertoni and the girl Buccazuppo, although against my will. Among the rest was the navigator, the brave Atto Turiglioni, who had from Fra Pietro of Sant' Angelo, at Simone's command, his charts of the sailors of those seas in which we should sail. It was arranged that the said Turiglioni, together with the others I have named, should stay by my side from Basra to Greater India and the land of Sinim, as well as two, one by name Micheli and the other Fultrono, to watch close over my body lest any should seek my life upon the way.

---

### 'BUT OF MONEY I HAD LITTLE'

*Jacob is in general discreet about money (as well as about the amount of his profits), but it seems from the manuscript that mediaeval Jewish merchants did not carry much cash with them, relying upon their representatives, family members and co-religionists to keep them supplied and to settle accounts. Commercial transactions were carried out on the basis of reciprocal understandings and trust, and by means of early bills of exchange and promissory notes. Under these arrangements, some of great complexity, a written or verbal promise by the purchaser to pay a sum of money in a place other than that in which the debt was contracted would be made, and the payment perhaps delivered to the vendor's agent. But there were many other forms: including letters of credit drawn on merchants' houses the length of the trade routes, and complex systems of discounting bills which might involve moving between currencies. In this activity the Jews (and the Italians) were expert in the middle ages.*

As we sailed forth from the harbour, I looking from the sea upon the high hill of Cònero, many were the fortunes apart from my own and that of my father, may his soul endure, and that of my brother-in-law, Baruch Bonaiuto, which hung upon my voyage. For my partners Ser Benvenuto and Ser Alberto de' Tarabotti[39] each had three shares, and Samuel di Nathan of Lucca, Levi di Abramo of Camerino, and Ser Domenico Gualdi of Florence two; the Tarabotti and the Tuscan to receive profits according to each man's share, as well as —, of whom I make no mention.

Thereafter the ship began to reach the open sea and the waves grew higher, I praying again to the Holy One, blessèd be He, that I should return safely. But once more a great grief seized hold of me for the ill that we have suffered. So that I began to weep again when I thought of my Sara and that I might not see her again, and my heart was heavy to leave my studies and my father, may his memory be blessèd, none knowing but God Himself what should be the fate of my voyage.

Thus, passing among the ships and galleys and sailing upon the sea towards the east-north-east, I composed my troubled mind for the voyage, resolving that I should always seek to observe the obligations of the Jew, that I should eat no unclean food and that I should neither embark nor disembark upon the Sabbath, God willing. I resolved also that I should not omit either to address my thoughts constantly to the Creator, exalted is He, or to use my phylacteries each day, and that if in a great tempest, being confused, I should come not to know where lay Jerusalem, God forbid, I would direct my

---

'PHYLACTERIES'

*Two square leather boxes, with straps, containing parchment scrolls upon which words from Exodus 13 and Deuteronomy 6 and 11 are inscribed. They are placed on the forehead and left arm as part of the morning devotions of pious Jews.*

heart and thought to the Holy of Holies, as Rabbi Judah, peace upon him, permits.

It was in the year 1270 ...

I vowed also that, however great my desire for profit, I should seek to conduct myself in the most honest fashion and without blemish, as has always been my habit. For it is often as advantageous for the purchaser to give benefit to the seller as for the seller to give benefit to the purchaser. Whether by a small payment in excess of a just price for certain goods in the first case, or by a small discount for certain goods in the second, one may come to have great favours cheaply in those things for which others will later pay richly.

Yet, since true profit to the soul can come only to him who is heedful to listen to God, may He be magnified for evermore, it does not serve if greed and avarice shall so come to command a man's soul that the Holy One is cast out from it, may I be spared for my words.

It was by such thoughts that I composed my spirit, but my body was made unquiet by the movement of the waves, and little by little, being of weak constitution, I became disturbed in my stomach, for which I gave up a quantity of food I had lately eaten. My legs gave way under me and once more I felt that I should die of grief, being far from port. But Berletto came to my aid and helped me to recover my senses and gradually I became better, God be praised.

At first light, the winds being more gentle and my body restored, I prayed to God, blessèd be He, placing my phylacteries upon my forehead and arm, at which many of the sailors seemed astonished. Yet the Jew, even among strangers, must do as he is commanded to do by God, by prayer which is heard as well as in the silence of his soul, provided only that by his will he does not seek to do harm to others, nor to interfere in their faith and practice.

Thus each may permit the other to worship God according to his belief, save only that a Jew may not feel respect for idols, nor for those who fold their hands and bow their knees to them. Lord God of Israel, there is no God like Thee. So we came this day to Zara, the rowers rowing with great effort, for the wind was strong and sometimes contrary, but my sickness was past, for which I gave praise to God.

Here we made stay for six days, during which fell the Sabbath Kedoshim, my duties being carried out among my brothers and all my goods loaded upon a more commodious and stronger vessel, according to the instructions which had been given to Sheshet Ha-Levi of Zara.[40] Here also I had undertaken to await the coming of Menahem Vivo of Mestre, may his soul endure, or if he had already arrived, as I found, we should then set sail together.

I had also to purchase every kind of provision as well as to hire, together with Vivo and those who should come with us from Ragusa, a vessel with three men to the bench and thirty soldiers under arms, each at the rate of sixty groats per month. Indeed, great were the expenses of the hire, of the provisions, and of the many mariners, for we must have a commander, an anchor-master, a master of the ropes, a master of the victuals, a carpenter for the timbers, a second helmsman and others who pressed to serve us in our journey to San Giovanni d'Acri.

At last, when all was prepared and provisioned, I departed thence, followed by the vessels of Menahem Vivo, and the vessels of Christian merchants, all being well-armed against the pirates of those seas, and not only of those about Famagusta. For unless they go under arms merchants are in peril of being robbed of all that they carry, the small islands and waters of Dalmatia being the lair of thieves, the people by nature being rough and much given to thievery even among themselves.

On the counsel of our captain we also flew from our masts the colours of Venice, in order to protect ourselves from their ships, there being still much enmity between our cities.

Thus we proceeded towards the south-east with a fair but cold wind, first to Curzola,[41] at which I purchased silver from Isaia ben Simone of that place and sold much wine, and

Menahem Vivo also, and thereafter went towards Ragusa. In this time, I observed my duties, God be praised, being able to avoid the necessity to embark or disembark upon the Sabbath. The star of early evening of the Sabbath Emor I saw at sea on my vessel, and ceasing thereupon from all labours, as from assisting Armentuzio and Pizzecolli in their calculations and giving counsel to the brave Turiglioni upon the charts, I sanctified the Sabbath, reciting the kiddush and the amotzi before my repast.

It was in the year 1270 …

For as Isaiah, upon whom be peace, declares, 'Happy is the man that doeth this and holdeth by it' and 'if thou because of the Sabbath turn away from pursuing thy business, I will make thee to ride upon the high places of the earth.' On the morrow, when I rose from my bed at first light, as is my habit, it being the Sabbath Emor, I donned a suit of fresh clothes, as the woman Bertoni and the girl Buccazuppo had been instructed by Sara to make ready for me on every Sabbath day, God be praised.

It also became my practice thenceforward, when at sea on the Sabbath, raising my hand to no labour, to traverse the whole length of the vessel, back and forth, as Rabbis Gamaliel

---

'I OBSERVED MY DUTIES'

*This is a constantly recurring phrase in the manuscript and can be taken to refer to the numerous daily observances of prayer and other ritual obligations – especially important in the sanctification of the Sabbath, through prayer, the lighting of candles, the wearing of clean clothes and so on – of the pious Jew. There are, in all, 613 separate mandatory and prohibitive rules and ordinances covering every manner of eventuality, which are each perceived as expressions of a love of God. It is plain from the manuscript that, even in difficult circumstances, Jacob is constantly aware of his obligations and his defaults, taking the trouble to record his performance of duty, although usually in general terms only. His constant praise of God in epithets and exclamations is also a practice enjoined upon the pious by the Torah rules.*

and Eliezer allow, and themselves did in sailing from Rome to Brindisi, as it is written, although Rabbis Joshua and Akiba permit movement of only four cubits, in reverence to the Sabbath law.[42]

Yet having arrived in Ragusa before the ending of the Sabbath Emor, which is to say the third day of Iyar,[43] I remained on board ship, despite the reasoning of my friend Vivo, peace upon him, who declared that it was permitted to disembark upon the Sabbath, provided that the ladder had been set in place for all, and not only for a Jew, as Rabbi Gamaliel teaches. Upon this, he made an address to me, but I remained unmoved, answering that the observance of the Sabbath weighs more than all the commandments of the Torah, for whose gift may He be thanked. Whereupon the said Vivo fell silent and said no more, as if so surprised as not to know what to say, my resolution being great.

However, I considered within myself whether, in the eye of God, to be so immovable should truly serve the glory of His name, or was to be stiff-necked. I therefore resolved, may God spare me, as when I journeyed in the Black Sea and to Alexandria, that, provided my heart was pure, I should pay heed lest I put my venture or the safety of others in danger. For even if a worthy man might say of me with good reason that I exceeded the duty even of the holiest of men, observance of the Torah is not in itself an end. Moreover the man of goodwill who breaks the rule under constraint is better than the dishonest one who follows the rule with ill-will in his heart.

With this reasoning I descended the ladder, yet unwillingly, fearing to do that which would be unworthy of my name or was in itself ignoble.

Having disembarked, I proceeded to the house of my brother[44] Leo ben Benedetto of Ragusa with a firm step, since to grieve on the Sabbath is forbidden, and believing that in my actions there was nothing for which I could be reproached. For if a man takes delight in the Sabbath and forswears labour, he does the principal thing which is required of him. Therefore, I, remembering the Sabbath day to keep it holy, forbore even to give a glance at my property on board ship, leaving it in the care of my faithful Christian servants. For to attend in thought upon the Sabbath to what is required to be done on the morrow is also justly forbidden by our sages, upon them peace, as being such labour as the man who fears God shall not perform.

At the house of my brother Leo, a factor, where I found many merchants gathered and at their ease, I was bade welcome to their table and to make my stay, all greeting me as a Jew of grand lineage and good repute. For they, who knew of my father's misfortunes and had often been his companions in the market, gave me no blame for what had befallen him.

On the contrary, they sought to aid me in every fashion, giving me much advice as to those places in Greater India where one may buy cheaply and sell well. But it being the Sabbath, and since time should be set aside on this day for the study of the Torah, I withdrew from their company to a quiet place. For as our sages of blessèd memory tell us, Sabbaths and festivals were given to Israel that we might devote ourselves to study upon them, each according to his conception and capacity.

Thereafter, having taken part with them in calling upon Elijah at the end of the holy day and, in company with them, having recited the evening prayers to the Lord that He should bless us and inspire Israel always to act justly so that the Temple of Jerusalem might be rebuilt in our days, Amen and Amen, I retired to my bed.

In the next days, while our vessels lay at anchor in the harbour, my cargo of oil, wine and corn was unloaded with great labour and carried to the market, some being placed in the trading house by the servants of my brother,[45] and the rest being sold at a just price to my profit. In the market were many men of Ancona who inhabit Ragusa in great number, being exempt from duties and taxes, and having many houses and ships.

There are also many hundreds of Jews here, Ragusa being a great port and a fair city, and they are among the richest of the place, concerning themselves much with trade in wine and other produce of our country, as cloth from Siena and oil from Arezzo.

At last, when the wind began to blow strongly from the north-west, the vessels having been repaired and reprovisioned, and all was in order at prow and stern, we put forth to sea after the Sabbath Behar, the ships of Vivo following behind, and also those of other merchants bound for Famagusta and San Giovanni d'Acri. Among them were the ships of Rabbi Isaac ben Isaac of Ceneda, Lazzaro del Vecchio of Ancona and Eliezer ben Nathan of Venice, they also each with a vessel of soldiers and with three men to a bench. But no pirates were to be seen, for which God be thanked.

Thereafter, we had constant winds and made fast speed as if to travel through the air; we made wings of our oars and the sky was clear, the mariners and the others content with their pay and food, and I with my health restored after my sickness. We passed by the island of Corchira, which has the name of Poseidonia, keeping close to the shore for safety.

Thus we sailed for many days in the Ionian Sea among other fair islands such as Ithaca, Zante and Chithera, where we stayed in order to obtain water and fresh provisions, I maintaining my duties upon the Sabbath Behukotai as I had vowed, and much attended to by poor Berletto. For I had taught him to serve me no meat but fish cooked in wine according to the ways of Sara, together with fruit, so that my kidneys be kept healthy and my water clear. Others ate in excess of meat, some becoming ill with fever, their water brown and with a stink of pestilence, which put me to great unease.

Thus the time passed as our fleet sailed towards Crete without encountering events that were worthy of being narrated, the weather being fair, the seas calm and there being

no pirates to be seen. At Crete, where there are many Jews, I
proceeded upon my arrival to the synagogue, having
determined that to disembark upon the Sabbath is permitted,
being present, God be praised, soon after the morning prayers
had commenced, and being greeted by Aaron Ebreo of
Eraclione who is also the agent of the Christian Pietro de
Todini, merchant of Ancona.

It was in
the year
1270 …

My fame as a pious Jew being known to all, and many
giving me greeting, I was called to the reading of the Torah,[46]
God be thanked, thereafter giving to the burial society of the
poor, and remaining also for the additional Sabbath prayers,
the better to contemplate the future dangers of my journey
and to pray to God for my safe return.

The next day, being the eighteenth day of Iyar and the day
of Lag Ba-Omer,[47] I remained in the synagogue together with
Rabbi Isaac ben Isaac, and would give myself to no buying
and selling. But Menahem Vivo, as well as Lazzaro and
Eliezer, did otherwise, while the captain of our fleet, learning
of my piety and that I would neither buy nor sell among the
Jews until the morrow, and the day after, grew impatient that
we prayed so long to the Creator. I would not be moved from
my will, but passed many hours in the study of the Mishnah
both on the day of Lag Ba-Omer and on the morrow also,
until I was content that my duty had been done. Upon the
fifth day, having made great gains, I parted from Aaron
Ebreo, peace upon him, with much brotherly love, many of
our nation, strangers to me but brothers of the same kind,
whom the Rock and Redeemer of Israel preserve,
accompanying us to the port.

Thus we set forth to Carpazzo and Rodi,[48] where I had a
fine sale of the cloth of Samuel.[49] Being of the best quality, it
commands a very high price among the nobles of that place.
At Famagusta, which we reached after much fear of the pirates
in those waters, whom we saw from a distance near the place
called Patara in the sea of Lycia, and also in the sea of
Pamphilia, but who were in turn struck with fear at the

number and force of our ships, God be praised, there were
many fine buckram quilts in the market. Of these I purchased
a great number, remaining several days in order that I might
obtain those which are best.

For in Manci they have a great desire for such things in
winter, and they therefore pay well for buckram. Here too I
presented to the priest Andrea di Famagusta the letter given to
me by Ser Simone, receiving from him a letter in the bishop's
hand for the friars of Manci. From Famagusta we then set sail
and on the thirtieth of May, having spent Shavuot on board
ship, our fleet, with my vessels to the fore and those of Eliezer
of Venice at the rear, arrived at last in San Giovanni d'Acri,[50]
may God be praised.

Here I disembarked the quicker to embrace my uncle, my
beloved Elia, may God protect his life, leaving my clerk
Armentuzio to take in hand the unloading of our cargoes. I
bade farewell also to Isaac of Ceneda, he having much
concern, together with his factor, to depart soon to Jerusalem,
may I be privileged to die there.

For here we were close to Sion, my true home, which is to
say the home of my soul and of the souls of all my brothers,
may the Lord bless us and increase our number a
hundredfold. In the harbour were many vessels from Ancona
and Genoa, but also of the Venetians, some even under their
own flag, at which I was greatly surprised. For after the late
war,[51] which brought much suffering to this city, a man might
think with reason that the Venetian merchants would come
here no longer. But the desire for gain conquers the greatest
fear.

Between the men of Ancona and the men of Genoa there
is, as in all the world, much friendship and love in San
Giovanni d'Acri, the district of the Anconetans, which was
given to them by Giovanni of Ibelino, and the district of the
Genoese, being close to one another. Here, the merchants of
Ancona, as a result of the gift of the Pope, pay no dues and
are thus settled in large number, having their own churches

and houses, shops, warehouses and hostels for the merchants who come here. Moreover, a merchant of Ancona, whether he be Jew or Christian, may trade not only in besants and marks but in his own coin even among the Saracens of the place.

It was in the year 1270 ...

The Venetians who caused the city such harm and grief are again permitted to trade, but the tributes they must pay here are high. Nevertheless, the conduct of all those who treat with them in the city is fair. For in a distant land merchants and mariners who hail from neighbouring places become kinsmen, whether they be of Venice or Genoa, Frank or Jew, and however much they may choose to quarrel in their own land. When men suffer the same troubles, as in a great tempest, goodwill may also be seen to increase, for the envy and malice of one for the other becomes less. But when the sun of good fortune shines upon them together, each will again go by his own path, and ill-will will once more come to guide his step.

In Acri there are two hundred and forty Jews, some of whom live in their own quarter, close by the quarter of the Genoese, and others who live in peace among the Saracens and Christians. Here the Saracens and Christians, although they will not eat together, also live in concord, even though the Saracens' great mosque where they worshipped Mahomet is made over into a church, for which they feel much bitterness in their hearts. Therefore their Christian lords have

---

'FRANKS'

*The name was first given in the third century AD to Germanic tribes of the Rhine valley, who were subsequently subjected to Roman domination by armies under the command of Emperor Julian (the Apostate). However, under Clovis (AD 481–511) they threw off Roman rule, conquered their local tribal foes, advanced through Gaul to the Seine and adopted Christianity; in their history is the history of the emergent kingdom of France. The term 'Franks' eventually came to be loosely applied, especially by those of other faiths, to Western Christians as a whole.*

given them a small cloister beside the church in which they are permitted to make their prayers.

Between the Jews and the Saracens there is much fellowship and association, even though the Jews of the city say among themselves that the Saracens often do them ill and are untrustworthy. Nevertheless, the Jewish and Saracen merchants of the place are often engaged in the same trade, buy much from each other, converse together in Arabic, and eat together in their houses.

Many of the Mahometans[52] give freely of their bread to all who are in need, unlike the Christians. But this custom is mingled with other acts and usages towards the Jews which are base. In addition, they sometimes express to the Jews hatred for the Christians, for to hate Christians is a natural thing for the Saracens, and sometimes they express to the Christians equal hatred for the Jews. Therefore, neither the Christians nor the Jews may have trust in the Saracens, for their hatred changes as the wind blows, blowing today from the north and tomorrow from the south, so that none may follow the movement of their spirits.

Yet although they are often a wicked people and kill each other also, they are more skilled in trade than the Christians but less skilful than the Jews, who are always able to get the better of them. Hence the Saracens serve the Jews well as factors in many lands, as in Greater and Lesser India,[53] for they are able to work on the Sabbath, God forbid, and have a love for merchandise, although they are also prone to steal, whether from the Christian or the Jew who takes no guard. All these things I have observed myself, for such is the best way to gain the truth, or have learned from others who have traded much in the lands of the Arabs.

Nonetheless, between the Jew and the Mahometan there is more love than between the Jew and the Christian, for the Mahometan declares himself to be the son of Abraam our ancestor and reveres our teacher Moses, may he rest in Eden and be quickened at the end of days. But those Christians who have made of a Jew their idol, may the Lord have mercy upon them for their impiety, but who have no learning of the writings of our sages, peace upon them, seeking rather to burn our Torah in the flames, may the Holy One strike from the earth and extinguish their names.

It was in the year 1270 ...

After a day of repose, it being the Sabbath Behaalotkha, which I spent at the side of my uncle Elia in study while the unloading of my cargoes continued, and in walking a little here and there with other pious Jews of the city, I went in the morning to the quarter of the Anconetans, where all were occupied with their Sabbath, save certain mariners who had carried me from Ancona, the girl Buccazuppo being among them and they, having too many Venetian groats in their purses, behaving themselves in improper fashion.

These I reproached, they declaring that their parting homewards was close at hand, that they might never meet again those who would accompany me to Basra, and that after many days upon the sea they had determined to spend the remaining hours in such festivities.

To them I replied that although they justly had fear for the morrow, for none might say what it would bring, it was to hold in disrespect their own Sabbath to act so, which the seed of Abraam cannot do, such behaviour not being worthy of men. At which they laughed in their drunkenness and even made to mock my grey beard, having lost their understanding and not able to remain upright. They had become as the beasts that perish, or brutish men who have no dread of sin, as Rabbi Hillel, peace be upon him, declared; swallowed up with their wine their tables become full of vomit and filthiness without God, even upon their Sabbath day.

From this place I therefore withdrew in sadness, but taking away from them the girl Buccazuppo on pain that she should otherwise be parted from the woman Bertoni, who is her cousin, and return in shame to our country, which she was loath to do, weeping to me that I forgive her for her conduct.

*51*

And thus she went away to her lodging in order to prepare with better sense for the morrow.

I for my part returned thence to the house of Elia, where I recounted what I had seen and passed the remaining hours of the day in thought and study of our sages, peace be upon them, and of the large book[54] of Armentuzio.

The next day, having ascertained with Menahem Vivo, Lazzaro del Vecchio and Eliezer of Venice that all our cargoes had been taken in good order upon many four-wheeled carts to the place called El-Gamalia, where the camels gather and from which the caravans depart to the desert of Syria, I made purchases of choice work in gold from a goldsmith of great repute. For there are some rich nobles of Greater India and Java the Less, as I had learned, who prize such Saracen work above all things on earth. Certain of his rings, in which rich jewels were also set, I concealed about me, together with the other jewels of which I have spoken. The rest I entrusted to the faithful Armentuzio and Pizzecolli, they swearing upon their lives that they should utter no word of it to our companions.

For these purchases I gave Elia the *suftaja*[55] by which he might have payment of Leo of Ragusa, factor, and Levi, banker of Ancona, whither he intended to go in the month of Tammuz with spices from Greater India, and other goods, God willing.

Having made other commodious purchases at great profit, I returned to the place of the camels, to which Elia came also, and there also had gathered my servants, Berletto being astonished to see such animals and in such numbers. He did not know what to say, being stupefied by so many hundreds of such creatures on their knees to be loaded for our journey, who bellowed as if in pain at the weight which each was to bear, I praying to God that He should have mercy upon them for their doleful cries, which rend the hearts of those who hear them.

It is the custom of the Arabs[56] to load these beasts in the

night as well as the day so that the traveller may depart at
dawn, but which they do very slowly, as they do everything in
these lands. Therefore, although with much assistance from
my servants and the servants of the other merchants, we were
constrained to wait under the great heat of the sun until the
caravan had been made ready. But the camels are most useful
beasts, since they carry heavy loads and cost little,
notwithstanding that they are not as fast-moving as horses or
mules.

Thus our caravan left Acri on the ninth day of June in the
year 1270, which is to say the eighteenth day of Sivan, 5030
years since the creation of the world, setting forth from the
Christian world towards the river Euphrates. There also
passed a caravan of old Jews on the road to Jerusalem, whither
they go to die – as is my desire, God willing – bearing with
them the bones of their kinsfolk, may their souls endure, to be
buried in the ground of the Holy City. These bones they carry
inside cloth sacks, a sight by which my heart was greatly
stirred.

Thus the dead among my brothers, peace upon them,
passed by on their last journey, while I, with my brothers
Vivo, Lazzaro del Vecchio of Ancona and Eliezer of Venice,
together with all our servants, being eighty persons together,
set our faces towards the north-east. In this fashion many are
the merchants among my brethren who range over the world,
seeking out not only those things which will serve to bring
them profit but also to satisfy their souls.

With a herd of many hundreds of camels, each bearing at
least six hundred pounds,[57] we proceeded thus towards
Damascus in Arabia, accompanied by many drovers who
urged on their slow beasts with whistles and whips. In this
fashion we crossed the rivers Leontes and Jordan and traversed
the great mountain of Hermon and came to the sands of the
desert of Syria, making halt at each setting of the sun and I
maintaining my duties, for which God be praised, together
with Vivo, Eliezer and Lazzaro of Ancona.

But on the fourth day, it being the eve of the Sabbath
Korah, it was necessary, as our sages, peace upon them,
instruct, to set three circles of ropes one above the other about
the place, the space between each rope being less than three
Venetian palms,[58] and this was done upon the shining of the
first star of evening to mark out the Sabbath that it is holy.
Whereupon, I said the kiddush and the amotzi before our
repast, which Berletto had prepared for us in accordance with
my instructions, after which, contented, we gave thanks to
God.

In the night, however, I was taken with much fear of the
drovers and their companions, they being a wicked and
cowardly people who steal freely from merchants, and with
cunning or violence, but more often with cunning.

Thus, all night long I remained with my eyes open, many
times walking among the camels which bore my goods,
together with my faithful clerks Armentuzio and Pizzecolli,
and my men Micheli and Fultrono, who bore their arms
about them, I praying to God that He spare me for my deed.
The two beasts upon whom I had concealed certain things I
kept close about me, beside the said circles of ropes. But the
others, being in darkness, since the moon was hidden, and I
having permitted that no fires be lit,[59] could not be seen. The
drovers, who were stirred from their sleep as we went about
them, were angered by our fears. But, there being many
impious men among them who think all Franks and Jews to
be rich, they will often devise stratagems in order to rob them.

In the morning the drovers whispered much among
themselves, also insisting that we continue our journey. But
this I forbade, it being the Sabbath Korah, and in this place
we remained until the next day, the animals resting also. For,
as it is written in the Torah, God be praised, thine ox and
thine ass shall also have rest.

From here we journeyed many leagues through Abilene and
by the river Abania towards Damascus. The way of life of the
country is that of those who revere Mahomet, being of

cultivation, trade and worship. There are many mosques, and learnèd men both among the Jews and the Mahometans, but also dark and empty souls who cause the traveller to fear. In the interior of this realm, on the margins of the desert of Syria, there are many who are very poor. Here also wander the families of the Bedouins who fled from us at our approach, even though some among the drovers were of their people, being sometimes timid and fearful but sometimes wicked and murderous without reason.

It was in the year 1270 …

Hence the traveller must remain cautious, neither too ready to drive them away, nor too ready to show them benevolence, whatever the heart might command. For there are some men who, from fear of others, may be either good or bad, as a dog that fears a man is unsure whether to wag its tail or bite his hand.

In Damascus, a great city with more than three thousand Jews, I entered through the Western Gate, together with my companions, leaving our servants to watch over our possessions. Here we had much conversation in the Arabic tongue with the brothers and cousins of Lazzaro del Vecchio, who are great merchants of the city, receiving gifts at their hands and much good counsel. Thus they informed us secretly both of their fear of the coming of the Tartars and, being privy to his desires, of the intention of Sultan Bonducdaro to expel the Christians from the realm of Syria, to the great benefit of the Jews. They declared that the armies of the Tartars, having conquered the lands to the north, would seek to conquer Damascus also, and that there was danger in remaining long, for marauders among them had already been seen a few leagues from the city.[60]

Therefore we decided, having made certain purchases from our brothers, and having obtained many provisions for the journey to Basra, that it was prudent to set off as fast as we could, for at noon the sun was every day growing hotter. Thus we departed from Damascus on the first day of Tammuz after the Sabbath Hukkat towards the river Euphrates, which is in the direction east-south-east.

For many days and nights we journeyed in the desert of Syria, which they call Hamad, towards Baudas,[61] and suffered greatly from the heat of the sun, so hot that it was a marvel. When the noon comes, since there is no shady place, it is difficult to stay alive in the rocky hills, and even the camels cry out in their dolour, the tears running from their eyes, may God have pity upon them. They limped at every step, and when the wind blew it was such that the dust obscured the very sun, making men and beast stumble together, so that we were constrained to wait until the wind had dropped. Great was the lamentation of my servants, who swore that they should not have left their homes, Buccazuppo pleading with me that she might return to San Giovanni d'Acri. But he that talks much with womankind brings evil upon himself and will inherit Gehenna.

So great was the heat that I felt twice-baked by the rays of the sun. No bird flew in the sky, nor creeping thing ran upon the sand, and even my blood was made dry. Yet I gave praise to God for keeping me in safety and called upon my Christian servants to do likewise. Some murmured against me, but in all men, provided that they be better than beasts, there exists an impulse towards God. For who but God, I asked, is the promoter of the natural life of the world?

But they, because of the evil works of idolatry, have no true conception of God, may the Unnameable One be exalted, who remains One and shall remain One to the end of days. For *that man* stands for them in the light of God, blessèd be He, whom they therefore cannot know. And if a

---

'THAT MAN'

*Jacob, like other pious Jews of the past and present, felt unable to name Jesus, not even as Jeshua ben Joseph, which can sometimes be found in Jewish texts. This periphrasis is also found in the writing of the twelfth-century rabbinic traveller, Benjamin of Tudela, e.g.* Travels, *London, 1783, p.73.*

rabbi should counsel them to pray to God, it is to *that man* and not to God that they turn.

It was in the year 1270 ...

Moreover, among them there were many doubtful thoughts, may God have pity upon them, some saying that none can foretell at noon even what manner of sunset the evening will bring, let alone man's fortunes on the morrow. To them I replied that truly the world and the heavens have no limit, and that as this day goes out and does not return, so does the sum of our days diminish without return. But the Holy One does not diminish, and in every place, be it ever so remote, wherever man declares that God is One, God, may He be cherished and honoured, will come to that man and bless him.

For more days we travelled with great slowness, since many were afflicted by fevers of the sun, to the place of the river Aurano,[62] in which no water ran, such was the dryness of the great desert. But in all these days, as upon the Sabbath Balak, I, together with Vivo, Eliezer of Venice and Lazzaro del Vecchio, carried out my duties, God be praised for the bounty which the Torah brings.

But in the depth of the night at this place of the river, I, not sleeping the whole night long, became much troubled in my spirit. The night was starry, but much grief returned to me at the thought of my wandering in the earthly world. The heavens above declared the glory of God, yet fears beset me and doubts also, may God have mercy upon my soul. For in the night I doubted where was the place of understanding and whence comes wisdom, seeing in the infinite sky not God's hand but, may God spare me, the void.

I wept much, alas, over my doubts, praying to God that He show me the way before the light of day return, so that I might not wander further in my own darkness of soul while the sun shone upon me. And this was the truth which He showed to me for His name's sake: that as the thought and wisdom of God are without limit, so also are the thought and reason of man, which have neither limit nor end, so that to man it is permitted to think also of the void. Moreover, there is no other proof of the existence of God, blessèd be He, than this immense realm of the heavens, and all that which exists before our eyes in the material world. Furthermore, by knowing his own soul, even in his griefs a man may come to know the nature of the Creator and the Creation, which knowledge is the end for which he has himself been created.

And for him who doubts that the hand of God is upon all things, let him know that some sages declare that in every moment the world is created anew and that, without God, it would indeed become a void. At which I truly felt fear as well as shame at my doubts, and at first light prayed to God for His forgiveness for my distress and the errors to which I had come. As Rabbi Judah teaches, a man should know what is above him, which are a seeing eye, a hearing ear and all his deeds written in a book. Thus, raised up by my own thoughts, I placed my phylacteries upon my arm and forehead, giving thanks to God for teaching me His wisdom in the night, and for conducting me towards the light.

In the days that followed, during which came the Sabbath Pinchas and the fast of Tammuz,[63] in which I performed my duties, we at last came to fertile places, passing close to Baudas, which is in the hands of the Tartars and become a wilderness frequented only by the Saracens of Syria and Aurano. Thereafter, we came to the great river Euphrates, journeying many hundreds of leagues along the western bank, where there are many inhabited places and where the country people have all the foodstuffs they need. Thus we continued in a fertile land of much plenty, in which all the things on which to live are found, I observing the Sabbaths Mattot, Masei and Devarim according to my duty.

Thus we drew near to Basra, seeing many lagoons, or rather marshes, on the left hand and on the right, as also many palms with dates, fertile gardens and much abundance. But on the ninth day of Av, when the heat was such as is unknown in any other part of the world, a heat which dries up the grasses and water of the earth and the sinews and blood of man, I mourned greatly, with Vivo, Eliezer and Lazzaro about me, all going without nutriment, neither food nor water, in grief for the ruin of our city, once great among the nations.[64]

It was in the year 1270 …

In the heat of the sun our suffering was great, and some were astonished, declaring that it made no sense that we forswore even water, Berletto pressing me often to drink, in distress that his master should seem on the point of death, and the servants of Vivo, Eliezer and Lazzaro did likewise, which pleased me to see.

But on this day was not the affliction of Judah greater, having passed into captivity and all her beauty departed, for the adversary had spread his hand upon her, as the Christian in our day sets his hand upon the Torah our queen? Thus we wept together, saying in our hearts to those who were around us, amid the beasts of the caravan, is it nothing to you, all you that pass by? Is there any sorrow like our sorrow? In this way we wept and when the day of mourning was past, we continued on our way to Basra, together with our cargoes and servants, entering the city, may God be praised, upon the thirty-first day of July,[65] which is to say three months and fifteen days after my departure from Ancona.

Basra, which in Arabic they call Al-Basra, is a great city which stands at a place where the great rivers flow together.[66] In this city the merchants make large profits, coming thither not only from all the lands of the Saracens but from Greater India, from the islands of Lesser India and even from the land of Sinim.

There are more than three thousand Jews in the city and also one hundred Franks, but for the most part the people worship Mahomet. From the city both the river, which some here call the river of the Saracens and others the river Iddacalo, and a canal, which is three leagues long and made with great artifice, take merchandise to the sea, where there stands a fair port called Saraggi. Here the great ships of Sinim

load and unload, and here the Jews also have trading posts,
and also build and hire ships for those who go to Greater
India.

In Basra you may find rich silk and gold baudekins, *nacchi*
and *nacchini*,[67] with lions, bears and other wild animals
wrought upon them in gold with great art. You may also buy
here at a good price horses for Greater India, where they are
much prized, as also dates in great quantity, which are held by
the merchants who come here to be the best in the world.
Here too they barter with silks and purple garments, and all
manner of spices. Among the merchants of the place many
Jews act as agents, acting also on behalf of the Saracens, and
by that acquire much wealth, as also in exchanging gold and
silver of different countries, in which they make great profits.

The women of the city, being worshippers of Mahomet, are
all veiled in thin silk, which is black or purple, so that they
may see but not be seen, as in all the lands of the Saracens.
But when they let fall their veils, as they do when they wish to
be seen, even by strangers, they are often of great beauty. I
have heard that the Frankish merchants declare them to be
not very chaste, although they wear veils which reach to their
ankles. But of the truth of this I could not tell.

The people eat dates, fowl and fish, and near the city are
fine baths, one which the Jews frequent and the other the
Saracens, in order to seek relief from the great heat of
summer. One also finds flies, horseflies and similar creatures
that trouble the people.

Of the rich Jews the greatest is Isaia of Ascoli[68] to whose
daughter my son Isaac was to be married. Him I greeted with
tears of joy upon my entrance to the city, clasping him to my
heart many times, the best beloved and most dutiful of my
sons, and he touching my feet to do me honour. Laying my
hand upon his head, I gave him blessings thrice over, he
weeping to be thus blessed, and I embracing him once more.

From him I sought to learn of the life of the Jews of the
city, since he had much knowledge of them. Here they

willingly eat and converse with the Saracens, and the Saracens, who depend much upon them, treat closely with them even as partners in the building of the great ships that voyage to Seilan. For the Saracens, although they here show cunning in many things, as in buying and selling, are less able than the Jews, to whom they turn for help at every step.

It was in the year 1270 …

Hence, only a few of the Jews are poor. Moreover, among the Saracens, unlike among the Christians, merchants are considered as kin to nobles, and many of the Jews have the wealth of kings. However, towards them there is also much envy, so that they must conceal their riches. Therefore their houses they keep locked tight, so that those whom they do not trust may not see what is within. For many of the Jews do not live in a quarter of their own, as I observed also in San Giovanni d'Acri, but without great distinction between the Saracens, Franks and Persians of the city, and even in the same lanes and courtyards as they. Some streets and alleys near the synagogues predominate with Jews, but even in these there are Saracens to be found, and there is much gentleness between them, the Saracens calling the Jews *malem*.[69]

For here there are no Christian priests to preach against eating and drinking with us, or to forbid spending time with us in our houses, as there are in Christian lands, but rather there is much friendship between those of different faiths who live in the city. Moreover, the followers of Mahomet permit the marriage of their men to those whom they call infidels, although it is forbidden by our rabbis, peace upon them and honour to their names.

The law of the Saracens also permits that a Jewish wife shall observe her customs and make her prayers inside the house, even admonishing her husband not to bring her to break the Sabbath, for which God be praised. Nor may he prevent her from reading in the Torah, for whose bounty God be thanked, provided that she does so in silence, but she may not attend the synagogue after her marriage to a Saracen, for which may a curse be upon them.

Further, here the taxes upon us are fixed[70] and we do not suffer the same pillage as the kings of other realms visit upon us. Neither are we compelled here to serve as usurers, which the Christians impose upon us in their lands to arouse the hatred of the common people. For in Basra there are not only traders among the Jews, but also tailors, workers in wood, leather and iron, makers of shoes and saddles as well as many apothecaries and physicians, from the great skill and knowledge of the Jews in the healing of men, and from the understanding of their nature.

The men all have long beards with points, and most are handsome. They wear dark-coloured garments, a vermilion cap bound around with silk cloth which is striped, and on their feet are permitted only dark shoes, by which to distinguish them from others, according to the decree of the sultan of the city. They are also permitted to ride on horseback, although they are Jews, but may not carry swords.

The women, who go without veils, are beautiful and graceful with black hair, yet have fair and clear skins, with eyes which are soft and black and sparkle from the powder which they put on them, may God forgive me for writing in such a light manner. About their waists they wear embroidered belts, have their hair braided and their fingernails dyed red.

---

### 'PERMITTED TO RIDE ON HORSEBACK'

*Denial to Jews of the right to ride on horseback or to carry a sword – perhaps because they were tokens in Christian eyes of chivalry – was a commonplace prohibition in Christian lands in the mediaeval period. To ride on a horse also elevated the rider, both symbolically and in fact, above the common throng, which Church ordinances sought to prevent in Jews, deemed unworthy of such distinction. A similar discrimination was evidently practised in Hormuz by the Saracens (p.81). To Jacob, seeing fellow-Jews on horseback was clearly sufficiently surprising for him to take note of it.*

In greeting a guest, they take his right hand boldly, kiss it and put it to their foreheads. Yet, for all that they conduct themselves in a modest manner, if an injury is received or at the death of a dear one they will cry out loudly, beating their cheeks and tearing their garments, but not such as are worked in gold or set with pearls.

At their repasts the Jews of the city sit upon the ground, the foods, which are wholesome and of rich flavours, being placed in silver dishes that they set upon their carpets. From dates and figs they also make a strong liquid, of which they themselves drink little but which is prized by the Saracens, with whom much trade in it is done. At the end of the Sabbath, when my brothers say the benediction over a cup of wine, they pour it thereafter upon the ground, saying that he in whose house wine is not poured out as water is not among those who are blessed by God, may their peace and plenty continue, Amen.

All this my son Isaac narrated to me while I made sojourn with him, may God protect him, or I saw with my own eyes in the city.

Our cargoes having been unloaded at Saraggi, for which one pays dues of one-fortieth[71] on all merchandise, and having been placed in the trading-house there of my brother Isaia of Ascoli, peace upon him, the drovers were well paid by Armentuzio and went away, our servants being given shelter at the trading-house of Isaia also, until the time came to set sail for Greater India.

But now a great and killing heat came upon the city of Basra after the Sabbath Vaethannan, these being the first days of August, which is to say the fifteenth day of Av. For in the summer there is a heat so great as is unknown in any other part of the world, a heat without measure. It was such great heat that it was hardly possible to suffer it, so hot that at midday one might not step upon the ground, the people betaking themselves to deep cellars beneath their houses. In the heat the people also lie much in water, as in the water of

tanks, in order to cool themselves, or take refuge in the palm
groves a day's distance from the city. It is also a time of
sickness, for when the hot winds blow many die of fevers, as
befell poor Berletto, of which I shall soon give account.

Thus, the people remain in their houses during the day
because of the great heat and dryness, and go out at night. At
noon nothing may stir, so great is the heat. Even the flies and
other insects sleep. All wait to catch a breath of cool wind in
order to lessen the great heat, but when the wind blows it
brings heat even greater. Indeed there comes upon you
sometimes in the summer a very strong wind of such heat
that it is not possible to survive it. For this is the driest
country in the world, and bitter were my days in this time of
heat, and bitter the days of my servants also.

Because fresh air is lacking and the harmful wind brings
putrefaction to all things, they cover meat and fish with a
cloth, together with much saffron and other spices, but they
stink from the heat in a few hours. For so full of disease is the
air of this city.

Thus, weary, I dreamed of great fountains of purest water. I
did not so much give forth sweat as a liquid which flowed
from my body, God forgive me for such an account, until I
feared that my very flesh would have been liquefied, which
God forbid.

In vain I sought relief from the heat, but there came a
plague of great flies as once tormented the land of Egypt, God
be praised, which were large as small birds and from which I
hid my head, so afflicted was I by such torments. Moreover,
so many were the stings of the mosquitoes that I suffered a
great itching from which I could get no rest and from which
came sores as a result of my scratching. But Abraam Hagiz, a
skilled doctor and apothecary of Basra, prepared me a salve
according to my instructions,[72] which eased the fever of my
skin.

Having spent one month in the company of my son, into
whose hands I had placed certain precious things until my

departure for Greater India and to whom I gave counsel for the future conduct of his life, and also having fulfilled my duties, spending much time in the study of Torah upon the Sabbaths Ekev, Reeh and Ki Tetze and in prayer, I came on the fifteenth day of Elul into the house of my brother Isaia, peace upon him. For the new moon of the autumnal equinox[73] was drawing near, and it was fitting that we should spend the festival of the New Year together, and pass the Day of Atonement in common, in preparation for the uniting of our families in marriage. For in the great recurrences are both ends and beginnings, it being just that repentance and joy, happiness and expiation, should attend one upon the other.

It was in the year 1270 …

In this time I became acquainted with my daughter[74] Rebecca, who was fifteen years old, a girl of grace and of modest behaviour, and most fitting for my son. In all things she was attentive to my wishes, seeking always that she should be in my favour. On the day of the New Year, a day of great heat, all repaired to the synagogue, which was only two hundred paces from the house of my brother.

Here the due prayers were said, I, as a Jew of grand lineage being summoned, with great honour shown to me by all, to read a portion of the Law. Afterwards, as is their custom, each said to the other, both in Arabic and Hebrew, May you this year be in good fortune and may everything that you do have a good outcome.

But where none could see me I wept also for the absence of my Sara, praying that God might keep her, and my father also, may his soul endure. In the rejoicing for the New Year, I ate at first with a stone in my heart, but this being an impious thing, for which God forgive me, I was thereafter in good heart, my son being at my side.

The heat continuing, I betook myself often to a broad and deep cave beneath the house of my brother Isaia, peace upon him, where a stream, passing through an aqueduct, fills the said cave. Here I gave thought, being able to breathe more freely and being at my ease, to the griefs of my father, may his

65

name endure. I prayed also that my goods were being kept safe by my servants and that God would preserve me upon my journey. Here, too, in the darkness, I thought much of the light of God's wisdom, which shines splendid and luminous upon the terrestrial world, but which cannot enter the hearts of the impious, being darker than any cave beneath the earth. As my friend Hillel ben Samuel, peace upon him, prayed, may the Knower of Truth continue to teach me such truth for His name's sake, Amen.

In this manner, often sitting against the heat in the cave of Isaia, I made myself ready for the Day of Atonement. Upon that day I prayed that God spare me for the doubts about all things which afflict my reason, forgive me for my sins against others, and punish those who have betrayed their word and stolen from our substance. In abstaining from food, I also gave my mind to God alone, and at the sounding of the ram's horn, my soul was raised in fear and joy as if to the Divine Presence. Then God again appeared to me to be the blessing of the intellect and not of the corporeal being, and that such was revealed, albeit in material form, to his elect by our teacher Moses in order to serve as a light to the whole human order. As to the sorrows and sufferings of the righteous, and the well-being of the wicked, which is about us all the length of our days, it is not in our power to explain.

Then came the days of the wedding of my son and daughter, days of much joy, in which there was a great feast at the house of my brother Isaia, with many girls and young men singing and dancing throughout the house. There was also displayed so much riches that one could not count it. I deemed it an infinite excess, for it is better that a Jew does not act in such a fashion that others know the wealth that he has.

Yet all declared that such a beautiful pair as Isaac and Rebecca had never been seen in the world, and that the bridegroom was one of the most handsome men who had ever been seen. But there were also those who said that Isaia of Ascoli had made such a wedding not out of his goodness and duty but for his own ambition and his own soul's sake.

But first I should say that during their nuptial I again wept for the absence of Sara, so that when the spouses both bowed their heads beneath the wedding canopy in order to receive the blessing, my eyes were blinded with tears, at which my friends Vivo, Eliezer and Lazzaro of Ancona came to me in order to give me comfort.

The spouses were so richly dressed and adorned that each seemed royal. For this was a great wedding, and my brother Isaia had spent a great deal. Indeed the house was not large enough for such a throng, so that he made some of them stay in another house nearby.

All the house was illuminated and many people had come from a great distance, even from Baudas, the city of Isfahan, and Cormosa, so that it was not possible to count the number, so many wished to watch my son tie the bond of love. When they were joined by their sacred vows, great was the joy of all to see my son take the object of his love by the hand, she being adorned from head to foot in embroidered gold, with a crown of pearls, sapphires and rubies – what gems! – of great workmanship, and with many rings on her fingers of great value.

Certain Saracens were also present, it being a commandment of the Torah to invite all, including such neighbours as are Saracens and even if they be foes. All exclaimed at the beauty of the bride, she having been bathed in cold water for eight days before her marriage, on the eighth day her hair dressed and her person hidden from the eyes of men.

Beneath the canopy, her face hidden by a fine veil, she walked thrice about Isaac and he once about her, upon which Rabbi Haim ben Joel of Baudas, peace upon him, joined them together. Then was the marriage contract between them read out, by which my brother Isaia undertook to furnish my fleet, as I shall tell hereafter.

To my son, whom God keep in his care, the said Haim

declared as follows, drawing the veil of the bride aside: 'Young man, lift up your eyes and see what you have chosen for yourself. Beauty is vain but a woman who fears the Lord shall be praised.' And at the shouts of good fortune after the seven blessings had been made, they broke upon the ground earthen pots that each of the principal guests carried in his hand, and not a glass, as is the practice among us.[75]

Whereafter, my son Isaac, may God bless him, took an egg which he made as if to cast at his wife, as if to say that he wished her an easy childbirth, which God, may His name be lauded, might grant. Whereupon the guests gathered in a great crowd about them, giving wine to a virgin to drink in a narrow glass, and to a widow to drink in a wide one, of the reason for which I make no mention.

Thereafter, the gifts of each person present were set before the spouses: belts of gold, rich clothes, precious stones, pearls, gold worked in a filigree with fine silver wire, silver so delicately carved that it was a marvel to behold, and a heap of besants of such value that it was not possible to count them. But seeing such things I also felt great unease, for does not our teacher, Rabbi Mose ben Maimon, declare that those things of which we have no need are without end, whereas those things which are needful are few? Moreover, many are those guests who, seeking to follow the ways of the rich, are constrained to borrow money in order to make such gifts.

In addition, great was the dowry of worldly goods given to us by my brother Isaia. Apart from other things, he undertook to furnish me on hire with a great ship and two galleys, a thing which was already advanced, as well as to provide half the pay of the mariners thereon, for my journey to Greater India and Manci, and for my return thence to Edente. I undertook for my part that half of their pay and the cost of their victuals should be borne by me, that he should have a certain part of the profits of the voyage, God willing, and that the ships should be brought back to Edente, to be at joint expense if any should suffer damage or loss.[76]

Having examined the gifts with much astonishment, the people thereupon gathered to eat. When all were arranged upon the carpets, each in his own place, I being the principal guest in virtue of my knowledge of the Torah, for which God be praised, the kiddush and amotzi were said by Rabbi Salomone ben Giuda of Basra, at which a great Amen was called.

It was in the year 1270 ...

Whereupon all fell swiftly to eating, but many comported themselves as gluttons, devouring many plates of meats and fruits until their eyes were ready to burst from their heads. For this was a grand feast, as I have said, all provided for my son by Isaia of Ascoli, peace upon him, in order to do honour to him.

Beside my brother sat his lady on his right, together with the bride, her sisters and the other women of the house. On the left side sat my son and I, together with the other sons of Isaia and their male offspring. Of the others, who numbered many hundreds, each knew the place on the carpets where he had to sit, some being in this room and others in others, among them those who were from foreign lands.

It was beyond all belief to see the magnificence of the clothes of silk and gold worn by the guests, together with so many precious stones upon them. For each person had striven to appear in the greatest pomp that was possible to them, which, to speak truly, is an unworthy thing. Before me was set a large bowl of pure gold, full of wine, and other beverages according to taste.

And when all had eaten and drunk, so much remained that a part of the food was given to the Saracen servants, and a part set aside for the poor of the city, may God have pity upon them.

Then thanksgiving was offered up to God, He who protects His people and smites the evil-doer, and all entreated Him that He give my son and daughter a long life and bless them with children. Also that He, may His name be unspoken, increase and multiply the wealth of all present. Also that the Jews of the city might live together in peace and goodwill among themselves and with their neighbours. To which all replied with one voice, Amen and Amen, others saying, May God do it, so that the rooms of the house resounded with their cries, while I wept salt tears for the absence of my loved ones.

Now, Isaia, with the address of a familiar calling me by the name Ciacco,[77] which displeased me, summoned me to speak first so that I might give my counsel to the spouses. I declared to them that life is both joyful and bitter, full of grief and laughter, of profit and travail, and of darkness and light. But however much it changes, and whatever God may bring, the duties of a man and a woman are constant, to their parents, to one another, to their children, and to their neighbours.

Hearing this, all cried out in agreement, and when those in other rooms understood what I had said, they cried out likewise, declaring that it was right in every way, praising my words greatly. And speaking well of my son, I further counselled my daughter to attend him with affection, saying that if she did so then would he likewise, praying also that she might soon be with child. Thereafter, when a great number of the guests had spoken, the young men and women, as I have said, began to sing and to dance, at which time they are permitted to embrace, a thing forbidden among the Saracens, but not to kiss. At last my daughter was taken away to be prepared for the night by the women and my son embraced me for a last time, swearing to uphold his duties to me, at which I was much pleased, and thus departed to his bride.

This ends the narration of the marriage of my son, at which I felt both joy and sadness, knowing that it is thus that one generation passes away before another, and that there is no new thing under the sun. Away flies the bird and there is neither bird nor shadow. But by the mercy of God, may He be exalted, all shall be renewed by the love of pious men for Him and His works, Amen.

# CHAPTER THREE

# Our Salvation from the Sea

As will have already become clear, Jacob's manuscript provides valuable evidence upon the Jews' conduct of commercial activity in the middle ages. It makes plain in what ways Jewish familial, religious, scholarly and trading relationships were interwoven and widespread, and how they paid relatively little regard to territorial and other boundaries. Thus we can see how the family of Jacob d'Ancona was linked by consanguineity, by marriage, by the search for education, by scholarship, by specific trading partnerships and by economic activity with other cities and small towns in the Marche region of central Italy, with Venice, Verona, Tuscany and Naples, with Provence and Spain, with Ragusa (Dubrovnik), Acre and Alexandria, with Damascus and Basra, and with India and the furthest East. The manuscript in particular shows that, by means of joint business ventures involving relatives in distant places, opportunities for profit were created which were difficult to emulate for others whose reach was less.

Thus, Jacob is able to hire vessels, acquire crucial trading information, secure payment and obtain redress through relatives or co-religionists. He found Jewish ship-owners and customs officials in Aden, hired vessels from his son's father-in-law in Basra, and held conversations in Arabic (and perhaps in Hebrew) almost wherever he went. The manuscript also shows how a son might serve temporarily in foreign outposts as a factor, or be married strategically into the family of a prominent merchant on a main trade route, in what might be called a dynastic trading marriage.

More generally, the manuscript indicates that in large trading centres, including on the Malabar coast of India, in Sumatra, and in Zaitun itself there were Jewish agents who acted both on behalf of single great traders and on behalf of numbers of overseas Jewish merchants. In the smaller ports, they would have maintained the trading-post, or *fóndaco* – with its counting house and warehouses – receiving, procuring and dispatching merchandise, accepting and passing on payments, as well as doing business on their own accounts. In addition, Jacob refers later to Jewish couriers, or messengers, operating between Cairo and Alexandria. Jewish merchants also appear from the manuscript to have employed the services of non-Jews, both Christians and Muslims, in the ports they visited, perhaps because they were needed should their vessel arrive, inopportunely for the orthodox, on the Sabbath and require to be unloaded; Jacob's manuscript documents his own scruples in the matter.

Conversely, we learn from him that in foreign ports 'many are the agents who are Jews and who act also on behalf of the Saracens, the Saracens being cunning in many things, as in the making of bargains, but not in the correct keeping of accounts, in which the Jews are the most skilful.'

But on the question of his own profits – and even of the prices he pays for most of his purchases – Jacob is notably discreet, as if he did not wish to disclose such matters in writing. As to such expressions of his trading ethics as he offers, they suggest an honest man, but one who is also ready to pay dishonest officials in order to secure exemptions from port dues and taxes. He is quick to identify sharp practice in others, as well as to reject poor quality goods, or what he calls 'poor stuff' or 'lousy stuff', that is, rubbish. From his own account of his business conduct, he seems shrewd and skilful, in constant search of benefit and advantage, but ready to pay a fair price for goods of high standard. A scholar he may have been, but he is also a recognisable market figure.

Apart from the personal family reasons – themselves linked with trading ambitions – which took Jacob to Basra, it is plain that his main purpose in his journey was, by extensive and profitable purchases, to try to restore family fortunes harmed by his father's losses and misadventures in the Black Sea trade.

In addition, we know that mediaeval international trade was largely dependent upon personal relationships. Given the slowness of communications by letter, the proper handling of business affairs was hard to secure. Local agents *(commissi)* and factors *(fattori)* tended therefore to be chosen from among settlers hailing from one's own home city, or (as among the Jews) from one's own co-religionists or family, for trustworthiness's sake. But all such relations required constantly to be renewed, or amended, by personal contact. It was a necessity which could drive a senior partner in a trading enterprise to risk life and limb in a voyage involving years of absence from home.

It is also plain from Jacob's intermittent references to such matters that there were particular problems for him to resolve. They would have included checking the work of factors and agents, and replacing them where necessary, dissolving certain agreements previously made, settling accounts and securing payments, and perhaps examining the entire running of a trading-base, where the factor generally lived and the travelling merchant stayed. A factor in the service of a company might be corrected or dismissed, for example for sending back to Ancona a poor quality of goods, or goods which had been adulterated, as well as for other forms of inefficiency and default. Or there might be fraud and stealing en route to look into, or too high dues and taxes might be being paid, as Jacob on one occasion complains, through insufficient guile in dealing with port officials.

Among such dues – which at one point Jacob describes as being 'no better than plunder' – were payments for warehousing where the trader did not own or part-own such facilities himself, harbour and road tolls, market taxes, transport taxes, payments to watchmen, bribes and arbitrary exactions, in some countries and ports levied on Jews alone. These exactions Jacob calls *malatolta*, or 'illegally taken'. It is at the western Indian port of Cambaetta (Cambaet, or Cambay, in Gujarat) that Jacob, recovering from illness, is most exercised by his factor's failures. In his angry criticisms of what he finds there he gives us a unique picture of the trials of the merchant of his time.

ow during this time there came to me from Saraggi, disturbed in spirit and burdened with their thoughts, the faithful Armentuzio, accompanied by the brave Turiglioni. They declared that, it being already the twenty-first day of September, for they came on that day which was the Fast of Gedaliah, the north-east wind would surely come within another twenty-one days. They said that I should make haste to return to the port, where everything necessary was being made ready, as also with the vessels of Menahem Vivo, Lazzaro of Venice and Eliezer del Vecchio. They also declared that there had been much sickness among my servants as a result of the air, Berletto being wasted, and the girl Buccazuppo said to be with child, which caused me to be greatly angered. They reported also that three ships and two galleys of the great merchant Aaron of Barcelona in Aragon were being made ready.

I replied that, whatever might be the winds, I should depart only after the marriage of my child, which fell upon the thirteenth day of Tishri, which is to say the thirtieth day of September. Moreover, a pious man might not embark upon the Feast of Succoth and Simhat Torah or upon the Sabbath Bereshit, at which they became greatly troubled. I therefore calmed their fears, declaring to them that after the eleventh day of October we should depart, which was twenty-one days from the day upon which they had come to me. Moreover, my son Isaac with the counsel of Isaia, peace upon him, having already purchased and dispatched to the warehouse of Isaia many cantars of choice dates for Manci, and with which to barter in Upper India, as well as three hundred baudekins worked in silk and gold, and one hundred each of *nacchi* and *nacchini*, while many other things had been purchased by Armentuzio himself upon my instructions and were already loaded, I declared myself to be well content.

However, upon the twenty-second day of September, I hastened to Saraggi to attend the better to my affairs. Here, alas, I found Berletto pale and thin, and the woman Buccazuppo lamenting upon her bed, fearful of my anger. To both I gave counsel, to the little one in his weakness of body and to the other in the blindness of her soul. To her I declared that the ladder of being has upon its highest step man and woman, who are superior to every other creature under the sun, and that such man or woman, whether Jew, Saracen or Christian, should therefore act in a manner worthy of their charge.

To this, in her grief, she made no reply, only lamenting the more, she and the woman Bertoni seeking my aid in order that the life in her should be destroyed. For so the Christian spits in the face of God, may He forgive me my blasphemy and may my tongue be cut from my mouth if I do not speak thus only to His greater glory, may He be exalted and cherished.

The ship of Isaia, being no *yehaz*, was of great capacity and carried as much as eight to ten thousand cantars of freight[1] and as many as four hundred persons,[2] of whom three hundred were for the sails, and for the oars when the winds were light. It had four masts and twelve sails, together with two other masts which they raise and place in position, and all was made with stout planking and well framed and with strong nails. It also had thirty cabins, each with its own lock and key, and six small boats attached to the outer sides of the vessel, in order to gather supplies when we were at anchor or to take fish from the sea.

Isaia, according to the dowry as I have recounted, also furnished me with two other vessels of sail and oar, each with ninety mariners, some under arms, to load certain choice cargoes[3] and to give help in time of danger. For there are many pirates who go about the sea of India in robbery from Cambaetta to Colam and loot the ships that pass.

Inside the great ship, which also had three rudders, the captains, who were men of Basra, were equipped with charts of the seas of India and Sinim, which, being made by Saracens who are wise in such things, were esteemed by them to be more accurate than those of the Franks.

They also displayed to me a compass of Sinim, made with great artifice and which is much prized by the mariners of these seas, so that they may tell where the ship lies by the meridian when the sky is filled with clouds and neither the sun nor the stars may be seen. But when the sky is clear, the Saracen captains are able to steer the ship by the signs of the earth or the stars, as is done among us.

Whereupon, having seen all these marvels, and given counsel to my servants, I went to the city for the Day of Atonement and the nuptials of my son, as I have written, as

---

'A COMPASS OF SINIM'

*This represents an early, although not the first, mention of the compass, which was already in use in the West in Jacob's time. It seems to be the fact that it is a Chinese compass 'of great artifice' which is of interest to Jacob, for it is probable that on his journey from Zadar to Acre his vessel would have carried one and that he, as a learnèd man, would have had an understanding of it. It had, however, been known to the Chinese for centuries before. It was a box or bowl made of box-wood, in the centre of which a magnetised needle turned on a small pivot and identified the south – and therefore all other directions also. These directions were marked upon a disc set into the box.*

also for the Feast of Succoth, Simhat Torah and the Sabbath
Bereshit,[4] when all my duties were done, for which God be
praised, returning thence to Saraggi in haste for my departure,
since the wind from the north-east now blew strongly.

Thus, when all the necessary provisions had been loaded on
our vessels, and those of Vivo, Eliezer and Lazzaro had also
been made ready, as well as those of Aaron of Barcelona, and
the sails of our great fleet began to swell in the wind, I bade
farewell to my brother Isaia and to my son Isaac, wishing that
God spare him and bring him fortune. Great was my grief,
and many my servants' troubles, while I feared that of our
vessels some would not complete the voyage without
shipwreck, or without being looted by pirates.

But these same ships in which I sailed, for so I reasoned,
had brought great riches to Isaia, may God be praised for His
bounty to our people. Thus, on the thirteenth day of
October, I set sail with a heart full of faith, as the Torah
commands us, undertaking to bring back the vessels to
Edente, as I have narrated, leaving in addition certain goods
in the hands of my son, to be sold by him in the event of
misadventure.

Now came some relief from the lack of fresh air and from
the heat in that dry country. It also befell to me that I should
calm the souls of Turiglioni, to whom the presence of the
other pilots was not welcome, and of the girl Buccazuppo,
who was much weighed down by her situation.

I told them that poor Berletto, who lay sleeping close
beside them, would not be long in this world, and that their
ills were little in comparison with his, and that true wisdom
comes from understanding that not everything is as one sees
it. Which is to say that even in grief and weeping there may
be a hidden ground of joy, as in the pain of birth there is the
beginning of felicity, or in the anger against a rival is that
pride which drives us to raise ourselves above others by our
greater merit.

However, from my counsel they seemed to take little

comfort, yet thereafter they became more attentive to
Berletto, for whom I felt great pity. For I saw that, despite the
medicine that had been given to him, his bones were without
flesh. Indeed, without any suspicion on his part, he was
already very close to death, so speedy was the advance of his
disease.

Thus, in trying to comfort him, I showed myself on this
day and those that followed compassionate to him, as I would
have been to a son, God forbid. For all men are alike in
suffering and their bodies grow weak and fail in the self-same
fashion. The energy of the Christian fails as does that of the
Saracen and the Jew, and his livid flesh corrupts and stinks in
death whether or not he be among God's chosen.

To him unwilling either to eat or to drink, I said: You would
be advised to drink. But he did not reply, such was his
weakness. Thus, our vessel, followed by the great fleet of all our
ships, proceeding by sail and in good order, passed onwards
along the coast of Suolstan in Persia by day and by night, and
in a fair wind.

After we had passed the island of Lar at the time of the new
moon, it came to be the eve of the Sabbath Noah, God be
praised, when I, having lit two Sabbath lights in my cabin,
gave myself to prayer, mindful also that now, having been
separated from my Sara for six months in my travel, I was
henceforward breaking my duty to her.[5] Whereupon there
came to me Armentuzio and the woman Bertoni, she weeping
and calling me to attend quickly to Berletto.

It being not only permitted but a matter to praise when the
Sabbath is neglected by a pious man for the sake of one who
is sick and close to death, for nothing in the world is of
greater value than human life, the Torah being given for the
sake of life, I immediately went to the bed of poor Berletto,
examining the eyes, tongue and pulses. His legs thereupon
began to twitch in the last agony of the quartan fever,[6] and
while the woman Bertoni gave herself up to moaning, I lost
the pulses[7] and knew that death had come. I felt myself

moved to pity, observing his thin body and thinking of his
kind service to me in my own sickness, all my servants
weeping about him. To whom I said, weeping may endure for
a night, but joy comes in the morning.

But many of them, seeing the young boy dead, seemed in
fear for their lives, for he had died of the quartan fever. The
girl Buccazuppo set up a great wail, crying that she had never
seen anyone dead and calling out many times, What has
happened?, and What is this?, in a strange manner. To her I
said, My daughter, it is a dead body, at which she was
quietened.

I then left them to return to my place, for he, being a
Christian, it was needful for them to say their own prayers
over him, which I called upon them to do. But since there
was a danger of contagion from his body, and I myself feeling
unwell, it was necessary to give thought what to do. Yet, the
child being dead and no longer a sick person for whom the
Sabbath might be further violated, I gave myself to study, as
on the following day also, during which time we came near to
the island of Cusam.

Having pronounced the sanctification for the end of the
Sabbath, I now myself felt the assault of the fever, yet
returned to Berletto. When I drew near, he appeared to have
been dead for a long time, being already in a state of decom-
position. Yet it was but eighteen hours since his death, so
speedy in such a place is the putrefaction of the body, which
begins to corrupt even after two hours.

It is the wise custom among us, even in the cold countries,
to bury the dead quickly, for a dead body when shorn of its
soul, and despite the respect which is owed to it, is an
abomination. So much the more then, because of the great
heat, should the dead of these countries be buried the same
day.

Yet by no means would my servants permit that the body
of Berletto be cast into the sea, Buccazuppo threatening even
to lay hands on me, declaring that he should have a Christian

burial upon the land. Therefore they had caused a coffin to be made by the carpenter, in the which they laid the boy, placing in it saffron and other spices of Basra against the putrefaction.

And thus we came to Cormosa, my body also taken by the fever. Here, traders come from Chesmacorano, from Greater India and from Sinim to purchase its pearls, horses, precious stones and fruits. The town stands on a river called Minao, by which vessels reach the city from the Indian Sea. It is fertile with oranges and apples and the sultan of the place is Roccan Mahomet, who is also called the *Calati*, and who commands all by his will alone and is much feared by his foes. It is said that he acquired his place by killing his brother and that all his family commit bloody revenges and other cruel acts, as is the way of the Saracens among themselves.

But it is an open place for all the world, in which there are above two hundred and fifty Jews, whom the Rock and Redeemer of Israel preserve. Some of them are very rich and most bountiful to their brethren, hospitably entertaining them, and follow the precepts of the Torah with great care. Their houses are also cleaner and better furnished than those of most of the Saracens. They know much of the Mishnah and Talmud, giving themselves to the study of the law both day and night, and speak the Persian tongue, but it is not the best there is.[8] Here there are bought and sold all sorts of goods and as much of them as any could wish, and nearly all the brokers of the place are Jews. So it is with the physicians also, and there are many families who are engaged in the dyeing of cloth.

All are compelled to wear a turban of yellow, at the command of the *Calati*. The women, who wear robes of vermilion or green, richly embroidered in gold at the bosom, do not hide their faces as do the Saracen women. Indeed it would be a sin to do so, such is their beauty. The men of this country are rich in gold, wearing turbans adorned with jewels whose value cannot be counted and silk vests over which they throw garments spotted with gold, and thus clothed they ride on horseback, appearing like the sons of kings.

But the Jews, save for the physician of the sultan, are not permitted to go on horseback, although they may go about on mules, the Saracens saying that a horse is too noble an animal for a Jew, a curse upon them. Nor are they allowed by the *Calati* to carry a sword, making as if to fear us. Moreover, when passing a mosque of the Mahometans they must go barefoot, and should a hand be raised by a Saracen against them they dare not reply, for their hands would be cut off as being raised against the true believer. Nevertheless, my brothers are treated justly in matters of trade and money, and many have grown rich by it from their ability and labour, the Saracens being less active and more given to ease. They punish with death by burning the Jew or Christian who blasphemes against Mahomet or their Koran, or who lies with a Saracen woman.

Here, so weak from the quartan fever did I feel that bitterness took hold of my spirit, it being a great anguish to suffer such torments, and yet to be constrained to seek my gain. The faithful Armentuzio and Pizzecolli urged me to remain on board the ship, at rest, yet it being my duty to restore my fortunes, I went about the market with my brother, Sanson Ebreo ben Mose, he who departed Ancona in the year 1259, and to whom my father, God rest his soul, had directed me.

Many were my troubles in this place. The soldiers of the sultan, seeing that my servants were bringing forth a coffin from the ship, were not willing to permit them to carry it to the cemetery of the Franks of that place. They summoned me to the port, and seeing from my beard and dress that I was a Jew, charged me that I brought some pestilence to their city, ordering that I open the coffin of Berletto before their eyes, may God spare me. Armentuzio therefore returned to Sanson Ebreo in order to seek his aid, since the king is secretly a great friend to the Jews, holding our faith in favour, for which God be praised. Nor has he ever seized upon a Jewish woman, God be thanked, as he has upon others, as the wives of his counsellors and sometimes their daughters also. This was told me by Sanson Ebreo.

Moreover, although for every Jew above the age of nine years a tax must be paid each year to the king, which in Saracen they call *kharadj*, Rabbi Asher ben Jehiel pays nothing, from the great respect in which he is held by the Saracens for his learning, being a truly wise man. Indeed, on the Sabbath the sultan goes in secret to his house in the *mellah* in order to hold discourse with him and to sit at his table, as the said Asher told me. Thus, although our brothers must pay the sultan so that they may have a synagogue and bury their dead, as also that the said synagogue may be open to the light and not hidden in darkness, we count ourselves blessèd not to suffer more, seeing that the sultan protects us.

Hence, as among us from Christian lands also, they fear the time of a new sultan, as we in our lands fear a new pope or prince, since such time is often a time of travail for our people, may the names of our enemies be erased. For a new ruler is often given not to do some kindness to us, but to extort new tributes and payments and other exactions, or to inflict punishments upon us for things we have not done, or even to expel us from the realm.

But to return to my theme, I therefore opened the coffin, praying to God that I be permitted to purify myself of such a deed by greater piety in the days to come, as upon the Sabbaths Vayera and Hayyel Sarah, saying in my heart to the Holy One that I acted thus only from great necessity, while I waited to be saved from these Hamans[9] by my brother Sanson and the faithful Armentuzio.

When I opened the coffin, great was the stink of the corrupt and greenish flesh, may I be preserved, at which the soldiers would have laid hands upon me and carried me to my death for bringing them a pestilence, albeit that it was the fault of my Christian servants that the body of Berletto had not been cast into the sea, as I had counselled. Neither was I willing to lay bare the corpse, although it might save my own life should no signs of disease be found there save those of the quartan fever, such was the abomination which lay before me, may God who gives and takes away life be exalted.

But now Sanson Ebreo came, declaring before the guard that I was of noble line among the Jews and no simple merchant, and that Rabbi Asher ben Jehiel would go before the Sultan Mahomet if they should attempt to harm me. Moreover, to each of the said guard he made payment in order that my Christian servants might carry the coffin to the cemetery of the Franks. Thus, after much debate and many speeches, I concealing my own fever lest everything go from bad to worse, my servants took the coffin away, I instructing them to quarrel with no one and to do everything in a quiet fashion.

Such was my weariness, I being of weak constitution and borne down by fever and the great heat, that I was now driven to rest, giving instructions to Armentuzio to treat with Sanson Ebreo, broker of the place, in the purchase of twenty horses and their fodder, which should thereafter be put in the charge of the men Micheli and Fultrono.

For a good and large Saracen horse, which may be had in Cormosa for fifty marks of silver, sells well in the cities of Greater India, even for four hundred silver marks, for so it befell later, God be praised. The horses of the Saracens are good runners and much prized by the noblemen of Greater India who ride them like devils. Indeed, so lacking in care are they of their well-being, God have pity upon the beasts, that they bring the strongest and swiftest horse to ruin in a short time, for they do not know how to ride. This Sanson Ebreo told to Armentuzio while I lay ill with fever, and so it is.

When I was somewhat restored, God be thanked, I made fine and great purchases of incense for the idolaters of Greater India and Sinim, for which they pay, and especially for the frankincense of Dafaro, which I found here of a quality at

which a man could marvel. For these things I gave Sanson
Ebreo 5 per cent, for the great gain which I should make. I
also purchased with his aid choice liquids of great perfume, as
well as turquoises of Scebavecco, indigo and fine blades for
Ser Antonio, as I had promised. I also found some good pearls
and had from my brother Sanson a few rubies of great value,
which are called *balasci,* and which he had himself from a
trader of Badascian.

The coral which I observed was not of the best, yet he who
wished to sell it sought the highest price. With him I treated
little, my brother Sanson putting me on my guard against
him, saying to me in our language, Watch that the person
does not rob you. I therefore determined, may God be praised
for instructing me in such caution, to make my purchases of
it on a better occasion. Here we also took on board oranges,
apples, peaches, nuts and pomegranates for our delight, so
that our hearts might be soothed, there being much fever
among us. For all the fruits of the earth are to be found in
Cormosa, may God be exalted for His bounty to man.

Thus I parted from my brother Sanson, many others of our
brethren accompanying us to our vessels, having left the
Christian Berletto in the earth of Cormosa, may his soul also
rest in peace, the other merchants of our fleet having made
great gains in this place, for which God be praised.

It was in these days of Heshvan, sailing in the sea of Oddo
beside the coast of Chesmacorano, so named for the
worshippers of Mahomet who live in these lands,[10] that the
wind from the north-east failed and we ceased to make way,
some of the boats with many oars continuing with great
labour towards the port of Chisi,[11] and others remaining with
us lest there be pirates. There also came a great heat, such heat
as dries and hardens the flesh but increases the fever. We were
without a breath of wind, the heavens were silent and the sea
as a mirror. My servants began to lament greatly, the girl
Buccazuppo given to much sickness from being with child,
and all wearied from such heat without measure.

Day after day[12] I maintained my duties, praying to God,
Who makes the winds blow, that He should have compassion
upon us. Thus, for one day after another, without
encountering any events that merit being narrated, I gave
myself to the study of Torah. For it is written that the book of
the Law shall not depart out of your mouth and you shall
meditate therein day and night, for then you shall make your
way prosperous and have good success.

Yet we were as pelicans in the wilderness, our hearts
withered and our bones burned as in a hearth. My servants, in
order to pass the time and from melancholy, slept the day
long without thought of God or man, God forbid, only the
faithful Armentuzio, seated on a bench, writing entries in the
large volume, as if he had been in his own place and in his
own country. But Bertoni and Buccazuppo whispered
together, the one with reproaches and the other with little
sobs, yet waited upon me still in my fever.

When the wind returned, God be praised, my fever eased
and we came to Chisi as though we again went through air.
Indeed the wind became stronger than before, since such
change of winds sometimes occurs in the Indian Sea, as the
brave Turiglioni, who remained much vexed with the Saracen
masters, declared. Thus I disembarked very weakly from the
vessel, as if with a paralysis of my legs, praying that God
might spare me and that with His aid I might soon recover
my strength.

But at Chisi I, together with my brothers, found more
travail, the new king, who had great hatred for the Jews, may
the fires of Gehenna consume his soul, having imposed
special dues and taxes of 15 per cent upon all goods, and
other cruel exactions of tribute upon the Jewish merchants
who come to his realm. These dues I therefore resolved that I
should not pay, at which the soldiers of the said king sought
to compel me by force.

Thus, although I was sick and trembling with the quartan
fever, my servants also being in great need of water and fresh

provisions, and I feared that the agents of the said accursèd
king would have me killed for my pride, nevertheless no Jew
should bend his neck to an unjust king even upon pain of
death. But Vivo, Eliezer and Lazzaro del Vecchio were not of
my mind, saying that we must treat with him, may his name
be erased, or lose our lives. Nor were the Jews of this place,
who number fifty and go in yellow turbans, ready to come to
our aid, being themselves frightened of the soldiers of the
king. Yet, reckoned together, the port taxes and the other
cruel dues that the king sought, may God shorten his life,
being nearly half the value of my goods, were beyond all
measure.

Whereupon the great Jew of Aragon who had traded much
with the father and grandfather of the said king, and whose
white beard a Saracen and even a Christian might honour,
entered into parley with the king's men. At the last all were
brought to agreement by means of silver, which is everywhere
the speediest cure of such ills, whenever a man knows how to
use it aright. To this sum I offered in addition a certain
amount to the poor Saracens of the place.

Thus released from peril, I found that the Jews live all
together in their quarter and their synagogue is close by, that
the laws of cleanliness in food are observed, and that they say
their due prayers, God be honoured. Yet here I encountered a
heretical Jew, much disturbed in mind, who said that he cared
nothing for Jerusalem or the Messiah, God have mercy upon
me for inscribing such impiety, declaring that only knowledge
of arms could exalt our people, by which they might have
possession of their own land and defend it from their foes.

He, may God forgive him, was much in fear of the king
and spoke thus from fear. But I reproached him greatly for his
wicked ideas, after which he attended me in my weakness at
the market. Here, together with Aaron of Aragon, I found
much musk[13] of good quality, for which the people of Manci
pay four times the weight of it in silver. There were also
precious stones from Cascaro, as well as black furs from

Chesimuro,[14] which I purchased as a gift for Messer Tarabotto that he might have a fine coat for winter. Here I also heard tell of the great plunder carried out by the Tartars in Chesimuro, which is in the northern part of Greater India, towards Bolor and Great Turkey, and of the bloodshed which was caused by Cane Cacciala[15] among those people.

From this place we departed upon the last days of October or the first days of November, but, such was the fever that again came upon me, I cannot say which day it was. As we journeyed towards Cambaetta with a fair wind, I was again taken with the quartan fever, and my kidneys also began to pain me. But it being the Sabbath Hayyei Sarah[16] when this affliction began, it was forbidden to rub wine of vinegar on my body, but only oil. In the night, being so much in travail and since I was killed all the day long, I prayed even that I might be no more,[17] God have mercy on me for my default, asking my soul why I should undertake such perils of the sea, the land, and different realms, and why God hid His face from me, a pious man.

Thus, O grief upon grief, I came into a parched place in the wilderness, and the world seemed to me bitter without end, so ill did I become. My legs and stomach were swollen with the dropsy, a horrible thing to see. But God, blessèd be He, Who knows all things, aided me in the correct judging of it.

But in my fever, although God kept me in His sight, yet I saw before my own eyes all my life depicted, sometimes as do men to whom death comes near. I was then the unhappiest man who has ever been in the world, and as if I were a child I wept in all my thoughts. For it was a great terror to me to be buried at sea, so that many times I said the Shema in order that I might not lose every hope, giving much thought to my fate, and lamenting that I was without the support of my familiars in my time of need.

My soul was also full of sighs for those whom I thought I should see no more, and in my grief my heart almost burst in my body. Thus I spent many days between life and death, attended by the woman Bertoni, while my travails drove me out of my mind. For the fever made me tremble all over and the pain overcame me, in my distress even the fleas consuming me as their prey.

At the last, it was as though my limbs were tied, so weak was I and unable to move. Even sweet and good water tasted bitter and harmful on my lips, so I thought I had eaten some bad thing, or had been poisoned by a beverage at the house of my brother Isaia.

Thus, full of grief, I prayed often to God for salvation, believing that my end was near and that I should die an evil death at sea. But God, may He be held precious, hearing my prayers, took me in His hand, and my fever slowly passed, and little by little my will to eat returned.

But very frequently I was constrained to go to the privy, I searching my excrement for signs of what my illness was. God, seeing all things, saw also my motion, helping me to discover the blood that was in it and to catch the fleas and other vermin in my shitty clothes. In the glass I saw also that my face was sallow and my legs thin, but in the next days I became less dropsical, and the sallowness also became less.

In this way I recovered from my quartan fever, the dropsy, and the fever in my kidneys, may God be thanked, for after

---

'I PRAYED OFTEN TO GOD FOR SALVATION'

*Mention of the recital by Jacob of the prayer called the Shema (p.87) occurs more than half a dozen times in the manuscript, the word always being written in Hebrew characters. Beginning 'Hear, O Israel, the Lord our God, the Lord is One', it is the fundamental Jewish confession of monotheistic faith, and is repeated three times a day by the pious (Encyclopedia of Jewish Knowledge, ed. J. de Haas, New York, 1946, p.513), as well as at the bedsides of the dying – who hope to die with the words on their lips. It is recited by Jacob at times of fear and danger. Martyrs at the stake of the Inquisition would say the words as the flames consumed them.*

my meal I was hungrier than before, for which my servants
also gave thanks to God in their own fashion. Altogether I
was ill for about one month, in which time I passed from
desperate pain to a contented state, according to the will of
God and the natural law.

On the fourteenth day of November in the morning, which
is to say the twenty-eighth day of Heshvan, we came to
Cambaetta, a great port of Gazurat, in which there are many
merchants from other countries, for there is fine cloth to be
found there, and where there live about two hundred Jews.
Here there are many Mahometans with fine mosques, and a
synagogue of the Jews, in which I passed the Sabbath Toledot
in prayer and study of Torah, giving thanks to God, blessèd
be He, for my deliverance from death.

In this place, the providing of apparel and other necessaries
to the court of the king is entrusted to the Jews, and all the
gold and silver ornaments with which his wives and
concubines are furnished are made by Jews, God be thanked,
who also make gold and silver lace.

Here, albeit still in great weakness from the passing of my
fever and constrained to go frequently to the latrine, I was
called upon to correct and instruct our brother Bekhor, factor,
who had wrought much harm by reason of his neglected
duties and other defaults. Those things for which he had been
asked he had not sent, or goods of poor quality, as discoloured
peppers, bad Passover spice, mixed indigo and other inferior
things, he refusing to make good the losses, neither putting a
halt to the thieving nor ceasing to pay every exaction that the
officers of the king demanded from him.

The wretch Bekhor I thus summoned before me, setting
the faithful Armentuzio and Simone[18] to check his accounts,
in which they found many grave defects, as of subtracted
income and other falsehoods, at the discovery of which the
said Bekhor trembled and wept, such a one having entered
into agreements with us and received all our favour, may God
forbid that we should again be treated thus, and that such as

he should take his profits from our purses. To him I said that while God calls every man to account for his deeds, and that everything can be restored except life until the Messiah comes, he must also give account to me. At which he only wept the more, pleading for my grace, and, taking hold of my cloak, laid all blame upon the desire of his wife for riches, and made other such excuses.

At this, although weak from my fever, I grew angry, demanding to know why therefore he had not collected all the money due to us, money which I burned to recover, and why, then, he had paid such amounts of money in dues and taxes. For such as he do not understand that if you behave with respect towards those who demand taxes, making them fitting gifts in goods or money, which should be neither too much nor too little, they will become more ready to value goods according to reason and not for plunder.

Yet, the said Isaac Bekhor had paid market taxes, tolls, warehouse taxes, dispatch taxes and all the wrongful exactions, but wept before me that in truth he had sought riches. To whom I replied that he had acted without intelligence or cunning, while sending to us goods that no man could sell save to the blind. At which he wept the more and fell to the ground, tearing his clothes and tugging his beard from his chin in a manner unworthy of a man.

But at this I felt no pity, being impatient, and Armentuzio also, to be free of him, for the factor of Menahem Vivo, his cousin Beniamino, an honest and upright man, was ready to serve me. Thus I sent him away without blows, telling him to thank God that I sought no greater compensation from him than that he should serve me no more. I for my part, as was my duty, made report to my brothers of Cambaetta of his default.[19]

In this I believed myself to have acted justly, setting aside my own losses, which may God repair, so that my brothers might punish the said Bekhor as seemed fitting, I declaring that such recompense as the wretch might pay should be given to the

service of their house of study. To this the rabbi of the place,
Meir ben Joel, peace upon him, gave his assent, at which I felt
much comfort in my heart.

Throughout this night I heard the buzzing of the
mosquitoes, which caused my soul much disquiet, being a
great plague to those of weak constitution. Yet in those hours
in which I could find no rest, I was restored by study and
thought. For to every created being the Creator, revered be
He, sets a goal towards which he aspires, as the fox to its prey,
the eagle to the skies and the pious man to the knowledge of
God and of the earthly world.

Many are the difficult things which only the wisest man
may explain, such as who was the wife of Cain who conceived
and bore a son to him, as it is written, and yet no woman save
Eve was on the earth. Or how should Abraam, our father,
peace upon him, have kept all God's norms and laws, as it is
also written, when they were not yet given to our teacher
Moses by God? To such questions I gave much thought,
lamenting at the same time that a learnèd man should spend
his days seeking his profit from trade with men. For as Rabbi
Hillel teaches, he who engages overmuch in trade cannot
become wise. But there also came into my mind the teaching
of Rabban Gamaliel, may he be remembered with a thousand
blessings, that all study of the Torah without worldly labour
comes to naught, and even brings with it sin.

By this I was much comforted in my heart, setting out
upon the next day with my friend Vivo, who was also much
afflicted with flies, in order to find good buckrams and dyed
cloth such as are much prized in Sinim. Of these we each
bought sixty bolts, designed in a strange and beautiful way
and six Venetian palms in breadth.[20]

I purchased here, in addition, much pepper for Sinim,
including good *custo*, incense for the idolaters, indigo, red
*kino*, and a cantar of mirobalan.[21] Of this last the price was
too low, or the merchant of Cambaetta, a Mahometan, made
a great error in the weighing. But since I had made much

profit of him in the other merchandise, I informed him of his mistake, God be praised. For as the Torah teaches, it is a more wicked sin for a Jew to defraud a Saracen or a Christian than a brother, since in addition to the fraud the Divine Name is profaned in such a case, may God have mercy upon a Jewish cheat.

Thus, well satisfied with my deeds and profits, and the vessels of our fleet having been refurnished, we left Cambaetta on the nineteenth day of November in the year 1270, after a stay of six days, setting sail to the south-east in a fair wind, may God be thanked.

Now we proceeded towards that part of Greater India which is called Melibar, passing many other great galleys that trade in these waters for spices. For here are found the best things for giving savour, the best perfumes, balsams, colours, medicines and waxes you may find in the entire world and from which the merchant can make great profits. And such are the fragrant woods for incense, for which all idolaters pay well, that there is no better trade than that with Melibar, provided that a man be blessed, God willing, with health and is kept safe from pirates and other misadventures.

Here the largest part worship the ox for their god, may the Holy One have pity upon them, and do not eat of his flesh, for they say that he is a sacred creature. The priests catch his urine in a basin of gold and his dung, God forbid, in a basin of silver, washing their faces in the first and with the second anointing their foreheads, their cheeks and the middle of their chests. By so doing, as a Christian may consider himself blessed by touching himself with water drawn from a well, they consider themselves sanctified with dung and urine. They also have many other beastly customs at which a man might marvel, and of which it is best not to make mention, but none which is more marvellous than to pretend to eat the body of *that man* and to drink his blood, as do the Christians.

They also count beads in the manner of the Christians, speaking in a low voice the name of this or that deity or spirit, their beads, which are held on a thread, being of a certain number according to which god they follow. I do not know how many beads the Christian counts in the same fashion, but all is idolatry, may God spare their souls at the last day. Among them, each day and even each particular hour is held to be governed by the fates, it being thought lucky or unlucky to encounter this or that accident according to the judgments of their wizards. Thus at certain times it is lucky to see a dog with food in its mouth, but at other times unlucky, likewise to see or not to see a man carrying butter, or an unladen horse, or a cat on the right hand, or a monkey on the left.

But the worst thing is that they worship not one God, may His name be exalted, as do the Jews and Mahometans, but many gods, as do the Christians, the number of whose saints no man may count. In the same fashion the Indian[22] worships many things, having thousands of gods, whether man, bird or beast in human form, may God have mercy on them. Indeed, their idolatry is without measure, men and women alike worshipping even effigies of the male member, upon which they place garlands. But the habit that is the most filthy among them is the said putting of the excrement of the ox and cow upon their faces as though it were a poultice, and upon the walls of their houses also, which stink therefore like the exhalations of Gehenna. Yet they wash many times each day and eat only with the right hand, saying that the left hand is unclean, things which are not to be understood when men mingle together that which is concordant with the reason and that which is not.

Moreover, although among these idolaters there are those who would kill no living thing, they also burn alive the wives of husbands who have died, sometimes the women casting themselves into the flames with great joy. Such madness and the smell of burning flesh, which they seek to cover with costly incense and spices, are abominable things. For it is

impious for a man to have the odour of human flesh in his
nostrils or to see the smoke thereof, while he who puts to the
flame another of the human species, whatsoever be the end of
the act, blasphemes against the Holy One, blessèd be He.

Yet among the Christians, who esteem the inhabitants of
Melibar to be savage people, this they do themselves with
those who offend them, as if there were no God to judge
them in turn. But between the one and the other no
difference is to be found. For whether naked save for a strip of
cloth or dressed in the habit of the friar, each acts equally
against God, may His name be magnified, whether it be in
the name of the sacred ox or of *that man*, before whom, made
into an effigy, they bend their knees. Of these matters I shall
speak no more in this place.

It befell, having set in order my affairs in Cambaetta and
having given instructions to Beniamino as to his duties, that
on the second day after sailing from that place Buccazuppo
was taken in the morning with a great flux of blood, and in
the hold a grey and stinking mildew was found, God forbid,
which covered the corrupted victuals.

The Saracens and the Christians held these things to be evil
omens, thinking the blood of the girl and the stinking mould
to be two effects of the same cause, or the action of the Evil
One. But I declared to them that the girl's flux was surely
brought on by a beverage given to her by Bertoni, and that
the mould came from a strong poison set in the fodder of the
horses at Cormosa by him, may a pestilence take his body,
who sold them to Armentuzio.

But this they would by no means accept, Bertoni denying
upon her life and the cross of her redeemer that she had
administered any harmful thing to the girl, and Armentuzio
declaring upon the head of his son and his holy ghost, God
forbid, that the seller of the horses was an honest man.

The flux of the girl I sought to arrest with a drink of
mirobalans boiled in water, together with a paste of salt and
cubebs,[23] and, thereafter, when the flux diminished, for her

strength and delight some dates mixed with honey, since she
wept greatly. Thereafter, I gave her twice daily the medicine
*asarun*,[24] since her body and mind became much disturbed.
Nor did I enquire with whom she had lain, yet reproached
her for her loose acts with men, counselling her that she think
well for the salvation of her soul according to Christian
teaching. But she, in her disturbance of mind, turned her
head from me, crying out that I leave her, that neither God
nor man had love for her but only the evil woman Bertoni,
and that God attended upon the wishes only of those who are
well favoured, may God have mercy upon her for such
blasphemy.

While I thus entreated her, the mariners threw the
corrupted provisions into the sea, the Saracens and Christians,
each according to their own fashion, praying that the evil eye
should not look upon them. For my part I was much stricken
that a pious man such as I should have fallen in such an
unclean state upon the eve of the Sabbath Vayetze, for my
hands were touched with a woman's flux and my very ears
were tainted with words which no man should hear. In my
heart there was therefore much grief, being separated by the
seas not only from my Sara but from my brothers Vivo,
Eliezer, Lazzaro and the great Aaron, although I could see
their vessels close at hand. I therefore washed myself and put
on fresh clothes, lit the Sabbath candles and said the kiddush,
doing all according to my duties, God be praised for sparing
me to do Him honour. Yet there was little joy in my heart,
may God forgive me that I should have greeted His holy day
in such a fashion.

Thus, in order that I might make amends for my impious
condition upon the sea, I asked that my lamp be taken away
by Armentuzio, I not wishing that Bertoni should approach
me, and sat the whole night in darkness. In this way I prayed
and studied not from my book but in my heart, nor the next
day, which was the eighth day of Kislev, did I seek out the
fleas, as was my custom on other days. For is it not forbidden

by our strictest sages, peace upon them, for a man to search
for fleas in his clothes upon the Sabbath? And is it not also
forbidden for a pious man to read by lamplight, lest,
unwitting of the Sabbath, he so forget himself as to move the
lamp so that the oil flow more abundantly? Yet if, by the
action of the sea, the lamp is thus moved it is permitted.

In this way in the darkness of the night and upon the next
day, remaining alone, I recovered my knowledge of God and
took heart, may God be thanked. The learnèd declare that
since all things are moved by a moving power, which is in
turn moved by another moving power, each superior thing in
the hierarchy of creation moves that which is below it. And
since, they say, there cannot be a number of movers which is
infinite, we must therefore reach the prime mover, which is
God, blessèd be He. But I do not find God in such proofs but
in the beauties of the material world, in its seas and
mountains, its leaping fish and its singing birds, and all the
other moving beings of the terrestrial world which God in his
bounty has given to us. For the earth is full of every living
perfection, and although the mind of God was the first
mover, a man may also talk too secretly of the beginning and
end of things, or of the alpha and omega of the created world.
Yet the light of understanding is truly the divine light also,
and in this light, which is eternal, all things have their
splendour.

But the nature of the world is also given to us to know by
our acts in the world as men endowed with reason, which
reason is the gift of God. Moreover, a man must take his place
upon the great sea of being, whether the light of God shine
upon him or not and whether he be Christian, Saracen or
Jew. Thus it appeared to me in my thoughts, may God be
praised.

Thereafter,[25] we came to a place called Mangialur, where
there are spices and incenses prized by the idolaters of Sinim,
as well as ivory, fine coral and other things from which skilful
merchants make great profits. In this place, where the men

and women are brown and slender and their food is rice,
serpents and scorpions abound, as also the tarantula, which
are numerous, and against which one must always be on
guard, for their poison is not to be resisted by any salve.

Here I bought many cantars of pepper, both black and
white, and of different kinds of each, for it is as much prized
in Manci as in our own realm. Here also are sandalwood, aloe
and other fragrant woods, together with rich incenses which
they use, in the manner of the Christians, for the worship of
their idols. There is also fine camphor, which idolaters
sprinkle upon the steps of their altars the better to please the
nostrils of their gods. It is of such quality that one may sell it
in Sinim for its weight in gold.

Thereafter, we came shortly to the country of Illi[26] and laid
anchor in the river. Here, where Vivo, may his soul endure,
was greatly robbed, the agents first came on board our vessels
bearing with them samples of their wares that we might
inspect them. But they have the custom of laying their hands
upon a table and covering them with a cloth, so that the
purchaser cannot see them, they receiving and making offers,
and speaking one to the other, by signs which are understood
only by them. Afterwards they return on shore to the
merchants who employ them, and thus matters are carried
forward, but not without great fraud, by which they make
their money.

But I did not have trust in them, they with the cloths put
upon their hands seeming great thieves. Thus he who would
not be cheated in this place would best first go ashore, having
little money about him and that under the soles of his feet,
and if he buys should weigh out the goods himself ounce by
ounce upon his own balance. Therefore, using our small boats
to reach the land, we betook ourselves to the Jews there, who,
although few in number, are among the leading merchants of
the place. They were not lacking in performing their duties to
us, being brothers although strangers to us, counselling
against the thievery of the men of Mangialur.

However, not all of them are rich, but they are well looked upon by the lord of the land, being strict in their observance, giving money not only for the support of their house of study but also showing pity to the poor of the place, God be praised. To us they sold fine cloves and cardamoms and good coral, which I bought in great quantity to take to Sinim. For it is very precious to them, since they place it around the necks of both their women and their idols.

In this place there are also many parrots of different kinds, large and small, some red and blue with yellow feet. There is also not to be found a tree that does not give off perfume and that is not of great use. When we parted from this place, the whole of our people accompanied us with brotherly love to our boats, and all necessary things having been prepared we set sail in fair weather, God be praised.

Thus we journeyed towards the south-east and after the Sabbath Vayeshev came at last to Singoli,[27] a country in which there are above one thousand Jews, and in a few days the ships of Lazzaro and the great Aaron arrived also. Here it is always hot, both winter and summer, and the Indians keep elephants as oxen are kept in the march of Ancona.

So frequented is this place by Jewish merchants and so rich the trade we bring that we are exempt from toll and tribute. Moveover, the Jews here are much favoured by the princes of the place, and enjoy tranquillity and honour. For it is the Jews who are given to acquiring knowledge of the world, as well as being proficient here not only in the Torah but in diverse languages and other arts, from which they reap much profit. Here the spice-sellers from among them also go about from town to town, since Ezra, peace upon him, made it a rule among us that we should sell our wares, so that the daughters of Israel might be able to adorn themselves.

But above all things they are of perfect faith, their Talmud being all in Hebrew, and they are diligent in observing its precepts. Thus they are always ready to aid and protect their brothers, giving them shelter and all other things which a

man could desire. Moreover they have been very long in this
place, I seeing certain writings on copper which were nine
hundred years old, and by which the king of Melibar, one
Baschra, may his name endure, granted to Rabban our
brother, peace upon him, the rights of nobility so long as the
light of the sun shall shine upon the earth, God be praised.

Thus was our brother Rabban granted to ride upon an
elephant, to have a herald go before him to announce his
name, to bear the lamp of the day, to walk upon carpets
spread upon the earth, and to have trumpets and drums
sound before him as he went.

Here, together with my beloved friend Vivo, may he rest in
Eden, Lazzaro, Eliezer and the great Aaron, with whom I held
much discourse in this place,[28] I kept a joyful Hanukah,[29] the
shining candelabra casting a pure light into my soul. Yet here
a frightening thing befell, God forbid, for a scroll of the Torah
was let fall to the ground, woe is me. Whereupon my brothers
set to wailing at the ill omen, Rabbi Salomone ben Mose of
Colam decreeing that all present must fast for a day, as our
sages command.

But many among my brothers, being most fearful, declared
that he who had let it fall, God spare him, would surely die in
the following year, and even those who had witnessed it, may
God forgive us, stood in peril of an early death, at which my
friend Vivo grew pale.

Therefore, in penitence, we betook ourselves to prayer,
abstaining from all food as Rabbi Salomone had justly
commanded, and fearing the wrath of God. For eight days the
oil of the lamps burned, we forbearing to stir from our prayers
with the pious Jews of the place, walking a little only at night.
In this time, the young men, knowing of my lineage,
addressed many questions to me concerning the Torah and the
opinions of the sages,[30] may their memories be blessed.

Thus, they enquired of me whether a poor man might go
before the Ark, I replying that he might, as well as a rich man,
provided only that his clothes were not ragged, in which case

it is the duty of the Jews to provide him, God be praised. For in ragged clothes he might not read in the Law, or go before the Ark, or lift up his hands in benediction.

A second enquired of me to know what was forbidden upon the Day of Atonement apart from eating, drinking and washing oneself, to which I replied that putting on sandals, and lying with one's wife, were also forbidden, although a king or a new bride are permitted to wash their faces, as Rabbi Eliezer teaches. But wherever there is doubt whether life might be put in peril when food is lacking, such doubt rules over all things. Thus a sick man is permitted to eat.

Yet another asked me how a man and a woman should clothe themselves upon the Sabbath, with many particular questions pertaining thereto. Thus I taught them that those women who go out into a public place with painted eyelids, or bands upon the forehead which are not sewn on the veil, or with rings in the nose, or with a vessel of perfumes in their hand, are breaking the Sabbath, as also those men who go in shoes that have nails. But a man who has lost a leg may go out with a wooden leg, provided it be attached well to his body.[31]

They also enquired of me what was permitted to a doctor upon the Sabbath, I replying that for the sake of life the Sabbath might be profaned, but that a doctor might not put right a broken limb or close the eyes of a corpse. One further asked me whether a finger might be put down the throat of a child to make it vomit, I replying that such was permitted only if its life was in danger.

And one also came to me on the following day while I was bathing myself and asked me a question, to whom I replied that a pious man may not answer in the bath, for it is forbidden to speak the words of the Law while naked.

When these days of penitence and study upon the Feast of Hanukah were past, and the Sabbath Miketz also, I came to the market with Baruch Ebreo of that place, in whose house I rested, the horses of Cormosa having been already taken by the faithful Armentuzio, with the aid of the men Fultrono

and Micheli, to be sold. These horses were eighteen in
number, God be praised, two having died from the mildew
which caused their stomachs to swell, and great was the price
they commanded, the stronger being sold for four hundred
silver marks and the weaker for three hundred. Thus from this
I had great gains, may God be thanked, being enabled to buy
ten cantars[32] of pepper, both black and white, and spices,
among which there was fine mace and nutmeg, for which I
did not pay too much money.

For I was given, together with Menahem Vivo, rare
counsel by Baruch Ebreo, may God protect his life. This
same Baruch, having traded greatly with Java the Less and
the land of Sinim, also informed me that sweet-smelling
woods, especially sandal and aloe, were much prized by the
nobles and rich merchants of Manci, who use them for the
pillars and doors of their houses, and that there was great
gain to be had from them. They also keep vases containing
choice perfumes in their houses with which to render the air
fragrant and their guests contented, burning rare incenses to
the same end. Therefore I bought from him in great quantity
of such woods and perfumes, as well as combs of ivory
delicately carved. For he recounted, and it is so, that the
noble women of Sinim make much use of perfume, which
they carry in silken bags hung from the band about their
waists, and in their hair set many combs of ivory. All these
things which he said were the truth, may God preserve him.

Thus I purchased well in this place and to my great
advantage, Armentuzio and Pizzecolli being greatly pleased
with our merchandise, upon which we paid no dues.
Moreover, this was a land of great beauty, with many trees and
flowers, including certain small trees that send forth a sweet,
red liquor. By this place my servants were also well pleased,
the girl Buccazuppo being restored and comforting herself in
modest fashion, according to my counsel.

When all our ships were provisioned and everything had
been put in order, the Saracen masters being greatly impatient

at our delays and the brave Turiglioni also, we set sail after the
Sabbath Vayehi upon the last day of the year 1270, may God
be praised.

Now we came to Colam,[33] the great Aaron having gone
before us, being impiously unwilling to do penance in Singoli
for the desecration of the Torah, setting riches before his duty,
which God forbid. Here, where I saw many spices which are
never seen in our country, as well as poor stuff which it would
have been foolish to buy, merchants come from every part of
the world, and it is one of the great ports of Greater India,
being much frequented by the merchants of Manci. In this
place, which is rich in ginger, indigo and pepper, they make
the elephants carry the trees, and there are three hundred and
eighty families of Jews, who are among the greatest traders of
Melibar.

Here I was as if in my own family home, having my cousin
Levi of Ancona about me, as also the Rabbi Eliahu ben
Elhanan of Colam, with whom I led the prayers upon the
Sabbath Vaera, for which God be praised. In this place, the
cemetery of the Jews, may their dear souls rest in peace, lies
outside the town and has many hundreds of graves which are
made of pure white stone, the letters of the inscriptions being
coloured black, and, as among us, those of the *Cahanim*,[34]
may their holiness endure for ever, have upon them hands of
blessing which are engraved with great art.

In the evening the Jews of Colam light aromatic candles of
incense which burn fragrantly and with little smoke. By their
light they sit in order to discuss the Torah and their
merchandise, there being here the sweetness of family peace
and of duty done before the Holy One, may He be exalted.

Here also, the shades of night fall in the twinkling of an
eyelid, leaving no time for the pious man to bid farewell to
the day and to thank God for having spared him, nor to
conclude his day's affairs and prepare for slumber. And when
night has fallen, they do not stir far into the darkness from

their fires and lanterns, in fear of the beasts which eat men in
these parts, which God forbid.

Here I had much debate with Eliahu ben Elhanan, peace
upon him, he being greatly learnèd in Torah, as whether a
bald-headed man or a man with other bodily blemish might
serve as a priest in the synagogue. He answered that in the
Temple, may it be God's will that it is built up again in our
own day, a bald man such as did not have a lock of hair from
ear to ear might not serve, nor a man without eyebrows nor a
man whose eyelashes had fallen out. Or if he had breasts like
a woman or his male organ was too big he was also
forbidden, for those without correct form might not serve
God.

To this I declared to the pious Eliahu that, according to my
judgment, although such prohibitions were fitting in the
Temple, in our synagogues they need not be followed. For
under such a strict law, which permitted only to those of
perfect form to stand before the Lord, there would be none at
all to serve Him, God forbid. Thus, I declared, provided that
a man cause no pain to the sight of those who behold him, he
is fit to read the Law before his brethren, and with this the
said Eliahu concurred, he himself being bald.

In this place I purchased such spices from the brother of
Eliahu as are greatly prized in Sinim. I also had good
buckrams through my cousin of this place, which are
esteemed to be the best in the world.

From here we set sail on the twelfth day of January of the
year 1271, voyaging towards the south-east by Comari and
thence to Seilan,[35] the vessel of my brother Vivo, may his soul
endure, sailing close behind us.

Now we came to the island of Seilan, and here I thought
that surely I was in Eden, the garden of God, may the Holy
One be blessed. For song-birds sang in praise of the Creator,
the pears[36] were the colour of roses and there was not a tree
which did not give off a perfume. The whole country is
scented with spices and exhales an odour so sweet that it is a

marvel. And in the light of the moon the beauty of the trees is also revealed, for in the day the sun is often too bright to observe all God's bounty, may He be praised.

Indeed, in all places and at all hours, our eyes must be ready to see, as our ears to hear, the beauty of God's creatures, blessèd be He. Yet when a bird sings to his Creator some ears do not hear the song, even when it is all about us, for our ears are given rather to the sound of lamentation and dolour, or of anger and strife, and, thus occupied, no other sound can be heard by them. And seeing is like this also, for that which appears must be seen by man, and not remain only in the eye of God. For a man has a duty to have regard to all creation that he may learn therefrom. They have eyes to see and see not, they have ears to hear and hear not.

The people of the island are very dark and all go naked,[37] except that they wear a cloth in front of their genitals and tie it behind. They are also much given to astrology and are very honest traders. The king of the island is called Paccambou, but the kingdom is much troubled, the Seilani being at war with a people to the north, whose prince is called Sundara, and who have conquered a part of the island for themselves, which they call in their language Ilam.[38]

Here, together with Vivo, may his soul be preserved, I bought pepper, ginger and cinnamon, for the cinnamon tree, which has leaves like laurel, grows in great abundance. I purchased a great quantity of it, it being much prized in Sinim as among us, together with oil made therefrom which they use for ointments and salves. Here there was also a good medicine for those who suffer from illness of the spleen, and oil of turpeth, which I purchased for Ser Bartolomeo.[39]

But of all the things the greatest which I saw were the jewels, which are the choicest in the world. For, disclosed to my sight, were jewels of the rarest beauty at which I marvelled, chief among them the rubies. Indeed for every created thing, the Holy One, blessèd be He, has set a goal of perfection, which it reaches and where it rests. Among the

trees this goal is the palm, among the beings with a soul it is
man, and among the jewels it is the ruby.

But here were also topazes, amethysts and sapphires, as well
as many others of great beauty of colour and form, which the
idolaters of Seilan say are the frozen tears of their gods.
Moreover, the manner in which they are worked is a marvel,
than which I have never seen better. Of all these jewels I
bought for a great sum,[40] God be praised. They also have the
finest pearls that a man may see, some white and some pink,
as those of Battala,[41] which they say are engendered in the
oysters by dewdrops, but which cannot be believed.

In this island, to which there is none equal in its bounty,
the greatest part of the people are idolaters. Indeed, many are
the pilgrims who come here, for they believe that this was the
home of their god Sacchia,[42] whom they call Buddum, and
that his footprint is upon the summit of a mountain of this
island. This footprint the idolaters venerate, climbing up as
far as the clouds with much toil, in order to wash their faces
and their eyes in the water of the hollow which they declare
was made by the foot of their god, saying, This is the water of
Sacchia, which will make us pure in heart.

But the Mahometans for their part say that the same
hollow is that of the foot of our first forefather Adam, may he
be quickened at the end of days, not the foot of Buddum, as
the Sacchiani declare, so that they often come to blows as to
whose foot it was. Yet although Adam was the first man
created by God, may He be exalted for evermore, it is not for
us to worship such unworthy things, for none can say where
our ancestor set his foot. Moreover, to revere a footprint upon
the ground is an abomination, being the work of the idolater.
But in the same way they also adore the tooth of Sacchia,
which is in a certain temple in the island and which is laid in
a golden vessel. Yet those who have seen it say that it is as
large as the fang of a boar, and not that of a man.
Nevertheless the faithful revere it, believing that it is the tooth
of their god.

Thus it is that the worship of idols has no bound, and that man's reason should guide him in such matters. For it is no guide to a man that he should believe that which is against nature. Rather, all nature was formed according to God's reason, may His Unspoken Name be exalted, Who created the world by His power. And although there be strange things which are difficult for a man to explain, yet the reason of such things can be found, and the laws which govern their being and movement can certainly be discovered. For God, blessèd be He, has made nothing which does not possess its own ordering conformable with the order of all things. And that which is not possible, as that a man should have a tooth as large as that of a boar, it is impious to believe.[43]

There are also in the island of Seilan one hundred and sixty Jews, but few among them who are given to the study of Torah. Indeed, most are without faith, God forbid, saying no afternoon nor evening prayers, and the morning prayer upon the Sabbath Beshallah[44] without devotion. Moreover, many eat abomination so that I could not stay among them.

From this place we parted on the fourth day of February, after the Sabbath Yitro, fifteen days having passed from our arrival to our departure, I in all things having continued to do as the Law commands, may God be praised. In this place I also spent much to my profit, at which my heart, troubled by the impiety of my brothers, was a little calmed. Thus we sailed towards the east-north-east, the masters of our vessels fearing bad weather, although the skies were still clear.

The way of a ship in the midst of the sea is a wonderful thing, as when the sails of a ship seem like wings. Yet, knowing that God may move where He wills, just as He may judge us as seems fit to Him, I forbore to give myself to my joy. For although some sages among the Christians say that the divine will is never mutable, our sages hold a different opinion.

For in the mortal and deceptive world, for all that a man may be for the time being content, he must weigh truly the

material stuff which, before God imposed order upon it, was
formed from chaos. Moreover, some sages say that nature
holds the earth firm in the midst of the universe and that
everything else moves about it, but we may not be sure that
it is so. There is no doubt that the potential force of the
material world lies both in the will of God and in the works
of the natural law, and who may question that the second is
the subject of the first? But the second is also a potential
force in itself, acting in accord with the laws which govern it.
These it is man's task to find out, so that he may come to
understand a little of the intellect of God, may He be
exalted.

But that the divine light surely shines upon us, and that the
existent world is given to us as God's blessing should not
make us blind to the confusion that sometimes comes both
into the world and into the hearts of men. Thus, the pious
man who discerns the greater order which stands behind all
that appears to us, knowing that not everything is as we see it
and as we experience it, should also know that the winds of
the sea may blow and the waters of the sea move in such ways
as may dash the hopes even of him who fulfils each duty to
the Holy One, blessèd be His name. For so weak is the flesh
of man and so firm is the substance of things that it is better
for us not to be overjoyed at our good fortune, since it cannot
endure. Thus, mindful in my heart of the uncertain fate of
man, I resolved to show more patience towards both good

---

'NATURE HOLDS THE EARTH FIRM'

*Jacob appears to be casting doubt upon the notion of the fixity of the earth. It can
only be that such sceptical reasoning was current among some of the more radical
thinkers with whom he had been educated, and who had themselves perhaps been
influenced by the much earlier doubts of the Pythagorean school. The Pythagoreans
are attributed with the belief that the celestial bodies, including the sun and the
earth – which was thus considered a planet – circled around a 'central fire'.*

and ill, praying to God that I might henceforth give myself to excess neither of grief nor of joy.

Now we came to the beginning of Lesser India, God be praised, which extends from the sea of Seilan as far as the sea of Sinim, the oarsmen toiling hard, for the north-east wind began to blow against us and the sea ran strongly although the sky was clear. The wind also changed, now coming from the north-east, now from the west, and now from the north, so that the Saracen masters, thinking to return to Seilan against the counsel of Turiglioni, yet could not turn the vessel in such heavy seas.

Thus Turiglioni prevailed, declaring also that to take another route was mistaken, seeing that the vessels of Menahem and of the others continued on their way, the great Aaron and his admiral also going ahead. And so we proceeded with much labour on our course, with sail and oar, following the vessels of Aaron of Aragon, I praying to God that He should make the winds blow more mildly and carry us safely to port.

So it was, God be praised, that we came to the islands of Nicoverano, which is to say the land of the naked. But the people of the place are not naked, since the men cover their genitals with a piece of cloth and the women cover theirs with leaves, with a string about the waist and two long streamers behind. Since these have the appearance of a tail, the people are said by those who do not observe them correctly to be men with tails.

Indeed mariners fear lest the wind should carry them to this place, for they also say that those of the island have human bodies but the muzzles of dogs, and that their way of speaking sounds like the barking and howling of dogs. But this is not so, since they speak in the same manner as those of Seilan. Nor are they only three and a half Venetian palms high,[45] as some have declared, being only a little smaller than us, and neither do they have beaks like birds. It is also said of them by mariners, for so the Saracen master told me, that they are ferocious towards strangers, being of wicked inclination, yet they showed themselves to us to be benign.

However, they have black bodies, and some have teeth like fangs and others do not cut their nails, so that they seem like the talons of hawks, yet one may treat with them as with other men. For they have much nutmeg, fragrant wood and cardamoms with which they barter, they having a liking for sugar which they willingly take for their spices. They also have a large quantity of Indian nuts, each large as a man's head, in which there is a clear, fresh water and a hard white flesh of delicate savour, which we took from them for our sustenance, and some rare fruits besides. It is said that these people have killed and eaten the bodies of mariners who have been shipwrecked in their waters, yet among them, as any man may see, they eat only fruits and the fish of the sea. Moreover, if there be in their eyes that which might make a man fear, for they often look at the stranger with suspicion, so do other men also whose nails are cut and kept well.

At our parting, against which some of the men of the island sought to warn us, pointing to the sky and urging us to disembark, at which the Saracens grew afraid, I prayed that God might spare us and our fleet. But the great Aaron was impatient to be gone, and thus we followed, against the counsel of Turiglioni also, this being the last time that I should see my brother Menahem ben David, called Vivo, may his soul rest in Eden.

Now we came to be lost in the deceptive world, and it was as if we were abandoned by God, may He forgive me and may His name be exalted. For upon the following day, the skies began to darken, and in the distance was the sound of thunder, the north-east wind blowing so hard against us that we could make no way. At which the brave Turiglioni came to me in my cabin, to which I had retired in order to pray to God, declaring that, as he had foretold, the sea and the weather were changing and that I should look to the safety of

my possessions since a tempest, together with a great
whirlwind, were approaching from the north-east.

Whereupon, as he had predicted, the wind began to roar
and the sea to boil, the lightning to flash and the thunder to
crash. Indeed, so great was the roar of the thunder that it
filled the skies as if they would fall, and the seas roared also,
and the fullness thereof. It became so dark, although the first
star had not yet appeared in the heavens, that nothing of the
other vessels could be seen. Thus it came about that in our
peril we seemed to be alone upon the great sea of being, yet
that God's might and power filled the world.

It was also as if it was darkest night, and the darkness and
thunder not that of the world of men but of Gehenna, may
God spare me for my impious words. The seas became so
high and our danger so great that anguish fell upon us all, the
mariners being able neither to sail forward nor to turn back,
nor to cease their labour, neither to keep their course nor to
take another.

In a short time, as the fury of the winds increased, my
servants came to me in great fear, I praying to God that He
might spare us from death, and telling them also each to pray
in their own fashion, remembering to give praise to Him for
having preserved them thus far. In this the girl Buccazuppo
was the most devout, seeking counsel from me as to what
words she should address to her god and dutiful in all things,
and thus went away. But Bertoni lamented her fate with great
sighs, declaring that our last hour had come.

Indeed now the tempest grew greater, going from bad to
worse and carrying us to disaster, the brave Turiglioni coming
to me and declaring that our vessel was in great danger, and
that if God did not help us we should be lost. For in the
storm the ballast which the mariners had placed in the
bottom of the hold had broken loose, with great force striking
the timbers of the ship within to left and right, so that the
Saracen helmsman was no longer able to steer the vessel.

Thus I also was now taken with great fear, God forgive me,

despite having resolved that I should give way to no excess, in my grief asking myself why I had put myself to such a long and perilous journey, and praying in the tumult of the winds that, being unable to swim, I should not sink in the water and die.

Many were those who wept about me, but Buccazuppo, who seemed not to fear to be drowned, gave comfort to the Christians, the faithful Turiglioni for his part going back and forth among the Saracens in order to give them counsel. Thus it came about that a rudder, being split by the winds and being about to be cast away into the waters, he, without fear hanging above the waves, tied it to the timbers. Yet soon the mariners, although fearing that our vessel would run against the boats, were forced even to cut the main rope, the ropes guiding the sails being broken by the tempest, so that now all seemed lost. First the prow and then the stern were submerged beneath the waters, the wind and waves as if seeking to smash our frail vessel, so that the sails were torn from the masts.

Now in the terrible roar of the thunder, I heard the anger of God, may all men tremble before His majesty and power. Indeed, it is the mind of God which holds the terrestrial world upon its course. Yet such was the tempest and the darkness that it was as if a fixed place in the world had been lost to men and that all was returning to the flux or chaos which preceded the first day, may God have mercy upon me for my thoughts. For it seemed that form and substance were one, without separation, and that the whole of Creation was dissolved in the black waters of the sea, which God forbid.

When such thoughts came upon me, I prayed in terror to God for the storm to abate, saying the Hear, O Israel, the Christians praying upon their knees in their own fashion with their hands folded, the girl Buccazuppo patiently waiting for deliverance by God, blessèd be He.[46] Yet so mighty were the roars of the winds in the darkness and the blows of the waves that I was not able to hear my own voice, but notwithstanding I fulfilled my obligation, as Rabbi Jose teaches. Thus I had turned myself to God and to whatever fate He might decree, weeping for my Sara and the loss of my treasure. For, at the last, the flesh of man is weak, and in fear of death grows weaker.

All night through, the mariners and oarsmen struggled to the point of death in order to steer the ship, but it was in vain, so strong were the winds and so high the waves. Yet by God's mercy, may His Unspoken Name be cherished, the vessel suffered no breach, neither were we thrown upon the rocks nor buried in the deep waters, but, remaining alive, we greeted the first light, giving thanks to God for our safety, may the Lord be praised and exalted.

Yet we found ourselves at daylight off our course for Java the Less, having lost six sails and two masts,[47] and thought ourselves to be alone upon the sea. But as the sun rose we saw near at hand our boats,[48] God be thanked, which carried precious cargoes, and upon the horizon, much scattered, the vessels of Eliezer of Venice, Lazzaro del Vecchio and the great Aaron.

But the ship of my brother Menahem, may his memory be blessed, could not be seen, and in my heart, alas, I straightaway knew that he was lost. For at our parting I saw that God had placed His hand upon him, may I be spared. Whereupon, thinking of my friend and knowing that he was no more, I began to weep and to say the Kaddish,[49] praying that his soul might be filled with pleasures in Eden, until he is quickened at the end of days, Amen. Much, too, was the rich cargo that he had had about him, together with many mariners and servants, may God have mercy upon them, and in my soul I saw all beneath the waters, brought to death and to the end.

And since there now came to us a calm after the storm, I declared to my servants that upon the sea the wind rules always, but according to the will of God. Moreover, it is better neither to lament to excess our losses, nor to be overjoyed at our good fortune, as I have written. Rather, it is noble to put up with all. Thus, recovering my senses, as the vessels of our fleet came to our aid and thus to draw us towards Java the Less, I gave thanks to God for having kept us in safety in the darkest night of our souls, praying, for so bitter is life, that the name of Menahem Vivo might be inscribed in the book of forgiveness. For he was a pious man, dutiful in all things, and it is not in our power, as Rabbi Yannai taught, to explain the sorrows of the righteous and the well-being of the wicked, as I have written.

In grave times the Jew cries out to his Creator, may He be exalted, Where is God that He gives me to my foe or to the waters of the deep, yet spares the evil-doer?[50] But God calls upon us first in one way and then in another, sometimes to life and sometimes to death. Thus in His majesty He cast the pious Vivo into the black waters and carried Aaron to safety, according to His will. For this I felt great grief in my heart, yet knowing that it is impious only to remember our dolours but not how, at other times, our hearts are made glad by God's bounty. Moreover, true knowledge comes not from the contemplative life of him who feels pain at the world and would be free of it, but from study both of the works of God in His creation and of the works of man, who is also His creature. He who enquires, finds out that which is to be found, but he who does not enquire knows only that which is already known.

At last, after much difficulty, the sky again growing darker and the thunder being heard to sound once more, we came after the Sabbath Tetzaveh to a place called Lambri[51] in Java the Less, the vessels of the great Aaron, peace upon him, having gone before towards the sea of Sinim, notwithstanding the great danger. Here, and at the port of Sarha,[52] because of the great storms of rain and the damage to the masts and sails of our ship, as well as to the ships of Lazzaro and Eliezer of Venice, we remained for ninety-three days until the month of May and its twenty-seventh day. Because of the bad weather I betook myself to the land, fearing that even in the harbours the ships might go to ruin. But the anchors held well, and in these places our vessels, praise be to God, were restored.

Having sat during Purim for a week of mourning for our brother Menahem ben David, called Vivo, may his soul rest in peace, and many remaining on board to protect my treasure and set the cargo in order, I found lodging, together with my brothers, and there remained for seven Sabbaths. During this time there also fell Passover,[53] and in all things I performed my duties, albeit that the difficulties were many, there being no Jews there. Yet we gave praise to the Lord, blessèd be He, singing our salvation from the sea under the command of Moses our teacher and that He sheltered us in His hand in a distant place.

Although it is very large, they say that Java the Less is an island, but that I cannot tell since I did not sail around it. It is a wild place, in which are found black spiders with poisonous fangs, one bite of which may kill a strong man, God forbid, in the flower of his youth. There are also great pigs from whose hair carpets are woven, and which a pious Jew may neither buy nor sell. The Saracens say that there are many sorcerers among the men of Java, and that they can change themselves into birds, beasts, or creatures of the water, but that I did not believe, for it is against nature.

In this place called Lambri, awaiting a favourable wind so that we might sail to Sarha, but the tempests continuing and the waters being so high, I suffered much anguish at the passing of the days and at the expense of the mariners, in grief for my friend Vivo and in fear lest my goods be spoiled. But of these last things Armentuzio and Pizzecolli took care, I continuing to fulfil my duties both upon the Sabbath and other days, may God be praised.

Yet my heart was often downcast, for the damage to my vessel was great. But my cargo being secure and my servants faithful, I had also ground for joy, even though my Sara was far from me. For I could give myself to study, God be

thanked, not grieving to excess either at my losses, for which
my brother Isaia of Basra was pledged to one half, or to find
myself in such a place, for even the trees and birds gave
testimony to the glory of God. Moreover, the pious man
should not give himself to lamentation, without reason, upon
his fate, or upon the discomforts of the world, such as rain or
cold or other things. For there is not a thing which does not
have its place, nor a man who does not have his hour, as our
sages teach, peace be upon them.

At last, on the fourteenth day of April at the time of the
new moon, the winds having a little abated and our vessels
being restored, we set sail for Sarha, which is a league's
distance from Sumantala, the place of the palace of the king,
who is a worshipper of Mahomet together with his people,
among whom there are also Jews.

In Sumantala, where we found that the fleet of the great
Aaron had taken shelter from the tempest, we were received
with much bounty by Efraim ben Judah Greco, man of
learning and factor, who, because of the default of time,
thought us to be dead, so many were the timbers from
shipwrecks that had been found upon the shores. With him I
stayed forty days, for it remained dangerous to sail, the
Saracen master and Turiglioni being of one mind that until
the last days of May we should not depart.

• In this place, as I have written, there are pious Jews, who
say their due prayers, observe the laws of cleanliness in food,
and are learnèd in the Torah. Moreover, the king of the
Mahometans is esteemed a friend to the Jews, holding our
faith in favour and permitting us to wear on our heads
whatever hats we may please. Thus, no one is constrained to
wear a turban of yellow or red, or a red cloak, or to do any
other thing by which to mark the Jew.

Moreover, there is to be found in the market and
storehouses of Sumantala all that the heart of the merchant
may desire. For here is the finest gold, that shining substance
composed of fire, air, water and earth and for which all men

crave. Here, too, is the incense white benzoin, which among
the Saracens is called *luban javi* and which is dear to the
idolaters of Sinim and Greater India and to the priests of
Rome. Here also are spikenard and the best camphor, that of
Fansur,[54] which any man may find but for which one must
pay a high price, even to its weight in silver. This camphor is
greatly prized by the idolaters of Sinim, they calling it *pinpou*
or flakes of snow, it being much superior to their own. Of this
camphor I purchased a great weight, that is three hundred
*libbre*,[55] at a high price, but knowing well upon the counsel of
Efraim Greco that I should be well rewarded, and so it turned
out, may God be thanked.

Here, too, were sandalwood, lac and lignaloes or wood of
the eagle, which smells of sweet honey and is much prized by
the idolaters of every land, the best selling for its weight in
gold. Of cubebs, mace, fine nutmeg, cloves and pepper, black
and white, there was great quantity and at a low price. Of
these, which Efraim Greco held in store, I bought two cantars
each of nutmeg, mace and cubebs, ten cantars of cloves and
twenty cantars of pepper,[56] some of which I should take to
Sinim, and some take upon my return. Of other things there
was also great abundance but of less quality than those which I
had from Efraim ben Judah. Yet there were many who sought
to sell me their spices and woods. To them I did as our sages,
may they be remembered, instruct, not speaking to them, for a
man may not say, How much is this thing?, if he does not wish
to buy it.

There were also those among the poor sellers of
merchandise who, having little and constrained to sell
cheaply, sought a small price for goods of great worth. One
such simpleton, having camphor of Fansur, the best there is,
for which he sought too little, Efraim, peace upon him, urged
me that I should buy, saying with a laugh, I am as a deaf man,
I hear not, and I am as a dumb man that opens not his
mouth.[57] Whereupon I reproached him that he should seek in
such a way to have the better of a simple man, as being

impious and against the teaching of our sages, peace upon
them.

Yet at our parting, when all our vessels had been made
ready and our masts and sails renewed, the same Efraim came
to me saying that he would willingly marry his daughter to
my son, should he be shapely and possessed of intelligence,
the better to carry forward our affairs. But this comportment
not pleasing me, I replied that all my sons were entrusted to
others, which he took ill, so that I had much to do to please
him, for in all things he had served me well, peace upon him.
Thus I was constrained to give him 5 per cent, at which in my
heart I felt anger but which I kept secret,[58] since he had
undertaken to purchase spices for my return.

Thus, in the last days of May, after the Sabbath Naso, we
departed from Sumantala, the masters having decided to
resume the way, and the time of the south-west wind[59] having
come. To the vessels of Eliezer of Venice, Lazzaro del Vecchio
and the great Aaron were now added those of other
merchants, so that we might be better protected, God willing,
from the pirates of these waters. For here many must go
together and well armed, in order to have defence against
them.

In these seas of Lesser India, through which we sailed with
wings towards the south-east, are islands which no man could
count or name,[60] so many are they, may God be thanked for
His bounty. Thus there are also many kingdoms, as of Sabam
and Sincepura, Mait and Bintano, in which last place there
are Jews who are great merchants in the wood of the sandal-
tree, but among whom I made no stay, the south-east winds
being so strong, yet who brought us food and drink in order
to bid us welcome.

Here, Aaron the Great bought sandalwood from them in
large quantity, and in Cacula,[61] where brazil wood is plentiful
and cheap, I bought much of it, as well as ivory, for here
elephants are abundant. In Cacula there is also much gold, of

which Eliezer of Venice and Lazzaro bought, hiding it from
their servants, and in Sondore[62] there is wood, of which
Lazzaro bought at a lesser price than is paid in Bintano, at
which the great Aaron felt much torment at the default of his
factor in that place.

Yet such torment I did not feel, it being unworthy of the
pious man who buys and sells to lament in this fashion, as if
God should make him free of every loss and tribute, and bless
him only with income and profits. For in the terrestrial world
no man has good fortune alone, not even the most righteous.
Indeed, many are the sages who, although wise, suffer much
pain in life, as when the unworthy and those who feel envy
for the wisdom of others show them spite. Nor can the
greatest wealth preserve him who possesses it from sickness
and death, just as the greatest beauty of the flesh must corrupt
according to the will of God, may He be for evermore praised
and cherished. Hence, to lament over money, as when in one
place a man has paid more for something and sees that in
another place another man has paid less for the same thing, is
folly.

To the great Aaron I told this, in the place called Sondore,
because of his great grief in the matter of the sandalwood, but
in his arrogance and cupidity he would not hear me. Rather,
he enquired of me whether I too was not in search of profit,
and I, by no means able to calm him, told him that indeed I
sought my profit, but in accord with reason. At this, such was
his anger that he made as if to strike me, the faithful
Armentuzio and Pizzecolli, hearing our words, coming
between us in order to ward off the blows.

He, however, in his pride, felt no shame, for such is the
nature of the scoundrel who sets aside his duties to God and
to man, thinking himself the master of the world, which God
alone commands. But gold and silver may not purchase either
wisdom or the souls of other men, nor may they be used
against reason. For in all things concerning men there are
bounds,[63] which God has set down in the Torah, and which

are also prescribed by the natural law. To these bounds both
our reason and our duty[64] command us, and, be a man ever
so great, he may not do violence to them. These things,
however, I did not tell Aaron of Aragon, for he had left me in
ill humour, he returning with his servants to his vessel.

From this place of Sondore we set sail towards the east-
north-east after the Sabbath Hukkat or the Sabbath Balak[65] in
the month of Tammuz, the wind continuing from the south-
west, and thus came to a place called Zabai which is in
Ciamba in the realm of the Comari.[66] Here they worship the
law of Mahomet, and the king is called Ciasinna, and they
have much aloes, as well as choice cardamoms of which I
bought. Thus, having fulfilled my duties on the ship as on
land, which my servants after so many days took for a
wonder, yet fearing that still at the last we might be assailed
by pirates, or come upon rocks in shallow water, or suffer
other misadventure, we entered the seas of the land of Sinim,
may God in His majesty and splendour be exalted.

It was upon the thirteenth day of August in the year 1271,
which is to say the year 5031 and the fifth day of the month
Elul, before Sabbath Shofetim,[67] that our fleet came to Zaitun
in Manci. Here I, Jacob di Salomone of Ancona, saw and
heard such things at which other men might wonder, and of
which I shall now tell with God's aid, may He be exalted.

## CHAPTER FOUR

# A City of Measureless Trade

THE CITY OF ZAITUN, LA *città lucente* or City of Light, was the main port of southern China in the thirteenth century. In foreigners' corruptions (or mis-hearings) of a Chinese name, it is spelt in other travellers' accounts – Arab, Indian and European – as Zaytun, Zaiton, Zaitum and Zeithum; also as Cayton, Saiton and Kaitam. It is clear from this that the sound of the first syllable was hard to grasp and to transliterate for non-Chinese speakers.

The question of the location of Zaitun was long debated by scholars who were undecided whether it stood at the site of the modern Quanzhou, or sixty miles to the south-west at what became Zhangzhou in Fujian province. Modern authorities have opted for the former site. In 1974 a large wooden thirteenth-century ship carrying quantities of perfume and spice was discovered at the bottom of Quanzhou Bay, providing further proof that Quanzhou was a major mediaeval seaport and shipbuilding centre.

Jacob also describes the city as the capital of its province, although there is some doubt about this. (The realm of Southern Sung was divided in 1270, the year before Jacob's arrival, into sixteen provinces, the whole constituting an area four times that of France.) But whether the provincial capital or not, Zaitun in the thirteenth century had displaced 'Sinchalan'

or Khanfu (Guangzhou, or Canton) as the main trading port of
southern China. Guangzhou's first heyday had been in the
eighth century, when it had an estimated population of
200,000, but from the eleventh to the fourteenth centuries the
more active port was Zaitun.

Thus, Marco Polo calls Zaitun, without qualification, 'the
port of the merchants of southern China' which 'all the ships of
India make their chief port of call'.[1] Historians agree that its
activity was on a far larger scale than that of even the largest
ports of mediaeval Europe. Moreover, in the Sung period,
China was the greatest maritime power in the world, and had a
combined population, north and south, estimated at 100 million.[2] In south-east China there was particularly intensive
circulation of goods and money. Indeed, the period in which
Jacob found himself in Zaitun – which he declares to have had
a population of 'more than 200,000' – is known to have been
one of unbridled consumption and luxury, of a continuing
influx of peasants into the urban centres, of large-scale imports,
and a consequent deficit in the balance of trade. In further consequence, there was a shortage of coins as a result of the export
of precious metals to cover the deficit, a shortage which was
itself a principal reason for that introduction of paper money
found so remarkable by mediaeval foreign travellers to China,
Jacob d'Ancona included.

It was a period, too, of considerable technological development, 'striking for its modernism',[3] in which large-scale use
was made of printing, and upon which Jacob – unlike Marco
Polo – has interesting things to say. In fact, the whole of the
Southern Sung realm appears to have been touched not only by
fear of encroaching conquest but by a great brilliance of activity, invention and expansion. In the 1270s, the capital of
Southern Sung at Kinsai (Hangzhou) – which Jacob, for
(much elaborated) reasons of his own, did not visit – is held to
have been the largest and richest city in the world, with an estimated population of over one million. By comparison, Venice
at the beginning of the fourteenth century may have had a

population of 100,000; Florence had between 45,000 and 65,000; Paris, with '61,000 hearths', may have reached a quarter of a million.

Zaitun was, from Jacob's account, a vast and teeming coastal metropolis, with a changing and heterogeneous population.[4] It was a city in social and cultural flux, with large foreign colonies of merchants, including Franks (Western Christians), Saracens (Muslims) and Jews. Confirmation of this degree of economic activity and movement along the seaboard has already been provided by archaeologists, who have found (and continue to find) Muslim, Nestorian Christian, Catholic, Manichaean and Hindu inscriptions in the area,[5] although no trace has yet been discovered of the Jewish synagogue and cemetery to which Jacob refers.

That there were Jews in both Tartar and Sung China at the time of Jacob's visit in 1271–2 and throughout the fourteenth century is historically well established, being independently confirmed in the reports of other travellers. Marco Polo makes passing reference to the presence of Jews in China in the Ramusio version of his *Travels*, lumping them together with 'Saracens and idolaters' and 'many others who do not believe in God'! Giovanni di Monte Corvino mentions them as being in China, while the friar Giovanni di Marignolli claimed to have had theological disputations with them at Khanbalik (Beijing) in the 1340s. Ibn Batuta also reports their presence at Kinsai in the mid-fourteenth century, but only Jacob d'Ancona, understandably, gives extensive attention to the topic.

However, despite all the evidences of economic expansion and social turmoil in southern China at the time of Jacob's visit, it has been asserted by some scholars that the Southern Sung economy, notwithstanding its great range and sophistication and its monetised commerce, was held back from development into a 'full-scale capitalist market economy' by bureaucratic controls, 'mandarin'-led discrimination against merchants and unenlightened political rule.[6] But Jacob d'Ancona's account of Zaitun – which makes it seem not dissimilar from the 'free trade zones' of certain entrepôts in the modern world – suggests otherwise.

It presents a picture of a thriving mercantile economy, vigorous manufacture and lavish consumption; in all, an intensely competitive entrepreneurial society almost 'modern' in its form. In Zaitun, in the flux and tension of the times – which Jacob describes with great verve – powerful and free-thinking merchants were not only engaged in a struggle for dominance with the 'mandarinate', but the 'mandarinate' was itself divided, some of its members being involved in trade themselves.

Other historians have come closer to an accurate judgment of the world that Jacob found, and upon which his manuscript sheds a unique light. 'New wealth and more accessible education bred a larger and confident elite,' write Hymes and Schirokauer. 'Intellectual life took on new energy and new political visions became available. The educated elite … tried to deal in thought, writing or action with questions of government and politics and their relation to society, [and] tried to understand … what government was and what it should or could do …'[7] This is strikingly confirmed by the manuscript, as is the same authors' view that, far from there being a lack of 'autonomy' in the Sung cities of the thirteenth century, it was a time of 'loss of faith in state activism'[8] and of decentralisation, a time when 'new local institutions, some voluntary, some state-sponsored, some a mixture, sprang up in great numbers'[9] – a time, in other words, not unlike our own.

Or, looking at it from another point of view, as does Gernet, 'the impression of order given by the southern China of the fourteenth century' – an order which Jacob did *not* find – 'is illusory … The edifice was fragile.'[10] It was also a world threatened by the Mongol foe, fear of whom is a constant and looming presence in Jacob's account, a fear which divided the city.[11] Yet Zaitun, both before and after the Tartar conquest, seemed anything but 'fragile' to the mediaeval travellers who called there, and who were all struck by its appearance and size.

To Marco Polo it was 'a marvel' and 'very large and noble'; to Marignolli a 'wondrous fine seaport and a city of incredible size'; to Andrea di Perugia a 'great city'; to Abulfeda a 'city of mark'. Ibn Batuta described Zaitun as a 'great city, superb indeed', and its harbour, where he saw 'about one hundred huge junks together', as 'one of the greatest in the world – I am wrong, it is the greatest!' Friar Odoric of Friuli estimated the city to be 'twice as big as Bologna', and thought its position 'one of the best in the world', but was most of all impressed by its port. 'It has shipping so great and vast in amount it would seem well-nigh incredible. All Italy,' he exclaimed, 'has not the amount of ships that this one city has.'[12]

It was here on 25 August 1271, the Chinese 'Year of the Sheep' as Jacob informs us, that the merchant of Ancona disembarked, in his fiftieth year.

rought with God's blessing to the land of Sinim and the city of Zaitun, in that district which the people of the place call Ciancio, a marvellous city and of very great trade which is one of the chief places of Manci, I disembarked with my servants and my rich cargoes of pepper, of wood of aloe and sandal, of camphor and choice perfumes, of precious stones and pearls, of dates, of cloth and of other things, God be praised, it being the Year of the Sheep, for so the Mancini name it, giving the name of animals, as dragon, ox and serpent to our years.

This city the Mancini also call the city ha-Bahir,[13] for so many are the lights of the lamps of oil and of the torches set in the streets that the city shines most brilliantly in the night and is visible from a great distance. And for this reason it is called by them (?)Hanmansicien,[14] or the City of Light. The country people give the city the name Giecchon, and it stands at the mouth of the Sentan river, opposite the islands they call the elder and younger brothers. It is the capital of this province of the realm of Manci, a realm which reaches to the banks of the great river which is called by the Sinimiani yellow, or Ouangho,[15] and by the Tartars black, or Carmuren. But those who have seen it say that it is neither yellow nor black, being dark brown.

To this city of Zaitun I carried so many precious things brought from India and its islands that I again feared for the avarice and greed of others and that, after much travail, I should be robbed before my fortunes were made. Moreover, although I was greeted with much love by my brother,[16] Nathan ben Dattalo of Sinigaglia, factor, who, together with the other Jews of the city, thereafter gave me all honour and praise and promised that I should be kept from harm, yet I learned also that the Tartars and their army were on the point of conquest of the realm of Manci, at which I felt great fear that I should lose all, both my fortune and my life, which I prayed to God that He should forbid. But first I shall tell of the port and merchandise of Zaitun.

It is a great harbour, greater even than that of Sinchalan,[17] which ships enter from the sea of Sinim, and it is surrounded by tall mountains which give a haven from the winds. The river upon which it stands is great and wide, running strongly from the sea, and the whole is filled with vessels which are a marvel to behold. For here there load and discharge every year thousands of great ships carrying pepper, besides a multitude of other vessels with other cargoes, so that on the day of our arrival there were at least fifteen thousand ships upon it, from Arabia, Greater India, Seilan, Java the Less, and from the far countries of the north, as northern Tartary,[18] as well as from our country and other kingdoms of the Franks.

Indeed, I saw here more ships, barques and small vessels at anchor than I have ever before seen in one port, more even than in Venice. Moreover, the vessels of Sinim are the largest one could think of, some having six masts, four decks and twelve big sails, and can carry more than one thousand men.

Not only do these vessels possess charts which are a wonder to
behold, so precise are they, but such are their geometers and
those skilled in the use of the lodestone, as well as those who
know the stars, that they may find their way to the ends of
the terrestrial world, for whose gift may God be praised.

There is therefore such a multitude of merchants here,
going up and down river, that one could hardly credit it if one
had not seen it. On the banks of the river are many great
storehouses with gates of iron in which the merchants of
Greater India and other parts keep their wares safe. But the
largest are those of the Saracens and the Jews, being like
cloisters, in which merchants may shelter their goods, both
those which they would sell and those which they purchase.

For this is a city of very great trade where merchants make
large profits, it being a city and a port in free state,[19] all
merchants being exempt from all exactions of tributes and
dues, about which I will write more in its place. Hence to this
city are brought articles in great abundance from every region
of Sinim, including from the land of the Tartars,[20] such as the
choicest silks and other things, and since every merchant,
large and small, can find means in this place to increase his
wealth, the markets of the city are wondrously great.

Once, merchants who came by sea from Greater India paid
5 per cent on all their richest cargoes, such as pearls and
precious stones, and gold and silver, for spices 10 to 20 per
cent and for cloth 15 per cent, unless their factors had gained
the favour of the *sciposo*, for this is the name by which he
goes. But now all such dues have been annulled, about which
I shall say more later, so that merchandise may pass in and out
of the port without charge. For they believe that whatever
harm may come to those of Manci who trade in cloth, or
spices or other things is equalled and exceeded by the benefits
of the very great revenue which comes to the city and its
inhabitants therefrom. For they say that that which is lost to
the realm from lack of dues is exceeded by the profits of the
markets, shops, taverns and other places to which the

merchants of all the world repair. Yet many are the traders who are driven from their counters and stalls and who become poor, God forbid, by the great concourse of merchants from other places, so that a man should feel pity to see them.

Nevertheless, to this city come so many merchants, Franks, Saracens, Indians and Jews, as well as traders of Sinim and from the towns and villages of this province, that for the whole year long it is like a very great fair, so that you also may find goods here from the remotest parts of the earth. But for the most part they make and sell to foreign merchants much silk cloth of rare quality, as well as many other choice things, purchasing from us spices, incenses, woods, cloth and other things, so that, as I shall tell, a man may see in Zaitun merchants even from Aragon or Venice, Alessandria, or Bruges of the Flemings, as well as black merchants and English.[21]

The demand for rare and costly goods, as well as for other goods, is so great that not only the port but also the roads to the city are clogged with carts and carriages. Indeed, the demand for goods cannot be measured, all, rich and poor, having burning desires even without the means to satisfy them. Thus, they crowd the markets both day and night, seeing there not only common things but the things of greatest value in any country on earth. Here are also all the things a man needs in order to live, but so great is the fever to buy and sell, as well as the greedy will for that which is prized, that the common man is not able to buy many things and is poorer than before, but others are rich beyond measure.

But first I should tell that the land of Sinim, or Mahacin,[22] is divided into two parts, that of the Cataini of the north who have fallen under the Tartars and their Cane, Chubilai,[23] and that of the Mancini of the south who live under a king called Toutson,[24] whom they call *tentsu*, which is to say the Son of Heaven. The Cataini are those who have origin from the realm of Cataio, and the Mancini are those of the realm of

Manci, and, although there is much likeness between them, they are as two peoples, for each is different both from the Tartars and from one another. From Zaitun, it is a journey of fifty days to the court of the Cane of the Tartars which is in Sandou,[25] twenty days to the court of Toutson which is in Chinscie,[26] and eight days' journey to Fuciu.

The Tartars, whom some call the Mongols, which means in our language the strong and the powerful, have laid waste the land of the Cataini. Moreover, the people of the cities of Cataio are under the guard of the Tartars, the soldiers of whose armies are placed at a league's distance from each city and who do not permit those under their rule to maintain their walls or gates.

Some say that these Mongols are descended from Gog and Magog, God forbid, the enemy of Israel to the north and a polluted people who ate human flesh, whence they were first called Magogoli, and that Alexander the Great shut them up in Tattaria so that the world might be preserved, which God secure. Those who have journeyed in the land of the Tartars say that they are very ugly, having small eyes and noses which are flat and that they have skins like hide, and that, being a cruel people who are much given to killing and plunder, it makes sense to have fear of them. But others say that the Tartars, having taken the lands and riches of the Sinimiani, have rather given themselves over to ease, and will have no clothes but those of silk and gold, and no food but that which is cooked with choice spices.

Their king, whom they call Chubilai, and whom the Cataini and Mancini call Scitsou, is the son of Tuli and the grandson of Cingis Cane,[27] a blacksmith. Some say that this Cingis was killed by lightning, others in battle, others that he was slain by his wife and others again that he died of sickness and old age. Thus is the truth of the terrestrial world hidden, when accounts of the same thing differ in such fashion.

Of the Tartars this also must be added, that, as did our King Solomon, may his name be recorded in the book of memory, so does their Cane have many wives and concubines, and many sons of them. It is said that in his palace he has many Saracen counsellors also. Thus those who would think, as among the Christians, for so I had it from Simone,[28] that the Tartars may stand with them in war against the Mahometans, are in error, for there is, rather, great love between them. Moreover, from the fear and hatred of the Tartars among the Cataini and Mancini, there are those who would call the Mongols the kin of the Jews. But they bear no resemblance to us[29] and know nothing of the Torah, may its words be cherished.

But are there not many who say of us, in like fashion, whatever it pleases them to say, the better to sow bitterness against us, whether that we too are cruel or greedy, and even, as I have heard tell, that there are certain fish that the Christian and Saracen may catch with ease, but not the Jew, may God keep us. Thus, when the Tartars entered Bohemia in our lands,[30] was it not said that they were of the Ten Tribes of Israel, may peace be upon all our true ancestors and kinsmen, in order that there might be even more hatred shown to them?

As to the people of Manci, I should say that they also have small noses, but black hair and white skins, unlike those of the Tartars. Their men also have no beards, or only a few hairs and thin, which the old men forbear to cut. The women have flesh which is very beautiful and white and soft skins, having no hair upon any part of their bodies, except their heads and their genitals,[31] may God spare me. But of this I shall write more in due place.

Their king, Toutson, he whom they call the Son of Heaven as the Christians call *that man* the son of God, may God forgive them, himself takes much pleasure with women, being a man of very great lechery who pays little heed to the approach of the Tartars, and who has women to attend upon him even when he goes to bathe. His ministers, of whom the first is called Ciasuto, rule the kingdom in his name, but first

I must speak further of the city of Zaitun, which is called the City of Light.

It is a city of measureless trade, and its streets are crowded with a vast ebb and flow of men and carriages. Moreover, being a *ouang*, that is to say in their language a great city, only the *cinsci* or the learned from among the greatest officials of the Son of Heaven may govern the city according to their law. Indeed, the confusion of persons in it is such, with so many things to be observed, that I do not well know how to recount it with ink and inkwell.

Thus in Zaitun there are so many people that no one could know their number, but they say that it is more than two hundred thousand, which is larger than Venice itself, God be praised. Indeed the inhabited places comprising the city and the surrounding towns and villages appear but one city, such is the number of buildings that are near to one another, so that the citizens and the country people are mixed together as though they were one people.

Yet in the city a man may hear the sound of one hundred different tongues, so many are they who come thither from other countries, so that, as I shall tell, there are also among the Mancini those who have mastered the Frankish and Saracen tongues. Indeed, there are many types of Christians in the city, even those who preach against the Jews, as well as Saracens, Jews and many other peoples who have, as well as their temples, houses of their own, each people being in its district within the walls. In these districts there are also hostels for each people, in which the Christians and Saracens of our fleet found shelter.

As to the Jews, they number two thousand and have a house of prayer, God be praised, which they affirm to be more than three hundred years old.[32] To this place I went upon the first Sabbath after the arrival of our fleet, which is to say the Sabbath Shofetim, together with Nathan ben Dattalo, Eliezer of Venice and Lazzaro del Vecchio, so that I might be among my brothers and to give thanks to God, may His name be

cherished, for our safe delivery from the seas. Here they
offered up prayers that King Toutson might be preserved, for
the Jews of the city were in great fear of the coming of the
Tartars.

Thus there live together in the city of Zaitun people of
every land and sect, may God save them, yet all are permitted
to act according to their creed, for they hold the opinion that
everyone can find his salvation in his own faith. Therefore the
priests may preach what they will without obstacle and
whatever the follies in which they may believe.

Of the idol monasteries, the greatest number are those of
the followers of Sacchia the Buddum, being found both in the
city and in the hills about the city. But the Christians of the
place alone seek the conversion of the Jews to their faith, but
of not one Jew have they made a heretic to betray the God of
his forefathers, may God be praised and exalted.

There are many Jews in the land of Sinim who came to its
shores in the time of our ancestors, Abraam, Isaac and Jacob,
peace upon them, and being so long among the Sinimiani
have taken their faces, customs and names, so that only with
difficulty may these be distinguished from others of the city,
having the same skin, eyes, noses and colour of hair as those
of the people of Manci. They also speak their prayers in a
tongue that I could not follow, being composed of the
language of Sinim and of some words of our tongue,[33] but
spoken in a strange fashion, as also is their Torah, all being
written in Mancino yet with whole words of our language
being hidden within it so that they may not be seen.

Yet they also have among them a Scroll of the Law which is
written entirely in our language, but which none of them can
read save their rabbi, a certain Lo Hoan, so that a Jew of
Frankish lands cannot follow their reading of the Law.
Nevertheless, they are Jews, for the Shema is understood by
them in our language, their foreskins are cut before the eighth
day and they observe the laws of purity in food.

But although they say their due prayers, as the morning

and additional Sabbath prayers according to our laws, as those
who know both our language and the tongue of the Mancini
declare, the Jews who come to them from the lands of the
Saracens and the Franks, such as merchants, factors and
learnèd men, pray among themselves in a nearby place. Here
I, having prayed upon the Sabbath Shofetim with the Jews of
Manci, betook myself thereafter, together with Nathan ben
Dattalo and the other brothers of my country,[34] of whom
there were many hundreds in the city, in order the better to
fulfil my duties, may God be praised.

They say that in the land of Sinim there are many tens of
thousands of Jews of Sinim,[35] as in Sinchalan, Penlian,
Chinscie and Suciu, and many other places besides. Thus in
the house of study of Chaifen are the lost books of the
Maccabees and the son of Sirach, which Nathan ben Dattalo
declared to have seen with his own eyes and which I think to
be true.[36] In Sinchalan, where the Jews are numerous, many
were slain long ago, peace be upon their souls, by one
Baiciu,[37] along with Saracens, Christians and Parsees, yet may
now go about in peace in that city, for which God be
thanked.

In Suciu, forty families of Jews live near the Se gates at the
north of the city, close by the Piscien temple. In Chinscie, the
Jews live between the Singte and the Ouangian gates in the
east of the city and are more than two hundred families. In
Zaitun, they live in the district of the Four-Span palace and
the Street of the Little Red Flowers, where is also found their
house of study. Their cemetery, peace upon the souls of the
dead, is outside the walls of the city in the district called
Ciuscien.

In all Sinim, which is to say in Cataio and Manci together,
the Jews, God in His great mercy be praised for ever, bear no
sign about them. For they are held in great honour for their
learning in many things, as well as for their riches, being great
masters of medicine[38] and of all other arts. Moreover, it may
be seen that from them the people of Manci have learned

many things, for, although they worship idols, it is contrary to
their faith that animal and vegetable substances be formed
into one weave and worn upon the body, which God forbid.
For, as it is written in the book of Leviticus that neither shall a
garment mingled of linen and wool come upon thee,[39] so the
Mancini do likewise, a custom that has surely been taken
from the Jews. Further, the proportions of the Ark of Noah
are as those of a ship of Sinim,[40] and, in the manner of the
Jews but not of the Christians, a man may not enter a
sepulchre or touch the body and bones of the dead, it being
among them also a profane and forbidden thing, save to
prepare such body to be buried or to find out the cause of
illness so that another may be spared.

Moreover, although the Tartars are surely not of the tribes
of Israel, as I have written, yet do they not call their princes
by the name of Cane, which in our language is *kanah*, which
is to say to become a possessor, as they have become of the
lands of others throughout the entire world?


But how shall a man speak rightly of the great city of Zaitun,
when his soul is thrown into such confusion in it that he
would go with ears stopped and eyes covered in order to
preserve his reason? For the noise and flux of men is so great
as to surfeit the faculties of everyone who goes among them,
and cannot be borne except for a short time, since the soul
requires repose in order to be apt for thought.

Thus I have forgotten to say of the Christians that among
them in Zaitun are many followers of a certain Nestorius who
have their own churches and bishops, and are much hated by
the other Christians of the city as being perfidious, not
because the beliefs of the Nestorians are more foolish than
their own, but because there is a prohibition from Rome
against them that reaches even to the shores of Sinim. As to
their beliefs, they say that there resided in *that man* not one
person but two, the one the corporeal form of the word of
God, may they be condemned for such blasphemy, and the

other a man, the former being placed in the latter as in a temple, or united with him as fire with iron, so these idolaters declare.

Over such dark theories, in which there is no light of truth, the Christians of the city quarrel, while the friars do nothing save to expel devils. For there are many among the Mancini who, believing that there are devils within them, come to the friars for succour. Then the friars, sprinkling with water those who have been taken with madness, bid the demons depart instantly from their bodies in the name of *that man*, and they afterwards seek baptism, thus exchanging one idolatry for another.

Of themselves, they say that a certain priest Alofeno came from Tatsin, which is to say Rome, more than six hundred years ago, bringing with him sacred books and idols of *that man*, and that King Taitsun, who reigned over them at that time, permitted the said Alofeno to teach his doctrine freely.[41] Of this I was not able to find the truth, yet it is certain that the Jews of Sinim came before.

But who might speak of God, whether the false or the true, in a city of cries and din so loud that one would not even hear the sound of God's thunder, may the Holy One forgive my words?

Thus, amid an uproar that would make a man mad, and in the midst of the carts, idols, and coming and going, thousands of merchants exchange gold and silver, groats, and

---

'THE CHRISTIANS OF THE CITY QUARREL'

*The Nestorian heresy (p.133), according to which the Virgin Mary was not the 'Mother of God' but of a man, was introduced into China from Persia in the seventh century. The doctrine was banned by the Roman Church in the fifth century. The Nestorians, while using the symbol of the Cross, did not depict a crucifixion upon it; it was a symbol for them not of suffering but of Christ's final triumph, or of a victory over death. Jacob calls them* cristiani nestorini.

money made of paper also, about which I shall say more in its
place, and such is the great frenzy and roar of voices, and so
great the clamour and shouting of the rich, and of the grief
and anger of the poor and fearful, that again a man could say
that the thunder of God would not be heard in the markets of
the city. Moreover, everywhere there are large workshops with
many hundreds[42] of men and women therein who work
together in the making of metals, vases of porcelain,[43] silk,
paper, and other things. In some of these workshops there are
even a thousand people, so that they are a wonder to behold.

There are also many places where you may have writings
and pamphlets of paper, which they call in their language
*tachuini*, and which are made with ink in their own fashion.
These little books are sold for a small sum and are thus
purchased in large numbers by those who have a will to know
the world, may God be praised. Moreover, every day in the
City of Light they place upon the walls a large paper on
which are written the decrees and decisions of the high
officials of the city, as well as of the deputies therein of the
Son of Heaven, as also the acts of citizens and other
information which are considered worthy to be mentioned.
Of these papers each citizen may have one for himself without
payment.[44]

Thus it is that many gather together like herds, the men
handsome in their own fashion but with beards of thin hair
like those of cats, but the women the most beautiful in the
whole world, may God spare me. Both prefer enjoyment
above all things, and that which they see and hold in their
hands to that which is promised or may not be seen. They live
by commerce and manufacture and are not given to arms,
preferring money to wisdom, although there are also many
wise men among the fools for whom wealth has precedence
over knowledge.

Above all, many of them make profession that all men are
equal not only in the eye of God but according to the law of
nature. Yet at the same time they seek among themselves for

greatness of wealth as well as for marks of honour over others. Thus for a man to receive a sign of favour from the Son of Heaven is the object of great envy, all craving the notice of the court, while at the same time professing to hold it in contempt.

Thus, from the beginning of my sojourn in the City of Light, I was greatly troubled in spirit and body, finding comfort in my duty and awaiting the Day of Atonement in fear for the sins of my heart and eyes, may my soul be spared. I found place in the house of Nathan ben Dattalo, peace upon him, together with the woman Bertoni and the girl Buccazuppo in order that they could attend to my needs, my other servants finding shelter elsewhere, and the mariners in the quarter of the Saracens close by their mosque, while I kept the faithful Armentuzio and Pizzecolli near to me also, so that they might help me to buy and sell according to my desires.

Yet such was the great fear of the Tartars and the confusion of the city that I could find no rest, nor be quiet in my heart, being disturbed first by one thing and then by another. So that little by little my soul went from bad to worse, contemplating the place to which I had come and the travails of the people. For albeit that it was a city of marvels, yet it was also a city condemned, may God save its people.

The bearded who go about the city are all of them Saracens, Christians or Jews from other countries, the Sinimiani having no beards or thin only. Thus a stranger may easily be noticed in the streets, but their number cannot be counted, so many are they. The Christians the people of Zaitun call the *elicoveni* and the Mahometans they call *hui*, of whom some are Mancini and others are merchants from other countries, as from Persia and the realm of Mitzraim. Indeed, so many are the Saracens, of whom they say that there are more than fifteen thousand, that they are divided like the Christians into sects, some who wear black caps being the most devout and others white, each having its own temple

where they go to worship their Prophet, and each in his own
fashion.

But many are those among the Mancini who think all
those from other countries to be alike, not distinguishing
between the Jew and the Saracen, or between the Jew and the
Christian. Thus they call the Saracens and the Jews by the
name of those who have large noses and who do not eat the
meat of the pig, God forbid, saying that both are *somaciun*,
which in our language means men with coloured eyes. Thus
even those things which are most different among men are
wrongly perceived, so great is the confusion. For the city is a
mixture of peoples, and each people in the city, of which there
are said to be as many as thirty, even those which have
inhabited it for a long time, has its own language. Therefore
the Saracens speak in Arabic, the Franks in the Frankish
language,[45] and every other people in their own language, so
that the city is as Babel, may God forbid.

Moreover, each people does as it pleases also, the Saracens
according to their custom, the Armenians according to theirs,
and all the other peoples in the same fashion. Thus, the
merchants of Greater India, who may easily be seen since they
are so brown and thin, and whose women, especially those of
Chesimur, are of great beauty, have for their food vegetables,
milk and rice, as they choose, but neither flesh nor fish, nor
will they eat as the people of Zaitun eat, nor follow their
customs. Each people lives according to its own way.

Therefore, the Zaituni, whose language and writing few of
the merchants from other countries know how to use, are
constrained to have many officials who are themselves masters
of the tongues of others, among them those whom they call
the *hunlusciaocini*, the *coscienfusci* and the *lipinueni*. Together
with them are those they call the *arguni*, of whom I will speak
more in their place.

Thus, a man may go about the streets of Zaitun as if it
were a city of the whole world and not of Manci, in one
separate quarter being the Mahometans, in another the

Franks, in another the Armenians who are Christians, in another the Jews, peace upon them, and in another those of Greater India, and in each quarter separate parts again, as in the quarter of the Franks there is a part for the Lombards, a part for the Germans, who are great eaters, and another part for those of our countries.[46]

For here there are Venetians who excel all others save the Jews in their skill, Genoese, Pisans and Anconetans, as well as Frenchmen, each of whom have their own hostels and warehouses. Moreover, here the Venetian and Genoese merchants live at peace with one another, there being much love among those of the same land[47] when all are far from their homes. Indeed, such is their concord that there is a council of twenty-four among them, composed of men of Venice, Genoa, Pisa and Ancona. Among them is one Vioni, a merchant of Genoa and long in this place, who told me that he had a brother in Tauris who died of the pestilence. The Saracens also have such a council, which they call *ortaq*.

And just as each people in the city has its own quarter, temples, walks, hostels and warehouses, so also the Jews, may God be praised, as I have written, have a hospital, a house of worship, a house of study, a school and a cemetery, upon those buried therein be peace, Amen. Indeed, the Christians, the Saracens and the Jews have each a cemetery beyond the city walls, but the idolaters of Manci burn the bodies of their dead, God forbid, as they do also in Greater India, in a manner horrible to see.[48] Of all the peoples in the city who have come from other countries, it is the Jews who have inhabited it the longest, may God be magnified and honoured. For, as any man may see, there is in the city our former house of prayer, more than one thousand years old, may we have peace and plenty, which, although it now lies in ruins, will endure in holiness for evermore. For so the Holy One provides for His people, Amen.

In the city the Christians are often united in marriage with the idolaters, but the Saracens who do this are few, and the

Jews never. For the base custom of the Franks is that when a
married man leaves his country for more than twenty days,
he, wherever he goes, can take another woman and the wife
another man, and neither of the two speaks of it. Among the
Saracens, the man may do the same, but the wife may not. Yet
both customs are an equal abomination, being against the law
of God, may He be exalted and His commandments obeyed.

Thus, the Franks and Saracens freely commit adultery and
do many other heinous and wicked carnal acts. Yet the
women of Zaitun, for their part, being of great beauty and
loose conduct, tempt many merchants to become enamoured
of them and to remain, so that they cast off their wives and
take new ones. For they say that their own wives do not
practise such arts as they, and they are thus beguiled to lie
with them, may God punish them. But to be weak in such a
fashion is not to be marvelled at in those whose lack of faith
extends to all things.

In the past they say that a Christian or Saracen could not
so conduct himself, since for a stranger to seek the daughter
of a Zaituno for wife, or to seek to lie with a woman of the
city, was held in great hatred. Moreover, in the past both the
men and the women of the city were of pleasing manners and
courteous, especially to foreigners, treating them with great
friendship and giving them every advice, saying that it was
their custom not to constrain anyone to remain in the city
against their will, nor turning anyone from their gates who
wished to stay among them. Indeed, in past times, they had
an official whose duty it was to defend from wrong the
merchant of other countries, and to punish those who sought
to cheat him with false goods. But now all is changed, and
among the Zaituni themselves quarrels have grown much
greater, as I shall tell, so that there is much bitterness and
hatred among them.

Therefore, the quarters in which the Zaituni live as
neighbours are no longer regarded as single houses. Likewise,
where they formerly received with goodwill foreigners who

came to them to trade, now in the confusion of the city many look askance upon them, as at those who should have no place among them.

Thus, in the trading-posts of the Franks and the Jews, the citizens formerly provided good wine from Taianfo and Uciaiano, as well as the spiced wine of Ciencian, for the comfort of their guests, although no pious Jew may drink it lest it have been dedicated to the worship of idols. The Franks, and the Saracens also, would gladly drink of it in times past, but such gifts are made to them no more. Indeed many are the crimes now committed against the stranger, even in the light of day. For if they can rob from a man of another country, such is the corruption of their manners it seems to please them the more, from the fear which is thus aroused in the hearts of those who have come among them. Over all such things, however, there are many in the city who make bitter lament, as I shall tell further in its place.

There thus being so large a number of Franks and other peoples in the city who have lain with the women of the place, a man may easily see their offspring as he goes about, whom they call *arguni*, as among us bastards are called *mamzerim*, or those who are the sons born of a woman of the city and a Christian.

It is from these *arguni* that those who serve foreign merchants are taken, since they are able to speak both the language of the Mancini and the Frankish tongues. One such, a certain Lifenli, who was twenty-four years old, I now took, having been eight days in the city, to be at my service, he being in appearance a man of Manci save for the eyes, and fathered upon a woman of the city by one Guglielmo, a merchant from Pisa. This man, who had much knowledge of the ways of the City of Light, was my guide therein, a man of fidelity and craft and much given to discourse upon the actions of others. Although esteemed by the nobly born of the city to be of low birth, he served me well, peace upon him, both prospering my trade and bringing me to the presence of

the sages and counsellors of the city, even though much travail
came to me from it.

After the Sabbath Ki Tetze,[49] upon which I performed all
my duties with a joyful heart, may God be praised, and
accompanied by the said Lifenli, for no man may find his way
in such a huge city without a companion of the place, I came
upon crowds denser even than in Venice at the time of the
great fair.[50] Indeed, such was the confusion of persons that it
was as though the world was overturned in chaos,[51] may God
forbid such a thing.

For in the streets of the City of Light there pass
continuously back and forth thousands of carriages and carts,
whose noise and number are overpowering. At all hours of the
day from earliest dawn, for the people of the City of Light rise
early from their beds, a multitude go to and fro on its
business, so large that one would believe it impossible that
there could be enough food in the city to feed them.

Yet, already at dawn, the stalls of those who sell food are
thronged, the passers-by eating pieces of mutton[52] and goose,
soups of various kinds and other hot foods, while others, both
men and women, are at large in the streets, some with rapid
feet proceeding in all directions as though burdened with
care, and others as if lost people or eating while in motion,
some with a definite end and others as if without purpose.
Indeed, such was the confusion that I observed a man
carrying a pot who fell in the tumult and another, also
carrying a pot, who fell upon him. In such a case, as our sages
declare, if two who are carrying pots are walking one behind
the other, and the first one falls and the second falls over the
first, the first must pay for the loss suffered by the second.

In this vast throng, which grew beyond measure with the
hours, were peasants and citizens without number, the rich
and the poor, men and women, masters and servants,
noblemen and miscreants, Sinimiani and strangers, and those
who go in silk and those who go in rags. There were those
who labour in the workshops of silk and clay, in the taverns

and the shops, merchants and sellers of food and other things, vagabonds, barbers, those who carry sedan-chairs, idolatrous priests, jugglers with dishes of porcelain, as well as soothsayers and astrologers, and those who go about with wild animals on a fetter.

The rich and nobly born wear long robes of silk that reach to the ground, and on their feet high shoes by which to make themselves taller, the poor a shirt which comes to the waist and breeches, and some go barefoot, may God have pity on them. There are also many mendicants in the streets and wretches who sleep on the thresholds, as well as those who fight over food or coins.

Thus, together with Lifenli, I came upon two arguing about such coins that they had found in the street, and a third who declared that they were his. In such a case, as our sages declare, if a man should find money scattered in the public way they belong to the finder, which is he who first placed his hand upon them. But if they are found in a purse, or in a heap one upon the other, the fact must be made known and the money may not be taken. This I told to Lifenli, who declared that each claimed to have placed his hand first upon the coins, and that the third was a beggar to whom they surely did not belong. I therefore counselled them that the coins, which were three, should be divided equally among them, and thus we went on our way.

The rich and noble of the city, however, carry their money inside their sleeves, in payment taking out such money and bowing, when they place it in the sleeve of another. For such is their custom. Moreover, they go about the streets carrying fans and walking with a proud air, or upon horseback, the saddles painted with lacquer, and their women in chairs with small doors, while the poor go on foot. Everywhere men carry goods which hang from poles of bamboo. There are also donkeys, mules and dogs without number, among which the people pass up and down in a confusion and noise which cannot be described. Even women of the greatest beauty, some in chairs and some on foot also, go close to such animals without fear.

Once it was, so Lifenli declared, that the wives of nobles, officials and rich merchants remained inside their houses, where they could not be seen. But now some of them have become merchants themselves, as among us,[53] and go everywhere as though they were men, not only serving at the counters but going to those who exchange money and purchasing from others. It is also said that some have sailed to Java the Less and Greater India in order to seek profit for themselves, but this may hardly be believed. There are also to be seen young girls in the streets, and about the hostels such as are frequented by strangers, who are prostitutes. For in the city of Zaitun many women give themselves to prostitution, going freely about the streets without modesty. Indeed, their very eyes are whorish, seeking by their glances to tempt the traveller, and should he look at one of them she will with a sign call upon him to follow, which God forbid. Others, although richly dressed, go about keeping their lips open, which is considered among the Zaituni to be a sign of lust. Of such matters I shall write further.

The city is encircled by great walls, a part of which have fallen, and many gates with towers, and at each gate there is a market, just as each district of the city is given over to a different profession and skill. Thus at one gate there is a market for silks, at another for spices, at another for oxen and carts, at another for horses, at another for grain which is brought to the city by the country people, and yet another for rice of every kind, at another for rams and goats, at another for the fish of the seas and the rivers, and many others in like fashion. Indeed, so great are the riches of the city that there are even many different markets for fish, both fresh and good as well as unclean,[54] for meats clean and unclean, for fruit and flowers, for cloth, for books, for incense, for porcelains, for pearls and precious stones, and both within and outside the walls.

At these markets, to which I was conducted many times by Lifenli so that I might make purchases there, great numbers of people may be found looking closely at the wares, which are of an abundance such has never yet been known in the entire world. There they see all that they desire, and which they are driven to possess by every means, both good and ill, some achieving their end with labour and effort and others by theft and vice.

Thus, about each market and in the streets which approach them, all is a noisy humming as of bees or other insects, as well as the thudding sounds caused by the movement of a great procession of people together with the cries of the vendors and the bellowing and braying of animals, both those which are for sale and those which wander the streets. Moreover, so close together and narrow are the houses, which are made of wood and bamboo, that in the streets often no man may move or pass, but must seek another way, and there are many and frequent fires, for so Lifenli declared. Yet there are also many great temples of the idolaters and other buildings which are carved and decorated with gold, such as shine in the light of the sun and are a wonder to behold.

In the shops, which are more numerous than in any other city of the world, every kind of merchandise, spicery, silk cloth, jewel, wine or salve may be found, of which I bought greatly. There you may find medicines against the cold, an ointment to ward off insects, a herb for the gall, and colour for women's eyes. One street, by name the Street of the Three Plates, is given over altogether to silks, of which there are no fewer than two hundred kinds, woven with such skill that they are a marvel to behold. Another is given over to gold- and silversmiths, of whom some are Saracens and some are Jews, another to apothecaries, and another to astrologers, who also dwell in their own district, although it is said that there is great enmity among them.

Indeed, one building, which stands in the Street of Harmony, whither Lifenli later conducted me, is the abode of

all their philosophers and astrologers, who make proof there
of their wisdom. Thus some astrologers and soothsayers who
go there, so Lifenli declared, watch for certain hours and the
conjunction of the stars in order to call on the people who
gather, being for the most part well advanced in years, to
place their foreheads upon the ground so that the Son of
Heaven, which is to say their king, might be appeased.

These astrologers, whom many hold to be wise, then cry
out in their language *que e*, which means, Go down. And then
they will call out *che e*, which is to say, Rise up, or *cho e*,
which is to say, Range yourselves on one side, or at another
conjunction will cry out, Put your fingers in your ears, and so
they do. And when they are commanded by their astrologers
to take their fingers out of their ears, this they also do, such is
the learning which the Zaituni think them to possess. Many
also are the taverns, both of good reputation and those which
are low, where men and women may dance together, and
others where fish or beverages of fine herbs are prepared. In
another district of the city, which is called in their language
*ouasu*, storytellers, singers and prostitutes abound.

Thus, the City of Light is a city in which all things are of
such an abundance, both of good and ill, as has never been
seen before. For there men may find shelter better than in
their own lands, yet it is a city in which many citizens come

---

### 'BEVERAGES OF FINE HERBS'

*'Beverages of fine herbs' and 'a beverage made of small leaves of a bush' which is*
*'bitter to the taste' (p.148) may well be references to tea, whose absence from Marco*
*Polo's account of his journey to China has led to doubt that he went there; see F.*
*Wood, op. cit., 71ff. Tea-drinking had been known to foreign travellers, and*
*remarked upon, since the ninth century. It is thought to have been drunk in China*
*since at least the second century BC and tea-houses would have been common at the*
*time of Jacob's and Marco Polo's journeys. However, tea was possibly unknown as a*
*beverage in Europe before the early seventeenth century.*

to a violent death, as I shall tell. But although the inhabitants run hither and thither at night as well as by day, as if they did not know where they went, yet time is measured by them with the greatest care. For in all the principal streets of the city are clocks[55] set upon towers, and at each clock a watchman attends, who strikes the hour on a shield of copper[56] which resounds even to the narrowest alley, he thereafter displaying that hour in their writing for all to see.

Nor is there any prohibition from going about at night as there is among us, those places where men go for enjoyment and in search of every pleasure, God forbid, remaining thronged until the rise of the sun. Thus many are the lamps and lights which the people of Zaitun place in the entrance-ways of their houses and courtyards, and without number the lanterns borne by passers-by as they make their way at night, so that the entire city sparkles, for everywhere there is light.

But despite the great wealth of the merchants and of many of the citizens also, the streets of the city are unclean, from the excrement of animals and of humans also. Indeed, even the carcasses of beasts are frequently left to lie for many days, God forbid, and many other dirty things are thrown from men's houses on the public ways without any concern. Nor does any citizen bring himself to touch them, looking always to others rather than to himself. Yet the Mancini, like those of Greater India, frequently wash their bodies, as also their hair, in cold water, and some every day, thinking it no shame to do so before strangers, but not in the presence of a woman, nor of a relation of a different age, whether older or younger. Neither are fleas to be found among them, yet they have many unclean habits, such as wiping their teeth and gums with a cloth, and their fundaments likewise, which is an abomination. They also stand within their doorways urinating towards the street[57] and spit in the same fashion, both of which are abominations. All these things I saw when Lifenli conducted me through the streets of the city.

It now being the time of the New Year, which fell this year

two days after the Sabbath Netzavim,[58] I, together with
Nathan ben Dattalo, Lazzaro del Vecchio and Eliezer of Venice,
the great Aaron having gone to Chinscie, went first to the
house of prayer of the Jews of Zaitun, those who are of Sinim,
and thereafter to the place nearby in the Street of the Red
Flowers, where the Jews of other lands are accustomed to pray.

In the first place were as many as five hundred persons and
in the second more than seven hundred, for which God be
praised, and here I did my duties as a Jew together with my
brethren, may God teach Israel always to do justice and
increase our number one hundredfold. Thus I praised the
Lord for having kept me safe, praying also with many tears
that my Sara, my father, may his soul endure, my sons and
my daughters might be held in His hand, and that I find
them preserved in health upon my return.

Upon the tenth day of Tishri,[59] abstaining from all food, I
prayed that all my sins committed against God might be
forgiven, and that for the sins I have committed against my
fellow men I should be given the health and strength to make
amends. I also prayed for the soul of my friend Vivo, may his
memory be blessed, weeping greatly that his body should have
been consumed by the seas and that he did not stand beside
me at this hour.

I also prayed that God would help me in a strange land to
take care of my soul and body, in the first by assisting me in
my study of Torah, and in the second by keeping unclean
meat from my lips. Of the two, the first is the greater by far,
nor are those who take most care of their bodies always those
who live longest. For disease may take the strongest man
when he does not expect it, but he who does not attend to his
soul suffers therefrom at the first, knowing his default, and
thus may amend it in time with God's aid, while he who is
sick of a disease which is hidden or which comes upon him in
a hidden way cannot aid himself, nor at the last can he be
aided by God, may God forgive me my words if there be
anything in them to give offence.

As to the food of the body which it is lawful to eat, it being part of the bounty of God, we should exhibit a good appetite but without greed, saying always that we love that which is given to us, so that we may return the generosity of nature with good grace, praising God with the kiddush and amotzi. Yet we should also not permit the abundance of food which may be given to us to turn our mind from study, nor in our greed treat badly the creatures of the earth as though their end was only to be food for the throat.

Thus, in the city of Zaitun everything that a man could want to sustain life is to be found, as I have written, and every type of foodstuff, such as wild game, including deer and birds, hens, and ducks so fat as could not be bettered, provided that their throats be cut in due fashion, together with many kinds of fish such as my eye had never beheld.

But the Zaituni, such is their greed, are given to eat other types of flesh which are unclean, not only pigs, God forbid, but foul things that not even a Frank would eat. Many are the good things which are to be found in the markets of the city, as rice and every form of fruit and herb, as well as a beverage made of small leaves of a bush which is much prized among them but which is bitter to taste. Yet they eat every kind of unclean meat such as kites, cats, dogs, owls, and even snakes and mice, God spare me for such words of abomination, which last they eat with ginger, calling them in their language deer of the house.[60] All these things I learned from the faithful Lifenli, or saw with my own eyes. But that they eat the flesh of children who have been cast away, calling it mutton with two legs, as some say, is not to be believed.

But of all the things which are eaten by the Zaituni, that which they eat with the greatest greed is the pig, whose flesh they are accustomed to cook in the street, and whose unclean parts they hold in the faces of passers-by, to the great discomfort of the Saracens also. Yet milk and cheese these same do not eat, for they consider them unclean, but they do not forbear to eat the meat of the ass or dog. Likewise, they

are able to suffer the great stink of a pig or of burnt oil, which
would make the head of a strong man turn and surely offends
the nostrils of God, may He be exalted, but not the smell of
garlic, which to them is an abomination.[61] Thus it is that
even the senses, as well as the tongues, of God's creatures, may
He be praised, differ among them, while to some are some
kinds of meat allowed by their law and to others are the same
meats forbidden.

Yet it is not permitted to us to say, since among men all
things are done both holy and unholy, that all things therefore
are of equal merit, just as we may not say that to eat a snake
or a mouse is as clean as to eat any other thing. For some
things are worthy of man and others unworthy, some things
harmful and others useful to the well-being of man, and some
things by their nature wholesome while others are by their
nature unclean. Moreover, if God should seek to guide us by
rule as to what is just and what unjust, what good and what
bad, let us bless Him for His bounty, for when such a rule is
lacking, man cannot live within due bounds and is lost.

As to the eating of food, some there are among the
idolaters who from piety do not kill animals, nor spill their
blood, nor eat their flesh. But there are also others who, while
professing great love for the Creator and His Creation,
nevertheless eat animals with a great will, getting others
among them to act as butchers while averting their eyes and
their thoughts from such deeds. Rather we should have
reverence for all life, God be praised, while at the same time
having knowledge of man's need for meat, acting in such a
fashion, according to reason, that we do not cause animals to
suffer torments, but stun them before they are killed. Yet
neither must we deceive ourselves nor deceive others about
our appetites and desires, for by these means the rule of
untruth is enlarged.

There are also those in the City of Light, so Lifenli
informed me, who, seeking to lead a simple and pure life,
believe that to eat little and digest well enables a person to live

longer than any other people in the world, even to a hundred years. They fast all the year round, not for penitence but for health, eating neither meat nor fish but only vegetables and rice, together with certain fruits and pure water. They say that thus one remains healthy and prolongs one's youth, but for others such a life is a hard trial and destroys their rest. Some, however, as in Greater India also, go beyond all measure and act against reason itself, saying that they would kill no animal in the world, not even a flea or a louse, because fleas and lice and other such things have souls like men. But in this they blaspheme, for only that which is made in the likeness of God possesses a soul, and not all things are equal in His sight, may He be praised.

For man alone, who is the crown of the terrestrial world, possesses both reason and soul, by virtue of which he is man not brute, just as those men who act against reason and who forget their souls become brutes, though they should have the faces and bodies of men. Thus our sages declare that a man should neither be so gluttonous as to become a brute, nor eat so little that his strength cannot be maintained. For this too is an offence against the Lord who has made us in His image.

To all these things I gave thought upon the Day of Penitence while faint from abstaining from food, may God forgive me for the wandering of my thoughts. Yet He recalled me to myself at the sounding of the shofar, setting my feet once more upon His path so that I might give Him praise, and gain the ends of my voyage.

Whereafter, with Nathan ben Dattalo and the faithful Armentuzio at my side, and with the aid of Lifenli, I began to make great profits from selling the merchandise of all lands that I had brought to the City of Light, my pepper, woods, incenses, cloth and precious stones gaining a great price among the traders of the city, for which God be praised. Indeed, so choice were my goods of Greater and Lesser India, at which other men marvelled, that never were such profits

made by a merchant of Ancona in the land of Sinim, for so
Nathan ben Dattalo declared.

Yet I was secretly troubled in my heart, not only fearing
that the Tartars, having entered the realm of Manci, as all
made report, should attack the city and I be taken, but since
all about me was such great confusion, greed, desire and pride
that a man might not know rightly how to conduct himself in
such a place. Moreover, my servants, being much given to the
pleasure of the city, I feared also that they might enter into
some snare or danger and thus be lost. So often I counselled
the woman Bertoni and the girl Buccazuppo that they should
have good care of their bodies and souls, and so often they
swore their faith, Buccazuppo praying also that I should teach
her how to read upon the voyage home. By this I now had
faith that she had a secure heart, yet I had no trust in Bertoni,
commanding her every day to do her duty lest evil come upon
her.

Thus I sought to still my troubled mind, but could find no
rest. For although the merchants of the city were very rich
and great, having more wealth than any heart could desire
from their trade in silks, porcelains, spices and other things,
and being of such numbers that they could not be counted,
such was their arrogance that it was as though they wished to
subject the whole city to their pride. Moreover, their cities
being bigger than our own, they boast about it, and where
once they had a fair name as honest men, now such repute is
no more, their greed and riches being so great. And should a
man enquire of them who it is that truly gives light to their
city, they believe that it is they, not their sages, nor even he
whom they call the Son of Heaven, who bring such lustre to
the realm.

Yet they grow fat not only on trade in Sinim and beyond
the seas but in the lending of money to the Son of Heaven
and his ministers, and from the profits of trade which was
formerly that of the king alone.[62] Indeed, so rich is their trade
that they are obliged from shortage of metal to use money

made from paper, which they call *fescieni* or flying money, and
with which they buy and sell without gold or silver, for they
may spend those papers in all the places where the king of
Manci rules.[63] On each piece of this money, of which five
have the value of one *sommo* of silver, one deputed to the task
by the king writes his name, placing his sign upon the paper,
while those of the Great Cane himself bear a seal of vermilion.

Among the merchants and craftsmen there were formerly
many guilds, as among the Christians of our lands, one for
every craft, as that of the jewellers, of those who change
money, of the merchants of food, of those who gild, of the
apothecaries and doctors, and even of those who take away
the night-soil from the city. Thus, as we in our *herem,* so they
also gave help to those among them who were in need, setting
a rule so that their lives might be well guided. But now their
guilds are fallen into great confusion, for every trade is open
to all who practise it, while many no longer follow the rule,
each making profits as he can, some becoming rich and others
being driven to seek alms.

But the richest among them desire one thing above all
others, which is to raise themselves to the rank of nobles. For
its part, the court of the Son of Heaven, itself being greedy for
the riches of the merchants and knowing of their desire for
honour, although they are not worthy of being honoured, is
ready to sell the title of nobility to those who are ready to pay
the price. Moreover, even those among the greatest and

---

'HEREM'

*Herem refers to the 'prohibition against belonging to the community', a system of
restriction exercised in the mediaeval Jewish community in order to prevent the entry
of newcomers to a Jewish settlement or trade. This was not only to limit competition
and thus protect livelihood – as in the case of the Christian guilds – but to inhibit
the concentration of Jews, and the growth of ill-feeling, in particular places. It seems
to have been instituted in Italy about the beginning of the thirteenth century.*

proudest merchants who have not been thus honoured adorn
themselves in the same silks, hats and high shoes of the
nobles, spending greatly on such a false show of favour. Thus
from foreign merchants they purchase the costly wares of
Greater India and the Frankish lands, in this trade the
Saracens and my brothers serving their folly and growing rich
thereby.

Yet because to give to the poor is justly considered to be the
duty of the rich, for which God be praised, and the Son of
Heaven no longer providing for the needs of the poor as in
former times, certain merchants of the city strive among
themselves to give help to the needy, even going to their
houses in order to know their distress, and to give money to
them with their own hands. Thus, those who do good also
make themselves happy. And although they do such things for
their idols' sake, yet do they also serve God, may He be
magnified and honoured. As for the Son of Heaven and his
counsellors, they declare that it is better that those who are
deprived of every good should be aided by the rich than that
they should be a charge upon the shoulders of the king.

Yet the merchants of the city, acting thus for the succour of
the poor, and bringing great riches to the place, seek also to
rule in every part. For they believe, as do some among us, that
it is right for those who serve the needs of others to govern
them also. But in the City of Light the merchants, behaving
as though they were kings, seek to reign in the place of the
nobles and the lords-official of the king.[64] But these same
merchants the well-born nobles and officials hold in
disrespect for their low birth, mocking even their wealth. For
they hold themselves to be the first, and that after them come
the country people, the craftsmen and last the merchants of
the city.

Thus is all in great confusion, each disdaining the other,
God have pity upon them. Yet such is the wealth of the city
and its great trade, and so many its people, that all seem lost
as if in the great flux of the world before the first day, may

God forgive me my words. For that which formerly had its
place in the city has its place no more, and he who knows
whither his steps might take him knows it no longer.

Therefore, those who in times of dearth and bad weather
received food and clothing from the king, as well as those who
suffered by flood or fire, do so no more. Neither are the
orphans and the sick given shelter by him as before, while
some of the nobles and lords-official take part in trade, which
was formerly forbidden to them by the Son of Heaven, a few
even having their own factors in Greater India and other
places. Moreover, some of the great shops and warehouses
belong secretly to the nobles and the officials of the king, who
grow rich by their hire, for such is the desire for wealth which
consumes the entire city.

Yet all make a show of noble conduct, this one bowing in
the manner of the seigneur while taking money, without
shame, of a Saracen, and that one, who is master of the rites[65]
and who declares himself to be angered at the corruption of
the times, himself takes 5 or 6 per cent for incenses and other
spices, as Nathan ben Dattalo declared. Though I now made
great profits in the city after Succoth, for which God be
praised, I saw confusion all about me and was much troubled
in spirit thereby, for all men said that those things which had
had their place had their place no more. Therefore, since a
pious man may not take profit from confusion, and since
some gained employment and others lamented over the same
things, I asked Lifenli to bring me to one of their sages, so that
I should have a better understanding of the great ills of the
city.

Upon the day after Simhat Torah, which is to say the
twenty-fourth day of Tishri,[66] and while I was laying my
phylacteries, the evil[67] Bertoni came to me, declaring that my
servant Turiglioni had been seen by no one for many days,
and that it was feared some harm might have befallen him.
Hearing our voices, for the woman Bertoni shouted that the
said Turiglioni kept bad company and frequented the low

taverns of the city, the girl Buccazuppo entered also and wept greatly, imploring me to find him. But I reproved them for coming to me with such tales while I was at prayer, God forbid, and sent them away. Lifenli now came to me, saying that he would bring me to a temple of the idolaters, which is called by them the temple of the Stone Phoenix, may God forgive me such sin that I, Jacob ben Salomone, should enter a temple of idols. Yet who is there who may speak truly of the Holy One that knows only Him and not the false gods also, before whom in their blindness other men bow their knees?

Thus, praying to God that I should be forgiven for entering a place of iniquity, I went with the said Lifenli to the cloister of the Phoenix of the Sacchiani, in which are to be found at least one thousand monks, God spare them, and not fewer than three thousand idols. For, as among the Christians so with them, there are monasteries and convents, friars and nuns, the curb upon the flesh and the impious cult of idols.[68] But these idolaters set their faces against the killing of men, while the Christians seek to gain glory from it, their sophists preaching without shame that which is contrary to the rule of their faith.

Yet for all that the Sacchiani, unlike the Christians, preach peace and the love of all things, they have suffered greatly in times past from the sacking of their temples and other harms. But now men no longer feel such hatred against them, for faith among the Mancini has become weak, and many are the priests without followers and monks without belief. Thus their temples are frequented only by the old, and there are few among the young who give themselves to the sacred orders of the idolaters, so that the priesthood is composed of men so old that they have lost all their teeth. Furthermore they say that in the City of Light the idols of the Sacchiani are no longer regarded with respect, and that the young laugh at the cult of the elders, having little desire even to enter the temples where their forefathers worshipped, although many are the works of faith done by them in charity, for which God be praised.

Yet their order[69] is weak and the vices and ills of the city are strong, the young mocking their rule, so Lifenli declared, counting it of little worth. For thus is the cult of the idolaters fallen. Rather, wealth and possessions are their gods, which God forbid, and the natural man their guide in all things. Indeed, it is even considered wise among the young men of the city to hold that the world contains nothing divine, may God have pity upon them and His unspoken name be exalted and lauded, nor anything which may not be understood by the light of reason. Yet others say merely that the priests of the Sacchiani are bald donkeys, and that when a priest goes to ride on horseback the head of the donkey stands higher than the head of the horse.

Moreover, as among the Christians and the Saracens, so among the Sacchiani there are hatreds unto death. For although these idolaters profess to worship the same idols, one sect of them persecutes another, as among the Christians, each accusing the other of heresy or deceit. Thus, just as some Saracens wear black caps and others white, as I have written, and dispute among themselves about the hour at which the holy fast of Ramadan may be broken, so one sect among the Sacchiani objects that another makes its holy turns about an idol from right to left, and not from left to right, as some say is enjoined by their sacred writings. Another sect declares that the forehead of the faithful should touch the ground in adoration of the idol, God forbid, twice and not thrice, as the others are accustomed to do. Yet another disputes in the same fashion as the Christians, whether three spirits may exist in one spirit, or whether the same spirit may exist in all.

And when no agreement can be reached among them upon such matters, that sect which is most offended will depart from the temple of its ancestors and create a new, so that there they may pass around their idols from left to right, and not from right to left as do the others, whom they call heretics, and unworthy to be in fellowship with them.

But the young, so Lifenli declared, have long grown weary of such follies, only the old occupying themselves with these matters. To which I replied that the faith of the Sacchiani, like the faith of the Christians, is a faith of a thousand idols but without God, for in the shadow of such idols, so many are they, God may be neither seen nor heard.

Indeed, the idolaters of Sinim have gods without number, may the Holy One forgive me, or they are of the number of the sands of all the seas. For since each man may make his own idol of earth, stone or wood, even setting it in his own house to watch over him, there are as many gods among them as there are thresholds. Of these gods, as among the Christians, some are carved in stone and some are painted with gold, but some also have many hands and heads. But that a man of Sinim may worship a creature with many heads upon one neck, or with three eyes, is not to be wondered at, when the divine being within all men is so denied that they fall down and worship false gods of wood and stone, as did the children of Israel when they turned away from Moses, our teacher. For then men do not have God before them, but altars only.

Yet in one respect the images revered by the Sacchiani are worthy of being praised above those of the Christians.[70] For the idolaters of Manci place before themselves not only the effigy of the Buddum but of wild animals, flowers and birds, all painted, while Christians place upon their altars only images of the griefs and sufferings of their gods and saints, as though death were a better thing than life. But this is to blaspheme before the Holy One, blessèd be He, it being contrary to the law of God and against human reason.

But contrary to the command of God, may He show me mercy, I set my own foot in the temple of the Sacchiani that I might better know the false gods from Him who is the true. And there I saw that, among them, each idol has its own name and its own feast day, and its own virtues also, as among the Christians.

I also saw that the statues of their gods are for the most part wooden and gilded,[71] upon which the priests place garlands of flowers, also offering up to them, God forbid, pans of hot food as if they should eat with their wooden mouths, which only a man without reason could believe. In this temple, as I saw with my own eyes, they also sprinkle milk upon the ground to their false gods, as Christians sprinkle water to theirs, believing that thus the spirits will protect them. They also make a great smoke of choice incenses before their idols, as do the Christians, which brings much profit to the merchants who supply them, for which God be thanked. Moreover, an old priest stands close by, who, bowing to the faithful, presses them to give incense to the idols which, they paying him for the incense, he himself burns, and from which come profits to the temple.

The priests also lead the people to believe that whatever good fortune comes to them is owed to the virtues not of the faithful but of the priests themselves, from which they also make gain, as also from the driving out of devils in the manner of the Christians.

But here I saw a few old men and women only who, having raised their hands on high to the idols about them, struck their foreheads three times on the ground, praying that such idols might bring them a good understanding and a happy fate. Moreover, believing that the spirits accompany them as they go, standing a few palms above their heads, they stoop towards the ground upon entering and leaving the little temples of the idols, so that their spirits may have space above them and thus suffer no harm.

For they believe that the soul of him who behaves ill towards the spirits descends to a lowly life and enters into another body, which God forbid, and may even be reborn in the form of a cat, dog or pig. But if such a cat, dog or pig perform well its animal offices, as by catching mice or finding out truffles, they do not say whether such souls may once more ascend the ladder of creation and enter once again into

the bodies of men. Yet according to such belief, albeit that it is
against the laws both of God and of nature and even though
they bow their bodies to idols of wood and gold, they
proclaim that all things in the universe are one, which any
pious man may also believe, since all things come from Him
who created all.

But we may not believe that the soul of man, who is the
crown of the created world, shall occupy the body of an
unclean beast, for thus would the divine order be rendered
null, God forbid. For such effect could be caused only by the
anger of God, may all idols be cast down and broken in pieces
and be no more.

They falsely teach also that this world itself is merely an
impression[72] and that therefore life is grief and suffering, since
we seek that which is not matter or substance, so that all must
end in deceit and error. But this too is a blasphemy against
the Holy One and His Creation, in whose form and
substance, is the very nature of God.[73] For none may say
without blasphemy that the world is made up only of
shadows, or that life is a mere waiting upon death. To say
such things, which God forbids even to our thoughts, shows
grave disrespect for the glory of the material world, which was
created by God, and destroys the duty of a man to be worthy
of the gift of his life.

Moreover, the priests of the Sacchiani, whom some say
possess great wealth and lead impure lives, declare that since
the terrestrial world is without substance, the living should
desire only to flee from it, averting their eyes from that which
offends them, for otherwise the light of truth comes to be
extinguished by the shadows of the world. Hearing this from
the abbot of the place, a certain Iunien, who declared that in
all things providence and patience rule, I again felt greatly
troubled in my soul, may God show me forgiveness. For in
the City of Light, in which many are rich and glorious and
many are poor, those who are without aid lacking even a
morsel of bread, yet in which there is the greatest trade a man

might see in the entire world, all seemed to me without order or reason, and as if abandoned by God, which God forbid.

It appeared to me also that I remained alone in a city so vast that it extended to the far horizon, wherein each looked only to himself, turning away even from his own idols, while the Tartars drew nearer. Thus, so fearful was I for my fortunes, believing even that I saw the sun glitter upon the swords of the Mongols, that I went down again to the city with Lifenli, in that night praying that God, blessèd be He, would spare me for having gone among idols, that my Sara and my beloved father, may his soul rest in peace, be kept safe, and that God, may He be magnified and exalted, hold in His hand even those idolaters who know Him not.

## CHAPTER FIVE

# In the Darkness
# and in the Light

THE HUGE AND RAPID GROWTH of Southern Sung cities, including Zaitun – which was some ten times larger than Ancona – has always been acknowledged by historians. But that they had suffered the scale of moral and social consequences which Jacob reports of Zaitun was not previously known, despite Marco Polo's vivid description of daily life in Kinsai under the Mongol conquerors. Such consequences can be surmised from the dynastic Chinese historians,[1] but the richness of detail that Jacob d'Ancona's manuscript provides is apparently without equal.

At the time when Jacob d'Ancona was in Zaitun – from August 1271 to February 1272 – the southern part of China, called (by Jacob) Manci, was on the verge of conquest by the Tartars (or Mongols). They were already in command of northern China, in those times called by foreign travellers 'Cathay'.[2] But in 1271 the great city of Zaitun, like the rest of Manzi, was still part of the realm of the Southern Sung emperor, Du Zong, whose capital was at Kinsai. Northern Sung, however, had long passed into the hands of the barbarian invaders, its Tartar ruler in 1271 being the legendary Kublai Khan.

China had always been subject to such invasion by nomadic northern tribesmen, and had frequently suffered rapine and conquest at their hands. In 1233, some forty years before the period covered by the manuscript, the Tartars, who came from the lands north of the Gobi desert, had taken Kaifeng, the capital of Northern Sung. Thereafter, step by step (and by modern standards very slowly), they extended their rule across the whole of northern China as far as the Yangtze river. Indeed, from the early twelfth century onwards they had gradually imposed themselves, under such rulers as Genghis Khan (1162–1228) and successive Khans, upon a great swath of the known world, the Levant included.

They took Kiev in 1240 and entered Poland; and in 1241–2, thirty years before Jacob's journey and when he was a student in Naples, they advanced into Bohemia – to which Jacob makes passing reference – Hungary, Dalmatia, Serbia and Austria. Thus, China, Islam and the European world alike felt the 'terrible trial of the Mongol conquest'.[3] In China, Mongol armies reached Sichuan and Yunnan in 1253. In 1264, six years before Jacob set sail, the city now known as Beijing (then Ta-tu) became the Mongol capital; from 1267 onwards – and while Jacob was in Zaitun – it was in the process of reconstruction as the new city of the Khans, Khanbalik or Canbaluc. And from 1268, the city of Xiangyang and the fort of Fanzheng on the Han river were under Mongol siege, which lasted five years and which is referred to in the manuscript.

Thus, by a concatenation of circumstances, the growing Tartar threat to southern China, remote as it might seem from the interests of a Jewish scholar-merchant from Italy, was on the contrary something close enough to his knowledge and concern. For the Tartars in their forays had even reached – before withdrawing from – the Adriatic coast across from Ancona three decades earlier; their conquest of Baghdad in 1258, and their marauding in northern Syria a decade later, had impinged themselves on Jacob's journey, as we have seen; and his interests as a Jewish China merchant were bound up with the fate of the Southern Sung dynasty. He therefore had an engagement of economic as well as intellectual interest in the fears of the city of

Zaitun, and this, I think, goes some way to explain the energy
of his brief involvement in its dramatic affairs.[4]

In the event, the manuscript reveals that, despite the loss of
the North and the growing fear in Zaitun (and its province) of
Tartar invasion, the economic and trading progress of the
Southern Sung provinces continued. But although Jacob con-
tinually registers his wonder at the economic activity and riches
he found – as at the quality of Sung crafts and manufactures –
he was plainly torn. He expresses both the excitement of the
merchant over his finds and purchases and the interest of the
'intellectual' in the political and moral conflicts which had
broken out in the city, and which were tearing it apart.

he next day, having seen my father's travails in
a dream, may he rest in Eden, the woman
Bertoni and the girl Buccazuppo, she again
weeping, came to me declaring that my servant
Turiglioni had not yet been found, and I was
constrained to reproach them for coming thus in the presence
of Lifenli, and for speaking before him of such matters in so
rough a fashion. Yet I was troubled lest from his own folly
some harm had befallen Turiglioni in the city, it being a place
in which flourished all human vices, and every sin and danger
which has yet been in the world.

Thereafter, having spoken with the faithful Armentuzio
and Nathan ben Dattalo concerning my fortunes, I set out
with Lifenli to the noble Pitaco, a man of great age and of
much honour in the city. For he had been formerly a prefect,
which they call *ciciu* in their language, the said Pitaco being a
noble and a *cinsci*, which means in our language a learnèd
man. For only a learnèd man may be the prefect of a city in
the realm of Manci.

But I continued to be greatly troubled in soul and body as I
passed through the streets, enquiring of myself how such a

city, with such confusion of men, gods, riches, and wills both
for good and ill, might justly be governed. For a man, be he
never so pious, might think that even the wisdom of the
Torah and of our sages, peace upon them, would not be able
to govern it aright. For so it must be wherever there are few
worthy to command and few ready to obey.

Thus we came to the house of the noble Pitaco in the street
which they call of Long Life, which is in the western part of
the city, and thus he expressed himself, Lifenli writing down
his words: 'The humble one declares to the learnèd one that
the learnèd one is welcome in this poor abode.'[5] To which he
added, 'May you find wealth among us.' To this I replied as
our sage, Rabbi Simeon ben Zoma, taught, declaring, 'He,
sire, who learns from all men is wise.' At which the said
Pitaco, Lifenli having put my words into his language, bowed,
folding his hands in the way of the Mancini.

Conducting me thence to an arbour, wherefrom rose the
water of a fountain, he spoke again as follows, I being
attentive to hear the words of the sage: 'The people act in a
manner contrary to heaven. Worship is neglected and the
ancestors are forgotten. Since the time of Angati, the Yellow
Emperor,[6] there have been no times worse than these. The
elders of the city are treated with disrespect and live in
darkness, and the lowly are considered to be equal to the high.
Men address words to the noble without invitation, while the
mean who are without merit occupy their places.'

Here, the old man ceased, and remained silent for a while
as though not willing to speak further. Then he resumed, and
expressed himself thus: 'Once the people were known for
their faith, holding in reverence those who went before them
or who were wiser than they: the son his father, the pupil his
teacher, the novice his master, and all worshipping those who
had led the worthiest lives, the better to find the way that
they should follow. But now men submit their reasons to their
desires, thinking themselves free to do whatever thing seems
fit, and no longer show respect to the elders of the city.

'Thus, the city of Zaitun is lacking in every virtue, for the
customs of our fathers are cast down and only the vestiges and
relics remain. But if the young have no reverence for the old
and for the ways of the ancestors, how can there be respect for
the laws?' Pitaco enquired. 'And if there is not such respect,
will not both the young and the city suffer together?'

To this I made no reply, thinking it unfitting that a
traveller from another country should speak ill of his city, so
that he continued as follows: 'I will treat the matter as reason
demands. The humble one served as a counsellor to the Son
of Heaven, having in youth committed to my memory the
writings of our great teacher and master Chun,[7] and being
always faithful to the rule of his wisdom. Therefore in
Chinscie I bowed with reverence to him who is the image of
the order of heaven, for in the universe all things are joined
together, the world of the gods and the world of men, the
realm of heaven and the realm of nature.'

To this also I did not reply, for a wise and pious man may
not believe that a king is the Son of Heaven, as I have written.
For although a man in his travails may wrestle with an angel,
as our ancestor Jacob, peace upon him, wrestled in the place
called Peniel, that a man may himself be an angel is not to be
believed, nor that at the court of Chinscie is a heavenly
kingdom upon the earth.[8]

The noble Pitaco continued in this fashion: 'But now not
only are the young rendered impious by greed, rejecting the
way of our master, which is the straight way of harmony, but
even the lords of the court no longer show piety towards their
ancestors, nor are learnèd in the writings of the sages.

'Do you think it is sufficient for a man to be wise only in
the ways of the merchant?' he asked me, at which I fell silent,
although I knew well that such wisdom did not suffice. He
continued thus: 'Once, for a noble or a scholar to enter the
market was held to be an unworthy thing, as also to walk the
streets or to enter a tavern. But now even the position of an
official is bought and sold, politeness is forgotten, and

officials dress themselves as they please. And since all men are held in this city to be free to do all things, even the *tunpan* and the *ciciu* are peculators,[9] yet they are not condemned. For that which they do is no longer considered an offence against heaven but a benefit of fortune. Once, those who received honours of the Son of Heaven were the worthiest of men. Now, since the basest receive them also, the worthiest feel shame that the honours at their waistbands are the same.'[10]

Whereupon Pitaco gave a sigh of anguish, for which I felt pity. Yet I made no reply, it being the office of a pious man to hear the woes of another, as our sages teach. Whereupon he added in a loud voice: 'Sinful are the *chuancen*', being angered at the high officials of the realm who go by this name. 'Gone are the days when the *chuancen* were held in honour and repute. For once they were known for their pure lives and fair judgment, and were devoted to their duty. Now they take part without shame even in trade, by their greed and unworthiness giving offence to the ancestors, so that the court is encompassed by deceit, and just reward is given not to merit but according to the scales. Thus the wise may wait for many years and receive neither reward nor grace, waiting in silence and alone. For when heaven does not favour a man, whatever his merits, neither do other men show him favour. Does not the greater man[11] agree with the lesser?'

I answered him as follows: 'I do not, for it is held by our sages that for the wisest man and him who is of greatest virtue to be abandoned by other men is itself an honour and a blessing, as well as the best token of his worth. For he who is truly wise rejoices before God, may He be exalted, and not before other men.'

But at these words of mine, which the faithful Lifenli put into his language, the noble Pitaco was so greatly surprised that he did not know what to say, looking at me for a while in silence.

He then continued, 'They bow down and worship the ancestors no more. It is for money and possessions alone that their foreheads touch the earth, as if those were gods in truth. Before, the one, but now the other receives their reverence. Respect for the old is rare, and few there are now among the young who consider that in old age there is wisdom, or that in white hair there is honour. Rather, the young are accustomed to go about closely in company, keeping themselves at a distance from their elders, so that the old go unseen in the streets like ghosts, and when they speak they are not heard.

'Indeed, so great now is the belief that an old man is a weight upon the shoulders of others that persons will say that they do not wish to live so long that the help of others becomes their need, and that therefore, when the time of sickness and weakness comes, others may kill them if they choose, which is a thing against heaven. And when an old man or old woman is dead, the body of the deceased is not kept for a due time in the house of their sons, nor is food given before the coffin, nor are figures burned at the grave in order that the dead one can have them in the next world, as is enjoined.

'For now only the devout perform such offices, death being considered a light thing, and the dead being abandoned without prayers or mourning. Now the festival of the dead is a day as all others, the lamps being lit at the door of the tavern but not in the houses of the deceased, the living going about their affairs without remembrance even of the day of death of their own fathers and mothers, a thing which is against heaven. Instead, the dead come to be buried in haste, the ungrateful son, his mind set upon himself, seeking thus to be made free by fire of the body of a parent. But what is worse than such unworthy treatment of a father or mother? For when the dead are carried to the place where they must be burned, they do not burn them out of love for the person, but for convenience. Although it is shameful to say such things before a stranger, when they see the smoke in the air, now sons think only that it is the hour to return home.'[12]

Although I, Jacob, had no wish to hear more of such impious things, Pitaco enquired of me for my judgment upon what he had said, God be praised, to whom I replied: 'These things are both against nature and extinguish the Unspoken Name, may He be exalted at the end of days by all mankind. For our sages declare that the body of a man, blessing upon him, must be washed, wrapped in a cloth and buried in the earth before the sun has set upon the day of death, and that only in a time of plague may a body be burned. For wherever there is a burning of bodies, there is also idolatry, which is an abomination. Moreover, we should show piety to the newly dead, for although the soul is separated from the body at the last breath, it remains attached to it for four days, as our sages, peace upon them, teach.

'As for him who neglects his father's or his mother's grave, he is as culpable as if he should have struck the body of his father or his mother in life and caused them a wound, God forbid, for which our judges in Israel condemn them to be put to death.'

To my words the said Pitaco replied: 'It is certainly to offend heaven for a son to put the bodies of his father and mother into the fire and to gather up their bones and ashes into a golden urn. For when the urn is too small, as often happens, the larger bones must be thrown aside and others broken into small fragments. Moreover, when several bodies are burned in the same place, as is now done among us and which is against the heavenly order, the ash of all is divided between each. In this the dead may be deceived, but not heaven. Yet, among all men who remain men, does not reverence for the dead bring a will to conform with the custom of ancestors? Is it not a pious and a just thing to do?'

These questions the nobleman asked of me, Jacob, God be praised, at which I began to weep for my father, may his soul endure. For I feared lest I should have failed in my duty towards him, having seen his sufferings in my dreams, may his memory be blessèd. Thus I gave assent to Pitaco in my

heart, being unable to speak, knowing him to be wise
according to his own faith, may God be honoured.

Whereupon he said: 'If the sons do not carry out the duties
of piety, how shall the sins of their fathers be redeemed?
Rather we should all strive to be like Sengsu, the most dutiful
of sons, who placed the piety of a son above all things. For
such piety teaches us to pay respect to our elders both in life
and in death, as well as to carry out the work of the ancestors
which was not completed, to gather in the same places as our
fathers gathered, to honour those whom they honoured, and
to love those who were dear to them. These are the highest
duties of a son.'

Thereupon he fell silent and said no more, but rose and
bowed to me, God be praised, asking me to come to him on
the following day.

Rising at dawn, I laid my phylacteries together with Nathan
ben Dattalo, peace upon him, praying thereafter for profit in
my voyage and a safe return, God willing. Whereupon the girl
Buccazuppo once again came to me in sadness for the loss of
the brave Turiglioni, who had not yet returned to his place,
the evil woman Bertoni reproaching me with a bitter tongue
that I had not troubled myself to search for him. This I
promised her that I should do after the Sabbath Noah but not
on this day, being bound to attend upon the noble Pitaco, at
which Bertoni replied with loud shouting and the girl
Buccazuppo again wept, but quietly, saying nothing.

But first I set out with Nathan to the warehouse in order to
speak with the faithful Armentuzio, who displayed to me
products of silk of all colours, including cloth of green and
gold silk which was a wonder to behold, the workmanship
never before seen in the entire world, yet of which you may
have forty pounds for less than eight Venetian groats.[13] There
were also rich satins,[14] whose name is from Zaitun, of which
the world has not seen the like, the richest being sewn with
small pearls. They had purchased for me also Tartar stuffs

woven with such art that not even a painter with a brush could have equalled them.

Of spices they had not yet begun to buy, I telling them to seek out the finest sugar, saffron, ginger, galingale,[15] cassia and camphor, and also indigo and alum,[16] but of porcelains they had already six hundred bowls made with great art, for which they had given two hundred groats, yet as fine as glass flagons although they were but bowls. These being the most beautiful porcelains in the world, I counselled them to buy more for me, for with such goods my fortunes would be made, God willing. But for the other merchandise, such as precious stones, pearls, country sugar, dark saffron for ills of the kidneys and stomach, and other things, we should await our journey to the surrounding districts. For the domain of the City of Light is one of much trade and manufacture, and of much buying and selling, in which a merchant may make great profits.

I learned also from Armentuzio, who had it from the clerk of Eliezer of Venice, peace upon him, that a great drought had befallen certain parts of the realm of Manci, and that the countrymen and astrologers of the city held it to be an evil omen of the coming of the Tartars. However, that there may be such omens a man should not easily accept. For idolaters are much given to such prophecy, as from the changing of the weather or the flight of birds, which reason cannot follow, and against which Rabbi Mose ben Maimon, whose memory be blessed, rightly counsels us, being unworthy of the wise man and a blasphemy for the pious.

Nevertheless, I determined to guard my merchandise more carefully, secretly ordering Armentuzio that my vessels be always at the ready, lest some misadventure befall the city. But my brothers Eliezer and Lazzaro, being without such fears, began to go freely among the towns and villages that belong to the city of Zaitun, buying greatly and to their profit, may God be praised.

Thereupon, I set out in haste with Lifenli to the house of

Pitaco, where I found many people gathered about him to
listen to his words, all of them treating him with great
honour, may his memory be recorded.

He declared as follows, Lifenli writing down his words as I
commanded him: 'Now so much has been lost that to recover
it is as difficult as mounting to the blue heaven. The mean is
forgotten, everything is sated, and there is no proportion
between big and small. Now, both young men and young
women are in a state of desire, not being satisfied with those
things which life brings to them, and being driven to wander
in search of pleasures and of other things which are acceptable
to them.

'Thus they find no rest. In the past, none could go at night
about the city without true need, for a guardian would say to
such a person, Where are you going so late? But now many
wander about the city at night, yet none without danger to
himself. Once, it was held that the true way is that which is in
accord with the mean, but now it is that which seems good to
each person. Moreover, that which appears good is now that
which will bring us some benefit. Indeed the ways of the
merchant have entered so far into us that only that which has
a price is believed to have a value, as though the whole world
were but a market. Hence few possess the will to decide what
is truly of worth and what without worth and merit, nor what
to love and what to hate.

'For all follow this way as easily as that way, without
distinction as to the better and the worse. Indeed, some
among the young say that to speak of good and evil is idle,
declaring that good and evil are not constant things but that
the goodness and ill of works and deeds come from the actor
himself and his will.[17]

'Thus they destroy the laws of good conduct, declaring that
to do so is itself a good thing, and thus they would bring
down heaven. And when the wise oppose them, they say that
no common rule may be found by men, and that if such a
rule could be found it would wrongly constrain those who did

not wish to observe it. Today, even some of our sages declare that it is wrong to teach respect for the law of heaven to the young, lest they be bound to faith, and others that neither the laws of men nor of the gods are able to make men good.

'Can we be surprised therefore that that which is in accord with nature, and that which is against it, can no longer be distinguished by many, or that that which is right and that which is wrong are thought to differ by little, and that upon such things the elders are held to be able to judge no better than the young?

'Thus it may be said that among us the divine order of heaven is lost and the order of men is destroyed also, so that we have fallen into the darkness wherein none can see his own way, since the lantern of truth shines no more.'

At these words, which the faithful Lifenli wrote for me in a clear manner thereafter, those who were gathered around the noble Pitaco murmured and fell into silence. Nor did I as a stranger venture to speak, albeit knowing that those who do not follow the commandments of Moses our teacher must live in a world devoid of every virtue, while those who also act without reason, as by permitting themselves to be ruled by lust or greed, cannot set their foot upon the just path, whether they be young or old.[18]

Pitaco continued as follows: 'Now there are even sages among us who teach not only that wrong may be right, but that good may be bad, so that all have lost the way. Moreover, should anyone say, We must honour the good and the wise, there are some now so lacking in virtue that they declare that to give such honour is to create a superior rank among men, in which some would be considered better and some worse, a thing which in their blindness they say is against nature.

'Or should another declare that the aged are deserving of honour, he will be opposed by those who see virtue only in youth. But in the souls of such men who think themselves wise, there is neither measure nor rest, since in them the roots

of the understanding have been cut, as when a man has his
eyes removed and can no longer see.

'Yet worst of all are those among us who say that a man
should not be judged for his deeds. Thus if such a man acts
without respect or merit, as when he shows no regard for
others, or even takes the life of another, they will say that the
fault lies not in him but in others, as his parents or his
teachers, or lies even in the times themselves. But they also
argue that the same man should not be taught that his deeds
are wrongful, since none may rightly judge such matters.

'Hence they have made a wilderness of the city, in which
the wild beast within man is unchained, the huntsman is
shorn of his weapons, and the prey placed before the wild
beast to harm as it pleases. When a man brings calamity upon
himself, there is no hope of escape. So it is of a city and a
realm.'

At these words of Pitaco, those who were gathered about
him seemed to grow angry, their faces becoming red, some
demanding to know what should be done, others calling upon
him to rouse the city to the perils which beset them, and
others sitting silent as if in despair.

To them, Pitaco declared as follows: 'The way of life of the
city is changed and is full of vices. In order that it may be
saved, it must first be rightly judged as to who are its foes.' At
this all fell silent, as if not wishing to pass judgment upon
such a matter, and Pitaco for a while also said nothing, as
though he himself did not know what to say.

He then spoke as follows: 'The merchants of the city have
taught even the common people to devour all that comes in
their path, as the silkworm devours the leaves of the mulberry.
It is they with their great greed who have brought unbalance
to the city, not even wishing to resist the Tartars, but hoping
rather to make profits from them after their conquest of the
city. They count everything but know the true measure of
nothing, yet now consider themselves to be equal and even
superior in rank to all.'

Thus the said Pitaco spoke, as if without fear of the hatred of the merchants of the city, or of any other citizen, but making his own judgment of good and evil, I too knowing that as the ox may be weary of toil, so may a man become weary of his possessions.

He continued in this way: 'But it is they who have brought the city to its corruption, so that even those mendicants who receive aid from others, as is just, conduct themselves without reason, doing violence to those who give them succour, declaring that it is not enough, so far is the measure of all things lost. Indeed, so great is the confusion under heaven that not only do violent acts go without report, so many are they, but our Son of Heaven himself, being attended by false counsellors from among the merchants of the realm, no longer knows which is the just path to take.

'For some tell him that to show much goodness to the poor is a wise thing, and others that it is foolish, making them unwilling to nourish their own offspring to the great loss of the kingdom's wealth. Once, the Son of Heaven provided them with grain and other cereals, as well as other things, and none who sought such help was denied, the succour of the poor having been considered a duty.

'But now the new counsellors of the Son of Heaven say that to seek help is the same as to beg, since all men may make themselves rich by their own labours. True it is, as some say, that greed and avarice have made all desirous, whether they are rich or poor. Thus all seek everything upon which they can lay their hands, but now the official says to the poor man, Go with heaven's curse, for if it loved you as it loves me, it would have done well by you.'

Hearing which words, I felt great anger, God be praised, it being contrary to the teachings of our sages to declare that the rich are favoured by God and that the poor are cast out by Him. But I, Jacob of Ancona, did not speak, still fearing lest a stranger such as I should be driven out if I did not show prudence before them.

Pitaco continued thus: 'And if a man, despairing, should go among our sages seeking the light of truth in their words, he will find that few know that which is proper to men of wisdom, and who have little therefore to teach to others. But while many of our sages are weak and sell soft wares, the people grow stronger and harder. So that others of our sages, being without arms, seek instead to make men subject to their judgments by the violence of their words.

'But some others of our wise men, considering themselves to be the wisest, do not wish even to know what others say, or to every opinion offer a contrary without concern as to whether such opinions be true or false. In consequence of these things, our young lack all knowledge of the way. Once, a son was taught that he might even escape the hand of death if he had shown piety to his father and mother in their lives. Yet which teacher now would teach such a thing, and who believe it?

'Yet those things which the wise have revered must not be treated with disrespect by those who know less than they, nor, being without wisdom, should they be permitted to subject others to their judgments. Nevertheless, it is the foolish who, being many, drive out the wise, who are few, from their places, so that great harm is brought to the young.

'For, as Menche[19] teaches, the common people become as wild animals if they are not taught the way of virtue. Moreover, the child who, harmed by his teachers, knows neither the way of virtue nor other arts can serve neither his parents nor the Son of Heaven.

'But now only that which offends heaven gains praise, while to obey one's elders is held to be the conduct of a weakling or a slave. Now, none admires the devoted son nor the faithful wife, for they are thought not to be virtuous but to act against their wills.'

All these things the noble Pitaco spoke of as if with a great weight upon his soul, after which I withdrew, it being the eve of the Sabbath Noah,[20] more of his followers and disciples gathering about him in order to hear his words. But Lifenli being little disposed to leave the house of Pitaco, I was obliged to command him to accompany me to the house of Nathan ben Dattalo, peace upon him, I thinking it perilous to go alone in the streets of the city.

Thus we departed, for upon the Sabbath the pious man must desist from all matters save those which are in praise of God, may He be exalted, or which seek His mercy, or which shall serve to spare the Sons of Israel from harm or danger. Therefore, a man shall not bite the nails of his fingers with his teeth, nor pluck a single hair from his head, neither must he listen upon the Sabbath day to the troubles of a city to which he comes as a stranger.

For this is not to remember the Sabbath day nor to keep it holy, from which default may God forever keep me, Amen.

In the morning following the Sabbath Noah the faithful Armentuzio came to me at an early hour after I had laid my phylacteries, counselling me to go in the next days to Chinscie, saying that my brothers Eliezer of Venice and Lazzaro intended to set out for that place. But I was troubled, fearing to be cut off there by the Tartars or other misadventure, and that I could as well purchase for my needs in the realm of Zaitun, where everything the heart desired might be found. For so Nathan ben Dattalo assured me. Moreover, of the silks and other stuffs of Chinscie, together with their chased silver, other ornaments and spices, I might have them as well in the markets and shops of Zaitun as in those of the other place. The woman Bertoni also came to me, imploring me that I should help to find our poor Turiglioni, which I undertook to do on the following day, whereupon the faithful Lifenli also came, and I saw that Buccazuppo fixed her eyes upon him.

Thereafter, accompanied by Lifenli, I once more set out for the house of Pitaco, thinking that thus I should learn more of the afflictions of the City of Light, the better to guide my

path in the ways of men. For he who journeys to the furthest
places of the terrestrial world should not only buy and sell to
his profit, but seek out the truth, if it may be found.
Approaching the house of Pitaco, I saw many gathered in the
streets about it, through whom I made my way with the
faithful Lifenli, the beard and hat which I wore causing others
to fall back at my step, out of the respect they had for my
bearing.

Within, I found even more than before were gathered at
the feet of Pitaco, he sitting upon a high seat so that he might
be better seen, and speaking of men who have faces and
bodies that are much like those of men, but who act less and
less as men should act, but rather like beasts, which God
forbid.

He spoke as follows: 'Slight is the difference between men
and the brutes, as Menche declares. The common man is often
without such difference, but he who knows the way preserves
it. But how shall those who have lost the way be enabled to
restore their worth as men, when they are given over to
baseness of heart, lewdness and idleness, and have in mind and
before their eyes every kind of wicked deed? How shall the city
raise them from their base condition, when many among them
have chosen it for themselves? However fierce the lion, it does
not devour its cub. Yet there are those among us who are given
to doing violence against their sons, and sons who would do
violence even to their fathers, so that they behave worse than
beasts, and without shame. For dragons beget dragons.'

These words the noble Pitaco spoke in a low voice, at
which many cried out, striking their fists against their chests.

He continued as follows: 'The very soul of the city is
consumed with hatred, and none is now more hated than he
who reproaches others for their misdeeds. Yet, in our
darkness, men more savage even than the beasts violate the
widow or woman with child and kill the weak for a coin,
while even mothers slay their children with an anger that
knows no bounds.

177

'It is as though the heart of men was consumed by flames, turning even the love of heaven to ashes. Once there was peace in the city and justice was severe, for the Son of Heaven did not wish either that anyone should suffer the least wrong, or that anyone should offend his neighbour.

'Indeed such was the fame of his justice that people left open their shops full of merchandise, and others let all their goods stand outside, and yet no one sought to enter or take anything away from them. All passers-by, whether in the day or the night, could go about safely in the streets without fear of anyone. Now all this is no more.'

In a weak voice Pitaco continued as follows, and as if he were weary of life: 'Once, all feared the law, knowing that whoever acted against it would be punished according to his deserts, so that the law was well obeyed. Now the four punishments[21] are themselves considered to be against heaven, or as if punishment were a wicked act against the malefactor, who, some say, deserves our pity. Indeed for every kind of crime, however cruel or violent, there are those who are quick to find the criminal to be without blame, so that the anger of the people grows, some revenging themselves on the malefactor with their own hands lest he go without punishment.

'Moreover those who once were judged worthy of death for their evil deeds go free, yet nobles are subjected to the law and judges take bribes without shame, such is the present disorder under heaven. Thus, the worst crimes increase, for there is nothing which men hold in fear, while the citizens, wearied by the confounding of everything, think that not even heaven can hear their cries.'

At these terrible words spoken by Pitaco, the anger of those present rose a second time, some shouting out to their gods for aid, and others with cruel expressions uttering threats to kill all evil-doers, so that, seeing them, a stranger among them might be brought to tremble. Pitaco continued in this way: 'Now, when there is a fire in the city, straight away the evil-doers, running like wild beasts, set themselves to rob the houses from which the citizens have fled. Once, each person came to the aid of his neighbour in order to save his possessions, but now each is a prey for the other. In the same fashion, even the stranger among us, to whom our fathers showed great courtesy, is now treated with disrespect, he too being robbed and assaulted as he goes about the city, by which heaven itself is destroyed.

'Moreover, who does not remember that in times past there was a guardian of those things which were found in the streets, and every man who had lost something made application to him. Thus it was that in the city of Zaitun almost nothing was mislaid, but now that which is found by the way is never restored but stolen. Therefore, is it not time that those who believe in their hearts that no man should be punished, and that even he who has killed another should go about the streets in freedom, are brought before the citizens in order that they may answer to heaven for their beliefs?'

This Pitaco asked in a soft voice, but was himself answered by all with loud shouts. He continued: 'For when twenty men on foot, with clubs and knives, jump upon the passer-by, rob him and flee without being taken by the guardians, are these not young wolves rather than men?

'But now we permit even the most savage among them to make excuses for their misdeeds, some saying that they acted from idleness, others in order that they might show their strength and that they were not cowards, others in order to emulate another wicked person, and others in order to gain fame for their misdeeds. Of these, some smile at the sentences of their judges, while beside them stand those who, confusing wrong with right, declare that the fault is not theirs, or that punishment of their wicked acts is not fitting, so that even the guardians must go in fear of their lives.'

Here Pitaco, being advanced in age and weak in body, concluded, all bowing to him as he went away. The things I had heard made my body and soul tremble, as to think that in

a city so great there should be such confusion among men.
Indeed so overcome was I by the words of the noble Pitaco
that, accompanied by Lifenli, I straight away returned to the
house of Nathan ben Dattalo, peace upon him, knowing that
in such fashion the world of the Gentiles should come to its
end. For the Jew should surely fear all that which afflicts and
weighs other men down, whether they be Christian, Saracen,
Indian or other idolater, since their ills bring dolour to us,
may God have pity upon His people and keep them forever in
His hand, Amen.

On the following day, which was the sixth day of Heshvan,
despite the cries of Bertoni and Buccazuppo for the lost pilot,
and having given further orders to Armentuzio, I returned
early to the house of Pitaco, may God spare me that on that
day I, so far fallen, did not lay my phylacteries but prayed
only in my heart. There I found a great crowd all gathered,
which was larger than before. For, as Lifenli informed me,
report of the words of Pitaco had been carried to all parts of
the city, and many wished to hear him. Nor did the guardians
or counsellors of the city seek to prevent his words, believing
him in their hearts to be an old man whose judgments were of
little worth.

Yet now the anger of Pitaco and of those who heard him
seemed greater, some crying out against the elders, and others
calling on him to lead them in order that the city might be
saved. To these he made no reply, but bowing his face towards
the ground, he spoke as follows, seated upon a throne: 'In the
brothel is a pit for the mass, in the gambling house a place to
be scourged, in the tavern a nest of wrongdoing, and in the
seeing and hearing of blood a lamp by which to light the
corpse in the coffin. For did not our wise men declare that
gambling is akin to robbery, and adultery to murder? But
today neither is considered wrong, but a delight, while for
some their solace is to kill. Moreover, our young men not
only dwell happily amid dangers, but look even upon the

*Merchants exchanging cloth for spices, detail taken from*
Livre des Merveilles (E.T. Archive).

*At the quayside,
detail taken from*
Livre des Merveilles
(E.T. Archive).

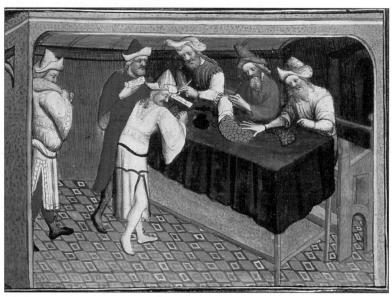

*The collection of taxes for salt, spices and wine, detail
taken from* Livre des Merveilles (AKG).

*A vessel with a compass, detail taken from* Livre des Merveilles (E.T. Archive).

*Pepper harvest, detail taken from* Livre des Merveilles (E.T. Archive).

*Merchants at sea, from a 1237 manuscript of Abu Muhammed
al-Kasim Hariri's* Makamen *(AKG).*

*Camel train, from a 1237 manuscript of Abu Muhammed al-Kasim Hariri's* Makamen (AKG).

*Dangers of the sea, from a thirteenth-century Western European manuscript* (Hulton Getty).

*Maimonides and his disciples, taken from a 1348 Spanish edition of* Guide to the Perplexed (AKG).

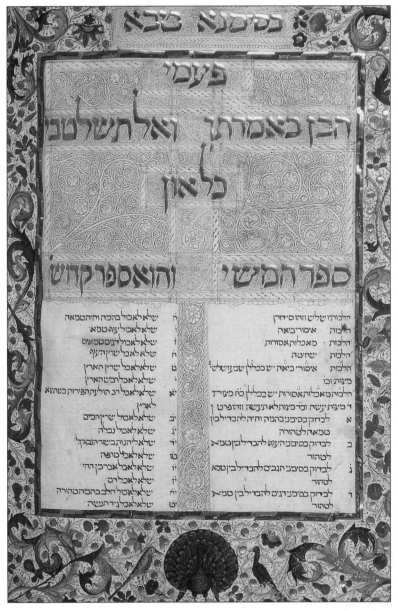

*A page from a fifteenth-century Portuguese manuscript of Maimonides'*
Mishneh Torah (British Library).

*Susskind von Trimberg (c.1250–1300), Jewish poet of Germany, portrayed as a bearded Jew wearing the distinctive pointed hat, fourteenth-century 'Manessian' manuscript, Heidelberg University* (Werner Forman Archive Ltd).

*The opening of the Book of Proverbs, Italian Bible, c.1300* (British Library).

harm which befalls others as a pleasure, for so great is the
disorder under heaven. Yet even if all find themselves at the
last deceived by such delights, they nevertheless run hither
and thither in search of them, thinking themselves at play but
only becoming more wicked. For he who follows the path of
evil himself becomes evil.

'Once, each family among us, having faith in its destiny
under heaven, prayed to the gods of the house that each
family member should be protected by heaven and have a
long life. Indeed both the realm and the city are founded
upon the tie between father and son. Thus when families are
virtuous the land is virtuous, and in order that the *chocia*
should have good rule, the family must have good rule also.
Moreover, when no father is able to teach his family, there will
be none to teach the realm, which is a family of all the
families of the land.

'Yet no longer are even old men of fifty given to purity of
life,while others, even the young, stay little with their wives
and have no care for their children, but go up and down
seeking the company of others while the children remain
alone with their mothers.

'Once, also, men would be very careful not to touch others'
wives in any circumstance, for they considered it to be an evil
and very villainous thing. Thus they would touch no other
woman than their wives. For their part, the women of the city
were chaste and moral, were careful of the honour of their
husbands and looked after their entire family well.

'But now there are children of whom none know the
fathers, while the girls of the city, who were once honest,
modest and observant of good behaviour, are often disorderly
and coarse and transgress every bound, so that some may be
found in taverns. They also display themselves without
delicacy and in too open a way, and are immodest even in the
presence of elders, lending their ears to unworthy
conversations. At marriage, therefore, it is rare that a daughter
is a virgin, having already permitted the snake to enter her

garden.' At which words many laughed, may God have pity
upon them.

'Once, sires, boys put on a cap in their twentieth year[22] and
girls put pins in their hair at the age of fifteen. But now many
lie with one another as soon as the first hair is to be seen.
Once the young women of the city were not only beautiful in
body but of good conduct, while no wicked girl who did ill
with her body for money dared remain in the city. But now
all, including the young girls, and whether or not they have
husbands, seek to sate their carnal desires whenever they arise,
being impatient to couple as soon as they feel the itch, and
having no concern for the outrage of their acts.

'Indeed, both young men and young women have become
equally wicked, girls not only showing their teeth in
immodest fashion, but going about the streets in summer
dressed in light stuffs through which the shape of their bodies
may easily be seen, and as if to offer themselves to whomever
may desire them.

'Thus, men now speak badly of women and with
contempt, as was once forbidden, for if a damsel has fat legs
or a great goitre in the neck they make reference to it without
any modesty or shame. Moreover, today, most men are
cuckolds since most women play the whore, while even the
youngest of girls lie with boys from idleness and as a pastime.
Indeed, it is of no greater moment to them than any other
pleasure that has the power to attract them.

'As for those men who lie with men, they seek to make that
which is against nature appear as if it were in accord with
nature, step by step making the citizen accustomed to that
which is forbidden, and to consider their base desires to be
good. Thus they say, first, that not all men are made happy by
lying with women, then that it is not more in accord with
nature for a man to lie with a woman than with a man, and
then that for a man to lie with a man is good, when it is proof
rather of the disorder of all things under heaven.

'Moreover, those men who love only men declare, in order

to confuse the citizens, not only that they too have pure love in their hearts, and that such love is as worthy of respect under heaven as the love of men and women, but that those men who put the member which man hides into the anus of another should be esteemed as worthy by all.' At these words, many of those who were around Pitaco began to shout out, shout upon shout, saying that such men deserved to die.

Pitaco continued: 'Yet fools among us proclaim that such conduct is not only in accord with nature but with the fashion of the city, or that men who lie with other men are milder and more tender than men who lie with women, pleading as if with reason for their own depraved and wicked pleasures. Others, pleading against nature in the same fashion, declare that, when men lie with men, women are spared much torment and that their bodies will not suffer in childbirth.

'At the same time, such evil ones tell to those who maintain the life of the city, by generating its sons and their own descendants, that to be a wife serves only men, and that therefore women should be freed from such duties, just as others say that sons should be freed from their duties to their fathers. But many of those who speak in evil fashion against the duties under heaven of mothers, fathers and sons seek only to make their own ways the common rule, wishing to escape the judgment of those who hold them in contempt, and to pursue their desires with nothing in their way, neither law, nor duty, nor the will of others.'

At these words, many cried out in despair, raising their arms to heaven, may God, the exalted One, have pity upon them and upon their city. Pitaco waited for them to become silent, and expressed himself as follows: 'All these things, sires, they say concern only the person himself,' which in their language they call *sou*, 'but it is not so, for they concern the future of the city. For when men walk openly in the streets in search of men, or dress themselves and go about in the manner of women, this is no longer *sou*, but a deed which concerns the people' – which in their language they call *cun*.

'Nor should those who seek the way avert their eyes, as if it were *sou*, from the habits and behaviour of young women. For in the past they were full of tenderness yet modest, but are now changed, some being like lions when they set eyes upon a young man, fleeing all restraint. Thus young women were once skilled in dalliance, but have become coarse from their loose habits and from the disrespect of men. Once, women overcame men by gentle wiles, but now they seek that a woman should conquer a man with her contempt or the brief desire of the flesh, and thus they fail to keep him.

'Moreover, if the woman seeks out the man in order to lie with him, he too is permitted to behave with her in any way he chooses, so that each comes to have contempt for the other. Yet if he is the first to seek out the woman, then women themselves now consider it wrong. Hence, few men wish to stay long with such women, preferring to remain alone. For not even a strong, courageous and handsome young man would wish for such a burden, but will pass swiftly from one woman to another, as some women pass from man to man, changing with each moon. Moreover, should such as they marry, their marriage lasts but a brief time. For no sooner have they made their promises than they find comfort with another.

'For respect and trust have passed away and wandering desires have taken their place, fewer being devoted to their spouses but desirous only of finding others who might please them more.'

Whereupon Pitaco paused a while, the men about him whispering in his ears and he seeming to give them counsel, at which they departed, Lifenli declaring to me that, such was now the anger of certain great merchants of the city at the words he had pronounced against them, those nearest to him feared for his fate. But, notwithstanding such fear, the noble Pitaco, rising to his feet and bowing low to those before him, concluded: 'When there is much to be said, one should say less than is needed, but the lowly one has spoken too much.

Moreover, so many are the opinions in this city that they are not yet digested. The wise man who takes pains[23] has been overcome by the sophist who acquires ideas as a merchant trades in vegetables or cloth. For all is traffic in goods, whether for the mind or for the body.

'Thus, today, everything under heaven is talked about in the same breath, and wise men and sophists make use of the same expressions, so that it is no longer possible to judge the worth of a man or of an idea. Whatever is cried as great in the markets or the streets of the city becomes great even for men of highest intelligence. So that from the laws of heaven the goodness has been boiled away, and only the lees remain.

'Now we live without any guiding idea, trying things here and there, as a blind man does. Nothing under heaven is reduced to order, but flies about our heads like the winds, that which is vice to one man being virtue to another. In our city, men forget today what they desired only yesterday, having no grounds for this desire or that, and going about in circles without cease. In one place they listen to men without faith, in another they see violent death and lust, in another they learn of impiety without measure. Thus there are many who know nothing but such fury and madness. At the same time, the counsellors of the Son of Heaven seek to prevent the effects of the very causes which they are promoting, while hoping that those who no longer feel any duty towards them will come to their aid.

'Yet each person has become uncertain of the future and prey to his fears, not wishing to grow old lest he be found weak and wanting, and searching, he knows not where, to be guided. Once, it was held that there was much benefit in being the humblest person in the city, so humble that even those who carried excrement might curse him for standing in their path. But now each wishes to have all things, thinking that none is more deserving than he, while those who have nothing demand help as though they were emperors, and, having received it, remain as ingrate as before.

'For now that which was forbidden in the time of our ancestors is not merely permitted but encouraged by those who, themselves spoiled, seek to harm others, in order that the worse should triumph over the better. It is as if men desire that that which is radiant should be hidden in the shadows, and that that which is obscure and shameful should be brought into the light.

'The world under heaven falls, princes grow feeble and the Tartars approach, but sage leaders do not appear. In the past, a man of noble feelings and wise counsel but poor in possessions was admired, but now others look upon him with contempt as if he had lost his way. For men and women now do as they please, thinking that even marriage is a curb upon their desires. Moreover, those without learning now feel no shame to make known their foolish judgments, as though they were wise.

'But, as in the time of Ianciu, when those above have no principles and those below have no laws, and when those above ignore the way and those below ignore learning, it is good fortune indeed if the realm should survive. This humble one, sires, has great fears also. Yet the way of benevolence and virtue can be found once more, and the law of heaven be again observed. Otherwise, to what will the citizens come unless the city is refounded with new rules and ordinances, which may protect it from still greater harm?'

With these words, again bowing, Pitaco said no more, I, Jacob ben Salomone of Ancona, having heard all this and taken it from the mouth and hand of the faithful Lifenli,[24] agreeing with many things and being made wiser thereby, for which God be praised.

To Pitaco I declared that he had expressed himself in noble fashion, saying that in casting out the wisdom of their ancestors the people of his realm had done as if the Saracens had cast out their holy book and the Jews their Torah, which God forbid.[25] To which Pitaco replied, asking, 'What is the noblest virtue, and what the virtue to be preferred?' To which

I answered, God be praised, 'Justice is the noblest, and health the preferred.' Upon which I took my leave of him, he bowing to me, God be thanked, and I went away.

It now fell to me to search for the helmsman Turiglioni, Buccazuppo imploring the faithful Lifenli, with many tears and upon her knees, to accompany me to certain taverns and other low places of the city, for to these places the said Turiglioni had gone from the first days of our coming into Manci.

Yet I feared greatly to go in such places, God be praised, for a pious man may not put himself in the way of that which is base, save only if he may thus rescue a human soul from the hand of death, as our sages, peace upon them, teach. But neither was it clear to me whether such was the case, so that I was in doubt about the argument, and to every appeal an objection beset my mind.

For if I should go in such dark places and Turiglioni were not found, I should see that which it is not decent for a pious man to see and would have broken the Law, which God forbid. Likewise, if I should go in such base places and save Turiglioni from death, yet not without having offended my sight with wicked things, and my sight have taken delight in them, I should also have broken the Law, which God forbid. But if I should not go, and the brave Turiglioni be found dead, his death occurring after I might have saved him, I should again have broken the Law, for a pious man should do that which he believes is necessary to save life, provided only that his belief rest upon a true ground.

Wherefore, it was required of me to judge whether there was some true ground for the fears of Bertoni and Buccazuppo. To which Lifenli, moved by the tears of the girl, declared that any stranger who went alone into the low places of the city, as Turiglioni had done, was in danger of his life. Hearing this, I summoned the men Micheli and Fultrono to my side and, with the faithful Lifenli as my guide, set out in search of the helmsman Turiglioni.

In the low places of the City of Light is found the common herd, among them many young men who, having no god, are without law or faith. Nor are they men of valour but given up entirely to idleness and vice, and, living like brutes in their stables, feed themselves by theft and other wrongful acts. Moreover, from living by night in the taverns and other places of ill resort, they are of a pale and unhealthy colour and often in their persons they are not clean, God forbid, as well as being drunken and ugly.

They also curse freely and with violent gestures, and each shouts or speaks brusquely to the other without grace, not caring who may observe their behaviour, some touching their members while they speak, and others being without modesty in other things. Others are slothful and fat, being unwilling to move themselves or to give themselves to labour. Thus they are wretched both in body and soul, and eat and drink in a bad fashion.

Many of them go about dirty and unkempt, as I have written, taking no care for their honour or for the persons who see them, for they never wash themselves or comb their hair. Thus these, contrary to the custom of the Mancini, who are much given to washing themselves, smell, giving off an odour which gives great offence to the nostrils, so that one must go about in the places where they gather with a cloth pressed to the face. Yet there are some among them, for of this Lifenli informed me, who are possessed of wealth, but prefer to go about dressed in rags and without fear that the dogs might bite them.

All those of whom I have written, and who make up the mass in the low parts of the city, have their own way of speaking, which others may not well understand. Many of them also, as I have written, are given over to rest and an idle way of life, so that such sloth leads them to a lowness of spirit.

Yet others are to be seen who are wicked and who know much of spells and magic, and some of these wear earrings of gold or set with pearls and precious stones, such people being

said by some to have come in times past from Greater Turkey
and by others to be Tartars.

But the lowest among the citizens of Zaitun know neither
the arts of the Evil One nor of any other, being unwilling to
learn the skills of their fathers, as in the making of silk,
porcelain, paper and other things. They remain resting and
sleeping during the day, making a home of their beds and
coming out of doors at night in order to go here and there
like vagabonds. Some drink opium and sleep thereafter as
long as three days,[26] while others go about the streets thinking
to ill-treat someone, and ready to do wicked deeds.

Of these I saw some with the appearance of beasts, with
faces like the muzzles of dogs, many of them dull of
understanding and like monsters from their idleness and vice.
Moreover, such brutish men have no fear of sin, so that there
is no ground to enter into talk with them, there being also a
great peril in it. For should they see in the eye or demeanour
of another that which displeases them, they may strike him or
do him other harm. Thus, observing them, I feared at the
same time both for my own safety and for the fate of the
brave Turiglioni.

For such men are of an evil descent who do not think it a
sin to do harm, to rob and even to kill. Indeed, some seek to
rob all those who pass through their streets, yet they are not
brave men but cowardly and wicked, striking and fleeing from
the passers-by, and fearing most he who is stronger than they.
Moreover, even when they do not seek to strike or rob a man,
they are of such evil habits that they chew and spit, and when
angered spit in the face of another. In such fashion, being
scoundrels, they are given to other sudden acts of anger or
violence, which I pass over in silence.

Wherefore, accompanied by Micheli and Fultrono, and
being led by the faithful Lifenli, I walked with great fear in
the streets of the taverns and other low places of the City of
Light, seeing also certain men, who are priests among the
idolaters, in hats of black silk with a border of gold, and

wearing black gowns with a cord of yellow or purple about their waists, together with shoes of black silk, and who alone may go about in such places without harm.[27]

In these taverns, they pass the entire day drinking, God forbid, and come out only to urinate in the streets. Inside, they always have their beakers to their mouths, and thus as the day passes they become truly drunk so that they are not able to stand, and are often drunk also in the street, shouting oaths at one another and at the passers-by. Indeed, in such low places none remains sober in his behaviour, but all drink and eat without measure and, when drunk, they sleep even in the street as if they were swine, or as if they were dead.

This being the bestial life, our sages and prophets, peace upon them, teach that a pious man shall be among neither wine-bibbers nor riotous eaters. For all their tables are full of vomit and filthiness, without God, and they are swallowed up with their wine and are out of their way through drink, they err in vision, they stumble in judgment, and are as cattle in a shambles.

Thus, entering these dark dens in search of Turiglioni, I was much afflicted by the bad smell, and it was a sad shame to see so many young men in such an unworthy state. For in them is the eye which does not see, that blind eye which looks upon the world without recording the place or the moment, and which may not know what may be learned from them, since the drunken are creatures deprived of understanding and ignoble. Here I saw that few were able to remain upright, and there were many other horrible things to see, since most did not stir or even appear to be alive, which God forbid.

For as has been shown by the most learnèd of our sages, following the noblest Aristotle, every being which is able to move itself is also able to be without movement for a certain length of time. Yet even in such things has God, blessèd be He, given of His bounty, for truly the sleep of the drunken and ungodly is of benefit to the world. But they are also as the beasts who perish, and who, like sheep, are laid in the grave,

as our David, son of Jesse, the anointed and sweet psalmist of
Israel, sang. Yet it is never the destiny of any man, whether he
be Jew or Gentile, to lie in this fashion in chains, not equal
even to the brutes, for such as they have placed the chains
upon their own bodies.

These men, who have neither belief nor aim, who neither
do good to themselves nor bring good to others, are not truly
in the rank of men, as Rabbi Mose ben Maimon, peace upon
his honoured soul, teaches us. Among the beings of the earth
they are lower than the true rank of men but higher than that
of the troop of apes. For they have the forms of men, and
faculties that are higher than those of the apes, but, lacking
the virtues of those who have been made in the image of God,
are in truth lower than the rank of men.

Moreover, when they are drunk, the men of Manci shout
and sing in the manner of the crying of cats in the night, and
are concerned only with the playing of music, singing and
dancing. Once, so Lifenli informed me, the young sang and
played music with such delicacy that it was a marvel to hear,
and had much festivity without drunkenness or coming to
blows. For, as our sages proclaim, when joy arrives none
should stop it, for to do so is unholy, dancing with one's feet
being a thing which praises the Lord, blessèd be He.

But in the taverns in the dark places of the City of Light
are heard the cries only of demons, God forbid, and not the
songs of the happy and fortunate. For here the drunken and
tormented give out the grievous sounds of the accursèd of
Gehenna, may God forgive me my words, with many wailing
notes ugly to hear, as of those who suffer great pain of soul.
Here they therefore rendered no sweet harmony or jingle, but
rather a sound of weeping struck me, which was like the
howls of those put to the flame, woe is me.

Together with Lifenli, and attended by Micheli and
Fultrono, I sought long in these sad and dark places, but
could learn nothing of the fate of Turiglioni, returning at the
last to the house of Nathan ben Dattalo, peace upon him.

Here Buccazuppo wept greatly before Lifenli, he being much
moved and giving her words of comfort in order to console
her.

Thereafter, after the sun had set, I set out once more with
Lifenli and accompanied by Micheli and Fultrono to the low
places of the city in search of Turiglioni. But first I prayed to
God, may He be exalted, that I myself be spared from
becoming unclean in drawing so close to that which is
forbidden. For it was beholden upon me to go yet further into
this base world, lest I be held to account by others that
without care I had consigned my servant to peril and death.

Hence we came to a great shining place of lanterns and
lamps, and of stages and prostitutes, near the eastern gate of
the City of Light where gather at night those who go in search
of pleasures and shameful delights, the like of which cannot
be found in the entire world and which no one even among
those who has seen them might believe. Here I, seeing an
army of young men and women coming towards me, and
fearing that they wanted to rob me, I took to flight but they
paid no attention to me, God be thanked.

In this place there was a great tumult and noise of shouts,
trumpets, kettledrums and the sound of hands beating
together, sometimes with shrill cries, sometimes a continuous
roar, and sometimes a buzzing sound as of a multitude of
bees. For here were many actors and singers, each troupe
upon its own stage, of which there were at least one hundred,
and about each of which there was a great crowd, some
waiting for the actors to speak and the music to sound, others
listening to those things that were taking place before them.

Thus all about was a great coming together of singing,
drums and speech, some of cries of grief and anguish terrible
to hear, and others of laughter, even of those who seemed
taken with a great fury to laugh, so that the air was torn by
the laments, groans and laughs of all those who were present.
Yet it was also as though I stood alone in a savage and desert

place, God preserve me, such was the empty roaring, furious and rabid, of a thousand thousand voices that echoed in the darkest night.

But when I drew nearer I saw such things as the heart fears to tell, may God spare me. For although the people of the city are not given to arms, yet it pleases them to hear and to see represented the images and figures of pain and suffering, while they stand at ease in places set aside for such things. Thus I saw a fight before my eyes in which were large numbers of men coming to hand-to-hand combat and others as if with death-wounds, all engaged in exchanging very great blows with swords and clubs, their hands and arms as if cut off and blood seeming to spurt and flow. It was as if it brought the young men of the city a bitter pleasure, for to them it is a great delight to hear the clash of swords, as well as the sound of the blows of clubs, the groans of the wounded and the red blood which they make to flow with hidden art.

Thus, to see gashes appear on the face and arms in a brawl, with vermilion all about them, is all their foolish delight, as also to hear the laments of women made widows and the cries of orphans, at which the young men laugh and shake their heads with pleasure, may God have mercy on them for their evil. Moreover, they cry out for the torture of others and in an instant the giving and receiving of cruel blows, and the cutting and striking off of feet and hands, are so presented to them that it is horrible for a pious man to see. Indeed, they so comport themselves as if they should like to go in gore up to their calves. Yet at the same time, so declared Lifenli, such as they are not willing to defend the city from the Tartars, at whose name they tremble in fear, but only to wreak harm upon one another. For it is as if they possessed the desire to slay their own brothers, as Cain, may he be accursèd, slew Abel, but not their enemies who stand at the gates of the city.

Hence it is not to him who is wise and of great cunning that they look, nor to him who is pious and given to duty.

Rather, they look to him who seems the lion among the savage beasts, and who strikes down and kills, making monstrous slaughter without end or purpose, yet they themselves are reputed cowards. Moreover, not only does it please them thus to see violent death but the drinking of blood, may God spare me at the last days for writing such words, does not seem to them dirty and wicked, nor even the eating of faeces, which abomination they bring in representation before the eyes of the mob, may curses fall in torrents upon them.

Thus I saw many young men, even thousands of thousands, and women and children also, stand in the shadows before the glittering lamps and lanterns, their faces pallid, and crying out with pleasure as though the blood which spurted and the other unclean things were nourishment for their accursèd and cheated souls.

Those who for gain display these things to the eyes of the people declare that they do not arouse evil thoughts, but rather, being fearsome, drive men from sin. But those who speak thus are themselves vicious, confusing not only good and evil, as do other men of the City of Light, but truth and falsehood. Further, having to do with evil they themselves become evil, and having to do with a false life they themselves become liars.

Thus, from such sights I turned away my face, God be praised, as from a corrupted body, for here were men without compassion for the sufferings of others. Here I saw youthful will directed towards wicked ends, and that which is abject and blind in man made into his delight. Thus it is that fear of God and love of man shall pass into darkness, as it passes into darkness in Christian lands where my brothers, upon whose souls be peace, are brought to the fire.

In the darkness and in the light I, Jacob of Ancona, saw a fearful and fearsome world made by demons; God have mercy upon me that a pious man should go in such places. For everything appeared blood, and those who stood before it fevered and a lost people. Nor could the brave Turiglioni be found among them, and of him there was no report.

On the next day, at nightfall, having done my duties, for which God be praised, and having attended to my affairs, I set out once more with Lifenli, Micheli, and Fultrono into places yet darker, to that part of the City of Light which is called the third district of the river, whither go all those who are in search of the most unclean pleasures, may God forgive me.

For here there were places of lust so foul that although everywhere there was light, and the lamps and lanterns shone here like stars, only the blackest souls have resort there, God forgive me that I should have set out among them with such light step.

Here, also, all mingle, men and women, without regard to rank, as also without shame that they should be seen there, with so many women of pleasure, whom they call in their language flowers, that they could not be counted, some beautiful and wanton, their bodies perfumed and attended by servants, and others low and vile, yet also without shame, who do everything which gives comfort and pleasure to men, may God spare me for those things of which my eyes had sight.

Indeed, so depraved are the citizens of Zaitun that the most beautiful of the harlots are considered as goddesses by both men and women, who follow them as they go, while the young seek to copy not only the manner of their clothes or the colours with which they adorn their faces, but the very sounds of their voices when they speak or sing. Thus, such harlots suffer no infamy for their vices, just as they feel no shame for their way of life, but go about in splendour as though they were queens of heaven, finding husbands even among the nobles of the earth. But others of them are married women who, being without virtue, freely play the whore, and others are constrained to such things by their husbands, who make their women commit adultery but feel no shame for it, may God spare me for having written such unclean things.

Other women there are who are sold by the hour or the night by traders in human flesh, others also who have been brought to the city even by their fathers and who are children not ten years old, and others in great number who are not harlots but give freely of their bodies to strangers for a day or a week or a month as it pleases them, so that young girls come very soon to be deflowered. Indeed, they compete with one another to be taken, and so light is their behaviour that when the merchant has had his way, God forbid, it is sufficient to give her a small gift for having lain with her, so pleased is she that he has chosen to have relations with her. Thus these give no value to being chaste, just as others think adultery no shame, nor even to bear children without concern, whom often they secretly kill. All these go about the streets wearing stuff so thin that a man may see their bodies, so immodest is their dress, may God spare me for what my eyes have seen.

There are also among them, so Lifenli told me, many wives who have been sent away by their husbands, even those who have borne children. For if any wife does not please him, the husband is able to chase her away and freely take another. But since women now seek equal liberty for themselves, they lack the power to oppose such a thing, and thus often come to live a wretched life, which God forbid. Moreover, so great is the confusion which is now among them that while some women give their bodies freely to all, believing that she who has had more men is more pleasing than the rest, others say, as among the Christians of our lands, that they would only marry a kind man who conquered them by the force of love or other proof of faith.

Other women, more men than maidens, well made and as strong as men, altogether refuse men, declaring it to be both right and reasonable that not for anything in the world would they lie with men. But these, although they have cast aside fine satins and dress only in rough silk or plain linen, yet, albeit professing lack of regard for men, nevertheless wear such clothing cut very close. Thus, with great art they permit others to see each movement of their bodies, arousing that which they deny, so that men do not know with what they deal. Some of these live alone, and others, it is said, lie with women, God forbid. But, nevertheless, these women refuse every entreaty to let themselves be vanquished by men, not, as Christian nuns declare, the better to devote themselves to heaven but from being averse to men, saying always that they will marry no one.

Yet, on the other side, I also saw, may God forgive the pious one who sees against his will, men who wore the clothes of women and of the finest silk, and others who so clothed themselves as to appear that they had fine breasts and large buttocks. For other men, so depraved are they in the City of Light, delight to think that they have before them not men but plump women, may God forbid such abomination.

Even these, who are much given to sinning against nature and thus live like beasts, do so with neither infamy nor reproach. There are also among them men and boys who sell their bodies exactly as the women, and these were once severely punished for their sins, but now have great power in the city, some also being of great wealth. Thus in certain low places into which I entered in search of Turiglioni, may the Exalted One spare me, I saw such things of which surely no man has written before, as men coupling without shame before the eyes of others.

Of such abominations, for which there can be no forgiveness, neither now nor at the end of days, may God be praised, they say in the City of Light that there are many different ways by which a man or woman may come to the highest pleasures of the body, and that each has a right to satisfy himself according to his desire, either in the rear or in the female passage or between the thighs.[28] Moreover, they say that no reproach may therefore be made of either men or women according to their choices, nor punishment be imposed upon them, however they may become sick and

unclean, such is the wicked reasoning that guides them in this
and other matters also, as I have already written.

Thus, those among the Zaituni who act as once they did in
the city of Sodom exercise their lusts freely, going about the
streets in search to satisfy their desires, since they do not hold
any form of lechery a sin. Hence, you may see those who
follow with their gaze the forms of youths, so that boys of ten
and twelve years old live and earn by the sale of their flesh,
not stopping day or night from running here and there, in
order to satisfy the desire of the member which man hides.

Yet our judges in Israel, peace upon them, declared that if a
man has connection with a man, he should be beaten to
death, and he too who pursues men may be delivered from
transgression only at the cost of his life, for the men of Sodom
shall have no share in the world to come, may God be
praised. For that which is so crooked cannot be made straight,
nor even may two unmarried men sleep under the same cover.
But in the City of Light the lust of all is unloosed, and every
desire may be sated for money, so that not even the monks of
the idolaters lead a more virtuous life than others, sinning
together freely in their holy houses, or lying often with
women.

Thus, with the faithful Lifenli as my guide, I walked in the
darkest places of the world in search of my servant, whither
come men to seek enjoyment for their flesh, forgetful of the
travails of the city. In these places, where men seek to calm
their erect members and girls display their haunches as far as
their natures, may God forgive me my words, disease walks
close by them upon the same path.

Moreover, although many women of the city are taken by
disease, they set a great value upon their beauty, as of their
hair, their mouths, their lips, their breasts and all their limbs
so that they be true. Thus, some compress their feet, even to
the breaking of the bones, so that they should remain small,
for they consider it to be more elegant and more beautiful,
while others paint their faces and necks white, and others eat

little so that they may be always slender. For those who become fat, and whose cheeks and breasts hang, fear to be turned away.

And thus it goes for these maidens all the year round, may God have pity upon them. Yet those poor people who have beautiful daughters are thereby made happy and even consider that whoredom is a great grace and honour, for each thinks that his daughter will marry nobly as the reward of such evil-doing.

In addition, many are the people of the City of Light who say that at the age of thirty the countenance of a woman changes, so that they strive to preserve their youth, seeking by every art to keep the appearance of their bodies as they were before they knew the trials of life, fearing above all lest their bodies dry out and harden, applying costly salves each day to their skin so that it may remain tender and soft. But to have firm flesh even at the age of forty is not all their desire, since among them it is not the quality of the person as such which receives the respect of others, but that which he carries on his back. Thus those who dress poorly are judged to be lesser, while those who dress in clothes of silk and gold are judged to be greater, God forbid. Yet as our sages teach, he that walks

---

'SOME COMPRESS THEIR FEET (p.198)'

*The deformation of the feet of girl children by binding them with regularly tightened strips of cloth was a Chinese custom held to give greater grace of movement when walking. The bones having been broken, the toes were pushed under the ball and sole of the foot, the mutilation producing a severely compressed stump – called a 'golden lily' – which might be no more than three inches long. It was an object valued by marriage-brokers (and a sexual fetish?) as well as a painful immobilising symbol of subjection. As J.K. Fairbank observes in* China: A New History *(Cambridge, Mass., 1992), 'the peasant masses ... imitated the upper class' while others – including the Ming emperors – opposed it. Seemingly not practised until the tenth century and here briefly noticed by Jacob, it continued into the late nineteenth century.*

alone by his way, and turns his heart to vanity, acts against his own soul.

Therefore, I went all my days in the City of Light among the lost, but in the darkest places beside the river I became myself as a lost soul, woe is me. Weak is the flesh when it is led by the eye and not by the reason with which we are endowed by God, may He be exalted. For, being among the many and entering with them into a place of infamy, I felt myself to be as them, God forbid, and as though I myself was turned into an unclean and roaring beast, may God forgive me for the desires which assailed me there.

Thus, while the noble Pitaco, may his name be recorded, preached against the sins of the city, for thus I learned, each day more assembling in order to hear him, and the faithful Armentuzio occupied himself with my brother Nathan in my affairs, I, without care for my beloved nor regard for my duty to the Holy One,[29] went with Lifenli in those places where men do not regard any lustful act to be a sin, and all engage themselves in carnal acts without shame, despite the sickness that many of them have in their skin and genitals from such congress.

For there one can do with any of these girls whatever one wishes as if she were one's wife, and be with her in great pleasure. Thus, when a merchant wishes to lie with a woman, he makes her come with him to a place which is set aside for the purpose. Indeed, there is no beautiful young woman here whom the merchant may not have, if he desires, according to his wishes, provided he pays the just price and provided it is with the accord of the woman.

In other places, the women, being agile and well-made with all their beauties, show their breasts and also their private parts to those who come there, dancing unclothed before them, may God forgive the sins of my eyes. And should the guards of the watch be approaching, those who stand at the door give a signal, and they cover their nakedness with a piece of cloth. Many of these women are beautiful beyond measure,

the most beautiful being held to be those with eyebrows like
willows and eyes like almonds, and these, having left aside
their clothes, come out naked, may I be forgiven.

Yet although the beauty of many is such that they would
cause the flowers in a garden to lose their colours, the
nakedness of a woman must be covered sooner than that of a
man, as our sages, peace upon them, teach. But these women
do not think that they do wrong, God forbid, saying that they
have no shame in showing their natures to men, and even if
they lie with men that they do no harm by it. Moreover they
declare that they have no more shame about one part of the
body than another, saying that we go about covered up
because we feel shame about it. Yet even if it is just that a man
should feel no shame for his body, it being a part of the
bounty of God and made in His image, he who is not modest
offends reason, for not all that which is of man needs to be
seen.

Lifenli, having heard from a certain Uaiciu, curses be upon
him, that Turiglioni had frequented this dark place or tavern,
and calling for Micheli and Fultrono to accompany him to
the Fifth Street of the Bridge, for thus it was called, I was left
in great fear to be alone in such a Gehenna, where no evil
deed remains undone and where incontinence is king.

Thus for a long time I held counsel with myself as to
whether a pious man might remain in such a place of infamy,
seeking God's aid that I might not sin further, for here I saw
that the women made a man touch them in many parts of
their bodies even against his will. Yet had I not also given a
promise to the faithful Lifenli that I should remain in such an
accursèd place, may God forgive me, until his return?
Therefore, I feared not to keep faith with my vow, being
bound also to the said Uaiciu, may his name be erased, to
whom Lifenli had given money so that I be kept safe in this
place, which, being a bond both of words and money, I might
not forswear.

Yet since a man may also not bind himself to an unclean end, I had much thought within myself as to whether my end was good or ill. For I came in search of my servant, yet my glances were directed, even against my desire, to the wicked things that were before me. For, as I have written, my will was rendered weak, may I be forgiven, by the beauty of the women about me.

But, seeing that my end was good, I not having come to such a place for the purpose of sinning, God be praised, but with a pure heart, and that a pious and learnèd man should strive even in the darkest places of the world to observe the ways of other men so that he be made the wiser thereby, neither did I turn my eyes from what might be beheld there, even though my desires were so sharp that I felt I might lose my own soul, which God forbid.

Thus there was presented to my eye one dressed in vermilion silk and with little shoes like claws, whose hair was as black as the plumage of a raven, her face powdered white, her eyes clear and her body as light as a flower, or like the stem of a blossom which bends to the wind.[30] Nor did she seem to be a harlot but was of modest demeanour, yet she showed me her legs and feet, God forbid, which in truth were so beautiful that it would not be possible to find more beautiful in the world. I was immediately tempted, may God have mercy upon me, because my eyes took pleasure in looking at them, such was the weakness of my flesh.

But, having made herself naked, God forbid, she began carnal sin with the thigh first and afterwards with the belly,[31] a strange fragrance coming from her scented body, so that a man might die of his desires. Moreover, they say that the most prized nature of the woman is that which is towards the stomach, for there it may be the more easily seen, may I be preserved from the wrath of God for such words. Nor did she have much shame in showing it, albeit with little hair, nor forbid certain men the touching of it, who, with swollen members, lay on a mat with the girl in great delight.

Whereupon I saw many obscene things, praying to God
that I might learn therefrom yet avoid beastly acts on my own
part in order to obtain the bounty of the Holy One, which is
the blessing of the intellect and the light of wisdom both as to
the nature of God and of man. Thus, one placed a silver clasp
about the root of his member, added a ring of sulphur and
spread an ointment upon his umbilicus. Whereupon he
parted the thighs of the said woman, may God forgive me for
what is written, helping her to raise her buttocks high and
with sputum making the interior part moist so that the way
might be made easier, and placed his member at the female
entrance. Thus he entered to the depths and soon the woman
came to the highest delights.

Other things I saw also, too unclean to be written, but my
sight was sated with naked flesh, and where I first felt
pleasure, may God spare me, now I felt weary in soul and
body. Moreover, while man and woman lay in infamy before
my eyes, coupling like the beasts, I saw not them but my
father lying dead, alas, his face pallid and his chin bound and
all gathered about him, upon the coverlet a small drop of
sputum of his last torment, may his soul endure and his
memory be blessed with a thousand blessings, Amen.

Being in a place of such heinousness, which is to say a stall
of beasts, I turned away my weeping eyes, may God forgive
me my great sinfulness. Yet before me I saw still not only my
father, peace be upon his soul, but also those who coupled
basely behind me. For it is hard even for a pious man to
forget the very things that are most harmful to him, so that
that which I had seen remained profanely in my mind, even
though I shut my eyes most tightly while they ran with tears.

Thus I learned bitterly that we should take much care
about the matters which we admit to our thoughts. For there
are many things which it were better we had never known,
although a man must go through the world in search of
knowledge, as our sages teach. Moreover, I saw that in the
appearance of beauty the unclean may be hidden. Likewise, in

the appearance of truth there may be falsehood concealed, or in the heart of the pious man a desire for that which is wicked and forbidden. I also knew that many men wish no curb to their desires, even preferring death to the denial of their delights.

But now, while I was taken with such thoughts, the faithful Lifenli returned to me, together with my servants Micheli and Fultrono, declaring that the body of the helmsman Turiglioni had been found. I therefore went with them to a dark passage, and saw there the corpse of Turiglioni greatly decomposed, with much black blood about it, and upon the chest and throat stabs and wounds, God forbid. But of those who had done such a thing or of the cause, nothing could be learned, for none would speak.

I therefore instructed my servants to carry him to the trading-house of the Genoese, where he had made his lodging, so that the fathers might give him due burial. Thus was my duty done to him who had sought to steer my vessel to its end, but had himself come to his death in a filthy place. For thus, as our sages teach, lust and incontinence may make an end of us altogether.

Whereafter I returned through the city, whose lamps sparkled in the dark like the glow-worms of our country, returning to the house of my brother Nathan ben Dattalo together with Lifenli, beset both by my vision and by the griefs of those about me, as well as troubled in heart by the manifold perils of so great a city. For I feared lest in its confusion and sin it fall to the wrath of God, may He be exalted, who should strike it down by the arm of the Tartars, and lest the evil of the idolaters be corrected by greater evil until the end of days.

## CHAPTER SIX

# Among the Learnèd

PROFESSEDLY AGAINST HIS WILL AT the outset, Jacob is drawn into discussions and debates taking place in Zaitun, including those among the learnèd of the city, who, according to his account, meet regularly in a kind of Academy, and also (it appears) have a law-making role. To the Academy also belong leading merchants, who are made out to be aspiring *arrivistes* among the learnèd. It is clear, too – although not clear enough – that the quarrelsome sages, most of whom Jacob seems to regard as 'sophists', belong to different factions, which appear to have been divided along political lines. The lines of division seem to have corresponded with, among other things, distinct views about how the city should be administered, and how it should be prepared against invasion by the advancing Tartars.

The situation, which can be glimpsed in outline from Jacob's vivid account, was evidently complex, for the threads of argument and conflict seem to have been many. Apart from practical differences about how (and even whether) the city be defended, there is a moral conflict of an age-old kind – in which 'Pitaco' is a protagonist – about a supposed ethical decline and confusion of purpose which are leading to the abandonment of tradition; there is a growingly acute debate about governance, in which Jacob claims to have played a part; and there is fierce disagreement about the values of mercantile freedom, in which the 'merchants' party' and its leaders adopt an aggressive stance.

Less certain however, is the actual nature of day-to-day civic government in Zaitun, since there appears from Jacob's description almost to have been a system of 'dual power', in which the rich merchants exercise, or are striving to exercise, authority over the city. It is as if an old order, that of the emperor's officials and the nobility, is disintegrating and a new order – centred on the merchant interest and supported by at least part of the common people, if Jacob's account can be trusted – is being born, while simultaneously the Mongol invaders draw nearer.

In addition to the regular meetings of the Academy of sages, at which Jacob speaks among other things on the (unlikely) topic of the misdeeds of the Christian faith, there also appears to have been an embryonic form of popular assembly, or at least a sequence of public meetings. Here the conflicting arguments in the city are aired in the search for a *via media* which will secure the best interests of all.

However accurate or embroidered Jacob's account of this may be, we gain a strong impression of the intellectual and political life of a Southern Sung city. It sheds as much light upon Jacob's moral, philosophical and political ideas as upon those of his many interlocutors; indeed, more light, since there are few subjects on which he does not pronounce in lengthy (alleged) orations or brief asides.

Yet, despite the city's 'travails' and Jacob's somewhat extravagant preoccupation with them, he remained attentive to his own merchant interest; flattered by the praises of his hosts, while continuing both to buy and, after his adventures amid the low life of the city, to perform his religious duties.

The chapter that follows is notable for the glimpses it gives of Jewish life in mediaeval Europe, for its observations on the relations between Jews, Muslims and Christians, and for Jacob's expressions of disdain, philosophical and moral, for Christian belief and conduct. In respect of the last, it should be said that

Jacob continuously breaches – or ignores – the Talmudic
injunction of the mediaeval rabbi Solomon ben Isaac of Troyes
(1040–1105), known as 'Rashi', that Christianity should *not* be
classed as 'idolatry'. The chapter ends with one of the great
prophetic visions of the ultimate fate of the Jews.

ow the girl Buccazuppo and the woman
Bertoni set to weeping greatly upon learning of
the death of the helmsman Turiglioni, Lifenli
telling them where his body had been found,
and how I, Jacob of Ancona, a pious man, had
gone in peril of the wrath of God to the darkest places of the
city so that I might discover his fate. The tears of the girl ran
without a check, nor did she cease at my reproaches, Lifenli
immodestly seeking to comfort her and the evil woman
Bertoni declaring that she wept so because Turiglioni had
earlier got her with child.

At these words I went away to my chamber, fearing to hear
of such misdeeds of the Gentiles, and lamenting that those
about me should act so basely, for a pious man may not stay
close to uncleanness unless it be to save the life of another.
Thus in my chamber I too wept bitterly that I had been
brought to such shame, first casting away my soul through
my eyes in dark places, and thereafter through my ears to hear
such evil, praying to God, blessèd be He, that He keep me in
His hand and turn my steps towards goodness and truth, so
that I might both make profit and serve others without harm
to my body or soul.

Whereafter, having laid my phylacteries upon my forehead
and upon my arm, God be magnified, and having resolved to
be faithful all the days of my life to the commandments of the
Torah, I straightaway received from the hand of Nathan ben
Dattalo a sign, which were three letters by Abramo ben Leo of
Mestre, a merchant arrived in Zaitun, telling that Sara my

wife was well, that my father was weak, that my daughter
Rebecca was with child, and that my affairs in Cambaetta
prospered. This was written by Beniamino Vivo, for which I
thanked God.

On this day, which was the twenty-first day of Kislev,[1] I
went also with Nathan and Armentuzio, again buying greatly
the most prized silks, as also choice porcelains that had been
brought at my command, and many other things. Yet, all the
while I was greatly troubled in my heart at my vision,[2]
thinking at each step upon the way that I should go at once to
the House of Prayer in order to recite the Kaddish, but fearing
to do so lest my vision had been false, albeit sent to me by
God, blessèd be he, as a trial of my devotion. The next day,
being the eve of the Sabbath Vayeshev, my travail grew
greater, the day thereafter being the eve of Hanukah,[3] so that
I lamented grievously that I should be thus without
knowledge of whether my father was dead, God forbid, or
alive, for which I prayed continuously, yet seeing always
before my eyes the same vision as before.

In these days, which were the days of Kislev, I also closed
the ears of my heart to the voices of the profane city, which
declared that the dangers in which it was placed grew at
each hour, and that those who followed the noble Pitaco
were greatly increased. Moreover, they said also that those
who gave support to the merchants of Zaitun, being
angered by the blame that Pitaco had placed upon them for
the ills of the city, demanded that he be cast into prison.
But to all these things I at first resolved not to attend, nor to
the cries of Buccazuppo, also forbidding Lifenli to come
close to her. Instead, fulfilling my duties in company with
my brothers during the days of Hanukah and upon the
Sabbath Miketz,[4] I praised God in the light of the Menorah
that my daughter should be with child and that my wife
Sara had been kept safe, praying also for the deliverance of
my father, may his soul rest in peace, but saying the Kaddish
in my heart.

Thereafter, the faithful Lifenli came to me, saying that a servant of the house of the noble Pitaco had brought word to him that I, as a pious and learnèd man who was also wise in the ways of men, would be received with all grace among the other learnèd of the city. These are accustomed to meet every twentieth day in their great chamber, that which is in the Street of Harmony of Zaitun, it being their task, together with the delegates of the Son of Heaven in the City of Light, not only to write the laws of the city but also for those among them whom they call the sages, as astronomers, astrologers, mages and those who are learned in the secrets of medicine and alchemy, to gather in order that they might exchange the fruits of their wisdom and experiments.

Here, no soldiers are permitted, since they are of low birth, but only the famous sages of the city who wear caps with long ears like those of asses, as well as certain rich merchants among them who, although lacking in learning, have made their way among the sages, declaring that, since they bring great riches to the city, it is unjust that any place should be forbidden to them. Yet rare it is that a wise man of another country, save only those who are greatly esteemed by the Mancini for their learning, should be summoned to come among them, for which God be thanked.

Thus I replied to Lifenli that I would esteem it a great honour to my merit to be admitted among them, of which he informed the servant of Pitaco. Whereupon, accompanied by the servant and Lifenli, I went at once to their place of meeting, in order to learn of the wisdom of their sages, and of what counsel they should give for the ills of their city in its time of travail.

Here I found a great feast already prepared, which, as Lifenli informed me, is called in their language to cook a dragon and to kill a phoenix,[5] God forbid, at which I felt greatly afraid lest unclean meats be laid before me. I also saw all about me great doctors of their holy scriptures whom they call *mincini*, doctors of their laws whom they call *minfani*, doctors of numbers whom they call *suansui*, and doctors of writing whom they call *sciusui*.

There were also men learnèd in history, in the study of faces and in geomancy, as well as certain magicians who search impiously for the secret of eternal life, as among us also, and who claim to have prepared a liquor of mercury for this purpose, but which is of great danger to those who drink it.

Some there were also who professed to be foretellers of the future, as do the impious among us, but who were without their learning.[6] Of them one is chosen by the Son of Heaven to serve him, as being more learnèd than the rest, who carried an astrolabe from which he might read the signs of the planets, the hours and the points. These, being astrologers and astronomers and other diviners, reveal from such study of the stars, numbers and points the day on which a man should make a journey, marry, give a gift or lie with his wife.

Of these, some appeared to be masters and learnèd in the sciences, but others were of great presumption, and others impious. For such are those who will not even move from their chambers without consulting one another whether it be a lucky hour. Truly, among all peoples there is a desire to know the future and to guard against misfortune. Yet, although there are many learnèd astrologers among us also,[7] albeit not so many as among the Saracens, when the will of

---

'GEOMANCY'

*A form of divination based on the interpretation by astrologers and others of patterns of lines and figures formed by throwing earth on the ground (or other surface, including paper). In these patterns and shapes, individual destiny could, it was held, be perceived and anticipated and correspondences also be found with the dispositions of the stars and planets. The practice was common to both Eastern and Western cultures in the mediaeval period (and later), but was frowned upon as superstitious by the followers of Maimonides.*

man surrenders to fate, he considers himself to be neither
good nor evil in his deeds but bound by the auspices which
govern the causes and effects of those things which he does.

Thus falls all right and wrong under the rule of the stars,
God forbid, and not under the rule of the Laws of God,
blessèd be He, which teach us what is good and bad in the
conduct of men. For as the wise Rabbi Mose ben Maimon
teaches, peace upon his name, neither the soul nor the will of
man, nor the deeds of men, are subject to the movements and
relations of the celestial world, a thing believed only by those
given over to idolatry.

Yet among the most feared of the sages of the City of Light
are those who live by augury and who write their prophecies
at dusk concerning the following day, these being placed upon
the walls and gates of the city at night so that passers-by may
read them in the morning. But they are no better than the old
country women of our lands who tell the fortunes of those
who will give them a coin. Nevertheless these seers are
considered as sages among them, albeit that they are false
philosophers who cannot distinguish between the truth and
the appearance of things, or between those things of which
there is proof and those things in which no man may believe
without impiety, being against reason, nature and the will of
God.

Thus, as I have written, on every twentieth day, all these
gather together in order to hold a meeting and a debate,
sometimes upon one subject and sometimes upon another,
and, after having eaten, discuss at great length the matter
before them, for which they prepare their opinions and
orations with great care, for so Lifenli told me.

But before their feast they also explain their discoveries to
one another, or bring ancient coins which they have found by
digging in the ground, or read from their new works, as of
their studies of the past, or of animals and plants and other
things. In this way, as among us, they philosophise according
to their estimation of what is true. Yet often, so it is said, they,

being arrogant and in their haughtiness considering all others to be inferior to themselves, speak only of empty things and neither of God nor of the substances of the perceptible world.

One such, a man very advanced in years and of arrogant manner, is called The Glorious Prince of Doctrine[8] in the Past and Present Worlds, believing himself to know all things in heaven and upon the earth, may God forgive me my words. Yet to those about him he laments secretly that he has written no great work, fearing that his name will be forgotten, but before others he is given to vaunt himself, pretending to be the greatest sage among them.

Moreover, such is his princely manner when he speaks, all, being deceived, believe that they hear the truth. But when they consider well what he has said, his words appear as they truly are, that is forms without matter. Such men, in the mode of their speech, may be said to be wizards, as declared my teacher Rabbi Jacob, peace upon him. For with words alone they seem wise to those who hear them,[9] yet are afterwards shown to have spoken not wisely or deeply but made only empty sounds and vain gestures such as will leave no trace in the terrestrial world.

In addition, among these sages there is great malice one towards the other, for so Lifenli told me. Yet, as I observed, they greet each other most genially, declaring that each is welcome and each wishing the other that it be for him a good year, or that the other have sons endowed with honour, and each asking the other, with a bow, that he be seated first. Yet such courtesies are false, for, as Lifenli declared, here hatred rules over many hearts, so that they are given even to conflicts and brawls, as I shall tell.

Three wise men preside over them, but in them the others, being full of envy, have no great faith. Yet they turn to them and seek their best counsel, but murmur against them when it has been given.

For such is the power of envy, in which the knowledge and fear of death rules over the reasons of men, that each, fearing

the fame of the other, seeks to destroy him, the envious man
being unwilling to be outdone by another. For, especially if he
is a sophist and not truly wise, he hates to think that he will
be forgotten, while the works and deeds of the other will be
spoken of by those who are to come. Indeed, even the most
intelligent and pious of men fears the forgetting[10] of his
name. But many here are led astray by hatred and envy, so
that they become governed by ill-will towards those who show
the greatest learning, to whom they display much malice. On
these they will turn their backs, or feign ignorance of their
writings or even of their names, and otherwise display their
spite. Thus they will say that those whom they know to be the
wisest among them are the least wise, or that they have
acquired their knowledge not from the great sages but at
random and are thus not truly learnèd.

Whence in their faces many bear the effect of such spite,
for a man may see that which gnaws at their hearts and souls,
which is envy. Thus some have the faces of sheep, but others
of foxes and wolves. Indeed not only their faces but their
minds also are turned[11] by the strength of their ill-will, which
lacerates them in both mind and body. But others were of
gentle appearance and some like countrymen, seeming to be
rough and rude. Thus some had skins as dark as liver, God
forbid, others had corrupted breath and others were so old
that they had lost all their teeth, while others had curvature of
the spine such as to suffer great discomfort. One stammered
and another spoke very rapidly, so that Lifenli could not
follow his opinions.

Yet others, among whom were certain merchants, spoke
without logic, for so it seemed when Lifenli put their words
into our language. But words which are untrue or contrary to
reason often receive favour in the world, for a man may gain
one step upon others by the force of his speech and two steps
by means of lies. Hence, I seemed to hear in this place many
words not of sages but of sophists, who had in them no light
of truth such as might guide the feet of others. For many

spoke not only without measure but without meaning, as if they loved to hear their own voices and had little care for the great ills of their city. Fewer words rather than more should suffice for a sage, for he that multiplies words occasions sin, but many of these seemed given over to objections without end.

Rather, as all things done by God possess reason, so also should all words spoken by men, as our sages teach. For words are the emblems of our minds and souls, and thus if such words are not wise nor teach the truth to others, it is a sign that our minds and souls are defective.

Moreover, the scholar who neglects all work which brings profit to himself or to his city, but lives at the expense of others, offends both God and man. Thus the wise, in order to deserve the respect of others by their counsels, must show their wisdom by their deeds as well as by their words, for it is the duty of the wise not only to revere the created world but to reveal and renew it.[12] Yet by a man's words he may also be judged, for so our sages teach.

There were truly some among them whose thoughts, when translated to me by the faithful Lifenli, were as wise as those of our learnèd men, but others who argued with false syllogisms that would make the wise man blush. Many were the sophisms I heard, and ponderous reasoning as when there is thunder and wind without rain, while to him who has two heads even the wisest cannot give a just answer.

Yet, with much presumption among themselves, those of Zaitun believe that theirs is the only true wisdom in the world and that those who do not know it are lesser than they. Thus, although they showed me courtesy fitting to my lineage, it was at first as to one who, coming from another country, could not have understanding of their science.

With one among them, Scipi, a grand master of astronomy, who in their language they call a *ciuncancien*, being truly learnèd, I had with the aid of Lifenli, peace upon him, much discourse upon medicine, philosophy and other things. For this Scipi declared that the natural order and the human order are one, and that a universal reason stands above all things, of which men by their learning can be masters. This is a thing that has been forgotten, so Scipi declared, having once been the knowledge of man, and that if it were to be regained, peace would reign upon the terrestrial world.

To him I replied that our sage Rabbi Mose ben Maimon, may his soul endure, held that reason is the property of man and of man alone, the intellect not being found in other beings of the created world. Moreover, Rabbi Mose ben Maimon also teaches that it is the highest perfection of man to acquire the rational virtues. For it is only thus, by the learning of the intellect, that a man can approach the divine and live longer than his material body, glorifying God and seeking always to become like Him by knowing that which He, in His bounty, has enabled us to know.

This I declared with the aid of Lifenli to Scipi, who replied, hearing and bowing, a large number of their sages being gathered about us, that such argument was akin to that of a previous age among them, in which the place of God was supreme, but that only when such belief was at an end, God forbid, might harmony be re-established among men.

It is true, I replied, that in his reason man is man, as our Rabbi Mose ben Maimon teaches, but whence comes his reason save from God? At this, when he had understood what I had said, Scipi, bowing once more, replied that, according to their sage Ciusi, reason is but an exhalation of the energy which among them they call the breath of the natural order, from which also comes, according to their teachings, moral truth.

To which, having understood what he had said, I replied that not only has moral truth come to us from the word of God, which was given to our teacher Moses, but the natural order is itself the creation of God. At which Scipi laughed with great impiety, God forbid, and made no further answer, for he did not know what to say.

Since the sages are much given to following the opinions of those who are strongest in the City of Light, whatever be the truth or falsehood of such opinions, the difference between wisdom and folly is in great doubt among them. Thus, if a rich man holds an opinion, they have a disposition to hold it also, even if it be wrong, but if a man who is without riches and power declares what they secretly know to be true they will oppose him. For such is their great desire for the favour of others that some are willing to betray that which they know to be good and true for that which they know to be bad and false, which God forbid.

Yet they do not become contented by such hypocrisy,[13] but find defect and default in all things, for their yellow eyes see all things to be yellow. Thus, this thing is too much and another thing is too little, for to each of them nothing appears just and right save his own judgment, and wherever their eyes turn they find something to displease them. For without faith their thoughts are never at peace. Thus they hold that it is not they who are lacking, but the times in which they live, while giving themselves over to so many different matters that their minds become confounded by the variety of things that occupy them.

However, few give thought to the nature of things as a whole, such as the travail and confusion of the city, but rather they spend their days in judging each other. Therefore, they have made a barren world for themselves, yet for which they blame others.

In addition, not only do they greet each other with such courtesies as if they were welcome to one another, as I have written, but many seek by the form of their conduct alone to be taken for wise men. Thus, unlike our sages, they think that without going out of doors they may know the whole world, without looking they shall see, and that without thinking they shall be wise.

Furthermore, while many of them declare that it is not just that men should be unequal, they themselves greedily seek

higher rank and honour. Therefore, the city turns this way
and that in its blindness, for none can distinguish between
those who are right and those who are wrong, nor does reason
command the counsel even of the wise. Instead, they are given
to arguments without end, at which they all show great anger,
so that the wise man no longer differs from the foolish and all
take part in brawls as though each was without duty and
conscience.

Thus, at the feast, of which I have already written, there
were eight tables, and upon each table thirty dishes set, and
after all had eaten and many had spoken, they fell into great
disagreement, some being of the party of the noble Pitaco and
some of the party of the merchants, but others of neither, the
last declaring that it is the duty of the sage to keep at a
distance those who unite into factions,[14] whatever be the
cause.

Nor was it sufficient for them to put their arguments and
objections, but they began to be feverish in their words,
clashing very bitterly, each party showing great contempt for
the other. Thus, from first speaking in low voices, they
commenced to shout at one another, soon baying like wolves,
so that each might get the better of the other.

For each party wished to hear nothing of the other but
took to curses and maledictions, as that the son of one might
become a thief or the daughter of another a harlot. Thus
without shame they called each other cuckolds, one saying of
another that he was as a dumb man who sees his father lie
dead in a dream, which God forbid, and although wishing to
tell his vision, cannot speak. And the other replied that the
first was like a blind man carrying a lantern who gives the
appearance of seeing clearly when he can see nothing. In the
same way, one said of another that he climbed a tree in order
to seek fish, and another that he was like a rat who gnaws the
letters of a book, learning nothing therefrom but rather
destroying the truth as he goes. So the faithful Lifenli
explained their angry words.

Thus they took to such great cursing that it was a wonder
to hear, praying even that another's body might rot, or that
his legs might break at the ankles. Even such sages as were
greatly advanced in years showed themselves to be mortal
enemies and to desire to fight rather than to have concord
between them.

So it was that they began to strike each other with their
fists, for so bitter was their argument upon the judgments of
Pitaco and upon the condition of the city, in which each
struck down his enemy of the other party with great ferocity,
may God forgive them, laughing to see him fall. But such was
the brawl that one, having knocked another to the ground,
spat in his mouth, God forbid, an abomination I have never
before seen, among neither animals nor men. Another, who
received the greatest harm, was wounded on the face and
nose, and a third on the arms. At the last, one, having with
his hands seized another by the throat, whose face was pale as
wax, the first, a great merchant by name Anlisciu, the second
a sage of the party of the noble Pitaco, I, Jacob of Ancona,
placed myself between them, God be praised, at which all fell
silent as though they were in great shame to have acted thus
before a stranger.

I then declared to them as follows, Lifenli giving them my
words: 'Rejoice not when your enemy falls, for so taught our
sage Eliezer ben Isaac, peace upon him. And let not your
hearts be glad when he is overthrown, lest the Lord see it, may
He be exalted, and it cause Him great anger.' At which, seeing
their astonishment at my boldness, I took fear at my own
words, being a stranger alone among them.

Whereupon one of the sages who was present said as
follows: 'You are mistaken to be afraid. For your counsel will
be heeded more than if you were of our country. Moreover,
we are accustomed both to the folly and the wisdom of those
who come here from other lands, and have learned to know
who is truly wise and who is foolish among you.' Having
spoken in this fashion, he bowed low to me, God be praised,

and all went their ways, I thanking God that He had placed
His words in my mouth, so that I might have honour in the
land of Sinim.

It was in these days of Tevet, after the Sabbath Vayiggash,[15]
that Eliezer of Venice, Lazzaro del Vecchio and Nathan ben
Dattalo, peace upon them, made preparation to journey to
Chinscie, which is the capital city of the realm and the place
of the palace of the king.

It stands at a distance of twenty days' journey from the
City of Light, but from the narrowness of the road the way in
many places is hard, with dark forests in which brigands are
found and torrents so swift that travellers may not pass. There
are also ferocious and very numerous lions and lionesses,[16]
lynxes, leopards, and other wild beasts, so that it is perilous
for travellers to pass through that country unless a large
number of persons go together. For the lion is an attested
danger. Indeed, many have been the traders who have
perished, God forbid, in the jaws of wild animals and
monsters on the way.

Furthermore, it being my custom when seeking choice
goods to go without an escort, or with but one or two
persons to give me aid, the better to find where the greatest
profits lie and lest others with little knowledge gain from my
judgment, I declared to them that I should not accompany
them but go only in the realm of the City of Light, where all
things desirable and needful are to be found. For, as I shall
tell later, there are many cities and towns at one or two days'
journey from Zaitun, where there is much trade and rich
profit.

In addition, I feared greatly not only the poisonous snakes
that are to be found on the road, but also the dangerous
monkeys with faces like dogs and wolves which cause great
harm to those who go by that way. Yet of all these beasts I
feared most those monkeys with a face very like a man's, and
which strike terror into travellers' hearts. For they seem in

very truth to be not beasts but men, which God forbid.
Indeed, such harmful creatures come upon the world, as our
sages teach, peace upon them, because of the profanation of
the Holy Name, may God be magnified and honoured.
Thus, so great is the idolatry among the Mancini that if the
traveller were to spend the night out of doors, he might fear
that he would be immediately eaten alive. Hence, in order to
display such peril to travellers, a large number of bones are
placed along the road, which serve as a warning to those who
pass by.

But I also had great fear of finding the Tartars on the way,
as well as that the Son of Heaven, being advanced in years,
might die, for then no man is safe, above all he who carries
rich goods upon the road.[17] Nevertheless, the said Eliezer and
Lazzaro urged me many times to go with them, to whom I
answered with the words of our sages that a wise man should
not seek out the courts of princes. Moreover, I kept from
them, God forgive me that I should say less than the truth,
that I had been summoned by the sages of the city to go
before them in order to speak of my land and faith,[18] and
thus to gain greater honour among the wisest of the place, for
which God be praised.

Therefore, having given many instructions to Nathan ben
Dattalo as to the precious things which I desired him to
purchase, I turned my heart to God, may He be exalted.
Whereafter, on the fifteenth day of Tevet, the Sabbath prayers
having again taken away the iniquity of my deeds, for which
God be thanked, I went with Lifenli to the great chamber of
the sages in order to speak there about my land and our
world, as they had requested me to my honour.

Here I found that there were again gathered a large number
of the sages of the city, who showed me much love and
respect, declaring that the words I had spoken earlier in order
to bring peace to their quarrels were those of a guide greater
than any who could be found among them, and that they
wished to learn from me of the way of life in my city, of the

lot of the Jews and the Saracens in Christian lands, and of
many other things.

Thus a certain Ociuscien, a great sage among them whom
they call a *sciansciuposci*, having said much in my praise as a
learnèd master of great lineage, called on me to speak and I
expressed myself in this fashion: 'I pray you, sires, insofar as I
know and can speak it through the tongue of another, to have
patience with my poor words. For I fear to cause you
displeasure, at a time when your city stands in such danger,
for this I have learned from the noble Pitaco, who is surely
among the wisest of men.

'Nor should I lightly think that I can teach any learnèd
man among you that which he does not already know. For
here are to be found those esteemed to be the wisest of your
city, which is truly one of the greatest cities of the earth both
in its riches and in its travails. But my father's home is a much
lesser city, that of Ancona, where my people have been for a
thousand years. The means of life of the said city come from
trade, Ancona being a great port, to which come large
numbers of ships and galleys, and which is subject to no king
but only to those men who are chosen by the chief citizens to
be their consuls.

'But among such principal citizens the Jews are not
counted, although some among them are both noble and rich.
For it is not permitted to them to govern the city, by
ordinance of the Church of Rome, even though my brothers
may freely come and go and may trade with whomsoever they
will, being greatly skilled in the manufacture and commerce
of the country, and having much wealth in ships, land and
other things. Among us, as well as great and small merchants,
there are also vintners and bakers, workers of cloth, as dyers
and tailors, and of metal, as of gold and silver, and fishermen
also, for there are among us those who are poor, may God
help them.

'In our language and means of life we do not much differ
from the Christians, many of my brothers finding their

companions, servants, nurses and even their cooks among
them, and living beside them even in the same streets and
houses. We also purchase eggs and cheese from them and they
meat from us, while we let our mills to them and they their
presses to us. So, too, our garments are cleaned by them and
their garments are dyed by us, and we also go to their tanners
in order that hides might be prepared for our Scrolls of the
Law, may God be praised for His bounty to His people.
Moreover, we give charity to their poor as to our own,
although they do not do the same.

'For, despite much love which is shown to my brothers by
the nobles of the city, and even by certain of their priests,
peace be upon them, and although the mark of Cain, which
is to say the red sign of the Jews, is not displayed by us
where other men may easily see it, but on the inside of our
clothes so that it cannot be discerned, yet it is the purpose of
the Church of the Christians to divide us from our
neighbours.

'I will treat the matter, sires, as reason demands, for, under
the protection of kindly princes, as in the mark of Ancona,
my brothers may live in peace, and we may govern our affairs
according to our Law, which is the Torah, having our own
place of worship, spiritual court, hospital and other places
besides, for which God be praised. Yet none of us may know
what our fate would be if a new noble or priest were to come
upon us like a Haman, our tormentor, which God forbid.
Nor may we find ease when for every misfortune, every
plague, and every sickness of man or beast the common
people blame us.

---

'FINDING ... SERVANTS, NURSES ... AMONG THEM'

*A decree of the Third Lateran Council (1179) formally forbade Jews to have
Christian servants or nurses for their children, but it was plainly flouted in Ancona.
(To have a Christian children's nurse was also forbidden to Jews by the Mishnah.)*

'In some places in the Christian lands, as in Bohemia and
Burgundy, my brothers are even taken in pawn by their
princes, may they be cursed, being exchanged among them
until they have no human use and are abandoned like beasts.
But in our land a Jew may live as a man among men, for
which God be blessed, although often a priest … will declare
that we come to sully the Christian life, they seeking either to
make our faithful convert, which God forbid, or by force to
hear their preaching against us, or even to drive us from
them.'

Thinking with great bitterness of the dolours of my
brothers in the terrestrial world, and of the cruelty of those
who profess the faith of love, for a moment I fell silent, upon
which the merchant Anlisciu rose to his feet and said as
follows: 'The lesser prays to know of the greater something
more of the hatred of the Christians for the Jews and the Jews
for the Christians, since we have little knowledge of its true
causes.'

To which I replied as follows: 'The Christians, sires, say
among themselves that the man whom they worship as an
idol was the King of the Jews, yet the Jews know no such
king. Moreover, they also declare among themselves that at
the end of days our people will be saved by this same messiah,
may God preserve me from the blasphemy of my words. But
in the meantime their friars preach that we are a depraved,
perverse and damned people because we will not bend our
knees to the Jewish God of the Christians, may the Holy One
be blessed.

'Thus, there was never such wickedness and folly, for in the
cities of my land, the princes and nobles, and certain of the
priests and common people also, greatly esteem the Jews,
protecting us from the cruelty of those who hate us. Hence,
they permit us to break the laws which would bring us to
wretchedness, even visiting us in our homes, eating at our
tables with a good heart, and permitting our learnèd men to
teach their children. Indeed, to some who ask it we teach our

language and the nature of our ways, so that there are even
those among the Christians who become Jews, despite the
suffering that will be theirs, and the peril that they should lose
their lives. But we are commanded by our sages, as our
teacher Mose ben Maimon also instructs, to love them more
than we love our own, seeing that they have chosen with their
own will to be among us, while we were chosen by God, may
He be magnified and exalted.'

After he had heard me, Anlisciu, bowing, sat down and
remained silent, and another, the sage Lolichuan, who in their
language they call *mincinciuscien* and who was much revered
among them for his learning, rose and expressed himself in
this way: 'The humble one addresses the pious doctor,
acknowledging with good will that he is the wiser. Thus the
sage one declares that in Christian lands some among the
Christians, learning of the ways of the Jews, become Jews. But
since the Christians, as you have averred, preach against the
Jews and condemn them for their errors, do not many Jews
succumb and themselves become Christians, in order to avoid
pain and death?'

To which, having understood his words by the mouth of
Lifenli, I replied: 'Alas, may God have mercy upon us, some
of my brothers indeed do so, either for their own good or for
the good of their sons, having no strength to resist, becoming
Christians not in their hearts but upon their lips alone.'

But having answered in this way, I was again constrained to
weep for the sufferings of Israel, upon which the said sage
Lolichuan asked what were the thoughts of a Jew upon seeing
the cross of the Christians. To which I replied that in his heart
he recoils, seeing extended upon the cross the idol of him
whom those who blaspheme against the Holy Name, blessèd
be He, declare to be both our messiah, which God forbid, and
the son of the Lord of Lords, God spare me, this being against
the law of reason, of nature and the holiness of God, may He
be exalted forever. The Christians say also that their idol was
killed by us, God forbid, maintaining that we are treacherous,

yet it was not we but the Romans who did the deed, if such a
deed were done. They say also that we are usurers, yet usury is
forbidden to us by the Law of our teacher Moses.[19]

'Moreover that law which the Christian preaches is not his
own law but the Law given to us by God, as that a man may
not kill or rob or be an adulterer or bear false witness. Thus
do we not with justice say that the Christian should forbid
evil-doing against all those made in the image of God and
against their possessions, seeing that he has learned the will of
the Lord from us?'

To which the merchant Anlisciu, rising and bowing in his
place, replied with much humility, asking which of the
teachings of the Christians were most unworthy for a Jew to
believe. Whereupon I answered Anlisciu in great anger, for
which God forgive me, saying that all is unworthy which
denies the evidence of the senses or is against reason, nature
and the will of God, such as the incarnation of God in man,
and the birth of a child to a woman without congress with
man. To which Anlisciu again humbly replied, bowing
towards the ground and wishing that in their city I might find
happiness and profit. Whereupon he asked that I speak to
them plainly about the nature of God, blessèd be He.

Hence I declared that God, may He be exalted, is neither a
body, nor a force in a body, nor can possess a body, nor may
become incarnate in a body. But the Christians, being
idolaters, falsely and impiously attribute to God, may He
have mercy and pity upon the world and upon Jew and
Gentile, both substance and place, quantity and quality,
relation and time, and thus give to the Unspeakable Name the
body of an idol, may God the exalted spare me for such
words.

Thus they see the Holy One as if He were in the heavens,
while we may say only that the Lord is Our God, the Lord is
One. But if we should speak of the hand or the arm of God,
this is not to speak of substance or of a corporeal thing, but it
is a figure composed of letters and words, by which to convey

the force of an incorporeal thing through the sound of our corporeal mouths.

Likewise, when we speak of the voice of God, which was heard by the ears of our teacher Moses, this was not the corporeal voice of God but a sound directed by God to the corporeal senses of man. For these senses, having little power, may hear and see only certain things, just as the understanding of man is not able to grasp the word of God, unless it accords with that which the mind of a man is able to know. Therefore, when the Holy One declares that nothing is unseen by Him, and speaks of His own eyes, it is not because He is a corporeal being, but so that men, knowing that the eye is the seat of human sight, may thus better understand the meaning of His word. But men themselves may not describe or depict the Holy One by such means, for thus idols are made, which God forbid.

The merchant Anlisciu again rose, enquiring whether a Christian might make an idol of his god by other means also, contrary to the teachings of the Jews. To which I replied that he might do so, as when he occupies the whole of his life with prayer. For to fulfil our worldly tasks in the company of other men is truly to worship God more perfectly than to pray to Him in solitude day and night, as do the Christians idolatrously in their convents. Thus, it is asked by us, Who shall go up for us to heaven and bring it to us that we may hear it and do it? To which our sages answer that it is they who lead a life of duty in the world, and not those who hide their faces from it, in thought only of their souls, who shall bring the truth of God to men.

With this answer, Anlisciu appeared much pleased, God be praised, and, bowing low, gave me thanks for my wisdom.

Now there rose to his feet another, a judge of the City of Light by name Cauiau, a man greatly advanced in years and with a goitre in his neck, who enquired of me with a smile what I should say of the Saracens or Mahometans, and whether they were to be thought better or worse than the

Christians. At which there was much laughter among the
sages who were assembled to hear my words, for which
honour may God be thanked.

I answered as follows: 'The Saracens are our brothers, for
we are together of the seed of Abraam, peace upon him, and
few there are among us who cannot speak their tongue.
Therefore, we are able to speak freely with them, which the
Franks may not do. Moreover, since we and they, but not the
Christians and other idolaters, hold that God is One, we are
also brothers in faith. Thus it is that the Christians' Pope,
having equal fear of us for our hatred of their idols, imposes
the sign of Cain upon both the Saracens and the Jews, a thing
that weighs equally upon us, may God remove such burden.

'The Saracen agrees with us also in the circumcision of the
male member as in hatred both of idols and of swine's flesh, as
also in reverence for the Holy City and in the eating of no
meat save that of his own killing. Thus in the houses of the
Saracens, our sages declare, a Jew may eat even their meat,
provided only that he has great hunger and that no other
good meat can be found. For the Saracen not only abhors the
pig but draws off the blood of cattle as is proper. Therefore, I
too have eaten among them, but only when my hunger was
great, may God forgive me if anything unclean has passed my
lips.'

Whereupon the merchant Suninsciou, a man much feared
in the city by reason of his wealth, rose, and with hands
folded as though in devotion, asked to know further about
the arguments which the Saracens and the Jews use against
the worship of idols.

To him I answered: 'In the whole terrestrial world the Jews
and the Saracens alone may not worship idols, for which God
be praised. For all others, among whom are the Christians,
bow down before images of wood and stone, touching them
with their fingers in reverence, which thereafter they kiss with
eyes raised to heaven or with a sigh, or place flowers and other
offerings before their effigies, even believing that such effigies

and idols may serve them in their sicknesses and misfortunes. For such is idolatry, it being the worship not of One God Who possesses neither human nor any other form, but of the artifices of men set in blasphemy upon an altar or a throne.'

In this fashion I, Jacob of Ancona, spoke in fear of the Lord, the sages of the city being so greatly surprised as not to know what to say, for they heard my words in silence while some whispered behind their hands.

Therefore I continued: 'Sires, the Saracens often profess love for my brothers, so that in their lands they even build their mosques near our houses of prayer, also following many of our customs and manners, as I have observed. Yet in times past, as all men know, their ancestors worshipped the sun, which God forbid. Moreover, as our teacher Mose ben Maimon declared, none has done such harm to Israel than the tribe of Ishmael, which is the tribe of those who worship Mahomet.'[20]

Whereupon another of their great sages rose up with intonations of anger, declaring in a loud voice that I was an ingrate, for he had heard tell that the greater part of the learnèd books of the Jews are written in Arabic, not in our language, and that thus, as the Sinimiani maintain, we are of one people and mind. To whom I replied: 'It is true, sire, that they are near to us in some forms of their teaching and learning, and that, being more learnèd than the Christians, they have shown more nobility of soul towards us than have the Christians, who throw our Torah in the flames,[21] may the Holy One preserve us and in Gehenna punish such transgressors. Yet a Jew cannot trust a Saracen more than a Christian, for each, when he is taken by the fever, may turn his anger upon us.'

At my words there rose another sage among them, who cried out that he had heard tell that the Jews lived in great wealth among the Saracens, being esteemed and loved by them as brothers, to whom I replied in this fashion: 'True it is that in certain lands of the Saracen, and of the Christian also, we have attained the highest rank and praise. Thus, in the times of Samuel Ha-Nagid, blessing upon him, a Jew ruled a kingdom in Spain of the Saracens as though he were its true prince. But the caliphs of Arabia drove out both Christians and Jews from their lands, just as the Saracens have left destroyed the sacred places alike of the Jews and Christians in the Holy City, for which may God's curses fall upon them. Nor is a Jew permitted to cancel from his heart that the Saracens drove both Jews and Christians upon pain of death to change their faiths, putting to the sword those who remained firm. Nor may a man of my city, be he Jew or Christian, not record that the Saracens laid its riches waste, also sparing neither woman nor child, may they rest in peace.'[22]

Whereupon, hearing these words, the merchant Anlisciu again rose and, with the demeanour of a brother, for which God be praised, declared that the Saracens being the foe of both the Jew and the Christian, there must needs be the more love therefore between them.

Hearing which, I grew angry, saying that the love of the Christian for the Jew was not increased by such things, from the difference of spirit between them.

There are also some who declare, for so I spoke, that the whole body of Saracens is evilly disposed to the whole body of Christians and they to them. But this also is not the truth, as the confraternity of all merchants in every place may show. Neither is it true that the whole body of Saracens and Christians is evilly disposed together to all the Jews, nor all the Jews to them, nor the whole body of Saracens and Jews to the Christians, nor they to them. Yet I have heard tell from a Christian that the Saracens and Jews together thirst for Christian blood, for it is as though each believes that the others, whether together or separately, intend harm to them.

But it is true also that in the eyes of the Saracens both the Jews and the Christians are infidels and have been together attacked by them, as by the caliph Al-Hakim and by the princes of the Berbers.[23] Yet in the eyes of the Christians, my brothers act secretly and in concert with the Saracens in order to bring harm to their Christian faith. But this may not be so, since the Holy Koran of the Saracens forbids to a Mahometan even friendship with a Jew or a Christian, lest the followers of Mahomet become at one with them.

And who does not know that the Saracens and Christians have gone hand in hand against us, at such times as they have not been given over to the slaughter of one another? For this is so even though my brothers live in friendship and trade with both, and have many partners among them, as with the great merchants of Fustat, Edente and Alessandria and other Saracen lands, and with those of Aragon, Marsiglia, Genova, Vinegia and other Christian cities. Moreover, each has separately engaged in the killing of my brothers, God rest their souls, as when in Medina, at the first beginning of the religion of Mahomet, the sons of Israel were put to the sword upon the order of the Prophet. And who does not know that in the time of Josef the Nagid, my brothers, peace upon their souls, were slain upon our Sabbath by the Saracens, may curses rain down upon the evil-doers?[24]

Yet, the Saracens call us their brothers in Abraam, for Ishmael, the father of the Saracens, was the first son of Abraam and elder brother of Isaac, may his memory be revered, who was our own forefather. But of Abraam the Saracens say in their scriptures that he was not a Jew, may God spare me, but not of the idolaters either, which God forbid, for he had surrendered in his heart to the Holy One. However, the Saracens, not being idolaters as are the Christians, may justly say of themselves that they are our brothers, they also denying in their holy book, God be praised, that the Jews killed *that man*, for which may God, the Exalted One, in His justice keep them also.

Whereupon I continued as follows: 'But the fear of the Christians for the Saracens is the greatest of all, so that to conquer them is their vain hope. Thus, the Christians look to

the Tartars to join with them against the Saracens, the Tartars
from their side and the Christians from theirs. Hence it is that
the Saracens, knowing of such stratagems, are the more eager
to establish themselves as counsellors to the Great Cane, so
that he may not join with the Christians against them. Thus I
have learned, sires, that at the court of the Lord of the Tartars
in the city of Sciandu the Saracens hold great power over the
Cane, some even claiming that he has been bewitched by
their astrologers, and others that the Saracens have charge of
all his treasures, so that he goes in fear of them.'

Hearing these words, for which God be praised, one of the
great sages of the city cried out that I spoke truly and that all
such things were known. At which others among them
laughed, while yet others, who were the larger part, urged that
I continue, chief among them being those of the party of the
merchant Anlisciu, to whom at my command the faithful
Lifenli spoke in their tongue certain words in grace, at which
the said Anlisciu was much pleased. I therefore expressed
myself in this fashion, some of the sages listening in silence and
others whispering among themselves: 'The Christians dream
that they may convert the Tartars to their faith, so that
together they may conquer all the Saracen lands and the sign
of the cross be seen in every place upon the earth, which God
forbid.

'Be warned, therefore, that the Franks who come to the
realm of the Great Cane seek only to drive the followers of
Mahomet from the terrestrial world. Moreover, they seek such
an impious end with vain hope, for, although it is said by
some that the Franks are better soldiers than the Saracens, the
Saracens show themselves to be so greatly fierce in the name
of Mahomet that they are more willing even than the
Christians to be killed for their faith.

'But it is no more to be borne that the Saracens should rule
over the Christians of all lands than that the Christians should
rule over them. For each is equally given to evil-doing against
the other, but both to evil-doing against the Jews, as I have

declared. Indeed, a Jew may not trust to be under the
command of either one or the other, for the Christian is
much given to spite against us and the Saracen to envy, so
that our dignity they call arrogance, our humility baseness,
and our anger against them treason.'

To these words the sages of the City of Light listened with
great approval, God be praised, so that I felt as a man who
had rightly served the Holy One and His people. Whereupon,
Ociuscien arose again, and, being learnèd in various faiths
and teachings, did me honour in his speech, for which God
be thanked, and expressed himself to the other sages about
him in this way: 'The lesser,[25] although little learnèd in the
matter of the Jews, for there is none whose learning may be
compared with that of the greater, knows that Abraam was
the founder of your faith, and that after Abraam came Moses,
who established the Law and gave the sacred books. In the
time of our king Migti the followers of Moses, to whom we
then gave the name *tachincho* and later *ciuhu*, came to our
land from Siiui, but some say that they came even in the time
of the Ciou.[26] Others declared that the *ciuhu* and the
followers of the prophet Mahomet are of the same people and
may not be distinguished from one another. For they say that
both are *oui*, the Jews being those *oui* who cut out the nerves
and sinews from their meat,[27] and the Mahometans being the
same *oui* who abstain from the pig.'

But, hearing such words, I denied that it was the truth, the
Jews and the Saracens not being the same people, while the
Jews also abstain from the pig, God be praised. Whereupon,
another of their sages, a certain Cian, declared without
knowledge that the Jews worship heaven in the same manner
as those of Sinim, as well that the true author of the Torah
was Abraam, may God spare me for my words, and that in
the time of Migti the Jews gave tributes of cloth from Greater
India to the said king.

To this Cian I replied that he did not have true knowledge
of our people, at which he, being a sophist, grew angry,

declaring as follows: 'We know that your law is to worship
heaven, to honour parents and to venerate the dead. It is
above all by duty to parents that you believe a prince is served.
Indeed you do not greatly differ from us, your Sabbath having
been observed by us in a more ancient time than that of
Abraam, and the letters of your language being like the letters
of the time of Ciou. We also know that you excel in
cultivation of the soil, in merchandise, in laws and in warfare,
and are highly esteemed for fidelity of every kind.'

I answered Cian as follows: 'Your words are of great truth,
little truth and falsehood, since we do not worship heaven,
God forbid, nor excel in war, nor venerate the dead, nor was
our Sabbath celebrated by others before the time of our
ancestor Abraam, upon whom be peace, nor is our language
akin to that of the people of Sinim.'

Whereupon another of their sages rose up, declaring that
the Jews and the Saracens are one, having coloured eyes and
noses like beaks, together with a hatred of the pig, at which
there was great laughter among them.

To which I answered that Jews have eyes as other men, and
noses neither large nor small but well made. Nor do we hate
the pig, although it is unclean, but only forbear to eat it.
Hearing which, one of their sages shouted in rough manner
that I was as all my brothers, having dark eyes and the nose of
a hawk, upon which Ociuscien, may his name be recorded,
rose in great anger, declaring that he wished to hear none of
such words and reproaching them in their lack of courtesy
towards a stranger of goodwill.

Therefore to Ociuscien I bowed with grace, saying that my
brothers, having been in the land of Sinim since the fall of the
Temple, may the perpetrators of the deed be cursed for
evermore, were worthy not of reproach but of honour. For
even the Christians say that it was my brothers of Persia who
first carried the art of making silk to Sinim, we having known
for many ages the way to raise the silkworm and to spin its
thread. Whereupon there was more anger shown to me, many

shouting that my words were false and that their ancestors
had known such art at the beginning of the world, which no
man may believe.

But now there arose again the said Cian, God forbid, who
declared that notwithstanding my words the Jews were
deserving of reproach and spoke as follows: 'It is certain that
even if the beliefs of the Jews, the Christians and the
Mahometans differ, your holy writings teach that you have
the same creator and father, for this I have rightly understood
from my studies. You must then be brothers, not according to
your faith but as men. Why therefore do you reject one
another so, and desire to do each other harm?'

To this question I replied as follows, for which God be
praised: 'You declare truly that we are brothers as men, for
all men are made in the image of God. Moreover, Abraam,
peace upon him, was father through Hagar to Ishmael, and
through Sarah, peace upon her, to Isaac, may his memory be
blessed, so that the first followers of Mahomet were of our
blood. And since *that man* who is blasphemously
worshipped as a god by the Christians was in truth a Jew and
his followers Jews also, it is from the Hebrews that their faith
has come. Yet we may not consider ourselves to be united
with them, for the laws and duties which were given to us
were given by God to no other, may God be magnified for
His bounty to Israel. Thus their worship is not ours, nor do
they forbear to preach against us in their mosques and in
their churches, for which may there be a curse against them
all.'

Whereupon Cian, not being content, asked as follows: 'But
how may we explain such difference of the injunctions of
God, if God be One?' To which I answered, God be thanked:
'It is because men are different, some perceiving God in one
way and some in another, and God granting to each that
which is most fitting to him. The greatest truth He
vouchsafed to that people which was most worthy to receive
His teaching, that we might thus be a light to other men.'

To which Cian, being a man without wisdom, declared in a loud voice, and without rising from his place: 'You therefore argue that hatred between the Jews, the Christians and the Mahometans is a natural custom.'

To which I replied: 'Hatred between men of reason is against nature. But fear of those who hold opinions which are against reason is not against nature, nor suspicion of those who act against their own beliefs, as do the Christians. Moreover, even if there is much understanding among us about our brief lives, or the marvels of the created world, how often are such concord and shared knowledge struck down by hatred, from which it is the Jews, may God keep us in safety, who are most frequently driven from their homes by the others, with the loss of their possessions and even their lives.'

To which Cian answered: 'But is it not you who are worthy to be blamed, for it is averred that you close your doors to others even when they wish you no harm?'

I replied: 'We have learned from our forefathers, peace upon them, that the opinion of others towards us cannot long be trusted. For he who loves us most today, should he think that we have given him offence, hates us most on the morrow, while many who seem to smile upon us when we are before them, speak evilly against us when we are at a distance. Therefore, we carefully guard our well-being, not knowing whom we may rightly trust.'

To which Cian declared that it was not our suspicion nor the hatred shown to us which drove us to stand apart, but our pride, from which we believe that Israel[28] alone possesses wisdom and understanding and that other men are in darkness. To which I again made reply that to reason that Israel alone possessed such things was not wiser than to argue that Israel alone possessed neither wisdom nor understanding, as the Christian friars reason, may curses be upon them. For not only are all men made in the image of God, but that which is truly spoken remains the truth, whosoever's the lips that pronounce it and whatever be his faith.

I also declared: 'If the son of a Gentile were to become more learnèd in a way that was appropriate to him than any son of Israel in a way appropriate to him, then that Gentile son would surely be nobler than our son and possess the greater soul. But should a Gentile study and master even our Torah, he to us is as worthy of honour as the High Priest himself, as Rabbi Meir has justly declared. Neither is it our pride which judges such things, although even the sea divided to let the Hebrews pass, and our lawgiver Moses descended from the mountain Sinai carrying the words of God as a guide for all generations.'

To which Cian replied in anger that thus I showed the pride of which all men made complaint, and that the Jews of the city of Zaitun, as well as the Jews who came to them from afar, were of like demeanour.

Whereupon I argued thus: 'The Jews have cause for their pride. For who does not know that our Jeremiah was the teacher of the Greek Plato, and that the great Aristotle, may his name be recorded, learned at the feet of Simon? Moreover, sires, every Jew in the world, however simple, is lettered. For the Jew who, being a bumpkin, is unable to study the Torah is no Jew, and must remain outside.'[29]

But at these words of mine the said Cian declared in the heat of his anger that thus I yet maintained that only the lettered Jew was worthy to be called wise in the entire world,

---

'JEREMIAH WAS THE TEACHER OF THE GREEK PLATO'

*The tradition that the Greeks derived much of their learning from Jews is a deep-rooted one (especially among the Jews), and even Nietzsche raised the possibility that Socrates was a Jew. In addition to the assertions of Jacob here, there is uncertainty — according to the Jewish intellectual tradition — as to whether Philo Judaeus was influenced by Plato or vice-versa. It is also believed that Aristotle studied the Septuagint, while the Talmud asserts that Rabbi Yehoshua ben Chananya engaged in debate with the sages of Athens (Bechorot, 8b).*

for only he who studies the moral law according to the Torah
becomes truly learnèd. To whom I replied that it is not only
the Torah but man's reason which teaches him the moral law,
permitting him to distinguish good from evil even if he is
unlearnèd, at which answer Cian did not know what to say
and fell silent, God be praised.

Thus I spoke of the Jews my brothers, may God keep them
in His hand, as was my duty, telling the sages of the City of
Light of our laws and customs, declaring also that in
Christian lands, with the sign of Cain upon us, our safety is
not a certain thing, and that all our blessings come from God,
may He be magnified and lauded.

For the Christian often takes our lives and possessions, as
when the priests set him against us in the name of their god.
Thus, although the entire world may be the native land of the
Jews, as some say, yet every man must lay his head at night in
one place and no other. Moreover, our true home is Jerusalem
alone, we having only sojourn in other cities.

And if a man should say, as is said by the Christians, both
those who oppress us and those who have goodwill towards
us, that my brothers are often sad and dolorous, then such is
the truth. For even in the gladness of the Hebrews can be
heard the sound of grief, yet for all these things, alas, there is
just cause, and thus I spoke before the sages.

At which, being much moved, the noble Ociuscien asked
whether, if the lot of my brothers had been often so hard and
without solace, it would be thus in the future also, to whom I
answered as follows: 'In the future I see both greater glory and
greater affliction[30] for my people, both the flowering of our
sages in all lands and great harm done against us, may God
shield us from our foes.[31] For in the face of a Jew a Christian
is taught by his church to see not a man like he, born like all
men to die in hope of redemption by God, blessèd be He, but
a Cain whom no evil should spare, whether his deeds be for
good or ill.

'Thus each of my brothers stands often not before a friend

but one who accuses him, and in whose eyes he may read his true judgment even when the other seeks to conceal such judgment with words of goodwill and praise. But such judgment is also a blasphemy, for only God may judge us truly, as those who accuse us will also be judged at the end of days. Of these foes, sires, the Christian is the worst, for he has the will for cruelty in his heart, and looks always to our defects, examining us more closely for our defaults than he examines himself.

'Thus, such a one is quick to find the Jew in us even when we act as do all other men, and swift also to bridle, as when the fur of an animal rises upon its spine, should he see in us that which arouses fear and envy in his heart from the force of our minds, and this even when we are poor in body and possessions. Indeed, he thinks us, even when we are poor and simple, to be rich in wealth and stratagems, wise beyond nature when we are cautious, cunning when we are prudent, faithless when we have our own faith, avaricious when we store our goods against our foes, ambitious when we acquire learning, and deceitful even in our good deeds, as though they were done only for the purchase of place or favour.

'Therefore, such opinions on the part of the Christian permit us to be safe with neither good deeds nor bad. For the more we seek to appease them, the more often they choose to act against us. Thus I see much suffering and death prepared for us, which God forbid and shield His people, even beyond all that we have suffered before, unless the ill-will of the Christian towards us be checked by the reason and goodness of other men. For there are those whose hatred of us is sated only by the shedding of our blood, or by the taking of our possessions, or by driving us away from their cities.

'Yet since we remain tenacious in our faith as well as in our labours for ourselves and for others, and proud of the splendour of our wisdom, that we are thus so firm and unyielding goads others to hatred greater still.

'Hence it may come about, which God forbid, that a new

Haman will one day arise who shall seek to make us like the
dust in the threshing and, woe is me, to kill us all, may God
spare us such trial. Yet God will surely not abandon us to
slaughter, but, as He made the waves to close over the
Egyptians, will destroy our foes, first placing the Divine
Presence between their swords and our bodies, and thereafter
bringing us safe out of the sorrow of our Exile to the Holy
Land.

'Thus I see the enemies of Israel as if armed for battle,
making ready for our slaughter by hanging, by poison and by
the sword, yet I cannot see the slain, for which may God be
magnified and praised. For in my thought I see only the
flaming effulgence of the glory of God casting back the foe,
whose sight is blinded by the majesty of the Lord, and
thereafter the smoke of sacrifices rising to heaven from our
altars in thanksgiving for our salvation, for which may God be
magnified and revered.'

Having spoken in this way, I, Jacob of Ancona, fell silent
and said no more, the sages of the city also remaining silent
for a while. For by speaking thus of the salvation of the Jews I
had brought concord among them, God be thanked, and
their quarrels were thereafter stilled. Whereupon, the
merchant Anlisciu rose and, showing me much favour,
besought of me that I should speak more before them upon
another day concerning the wickedness and hypocrisy of the
Christians of the Frankish lands. And thus, accompanied by
the faithful Lifenli, I went away, all bowing low before me as I
passed, for which God be praised.

In the next days all my pious duties being fulfilled, for
which God be thanked, and the words of my oration to the
great sages of Zaitun having been carried to each part of the
city, for so Lifenli informed me, there came notice of many
brawls and clashes in the streets of the city between those of
the party of the noble Pitaco and those of the party of the
merchants and the people, so that all were obliged to remain
for safety within their houses.

Whereupon I was much beset by the evil woman Bertoni and the girl Buccazuppo, for the helmsman Turiglioni having been but lately buried, she had at once conceived a love for the faithful Lifenli, God forbid. For thus Bertoni secretly declared to me, swearing that it was so upon the heads of her children, and with many false tears lest the girl should find harm from it. For to Buccazuppo, being much taken with grief for Turiglioni, Lifenli, having become acquainted with her sadness, had spoken words of comfort and thus gained her love. Therefore, learning this, I summoned Buccazuppo to my presence, declaring that since she had been placed in my care in order that she should serve me, she might not stray from the path of her duty but was to consider only the danger to her soul. For I was compelled to speak thus in the manner of the Christian, for which may God forgive me. Nor might she think to remain in Manci with any man of the place without great danger to her life, the city being in peril from the approach of the Tartars and from the troubles among the citizens, so that each stranger should rather give thought to his escape. I told her also that I had ordered my ships to be prepared against the danger, and that we should soon depart.

At these words she wept greatly, declaring first that Bertoni had spoken falsely, and thereafter that the faithful Lifenli knew nothing of her love, it being hidden in her soul. Hearing which, I had now tender thoughts for the lost one, saying that it was better for her to keep silent before the woman Bertoni, also that I should keep her the more in my care so that no harm might befall her, and that although Lifenli was a man worthy of her love, she must think rather of her return to her native land. Moreover, I declared that for her faithfulness I should teach her her letters upon the voyage. Thus she went away, yet weeping still.

In these days, upon the twenty-fourth and twenty-fifth day of Tevet after the Sabbath Shemot,[32] there also came messengers to me at the house of Nathan ben Dattalo, the first that of the noble Pitaco, praising the wisdom of my

words before the sages of the city, of which he had received
report, yet warning that I would be better to stand well upon
my guard with those who sought my counsel. Thereafter,
there also came a messenger from the merchant Anlisciu,
who, declaring me to be a sage of sages, humbly called upon
me to attend with him at the house of the great Suninsciou,
so that thus I might learn more of the opinions of those who
secretly commanded the city.

To these having replied with the aid of Lifenli, there came
news from my brothers Nathan ben Dattalo, Eliezer of Venice
and Lazzaro del Vecchio, peace upon them, that, having
found great wonders of merchandise and art upon the way to
the city of Chinscie, they had purchased to great profit, for
which bounty they gave thanks to God, blessèd be He.

# CHAPTER SEVEN

# The Law of Freedom

AMONG THE MOST REMARKABLE PASSAGES in Jacob d'Ancona's manuscript are those describing the political debates that took place in Zaitun during the winter of 1271–2, as its elders and sages struggled with issues relating to the defence of the city against the Tartars and with even wider concerns as to government and order in general. Jacob's comments upon, and contributions to, these debates – if his account can be credited – also raise profound questions about the nature of his own views, for which further study will be required.

In my rather arbitrary division of the translation into chapters, we have in what follows an account of his 'private' exchanges with a rich merchant, whom he calls a *grande popolano* – literally 'man of the people' but which I believe to mean citizen and 'burgess' – on riches and poverty, on trade and profit, and on the virtues and vices of what we would now call 'welfare' and the 'free market'. The argument between the two merchants upon the duties of the rich and the expectations of the poor, and upon the benefits and risks of mercantile freedom – however it may have been elaborated after the event – is a sharp one and is terminated abruptly by the anger of Suninsciou at some of Jacob's responses. But its themes are not absent for long from the text, as Jacob is drawn – or permits himself to be drawn – deeper into the labyrinth of what he calls the travails of the city.

In the course of the discussion we are also given a tantalising glimpse of the 'life-style' of the rich merchant of the Southern Sung empire, with its 'conspicuous consumption', luxury and (in Jacob's eyes) greed. The merchant in him admires; the moralist in him condemns. Indeed, it was this tension between contrasting aspects of his character – the manuscript is a delightful mixture of witting and unwitting testimony upon Jacob's complex personality – which drove my translation on: the man stands before us in his many-sidedness, engaging fully with the dilemmas and challenges, moral and practical, which he believes confront him.

There then follows an account of Jacob's first attendance at an assembly whose exact political status is unclear, set up to debate the city's problems. The word Jacob uses – *concilio* – for this assembly would have meant to him a meeting of high functionaries, ecclesiastical or lay, for a special purpose, rather than a standing 'parliamentary' body; Jacob also uses the word *parlamento*, but only in the sense of a 'great parley', or (as we might say) 'talking shop'. The word, for him, seems not to have the sense of an assembly of representative citizens, despite the contemporary development in many parts of thirteenth-century Europe of 'parliaments of the estates'.

In this he may be considered 'old-fashioned' for his time, or perhaps in his piety unaware of (unconcerned with?) developments in the governance of Christian Europe. Nevertheless, the intensity of Jacob's engagement with the political problems of Zaitun, an engagement which grows almost to the point of obsession as the manuscript proceeds, reveals that he did not come unprepared intellectually for the arguments in which he claims to have been involved.

For Jacob's time was one in which the works of Cicero, especially his *De Officiis* [*On Duty*], of Avicenna and of Averroes influenced thought and discussion among scholars, Jewish, Christian and Muslim alike, on worldly matters, those relating to government included. Scholars traversed easily the boundaries between the worlds of God and of Caesar. Under the influence of Aristotle in particular, the nature of the body politic was a fit subject in mediaeval times for the speculation of the Jewish sage. Indeed, there is an old Judaic tradition, which was known in mediaeval Italy, that Aristotle himself became a convert to Judaism in his old age.[1]

But setting aside his 'old-fashioned' use of *parlamento*, to what extent does Jacob d'Ancona reveal familiarity with contemporary thought and argument in Italy upon how a city and realm should best be governed? The manuscript, in its discussion of political questions, freely uses Italian words current in Jacob's day, such as *città* and *cittade* (city), *cittadino* (citizen), *governo* (government), *regno* and *reame* (realm), and *terra* or *patria* for 'country'. We find *terra natio* also for 'native land', but it was of course too early for Jacob to have employed such terms as *stato* in the sense of 'the state', or *nazione* (nation).

However, he later shows himself 'modern' enough – certainly in relation to the more benighted thought of his own times – to suggest to his Chinese interlocutors that city representatives were required to be summoned and consulted on the plight of the city. (This can only mean that those present at the *concilio* were not formally chosen representatives as such.) He is also averse, in the Judaic tradition, to the monarchical principle and to absolutist rule. But, like Aquinas, he seems rather unaware of (or unengaged with) the then emerging contemporary belief, already held by some mediaeval jurists – and practised in some cities, including in Italy – that decisions concerning the people should be 'democratically' approved of by them, including by the rule of majority decision, even if such approval were to be given on their behalf by the majority of the principal citizens only. Moreover, it is most probable that Jacob's own city of Ancona already had a form of representative standing council in his own time.

The first documentary mention of a *podestà* (roughly, mayor) and consuls in Ancona is in a document found at the monastery of Tremiti and dated August 1128; these figures would most likely have been appointed or chosen (perhaps by majority vote) by a standing body of select citizens of Ancona qualified by birth, wealth and status, and almost certainly excluding Jews. Moreover, the principle of representation, whether by appointment or election, was also well established in the councils of the Church.[2]

Eventually, such early 'democratic' ideas and practices were challenged and supplanted, especially in the early and mid-fifteenth century, by such doctrines as those of absolute papal authority and the divine right of kings. But in Jacob's own day, political thought and practice ranged wider than his own observations and counsels reflect. Although his quick intelligence enabled him to understand the implications of the political and social turmoil he found in Zaitun, he does not appear to have been familiar with contemporary Western debate on such matters. Although tempered by his 'humanism' and scepticism, his political ideas seem (with the benefit of hindsight) to be, in their general tenor, more 'mediaeval' than 'early renaissance'.

There are good reasons, I think, for his relative distance from such questions. The best of them is that, as a Jew, albeit well connected and in good standing, he was (probably) not a citizen with full rights in his own city, while to the issue of conciliar rule in the Church he would, as a Jew, have been a stranger. Indeed, it is an irony that a man such as he should later have enunciated a theory of civic duty to the elders of a foreign city, as he claims he did, when it is most unlikely that he was a citizen himself.

Jacob's vivid account of the conflicting arguments between officials, merchants and others at the first session of the *concilio* largely ranges over issues he had debated privately with the merchant Suninsciou, upon the nature of freedom and the demands of order. In his own contributions moral concerns typically are uppermost, whether on the subject of the just price, or free will and choice.

The chapter ends with Jacob's description at second-hand of the Southern Sung capital Kinsai, and with a discussion upon the rights and comportment of women.

～

O n the twenty-seventh day of Tevet,[3] accompanied by Lifenli and Anlisciu, I came to the house of the great merchant Suninsciou, a man still young but having great riches and much feared in the city, as I have written. His was truly a grand palace, with many gateways, pavilions for feasts, and gardens, and its floors were inlaid with silver. For merchants newly grown very rich live with as much delight as if they were kings, and their women as if they were angelic beings, may God forgive my words, clothing themselves in the richest silks spun with gold.

Their houses are also richly worked and they go to huge expense to purchase ornaments, pictures and furniture. In addition, they buy much rare perfume, incense and medicine from the merchants of Greater India, sparing no expense upon choice things so that others may feel envy towards them. Moreover, in their habits and manners they follow the ways of the nobles, for they seek not only to live but to speak like them, so the faithful Lifenli informed me, so that they become objects of contempt for others. Nevertheless, they have possessions of great variety, to which they themselves pay great honour as if such things were the aim of their lives, which God forbid.

Of these possessions, of which some are of the greatest price which a man may pay, there are many of great beauty but without human use, as trees with leaves of gold and silver that by great art are made to rustle, and golden and silver birds, which stand among them, to sing. In addition, they go about the city upon horses with silver bits, yet at their feet are filthy things to which the horsemen pay no regard.

This Suninsciou is a grand burgess[4] with more than fifty servants who wait on him continuously. Thus when he takes his seat at table the dishes are brought to him in such a quantity that it is a marvel, and sometimes they feed him as if he were a pet bird, even putting the food into his mouth, a thing it is shameful for a pious man to see. Indeed it is said

that so rich is the said Suninsciou that in a hill to the north of
the City of Light he has hidden a store of gold and silver, so
much that it is greater even than the treasury of the Son of
Heaven. Yet, for all his wealth, he is said by many to be given
to great cruelty, whipping his children even in front of his
servants, but others declare him to be good and kind, while
others again declare that he is a robber who steals even from
the poor, God forbid.

Of his dress he takes great care, his shoes being of satin and
all his clothes of the finest silk, and he was perfumed in a
manner more fitting to a woman. Indeed, when he finds fault,
however small it be, with his dress he at once summons his
tailor to his presence in order that it be set right without
delay, but of the beggars who stand at his gate it is said that he
takes little care. Moreover, he goes about the city without
concern that it should be kept clean and that the stink of
night-soil be taken from it, yet when fruits are set before him
he would not eat them if they had not been washed.

The women of his house also wear silken robes of such
beauty that they were a marvel to behold, wearing in their
hair not only golden ornaments choicely worked by their own
craftsmen, but combs of ivory from Greater India and
Ciamba, and going about with their hair uncovered, the
better to display them. Moreover, at great banquets the wives
of the richest merchants of the city also wear coronets of
pearls upon their heads, so that a man should think not that
they were a new people[5] but truly noble. In addition, washing
themselves in water of sandalwood and alum, and carrying
much perfume about them, they smell most sweetly, so that
even within doors they seem as the flowers of a paradisal
garden, for which God be praised.

Yet, of such women, it is not only said that they pour out
gold and silver like water from a well, but that, although they
seem like beautiful foxes, they satisfy themselves in the
manner of dragons and lionesses. Furthermore, all the
desirous will of the richest among them is to be called to the

court of Toutson in Chinscie, and to take their places among
the lords and other great ones whom he feasts at his banquets.

Thus they seek that they and their consorts should live as
the nobles do, as I have written, summoning poets and singers
to their houses in order to give pleasure to their guests. But so
many are the followers whom they have about them in their
halls and gardens that the said accursèd[6] Suninsciou, although
yet a young man, appeared not as a merchant but as a prince
amid his vassals, and with riches so great that it was contrary
to reason.

Therefore I declared to him that our rabbis, peace upon
them, teach that even the richest should strive to live not only
according to reason but within the bounds of nature. To which
Suninsciou replied with disdain, saying that their sage Latsu
taught that nature not only shows no goodwill towards men
but has no care for them, making all things serve her purpose,
which may God forbid.

Having spoken these impious words, he continued as
follows: 'Those who follow the way[7] say that the highest
virtue obtains everything, but in the material world it obtains
nothing. Moreover, to seek riches is not in itself to fall into
avarice, just as poverty is not ordained by heaven. Only if the
rich man and the merchant use their wealth for wicked ends,
or deny the gods, are they to be condemned. For all depends
upon man's will for good and evil, and not upon the good or
evil of money in itself. And if trade is a danger to the soul, as
the Frankish priests who have come among us preach, how
else shall Zaitun live? Or do you too confuse wealth with
wickedness, and poverty with virtue, as do the Christians?'

To which I replied that not being a Christian, which God
forbid, I did not hold such an opinion, but rather that a rich
man ought to spend his wealth wisely, succour the poor, live
according to the laws of God and not yield to excess.

But for my words Suninsciou again showed disdain,
speaking as follows: 'Those who scorn comfort may do as
they wish, but he who is nearest to the fire is soonest

warmed.[8] Moreover, actions that cause men to rejoice in their souls are not those which are always good, nor is he who is ready to serve others always a man of virtue. Rather, he who depends on his own strength and pursues his own ends will attain the greatest happiness, while he who looks always to others, whether to please them or to gain succour from them, and whether they are gods or men, will never be requited.'

Whereupon, hearing such wicked judgments, which no man before had spoken into my ears, the great merchant Suninsciou having no praise even for the merit of giving, I replied as follows: 'I, sire, am also a merchant who seeks his profit and his own ends, venturing even to the furthest places of the terrestrial world in pursuit of gain. Yet, being a pious man, I seek also to obey God, blessèd be He, and to follow the teachings of our sages, may peace be upon them. Thus it is not given to us, however rich in possessions, to make other men believe that we have powers without end, for such is a blasphemy against the Holy One Who alone commands the heavens and the earth. Nor shall any man set his face or his hand against the poor and those who have need, but give them aid. For such is our duty both to God, may He be exalted, and to men.'

At which words, Suninsciou, his face becoming red, grew angry and his voice so loud that a man might have trembled at it, his servants being as though their bodies were frozen as the dead to hear its sound. He spoke as follows: 'You may give to another whatever you wish, for such is a matter for the free judgment[9] of man, but he who receives aid that is too large or too frequent becomes lazy and vicious. For he comes to beg for his bread as if it were justice, and takes that which is offered to him not as if receiving but as if granting a favour. Thus those who seek help will come to say not, We pray you to be willing to requite us, but, We are here to claim justice, or, We demand that you be willing to do your duty by us, while those who observe such vice say that for all this there is no help but in patience and prudence.

'But as our book of odes says, The gentleman enjoys only the food which he has earned, but the ignoble man takes pleasure in reward without merit, thinking that he has made a profit thereby. Indeed, such as he seeks out only that which he thinks to be his right and cares nothing for his duty.' For so the merchant Suninsciou declared, to whom I replied that he too seemed to have little care for his duty, for such are those who pursue their own ends without care for others.

To which words of mine he answered, showing me great scorn: 'The dog is a good judge who bites those who go in rags. Here each person has that which is necessary for a man's body upon which to live. Moreover, the air of the city makes a man free, while in the fields a man is slave to the soil. The citizens of the City of Light have a sweet life.'

To which I replied without fear, God be thanked, in this fashion: 'On the contrary, sire, there are some who have a sweet life beyond reason, many who have sufficient, many who have little, and others who have nothing. Moreover, although the City of Light is the greatest of all cities in the riches of its trade, so that nowhere in the entire world may be compared with it, yet its vices and perils are so great that a man must go in fear for his life and his possessions even in the midst of its great houses and ways. In this city there are also to be found pleasures and delights that bring shame both to the body and to the soul of man, so that even now the sword of God's anger, blessèd be He, stands ready to strike it down, for the Tartars approach its gates. Yet at the same time the citizens are divided among themselves, some being for this party and some for that, so that none can find the good path.

'In addition, among your great sages there is such hatred and evil-doing that the truth can no longer be found by them, and in the temples of your faith there remain only the old, for the young no longer follow the cult, as the noble Pitaco has declared to all. Yet the rich in their pride vaunt themselves upon their possessions, thinking that by trade and money alone come the blessings of human life, and that those who

have little may, by the strength of their wills, gain more and
thus become content. Fine silks and porcelains and other
things you have in abundance, yet all about you, sire, are a
thousand thousands who have lost their way and their souls,
of whom the great part, being young but unwilling to follow
the paths of their fathers, have lost even the means of life.'

In this way I reasoned, after which the great merchant
Suninsciou fell silent, looking closely upon me yet as if sunk
in thought, his servants also standing in silence about him,
and the faithful Lifenli as if taken with great fear.

At last, Suninsciou spoke as follows: 'You are too hard and
severe. Various are the defects to be found in man, but various,
too, are their virtues. For who does not know how to do at
least one thing better than others, even if he does other things
worse? But no one at all knows how to do everything, not
even the greatest of sages among us.'

Here he fell silent, so that I, Jacob of Ancona, began to
speak again, but he bade me hold my tongue and himself
continued as follows: 'In one thing alone we err, for our
offspring are in number without bounds, so that there is such
a great multitude of people in Manci that no vacant land will
remain that can be worked.'

To which words I replied: 'Then, sire, you wish free
judgment in all things save in the generation of men, yet it is
impious for men to interfere in the design of God, may He be
exalted.'

To which Suninsciou replied in great anger, so that it made
the words of Lifenli tremble, that I should have more care for
my own land which had need of my counsel, but that in his
own city all would be well at his command. Hearing which,
Lifenli advised me quickly in our tongue that we should
depart, but I chose, at God's will, to hold my ground,
declaring that it is man's duty to give care to the needy poor.

To which the merchant Suninsciou answered: 'The needy
poor who cannot raise their own children may give or sell them
to the rich, for in their houses they will be better brought up.

As to those who are healthy, they must be obliged to practise some trade, for when those who are neither sick nor advanced in age have no will to do so they instead cast themselves upon the mercy of others, or rob them as they pass.'

To which without fear I replied, God be praised: 'But I have heard tell from the noble Pitaco that the Son of Heaven no longer serves the poor with goodness in his heart as once he did, but having been counselled that to succour them in their need takes away prudence and strength from their souls, he has turned his face from them, which God forbid.'

Suninsciou, again showing contempt for my words, answered: 'It is not the duty of the Son of Heaven to serve the poor, but the duty of the poor to serve the Son of Heaven. Moreover, all men under heaven, be they rich or poor, noble or of humble birth, must make their way in the light of the sun or in deep darkness, according to their fate. Yet each, possessing his own good sense and strength, may also by his own will choose to live well or badly, faithfully or without faith, and with this purpose or another. Therefore, it is not the task of the Son of Heaven or of the rulers of this city to restrain men in their choices, for this is to make them less than men and to undo their virtues.'

Whereupon I replied as follows, the faithful Lifenli being at my side: 'Nevertheless, the poor murmur that their sicknesses are neglected and that only the rich are cured, that the water of the wells is no longer sweet, that children wander in the streets and that those who took night-soil to the gardens and fields beyond the city no longer carry out their tasks.'

To which the merchant Suninsciou replied in this fashion: 'You know nothing of our affairs, for the poor are of our party, and not of the party of Pitaco and the old men about him, who seek only their own ends and to return to the ways of their forefathers. For both the poor and the rich among us wish no obstacle to their desires, preferring even the Tartars to the curb of duty. Now there is no office for the protection of children, but neither are there dues for merchants of other lands, nor must a man any longer pay secretly to the *scibaso* so that his goods may be exempt from tax. Instead, just as men pass freely in the streets of the City of Light, so all merchandise may pass freely in its port, and all may grow rich. With such ends the Son of Heaven is also in accord, for, loving his people, he wishes their good fortune, knowing that, when the need of war arises, they will be the readier to pay for the defence of our realm, the more freely that in time of peace they may pursue their own desires.

'Moreover, no longer in the City of Light must the merchant fear the *cianinpancian,* nor is the trader from other lands constrained, whether he will or no, to sell gold and silver, and jewels and pearls, only to the Son of Heaven.[10] The ruler Ouaninsci is no more, for so we have decreed, and each may seek his own ends as he pleases, so that all may be contented in their own manner. For this is the law of freedom[11] against which no man can be a rebel, except those who would destroy the riches of the city and put out its light.'

These things the merchant Suninsciou spoke in a loud voice and full of haughtiness and pride, as if to bring fear to those who heard him. But having no fear, I declared that for each to do as he wills in order to gain his own ends is not the law of men but the habit of beasts, at which the said merchant became swollen with rage and his expression distorted.

To whom, again without fear, I spoke these words: 'If I should sell my noon and my night upon the market, God forbid, neglecting my duty to God, blessèd be He, there would remain nothing for which to live.'

Then Suninsciou demanded as follows, as though his throat were narrowed: 'Can a man feed and clothe himself who keeps only the truth and the just way before him, and calls in no evil to his aid?' To whom I replied that even if the wicked man gave himself to traffic in prayers and blessings, may God spare me for my words, yet his goods would remain accursèd.

To which Suninsciou, ordering me to leave his presence, replied impiously: 'As in cold weather fire burns with a clearer flame, so in matters of trade we should not permit excess of virtue to obscure its light,' at which his servants gathered closer about him as if before a foe.

Whereupon I took my leave of him, declaring that the first star of the Sabbath Vaera would very soon appear in the sky and that thus I was summoned to prayer, may God be praised. To which the wicked Suninsciou, laughing, answered thus: 'Wherever men are not put in mind of their duties by priests and sages they prosper and are at peace with one another.'

Having heard this, God forbid, accompanied by the faithful Lifenli I went away.

Now in the following days, which is to say at the beginning of the month Shevet,[12] there came news that in the city of Zaitun certain men had been killed who were of the party of Suninsciou, and others killed who were of the party of the noble Pitaco, so great had become the enmity that had arisen between them.

Therefore, in much fear for the safety of Nathan ben Dattalo, Lazzaro and Eliezer of Venice, peace upon them, I sent a messenger to them in Chinscie, so that if they were still to be found in that city they should make haste to return. Moreover, lest my life and hopes be lost, God forbid, if the confusion of the city should bring peril to all, I again ordered that my ships be made ready so that we might depart as quickly as we could, that my wares be loaded in good order, and that the mariners stay close to the harbour since none might know the day of our departure. The same things I told to my servants Bertoni and Buccazuppo, as well as to Rustici and Pecte, at which the face of Buccazuppo became pale, for it seemed that she had conceived a desire to remain in the city, albeit that she would give no answer to the questions I addressed to her, nor to the questions of Bertoni.

In these same days, which were the second and third days of the month Shevet,[13] a messenger also came to me from the house of the noble Pitaco, telling that the great officials of the province, whom they call in their language *ciciu* and *tunpan*, had ordered that the citizens of the City of Light should reach concord among them, for such was the command of the Son of Heaven. Therefore, they were bidden to come together in an assembly so that there might be a debate between them, rather than that one citizen should spill the blood of another. Moreover, since here they should discuss together all the travails of the city and consider rightly how it ought to govern itself, and since I was a man who had shown himself to be wise in such things, I too, although a stranger among them, might attend such assembly in order to hear the words that were spoken there. Thus the messenger of the noble Pitaco declared that, although I was a merchant of great renown in all lands, I had shown myself not to be of the merchants' party, but rather of the party of those who followed the way of goodness and truth, may God be exalted.

With the words of the messenger I was much pleased, declaring that I gave my humble thanks to his noble master, and that I should attend in duty to hear what was spoken.

Thus on the fourth day of Shevet, accompanied by Lifenli, I betook myself to the great hall of the prefect of the city, where were assembled all the higher officials and lords-deputy whom they call in their language *chuan*, together with a great number of merchants, sages and other citizens, among whom were also soldiers and guardians of the city. Indeed, such a throng was surely never before seen in an assembly, so many thousands were there gathered together in order to hold a great parley.[14]

Before those assembled in this place, the prefect spoke as follows: 'Sires, we are gathered here to make safe the city and we must let all speak in peace. For there is great disorder among us, so that we have become enemies to one another, each believing that he knows the way and that the other walks

in deep darkness. We must therefore go to the root of the
matter, determining what is the major point and what the
lesser, but treating all things as heaven demands. Nor should
we think that anyone is right in every way, for in each some
part of the truth may be found, as you will be able to hear.

'You know also that the chief counsellors of our Son of
Heaven, the sages Ciumin and Gaiudincia, being followers of
the wisdom of Menche, have guided him to decree that in our
city goods should be exempt from taxes. For, as the wise
Menche taught, where goods are exempt from taxes, there
traders will be pleased to come. Likewise, where there is no
tax to pay at the confines of a city, then travellers will be
pleased to unload their wares in such a realm, as also to go by
way of its roads, thus bringing wealth to such a city.

'Moreover, when such freedom is permitted to the people,
as the wise Menche instructed his disciples, then will they look
up to the governors of the city, which will thus have no equal
in the world. For by such measures the citizens will not only
become rich from the greatness of trade, but will work with
greater desire, being free from their former burdens. Thus, in
turn, the Son of Heaven and the city will each be unburdened
of their duties to the citizens, for these will be the better able
to avail themselves of their own means and labours.

'In this way our city has come to be ruled according to the
wisdom of Menche, so that each citizen may the better seek
his ends according to his free judgment, and by attaining such
ends bring benefit to the entire city. For the Son of Heaven
and his counsellors wish that in this city those who rule shall
be servants, not masters, of the people, and that each citizen
shall live freely with his fellows as a free man in a free
condition.[15] Moreover, the sage Ciumin has declared that in
such condition and in a great city the purposes of a citizen are
too diverse to be governed by a common rule as in other cities
of the realm. Instead, each must act with goodwill towards the
other, for it is not possible that a guardian should be placed in
every house and every street.

'Therefore, in order that men shall continue to live in free condition with one another, none should take up arms against the other, but permit each to go about in pursuit of his own ends, provided that such ends be lawful. For by these means each will find his wealth and happiness. But if he stands in the way of others, and others stand in his way in turn, all will be in great confusion under heaven, our riches will be lost, and each man will suffer harm.'

But hearing these words, the noble Pitaco, not permitting the prefect to continue, declared very bitterly as follows, many at first shouting against him: 'With such foolish arguments the Son of Heaven has been persuaded, not seeing that each liberty gives rise to another until all order is lost and can only with great difficulty be restored. For when a man is freely given to the pursuit of whatever thing he may choose, the curb cannot be reapplied without great complaint.'

Whereupon, many among the merchants and the people cried out against him, yet he continued as follows: 'In times past, we converted the barbarians of the north to our customs and usages but we were not converted to be as them. But now there have come among us those who, lacking true understanding of the wisdom of Menche, act in a manner which is against the law of heaven, destroying the ways of former days and turning their backs upon our teachers. A man may come from a dark vale in order to settle in a tall tree upon the summit, but he may not forsake the tall tree to descend into the dark ravine.'

To these words there were many shouts and cries, Pitaco in a loud voice adding as follows: 'Nor did Menche declare that the guidance of the city should be entrusted to its merchants, and that thus it should be brought to its ruin.' Hearing which, none would permit the noble Pitaco to continue, so great were the shouts of the throng, until the soldiers and guardians, upon the prefect's command, with heavy blows brought all once more to silence.

The noble Pitaco then spoke of their realm in this fashion: 'So far have the counsellors Ciumin and Gaiudincia led the mind of our Son of Heaven that they have turned him altogether from the just way, so that even the buying and selling of salt, of wine, of incense, and of all other things over which the realm had power may be conducted by anyone without hindrance. Indeed, even the prostitutes, whom once our Son of Heaven furnished to the ambassadors of other lands for their greater comfort, it has become the task of our merchants to provide.'

Whereupon, there were many shouts of anger against Pitaco, who nevertheless added: 'But now also the lands of the realm are sold, as well as the mines and the marshes. Yet, once, the Son of Heaven gave loans to the countrymen and administered the grain markets, and many were the workshops and warehouses of which the realm was formerly the possessor. But now all have fallen into the hands of the merchants, to do with as they choose.'

Yet the party of the merchants, of whom there were present more than one hundred, would by no means allow the noble Pitaco to continue in this fashion, the merchant Anlisciu crying out against the great officials, whom in their language they call *chuanceni*, as follows: 'But for how many lords-delegate and lords-deputy of the Son of Heaven were we constrained to find lodging out of our own pockets? Were there not three or four hundred of such idle clerks in our city, whose only task was to chase flies, finding default in all things, so that no man might move a stone from here to there without their permission? Now, let grace be shown to our noble leader Suninsciou, whose power shields us from such folly.

'For the office for ships is no more a burden upon our backs, nor their brokers who robbed us of our gains, nor is the office for buildings and houses-with-storeys permitted to spoil our labour. Neither is the trader from other countries forbidden to sell in the shops of the city, for we are all now in

a free condition, the demons who bit our flesh having lost
their teeth and claws.'

Whereupon, at these words spoken in a loud voice by the
said Anlisciu, there was much laughter among the merchants
and the people. But some also cried in anger that the sick
were no longer healed nor were children any longer under the
protection of the Son of Heaven, declaring that their houses
had been closed and those who were in them sent away.[16]

At which words, a certain Anscinen, being also a great
leader among the merchants and vying with the noble Pitaco
for speech, was given favour by the said prefect and the
guardians, replying as follows: 'Yet, sires, those who sold
medicines, being servants of our Son of Heaven, were guilty
of great wrongs against us. For those precious things which
are brought to us from other lands, and by which every man
may be cured, they sold only to the *chuanceni* and the other
officials and to the women of the court. Noble Pitaco, to such
unjust things we have brought an end, for now the merchants
of the city have them in their hands. Neither shall we permit
to continue the cruel power of those who command our
prisons in the name of the Son of Heaven, nor those who,
themselves inhabitants of darkness, teach only the oldest
things to our children. But we shall put in charge of both our
sons and our prisoners equally those who are best fitted to
bring light and yet more light to the city. Nor shall we
exempt the places of worship, for we declare that the debts of
the monks must be paid from the gifts of the faithful, it being
no longer just that it should fall upon the city to sustain
them.

'Nor shall we give aid[17] to the citizens as we gave it before.
For to give in excess to the poor is to do them harm, while to
give in excess to a very large number of families causes harm
to the city.'

At these words of the merchant Anscinen, there were now
great shouts of anger from among the people, of whom one, a
certain Oantatte, spoke with bitterness as follows: 'But why,

sires, should not the Son of Heaven give as before to the families of the poor according as one requests, such as for clothing in the wintertime? For is it not an act of goodness in itself, and also better that among the citizens there should not be any in great want? And is it not a worthy end to help the people so that they are able to live, work and increase their goods?'

To which the noble Pitaco replied as follows, all falling silent: 'As Menche teaches, a king cannot keep his realm within the four seas[18] unless he shows benevolence.'

Whereupon the merchant Anscinen asked him in anger: 'What then is the giving of help to the needy, according to your teaching?' To which Pitaco replied: 'It is an act of benevolence in accord with the command of heaven.'

At which words, Anscinen spoke as follows: 'But when such an act of benevolence is done by the rich, not at the command of heaven, but by means of dues imposed upon them, is it not the taking from one to give to another? Or should men leave their own fields to till the fields of another? Did not the same Menche teach that a man of true benevolence, such as our Son of Heaven, should not take from one in order to furnish another, but should seek to provide from his own pocket, leaving the rich to give when they choose and when the needy come to them for succour? For only thus are all enabled to act according to their conscience, being free to listen to its commands or not, according to their will.'

But at these words of Anscinen there was great derision on the part of some among the throng, upon which Oantatte, who stood in the ranks of the people, spoke as follows: 'It is the duty of the rich to give to the poor and, to those among the poor who are in need of work and gain, to furnish them so that they might live. For to such things they have a good right, being men among men.'

Pitaco replied: 'They do not have a good right to such things, but what is expected of the gentle heart are good

deeds. But even good will is harmed by those who say that
each should act according to his conscience.'

To which Anscinen answered with scorn that from the
counsels of Ciumin and Gaiudincia came riches, and from
riches came benevolence, at which many cried out in anger
against him.

Whereupon the noble Pitaco declared as follows: 'But you,
sires, destroy the very will to give succour to others.
Benevolence is a good in itself of which the poor also are
capable. For it does not derive from riches, but from a good
soul, of which the counsellors Ciumin and Gaiudincia have
no understanding. Moreover, whether you take half or double
or nothing of the tax which you took before, itself counts for
nothing, if you are unable to improve the virtue of the
citizens. For without virtuous citizens you will lose all.'

To these words of truth, for which God be praised, the
merchant Anscinen made impious reply: 'You mean by this
that we act without just principles. But our principles are
those of Latsu himself, who, declaring that the universe was
governed by fixed and natural laws, held in great contempt
those who sought to go in vain against the course of heaven
and to obstruct the will of men. Thus, none may seek,
without harm to all, to govern him who buys and sells
according to his choice and need. For each must be free to
pursue his way as he sees fit, since the will of man is the first
mover of all that brings bounty to the city. By destroying
such force the city also is destroyed, those who seek its
destruction in such a manner being greater enemies to us
than the Tartars themselves.'

But now, alas, there arose the learnèd sage Ociuscien, a
man tall and thin, who spoke in favour of the said Anscinen
as follows: 'The conduct of the merchant, sires, is neither
good nor bad. Moreover, having no concern for right or
wrong, it cannot be said that the merchant acts in order to
oppose the good. In addition, as Cienlian teaches us, we must
judge an action by its effects rather than by its causes, as we

must judge a man not by his robes or by his principles but by his deeds. Nor can it be said that the merchant brings danger to our city for, on the contrary, he brings to it the goods that it desires. Furthermore, the more goods that are sold, the more that are bought.'[19] At which foolish words many among the people could not forbear to laugh.

Nevertheless, Ociuscien continued as follows: 'Moreover, by his trading the merchant creates riches for others as well as for himself. From these riches spring many benefits for the poor, while, from his getting, carrying and selling, like an ant he sets an example to others of constant labour and gain. In addition, through his powers and those of his brother merchants, a means is gained not for the pillage of the city or for the destroying of its ways, but for the protection of the city from the tyrant who would seek to oppress its citizens with unjust tithes and dues, or otherwise to thrust himself upon them to their great harm.'

To him the great merchant Anscinen, bowing deeply, replied: 'The learnèd Ociuscien has spoken wisely. For, as Latsu teaches, fishes must not be taken from the water, nor man kept from the market, for the market is for the exchange of that which a man has for that which he lacks. Nor does it require anyone to oversee those who go thither to provide for or to find their needs.'

To which words Pitaco again made answer: 'Then you declare, sire, that it is better that the merchants should not only be without government, but that they should govern all things', at which many among the people shouted to him with praises. Whereupon, Pitaco added as follows: 'Moreover, you say that the merchants should be free to do as they choose without any to oversee them. Then why is it that you wish the judges of the city to carry out immediate justice if any dispute occurs among the merchants?'

To this question of the noble Pitaco, in which lay hidden the truth for all men, Anscinen answered in this way: 'We do not deny that justice should be done among us. However, we

declare that when the laws that govern us are bad and too
many, the people grow poorer and the realm is thrown into
confusion. The poor may even suffer great hunger not
because they are idle but because the officials devour all things
with their laws, while the more laws and decrees, the more
thieves and brigands there will be. Rather, you must govern a
realm as you would cook a small fish.[20] Thus, when the
people are difficult to govern, it is because those who rule are
foolish and their laws bad.

'Wherefore we say that the people should not be confined
within narrow bounds, nor their lives made weary by law.
Moreover, if the ruler does not weary the citizens, the citizens
will not grow weary of him. Therefore, the sage man says, So
long as I do little, the people will find their way.' At which
words of the merchant Anscinen, many shouted out their
praises of him, so that for a while none could be heard.

Then the noble Pitaco spoke bitterly as follows, some of
the merchants and the people showing him great scorn: 'That
is not all you say and do. Nor do we deny the teaching of
Menche, who declared that only that realm which is wisely
governed will have enough means to meet its expenses. You,
however, seek to destroy all that which for you serves no
purpose, such as the customs of our ancestors and the most
cherished ways, as well as the laws and even the buildings
which to you are without value.

'In the lands of the barbarians, which are without city walls
or embassies from the kings of other countries, as also without
public office and civil occupation,[21] and thus no public
domain, then a man might see more reason in your counsels.
But in this realm and city, our ways may not be so easily
thrown down, nor may order be maintained, nor happiness
attained, nor the law of heaven be observed without respect
for that which was held to be truthful and just by the wisest
rulers and sages of past times. For they gave care to all things
under heaven both high and low, both those things which
pertained to the gods and those which pertained to men,

while you give thought only to your desires and your
possessions.

'Likewise the Emperor Oaou and the Emperor Man
decreed that the making of iron and salt should never descend
into the hands of merchants, yet in your pride you have taken
even these to yourselves.[22] But the emperors were wiser than
you, sires, knowing that such things, being for the good of all,
should not be at the command of the rich alone.

'Moreover, what was a wrong for them is a wrong for us
also. For in the heart of each man in all times is a clear idea of
justice, such a man being offended at all times by the same
things which seem to him unjust.'

To these words of Pitaco, peace upon him, the merchant
Anlisciu, a man coarse and rough, as if unwilling to hear more
of such things, cried out, O patience, at which many others
shouted his praises, he declaring as follows: 'The realm can be
no merchant, nor can such as Pitaco weave silk, nor any
official bring to the people the goods for which they crave.
Thus, it is just that all things should be governed by those
who best serve the people in their needs, and not that those
who serve them least should take their light, or ride upon
their backs.'

Hearing which, Oantatte, who stood in the ranks of the
people, spoke thus: 'You are right, but why do we remain
poor under your rule, with not enough money even to renew
our strength for the next day's toil? If matters are as you say,
why are the drains that carry the foul waters no longer cared
for? Now, stalls and shops are dispersed all about the city, so
that no one knows where anything is to be found, for all is in
confusion.'

Whereupon many of the merchants laughed at his words,
may God punish them for their hardness of heart, another
from among the poor adding as follows: 'Sires, even when
good fortune comes to a few of us under your rule, the high
and the low gain unequally, so that the rich grow fatter and
the poor leaner. But since the poor may no longer seek aid as

they once did, there should be a law ordering that the rich man and the poor man should be equal.' At which words of the countryman, may God have pity for him, there was again great laughter among the merchants, nor did the guardians permit him to say more, for he would speak of the rebels[23] of the City of Light, crying out that the gods of heaven would surely punish the merchants for their pride.

Whereupon there rose in the ranks of the party of the noble Pitaco a certain Cianianmin, a man of great age and a master in medicine, who spoke to the merchants as follows, all falling silent to hear him: 'The poor men both of the country and of the city, being without land, have become poorer than before. For now they see before their eyes not the spirits of their ancestors but the ghosts of such things as they desire but may not have. You also claim yourselves to be those who have brought light to the city, but by your actions you cause only great bitterness under heaven and danger to the common good. For, having no concord between us, how shall we defend ourselves against the foe who approaches, and cure the ills of contention and violence which beset us in our cities?[24] You, sires, act contrary to heaven and will thus bring down ruin upon us, both rich and poor.'

To whom the merchant Anlísciu, hot with anger, spoke as follows: 'The words you pronounce, revered sire, are not the truth. For, because of the greater buying and selling, all those who have the will for labour can gain greater benefits than before. Your ideas are as cloth eaten by moths and your words as the sounds that rise from an empty cave.'

Hearing which, many in the throng began to shout in loud voices one against the other, some even seeking to strike those who were near them, so that none might hear the words of the aged Cianianmin, peace upon him. But after the guardians had gone among the throng, striking that one and this, the old man continued as follows: 'You lack respect for both gods and men, in your arrogance believing yourselves even to rule over the whole of nature itself. For how else should you think that the very earth, the metals within it, the waters, and all the animals of the land and sea should belong to you? Rather, as Latsu teaches, water is of the highest goodness and, provided that it not be in excess, brings benefit to all things and thus belongs to all. So with other bounties also, which no one may claim as his own, they being given to all men so that their lives may be maintained.'

For these words of the learnèd Cianianmin there were great cries of praise, to which the merchant Anlisciu replied: 'It is the honest countryman and the honest craftsman, the goldsmith and the tailor working upon their wares, who sustain the city and the realm, not the sage whose head is full of learning but who cannot draw water from a well.'

For these words of Anlisciu there was also great praise from among the merchants and the people, some shouting one thing and others another, the sage Cianianmin declaring in anger as follows: 'If your honest goldsmiths were to renounce the stealing of gold, their families would starve to death, and if your honest tailors were to cease stealing cloth, their wives would go about naked.' To whom Anlisciu made answer thus: 'You scorn the merchant while buying his wares, and look up to heaven while other men must till the earth. Is this a just way to proceed through life? Moreover, while other men seek out new paths on which to set their feet, you not only follow the old but seek to turn men from the new, bringing peril to all.'

To these charges, the noble Pitaco now made reply: 'Even when your errors are shown to you by those who are wiser, you continue on your way without heed. Yet, as Menche teaches, when a man knows that he has lost his way he should stop at once. But you who have seized greedily upon the goods of the city which formerly served the needs of all, while leaving many things desolate without just cause, are surprised that in their confusion men should now turn against each other. In your own eyes you are worthy of praise, for you labour for your riches from morning to night, so intent is

your will. But he who rises with the cock and never tires of
labour for his own gain is little better than a thief. For he is in
concord only with that which in the entire world is the most
sordid, the desire for riches.'

Now, since it seemed that the party of Pitaco had the better
of it, the prefect called on the great merchant Anscinen to
answer, who spoke as follows: 'The market is not the place of
cupidity but of work, and the satisfaction of desires and needs
among the people with goods and other things. In the City of
Light does not the abundance of all things spur men to
possess them, and thus to work the harder in order to obtain
them? For he who desires to possess seeks to acquire the
means thereto, and, having acquired such means, he in turn
satisfies those who have provided him with what he desires.
Thus it is that the wheel of trade turns,[25] nor can it be a good
thing to stay its turning and to hinder its passage with this or
that stone placed in the way. For to do so brings benefit to
none, while from the free movement of this wheel the entire
city prospers.'

For these words the merchant Anscinen again received
great praise, to whom, the noble Pitaco seeming wearied, the
sage Cianianmin made reply: 'In the present day, sires, men
spurn moderation and pursue excess, and will therefore
perish. As Menche teaches, there is nothing better for the
nurture of the heart than to reduce the number of desires,
while those who treasure pearls and jade above all things are
sure to suffer ills. You of the other party think yourselves great
men because you are great merchants, but you are great only
in your riches. Better would it be to study Latsu, who teaches
that he who is truly great stands firm upon the hard ground
of truth and not upon the form of things, however adorned
and embellished.

'Thus, there are some who drive chariots with four horses,
but in what way is it better than sitting still? If a man prides
himself on his treasures of jade and gold, not only may he not
guard them all but he hastens to his own fall, just as he who

raises himself on tiptoe[26] cannot stand firm, and he who keeps his legs too wide cannot walk. But he who knows when he has enough will not be put to shame, nor he who knows when he should halt come to harm.'

To whom the rough merchant Anlisciu shouted in answer: 'You old men speak well, but you are not honest, you who walk the streets and markets marvelling in your souls at what the merchants offer there, pretending to disdain such things as though they were unworthy of your sight. It is as though a pan of hot beans[27] caused you pain not only to devour but to see.' At which words all the ranks of the people laughed very greatly, for which God be praised.[28]

To whom Pitaco responded as follows: 'You laugh, but those who are led always by thought of gain and the satisfaction of desire, how can they awaken to the suffering of others in our drought and famine? It is heaven that gives life to the five grains in order to nourish the common people, and bestows good fortune upon the rich so that they may help the poor. But of such things what do they know who think only of their own profit? When rice is dear and the poor cannot buy, and none take pity upon their state, does it concern them what heaven will say, those who are deaf even to the cries of their neighbours?'

At these three demands there was a great silence, as if none knew what to say, until the great merchant Anscinen answered as follows: 'It is the man who gives no thought to the morrow who makes his neighbour pay. There was never an age without flood or drought, sickness or cold. Yet you would have the people for ever without foresight, when it is the duty of every man to protect himself against the accidents of heaven.'

To which the noble Pitaco replied: 'It is true. But in the meantime must the hungry, trembling with fear and without means to buy, merely stand in their places, looking from one to the other in silence, and thus go to their deaths without demur? And will you, observing all, blame them for their lack, whether it be their fault or no? Moreover, if the poor lie in the ditches and streets, or flee to other places, who will till your fields[29] and bring food to your tables?'

For these three further demands of Pitaco there was now great praise among the people, many crying out in their places against the ranks of the merchants, where before they had praised them, so that Anscinen was constrained to speak again in this way: 'But it is men like you, noble Pitaco, who are simple-minded, knowing little of the world, and who are yourselves the cause of all our ills. For you look with disdain on all those things which it is most common for living men to do, whether it be the lying of man with woman, buying and selling, the seeking of pleasure and many other things. To the idle your disdain gives licence, although this in your pride you do not see, while to those with no concern for the morrow your care for them permits further folly, so that they set nothing aside, turning always to you for aid. Moreover, you, with your noble demeanour, who never laboured a day in the field or the workshop, think that the rice which is given to the hungry man has more virtue than that which he grows by his own hand. You think also that to be a merchant is to descend the scale of heaven, and that for a man to sell the work of his hands is not better than for a woman to sell her body. In your arrogance, you hold in contempt all those who gladly go wherever a profit may be made, save those who come here from other lands, to whom you unjustly show honour.

'But of all bad things, the worst is that you teach that the people should seek the less rather than the more, that to fail is of greater virtue than to succeed, and that the poor are nobler than the rich. But by such instruction, the city itself must fail.'

Now the party of Pitaco, and the ranks of the people also, fell silent, for it was as though all sought the truth, for which God be praised. Thus Anscinen was able to speak freely as follows: 'It is in the matter of buying and selling that the noble Pitaco and the men who are about him have least knowledge, so that their contempt for the riches of the city is also least fitting. For it is as though they despised the plenty which they see about them, as my brother Anlisciu has declared according to his manner. But only where there are divers things from which a man may choose, as between different kinds of rice or fruits, is he able to satisfy his desires by buying that which is fitting for him, according to his taste or his purse. Moreover, in buying this or that thing, he gives the merchant knowledge of what pleases him and what does not. Thus the merchant, ever constrained by the presence of other merchants to raise the quality of what he sells yet not to drive away him who buys by seeking a price which is too high, is better able to choose the wares which he sets out before him. By such means each comes to know of the condition of the other, he who sells as to the tastes and pocket of him who buys, and he who buys as to the goods which are to be found and the price which he must pay. Thus, when both may freely act as they choose, according to their will, each in this fashion may satisfy the other, and in the round of buying and selling, in which all take part, the city becomes both rich and free.'

But the heart of the noble Pitaco was not stilled and, although greatly aged, he replied as follows: 'The people desire more and yet more still, without end, each seeking like a child for what he does not possess. But they are not rendered happy by having in their hands what they have sought, even throwing it aside and crying out for a new thing once more. Thus is all custom broken, for only that which is new has value in their eyes, and restlessness, not peace, flourishes in all men's hearts.'

To whom the coarse Anlisciu answered in this fashion: 'Some prefer turnips to pears, since each prefers that which he prefers. Are you to say that they are wrong, or shall we not leave each man to eat turnips if he desires?' But at these words there was so much laughter among the people that for a while no single voice could be heard, until the aged Cianianmin replied as follows: 'You could be compared with Ianciu, who also thought only of himself, but he was a sage', at which words there was again great laughter even among the party of the merchants. For such was their enjoyment, as well as their bitterness and anger, in discussing these things among themselves.

But the merchant Anlisciu, feeling sorely the scorn of others, declared in a loud voice: 'It is just for me, as for all other men, to pursue whatever pleases and exalts me. If I am exalted by possessions, by fine clothes and by beautiful women, it is right that I should pursue them, for it is in the nature of man to seek his own ends.'

To whom the noble Pitaco, may his name be recorded, replied as if he truly heard in his heart the word of God, for Torah wisdom may be understood and learned by the Gentile also, may God be praised. 'All men, sires, share a desire to be exalted, as Menche teaches. But in every man is that which is already exalted without need of possessions, fine clothes and women. That which he has is his soul, yet in some persons such truth never dawns in their minds. But what exalts you, my friend Anlisciu, is not itself exalted, while that which is truly exalted you have never seen nor known.

'Moreover, if there is nothing which you want more than pleasure, why should you trouble yourself about the means, so long as it serves to bring you what you desire? And how may others put a curb to this, if happiness and the seeking by a man of his own ends are held to be the same thing? Rather, it is your greed which is the great enemy of our city, and not the means by which it may be made strong, rich and safe from its foes.'

But at these words of Pitaco, as though someone had given a signal, all the merchants rose in their places together, crying out in anger that they were thus accused of being traitors to the city and friends of the Tartars, some making as if to strike the noble Pitaco and master Cianianmin, so that the guardians ran to their aid, the people shouting for this party and that in great confusion.

At last, the merchants were constrained to push Anscinen forward with their hands,[30] for he was no longer willing to address the noble Pitaco, such was the anger of all his party at the accusation made against them, most being resolved to leave the assembly and to parley no more.

But I, Jacob of Ancona, stepping from my place with the faithful Lifenli, and grasping the merchant Anlisciu by the hand, besought him in the name of God that the men of his party should stay, for it would bode ill for all the merchants of the city, whether of Manci or of other countries, that they should incur blame for such a quarrel. For I declared that so they surely would, if part of the people should descend with them to the streets with anger in their hearts, may God be thanked for placing such wisdom in my mouth.

Whereupon the merchant Anscinen, who had been uncertain whether to remain or take his leave, now spoke as follows: 'This treasure, which is to be free men in a free condition of life, we shall not only defend from those who seek to restrict it but shall strive to make it yet larger. Upon it, contrary to what Pitaco has spoken, depends the happiness and wealth of the entire city, including of those who are now poor and needy. For, as Sumacien teaches, when each person works at his own occupation and delights in his own affairs, then, like water flowing downwards, goods will flow forth according to the laws of nature[31] without cease day and night and without having been called forth, for the people will produce those things that others need, without being asked. Indeed, in this City of Light, as in no other city in the world, so wise is our order of freedom that each person makes the greatest effort in order to arrive at the mastery of his task.

'For since in our city every man is free to act and to reap the fruits of his effort, so he acts with greater will, knowing that it is right for him to do what he does and to keep what he has gained. Therefore is this city fruitful in great riches, strong against its foes, and ready for battle with those who would strike against its faithful company of merchants.'

At which words very many of the people shouted out in praise with so loud and violent a sound that it was a frightening thing to hear. But the party of Pitaco was not made afraid, he himself declaring: 'You speak, Anscinen, in noble fashion, yet much of what you do is unlawful and against the order of heaven. You oppress the poor without mercy, cheat each other, give false measure and all from the desire for gold. In the name of free judgment, the rich do all that they want to do and the poor all that they can do. Thus, every sin comes to be made licit, whatever our law may prescribe. Therefore, when the citizens rob and cheat others, they do not think they commit any crime, so that now the city stands upon the edge of the abyss. The realm, sires, cannot be governed as if it were the house of a family, for then the ends for which men come together and live in human concert are lost. Yet now you argue that in the City of Light each man should freely defend his possessions as he chooses, saying that since there are so many men who go about, day and night, with swords and clubs in their hands, so each inhabitant may justly defend himself and his possessions from his neighbours with such means as he requires.

'Thus, now, no man can justly be deprived of such means, for without them each becomes a prey of others. But when someone says that you have therefore placed all men not in safety but in great danger, you reply that it is better that all should have arms than only the strong or those who are given to violent acts. Indeed, there are some among you who say that it would be better if each man had a duty to carry a knife about him, as if thus all might be safe.

'But this is the way of death and not of life, in which none can be safe. For when each man goes about the streets with a weapon in his hand, quarrels must come to be settled more often by the shedding of blood than by the force of reason. Yet you say that those who would do harm are prevented from evil-doing by the knife each man carries, even arguing that peace is better kept thus than at great cost to the realm. But

this too is a wicked teaching, for justice cannot be maintained
by the sword and the knife alone.

'Moreover, there are learnèd men who come among us from
other lands who marvel at our riches but look with fear and
shame upon our ills. Let one such speak in his own tongue
who is truly the wisest of men, for he is both the greatest
merchant and the greatest sage of his people, as well a man of
piety as of riches, learnèd in the Law of the Jews and many
other things, who is thus most fitted to reason before us.'

In this way did the noble Pitaco give me, Jacob di
Salomone, merchant of Ancona, great praise and honour, that
I should have been chosen from among all men, whether Jew
or Gentile, to speak thus, by the aid of the faithful Lifenli, in
the great hall of the prefect of the City of Light before a
throng whose number might not be counted: 'Sires, has a
realm ever heard such evil things from its merchants as may
be heard in this city since the world was divided into diverse
territories? Of so many excesses and follies have I been witness
since my coming to this place, that none in other lands would
credit my tale. For how shall any man in whom there is the
light of reason believe that the rulers of a realm or city should
permit those who dwell there to act so freely, that none may
deny a citizen to choose whether he go about with knife in
hand, or lie with a woman in the sight of others, or play the
beast with man, or any other thing, all of which may God
forbid.

'Nor would it be believed that, in pursuit of riches, the
rulers of a realm or city had ceded to its merchants not only
the liberty to buy and sell according to their own wills and
exempt from impost, but had sold to them their buildings
and ways, lakes and conduits, and even the abandoned
temples and altars of their ancestors. For in doing such things
there is a foolishness so great that only the mad could judge
the doers wise. For has such a thing ever been heard that men
should of their own will seek to let their city fall into ruin[32]
and turn its citizens into enemies of one another?

'Although, sires, I too am a merchant, I judge that these things are not the fruits of the reason or wisdom of man but have come about by the work of devils, God forbid. True it is that without the liberty to come and go, and to buy and sell, which are powers not enjoyed by men who are unfree, there should be no trade among them. But such freedom is a useful right not a natural right, nor is it absolute, for so the sages among the Franks correctly declare. As to riches, the noble Pitaco speaks justly that in excess they harm the soul, even when they fill the treasury of the merchant with gold and silver.

'Thus, although the words of the merchant Anscinen might be pleasing to the ears of one such as I, a merchant also, they displeased and disturbed my soul. For this city, rich as it may be, seems as though ruled by folly. Being a pious man, may God be praised, I therefore hold such greedy and blind incontinence of the desires as I see in your city to be not worthy, but base and wicked. For a man has a duty to himself as well as to others neither to give way to everything he wishes to do, nor to seek everything he desires to possess.'

Whereat, the faithful Lifenli having with great labour translated my words from my own tongue, with one voice the party of Pitaco greeted my speech with great praises, calling upon me to continue.

I therefore spoke further as follows: 'Some of our sages permit merchants to trade freely, provided only that they do not cheat those to whom they sell. But others of our sages warn of the sin of those who lived when the world came to be deluged, declaring it to be an evil thing that a trader should demand to do whatever he wills for his own gain. For they say that this is the direct way not to riches but to the profanation of the Name of God. Thus, should any man be freed from the bonds of law and be permitted to act with neither moderation nor care for his fellows, then all law and right must come to confusion, since each man is disposed to imitate his fellows, and that which is allowed to some must come to be allowed

to all. Rather, men must be constrained to act justly towards
one another in all relations and in all things, whether master
to servant and servant to master, husband to wife and wife to
husband, or seller to purchaser and purchaser to seller.
Therefore, as to the last of these, there must be a just price
established between them, so that both may be content
thereby.'

Whereupon the merchant Anlisciu shouted out: 'And in
your judgment, O wisest of the wise, what is a just price?' To
whom I replied: 'Sire, you may tell me first.' To which
Anlisciu answered: 'Any price is just which is established
between the seller and the buyer.' To whom I replied in turn:
'This is no more than to say that a thing is worth as much as
it can be sold for.'[33] At which the foolish Anlisciu declared:
'This is our belief also.'

To him I said in turn: 'But there are some who argue that
the price of a thing depends upon its usefulness and upon the
need of those who purchase it, as our great Aquinas[34]
maintains.' At which Anlisciu declared that the words of
Aquinas were not different from the first,[35] saying: 'If the
purchaser finds a thing useful to him and wants such an
object, he will pay the just price for it, which is also the price
at which it can be sold', whereupon those about him laughed
without understanding, may God have pity on them.

Therefore I asked as follows: 'But where is the justice in
such a just price? Is the starving man who is in need of bread
in order to fill his belly to be asked fifty groats because in his
hunger he is willing to pay it?' To which the wicked Anlisciu
replied: 'If he is willing to pay the baker such a price, why
should he not? Are you to forbid him, in your great wisdom,
from paying whatever he wishes to pay? And if he is willing to
pay it, why should the baker ask him for less?'

To whom I replied in turn, God be thanked: 'Then, sire,
there can be no justice in the world.'

These words of mine having greatly displeased the ranks[36]
of the merchants, many stood up, calling upon the prefect

that, being a stranger, I should not be permitted to speak
further. To this, many among the people also cried out in
agreement, but others that I should stay, saying that my words
were wise, God be praised. Whereupon the noble Pitaco,
peace upon him, declared that the merchants of the city were
put to flight by one who, being a merchant, rightly judged
their faults and had no fear to speak of them. Moreover, that I
was a Jew and a stranger among them could not turn truth to
falsehood, nor make evil my pious words.

Therefore I was permitted to continue: 'True it is that the
merchant of all lands has liking neither for taxes in excess nor
for those who would obstruct his path. For he wishes to
conduct himself freely, to decide to which lands to direct his
fleets according to his judgment, and to choose when to buy
and when to sell. Moreover, the merchant wishes for the
protection of his king or of those who govern the city, but not
that they rule or stand over him, for he knows better than
they what should serve him.

'But shall the city therefore not impose taxes, or take care
of the water which men drink from its wells, or relieve the
poor and the sick, or punish the lying of men with men, or
say who shall enter the market and who shall not? How then
shall a city be well governed and the common good be
maintained? And may men deny air, water and fire to others
except at a price? May they buy the heavens, the oceans and
the rivers, and the burning flame? Rather, he who thinks
himself free of all restraint and abandons himself to whatever
his will decrees, without regard for others, shall have no share
in the world to come, for so our sages teach, may peace be
upon them.[37]

'Yet among us, too, there are many who seek only to stand
above others and to do what seems right according to their
own wills, but such conduct cannot furnish a rule as to good
and evil by which all men may live. For a man may not
choose whether to act well or ill towards others according to
his own judgment, since thus the world comes to be without

law or justice. Hence, sires, it is clear that you have set your city upon the wrong path, by which you will come to ruin, may God have pity upon you.'

To these words of mine the coarse one was driven to reply, albeit that the party of the merchants had not wished to hear me more. But now the expression of the merchant Anlisciu was much changed: 'You are a Jew who speaks without end of good and evil, and a merchant who betrays his fellows, as do all the Jews. You make profession also to be learnèd, discoursing as if sagely, for this our leader Suninsciou and the wise Cian have told us. But it is you, not we, who are in great confusion, and I too am wise. Thus, you complain that we hold it in favour that each man should seek his own ends, just as he chooses that which most pleases him between this cloth and that, or this and that fish in the market. Yet, for all that you speak your Jewish things of good and evil, if a man cannot freely choose between the better and the worse, how can he choose between good and evil, or right conduct and wrong? Moreover, if there is no choice, man cannot be blamed for his actions and all judgment fails.'

In this way spoke Anlisciu, who was not truly wise, yet those about him laughed, pointing their fingers to deride me, God save them. To whom I replied with faith and strength as follows, God be praised: 'I do not deny, sires, that by virtue of his nature and endowment by God a man may do whatever he wills or chooses in those things for which he has capacity, as to choose between one path and another, one companion and another, or one sack of spices and another. For, as our Jewish sages declare, all is foreseen, but to men freedom of choice is given. But he who chooses this bolt of silk or that, or this quality of pepper or that, is not choosing between good and evil but between two qualities of matter. Thus, to be enabled to choose between them provides no principle for the moral life. For he who conducts himself well rather than badly does not make a choice between them, but is guided by his soul and by his sense of duty.'

To this Anlisciu could make no reply, all the merchants
about him being in great confusion, for which God be
magnified and praised. Thus, some shouted to me that I had
no place among them, and others complained that Anlisciu
made no answer. Whereupon, many in the ranks of the
people went away in anger, lamenting that neither the party
of the noble Pitaco nor of the great merchant Suninsciou
might lead them, one crying out that it was the Franks and
the Jews, God forbid, who, from their desire for profit, had
driven on the merchants of Zaitun beyond all measure. But
the noble Pitaco bowed low to me in honour, for which God
be praised, declaring that through my words the side of truth
had had the better of the side of falsehood, while the
merchant Anlisciu, coming to me also as I departed that
place, prayed again that I should speak more of the Christians
and their hatred for the Jews, saying that all wished to hear my
words. To him I answered that I judged myself to be both
honoured and bound by faith and duty, he declaring me
before all to be the wisest of men.

After the Sabbath Bo,[38] the month of Shevet being well
advanced, my brothers Nathan ben Dattalo, Lazzaro and
Eliezer returned safely by ship to Zaitun,[39] being fully laden
with goods of silk and gold, perfumes and salves, and of a
value which may not be spoken, for which praise be to God.
Nor did they have concern for the troubles of the realm or for
the great confusion of the City of Light, speaking only of the
wonders which they had beheld in the city of the Son of
Heaven.

For they declared that Chinscie, which is to say the
capital city of the realm of Manci and the seat of King
Toutson, is a city all painted in gold, with the highest walls
in the world, together with many lakes and gardens, a
thousand temples, fifty monasteries, more canals than may
be found in Venice, four thousand bridges of stone and
more than nine hundred thousand hearths.[40] Thus it is the

greatest city upon the earth, requiring four days' journey to
go round the walls.

The king lives in a grand marble palace with more than five
thousand rooms, all adorned with gold and jewels. For such is
thought fitting for him whom they impiously call the Son of
Heaven, as the Christians call *that man* the Son of God,
although it is not more foolish for the one to be called so than
the other. In the palace of Toutson, all is hatred and plotting
among the nobles of the court, as it is among the cardinals at
the court of Rome. Moreover, just as the Pope bestows ranks
and honours upon those who crowd his chambers, so the Son
of Heaven of the Mancini does likewise, presiding over the
cult upon a golden throne in the manner of a pope. In the
same way, the relatives and concubines of those who are of the
court of the Son of Heaven, as of those of the court of the
Pope, gain preferment to power, so that lust and greed, not
virtue and justice, rule over the one as over the other.

The Son of Heaven is surrounded by eunuchs, scribes,
servants, astrologers, women and others given to idleness,
together with keepers of the animals of the king, as masters of
the hawks and gyr-falcons, and servants even of his fish,
which they keep for his pleasure in a certain lake close beside
the palace. All these and many others beside, to the number
of ten thousand, receive from the Son of Heaven what their
occupations have need of, and all in turn prostrate themselves
before him. Nevertheless, it is said that the king is so free with
those about him that some among them see him even when
his hair is being cut and when he is naked, as when he bathes
himself, which is an abomination.

The Jews of Chinscie, who number about two thousand,
live upon the Hill of the Phoenix, which lies to the west of
the palace of the said Toutson and is called by the Mancini
the Hill of the Franks, for there the Franks, as well as the
Saracens, also live. The Saracens have their temple and houses
near the Bridge of Riches and the Jews their house of worship,
God be praised, in the Street of Blessings. Yet to hear all these

things from my brothers Lazzaro and Eliezer of Venice, whether of wonders or of things forbidden, no longer moved my soul, nor even to see the choice things they had brought, among which was much to my profit also.

For that a man should call himself king and take to himself many wives and amass for himself silver and gold more than a man requires, is neither to be wondered at, nor praised, while my eyes looked without lustre upon the goods set before me by Nathan ben Dattalo, for my soul was wearied of such trade. For neither the king or pope who proudly sits upon his throne, nor the silken robe, nor the golden ring, are the true lights of the world, but shadows only, beside which the lamp of the Torah shines with a flame which may never die, may God be exalted for His bounty.

Moreover, I was greatly beset by contemplation of the troubles of the city, which increased day by day among the people, some being for this party and some for that, so that I saw that those things by which it was riven were the same as cause woe to all men. Thus, upon the Sabbath Yitro and the Sabbath Mishpatim[41] I prayed that God, blessèd be He, might vouchsafe me wisdom to guide my thoughts and words before the great assemblies of the city, so that its rulers who besought my counsel and gave me great praise, God be thanked, might be brought with my aid from darkness to light. For such is the duty of the pious Jew, as our sages teach, peace be upon them.

But now in these days of Shevet yet another travail came upon me, for my servant Buccazuppo, who had grown into a fair woman, God forgive me that I should so praise her, was given to much weeping and sighing without cause. Therefore I, thinking that she was too much in the company of the evil Bertoni, besought the faithful Lifenli to bring to the said Buccazuppo his sister, a certain Liciancie, who, since she spoke our tongue, might serve as a companion to my unhappy servant. Thus, they passed many hours in talking together, but I knew not, alas, of what things, I being much occupied about the city, so that even my pious duties I did in haste, may God forgive me. At last Liciancie was brought before me, so that I might talk with her, God forbid, for I did not wish that my charge of Buccazuppo should be neglected, for such was my pledge.[42] Whereupon I found that Liciancie had a brazen manner, which was little that of a woman, she having contempt for men, her dress disordered and with an unchaste and ready tongue, so that she spoke of things of which no women should speak, whether to man or woman.

Of such women, from whom all men are wise to keep distant, there are many in the City of Light, so Lifenli declared. Thus, those among them who are married are accustomed to treat men with great harshness, not only driving them from their beds and refusing to lie with them, God forbid, but also refusing them other services, so contrary to reason and nature are their actions. Indeed, it is said that their husbands, becoming fearful of them and glad to escape their presence, lose the very will to lie with women, for all become hateful to them at the last. Yet these same women are by no means friends among themselves, being much given to arguments, even to the exchanging of blows.

Thus Liciancie, when I enquired about her beliefs[43] as to the lying of man with woman, may God forgive my deed, answered that such act gave no pleasure, nor should a woman give her body to the lusts of men. For men seek only to employ the bodies of women for their relief, being without modesty or honour. Wherefore I asked her how might a woman bear a child if she were not willing to lie with a man, to which she replied that it was not necessary to give birth, there being many children at large in the city whose mothers were no longer to be found.

I therefore answered her as follows, God giving me the strength to deny her impiety: 'That a virgin might conceive without coupling with a man only the Christians in their folly may believe. But that a woman who desires no congress with

man should seek to possess a child, without having borne it in
her womb, is also contrary to nature. And how shall a
woman, being without man's aid, come to provide for such a
child?'

To which Liciancie answered as follows, Buccazuppo
listening to her words, even though I had forbidden her: 'As
the wives of mariners do.' To whom I replied in turn: 'And
how without the partnership of a man may such a child's
needs be served?' To which she answered, taking Buccazuppo
by the hand, that the friendship of a woman was all that she
desired. To whom I replied that hers was therefore an
unhappy soul, at which she became greatly angered, treating
with me as though she were a man and even as though she
would strike me down, God forbid.

Whereupon I declared as follows: 'You have no regard for
the ways of others, and seek to do whatever is fitting for
yourself, yet grow angry if you come to be reproached.' To
which the said Liciancie replied without shame in this
fashion: 'But you also demand that your desires be satisfied,
seeking to do with a woman as you wish and growing angry if
you should be denied.'

To whom I replied, having sent Buccazuppo from the
room: 'The single life, especially when it is practised by many,
is against nature, being against the law of creation. Nor may a
woman beget a child upon a woman, nor a man upon a man,
God forbid. For the seed of man cannot flow from a woman's
nature, nor a womb be found in the belly of a man. Thus
your judgments are against nature and reason, although you
speak with passion, believing yourself to be right.'

Yet such was the great confusion in the City of Light that
Liciancie, although a woman, answered as follows, may the
Holy One spare her at the end of days: 'To be a man like you
is to be imperfect, for a man, but not a woman, must be prey
to his desires, he being unable to turn his face or his thoughts
from that for which he feels lust, and being quickly tired by
the body of a woman who no longer gives him pleasure. But

who does not know that after a man's fortieth year his strength
declines from year to year, after his fiftieth from month to
month, after his sixtieth from week to week, and after his
seventieth from day to day? Yet although the strengths of his
body become weaker, the thoughts of his mind remain, so that
he despairs that his life is lived in vain. Hence, he for ever
seeks to put in chains the woman who loves life without lust,
for she brings to his eyes the baseness of his own thoughts.
Moreover, he is driven ever more into the company of men
who are similar to himself, and thus comes to still greater
despair. But men may not live justly at the price of women's
souls and bodies, nor suck their blood like leeches.'

At these words of Liciancie, she being a woman young in
years, I was greatly surprised and troubled, for it seemed that
no woman had spoken such things since the beginning of the
world, when the Holy One first gave life to all things and
established the laws of nature, may He be revered. Therefore,
calling my servant Buccazuppo so that she might hear my
words, I said to Liciancie that the savage part of woman is
surely akin to the savage part of man, both being unworthy of
human society. For since certain men behave wickedly
towards women, which God forbid, so it makes sense that
certain women may do likewise towards men, which God also
forbid, for each partakes of the nature of the other. Likewise,
as the women who purchase victuals, put the house in order,
and hold and watch over the children are of the good part of
women, so the men who furnish their wives with money,
guard the house against robbers and instruct the children in
right conduct are of the good part of men.

To which the brazen Liciancie replied that the things of
which I spoke as to women were the works of servants and
not of free persons, and that all men order their wives to serve
them in all their needs. The woman also added as follows: 'No
longer shall we be taught only to sew and to cut out gloves
and other such work. For every wife who strives to show
obedience, in order to please her husband, binds herself and

him also in the saddest of travails. Or shall we accept a
different truth from those who bind our feet and call them
golden lilies,[44] or teach that a wife should follow her defunct
husband even to death?

'Such men now see us as stinging scorpions, yet for how
many generations have they served us ill? But no longer may
men judge us as if we were beasts in order to see that we are
not ugly under our clothes, for when a man was gross, or had
bad breath, or was a wicked person, which women might say
so? Now, we shall no longer permit men to disparage women,
speaking of us as though only men possessed reason, or as
though we lightly changed our wills and men alone were firm
in their resolves. Rather, women must seek contentment for
themselves, no longer doing those things that men say they
require us to do, but those things which it most pleases us to
do, each according to her choice.'

Whereupon, hearing these words of Liciancie, I again felt
greatly troubled lest Buccazuppo be rendered unhappy by
such a mixture of things foolish and true, may God forgive
me that a pious man such as I should have been compelled to
engage myself so closely with them. For, in order that truth
might vanquish folly, I was driven yet further before the eyes
of my servant Buccazuppo, speaking as follows to Liciancie:

'Men do not have the intent to wound unjustly, nor do
women have a better understanding of their own natures than
do men of theirs. Rather, both are made in the image of God,
blessèd be He, and both are frail in the same fashion.'

To which Liciancie replied as follows, causing me great
shame: 'Men take delight only in the bodies of women, even
to rape, although they may speak to them tenderly of love so
that they might the sooner possess them. Instead, women
should choose with whom they lie, and whether they would
marry and bear children, according to their own wills and not
according to the wills of men. Moreover, in the act of love
they should not be surmounted but should be placed above,
for thus may the pride of men come to be humbled.'

At these words, both women took to laughter, God have
mercy on them, so that never before did I feel such grief to
observe the wickedness of humankind, declaring that to speak
and to laugh so, being without modesty, was against nature.
To which Liciancie replied without shame as follows: 'Such
men as you teach women the laws of modesty and faith, but
are yourselves given to incontinence and lust. You wish us to
be mild and gentle, while you are proud and cruel. Now, just
as a man takes a concubine for his delight, so may a woman
take a lover to herself for her own pleasure, according to her
choice and will, and in order to satisfy her desires. Moreover,
just as previously women turned their eyes away at men's
command, so now must men do likewise. To make men
cuckolds[45] is our right.'

But the first star of the Sabbath Mishpatim being now seen
in the heavens,[46] I sent them away from me in great anger,
God be praised, ordering that Liciancie be barred from the
house of Nathan ben Dattalo in order that my servant
Buccazuppo might be kept from harm. Whereafter I betook
myself to prayer, God be praised, in order that my heart
might be made pure and come again to the throne of God,
fearing also that I should lose my way in so accursèd a city,
where every wrong was made right and truth itself overcome
by the folly of men.

## CHAPTER EIGHT

# I Spoke the Truth of God

THIS CHAPTER IS NOTABLE ABOVE all for Jacob's second and more extensive diatribe, or tirade, against Christianity and Christian misdeeds, as he sees them. At a distance of more than seven hundred years it still has the power of an argument from living faith, whether such argument was put forward in public before the sages of Zaitun (in early 1272), as Jacob describes, or, as I believe, was much elaborated upon in the writing, after his return to Ancona the following year. (I point out intermittently in the notes those passages which were plainly the product of further thought.) But there can be no doubt of the ring of truth in the savage exchanges with the Franciscan – as I suppose – Fra Bartolomeo, or of the ardour and bitterness of Jacob's views. It is also as if we heard the accents of the Inquisition in the charge and counter-charge, and in the animus and defiance of position and counter-position. In the exchanges we are also provided with a great deal of information on the lot and standing of mediaeval Jews, on Church practice and malpractice – including the malpractices of simony (or profiting from church office) and usury – and on the outrages to Jewish feeling of false allegation and imputation against them.

Moreover, the power of Jacob's sentiments derives from a particular (or egregious) sense which he possesses of election and obligation to 'speak the truth of God'; in the heat of the moment, he reaches great heights of inspired eloquence and passion, however offensive to the religious sensibility of others his words may appear. There is a kind of *rage* in what he says, but it is the rage of a man who feels a rankling sense of injustice at what he feels has been done in his time, and in previous times, to his 'brothers'. In the light of what was to befall them in future centuries, the quality even of Jacob's anger and argument, painful as it might be to those with no sympathy for them, must be regarded as a puny thing indeed. Nevertheless, the force of his charges against Christian hypocrisy – that Christians do not behave (including towards one another) as they preach – can hardly be gainsaid. Against such charges, his more theological arguments as to 'idolatry' and so on, offensive as may be (and contrary, as we have seen, to the injunctions of the rabbis themselves), seem to me to be of less significance today.

It is interesting, as Jacob's first tirade on this subject also disclosed, that he should have been put to the test not only (as in this chapter) by a Christian adversary, but also by 'scoffers' among the sages, and even by the tenacious Lifenli. Of course it can never be finally shown whether Jacob has put in their mouths the questions they ask and the sentiments they express. But his exchanges with the young and 'impious' Lifenli – a kind of Judaeo-Platonic dialogue – are illuminating of Jacob's own beliefs; he is driven to clarify and to explain his faith and his philosophy under pressure, but now with anger, in a fashion that enables us to see clearly the nature of his own piety and thought, in their weaknesses and their strengths.

The chapter also contains an account of a short journey made (for purposes of trade) by Jacob in the environs of Zaitun – as the impatience of his servants to return to Italy mounts – and of a debate in the *concilio* as to the virtues or otherwise of an armed defence of the city against the Tartars. In this debate we are made aware of the existence in Zaitun of both a 'pacifist' and a 'military' school of thought, with the merchant-interest seemingly preferring harm-free acquiscence in conquest, and

their opponents counselling fortitude, wall-strengthening and
resistance to the invader. It is in this debate that 'Pitaco', for
whom Jacob shows increasing admiration, denounces the cowardice of the party for surrender, and Jacob makes (or claims
that he makes) his own modest contribution.

ow, on the second day of Adar,[1] having fulfilled
all my duties, the merchant Anlisciu, showing
me great honour, sent to me in the name of the
great Suninsciou that I, together with Lifenli,
should accompany his servant to the chamber
of the sages of the city in the Street of Harmony. There I
found many gathered to hear my words upon the wrongs of
the Christians and their evil conduct towards the Jews. For
my fame had grown great among them,[2] for which God be
praised.

Thus I entered the chamber of the sages, where no place
remained so great was the crowd, I being commanded in my
heart by the Holy One to declare without fear or burden
upon my soul the truth of my faith, and the wickedness of
those who speak always of love and forgiveness but whose
hearts, being hypocrite, are filled with hatred and false
accusation against us.

Therefore, when the sages Ociuscien and Lolichuan, a
master of great lineage, having praised me for my wisdom,
called upon me to speak before the learnèd of the city, I
declared as follows:[3] 'Sires, I come to make all things plain,
as never they were before, as to the nature of the Jews and
the evil of our foes, and if I should speak falsely, then God
grant that I may die a Christian,' at which words there was
great laughter among them. Whereafter, I continued: 'The
truth of these things is particular, for those who preach
brotherly love to the world are our persecutors. For in no
place do Christians leave us quiet for long, let alone love us,

before they find some reason to commit wickedness against one or many of us. And this is not because we in turn have committed some fault against them, but because we are Jews.

'Moreover, if the Christian may benefit from the Jew he permits him sojourn, but when he finds that the Jew no longer serves his Christian purpose, he finds reason to send him away, unless it should serve his purpose the better to set the common people upon him. Thus in Frankish lands we owe our safety to the greed of princes, not their love, when they would rather take our money than our lives. And if the Jew should claim that which is his due as a man among other men, Christian love demands, alas, that he shall first abandon his faith, which God forbid.'

I, Jacob of Ancona, further declared in a great voice as follows, knowing that I spoke with God's blessing, but also hearing a bitter cry at which I remained unmoved: 'Further, it is their priests who are the most wicked among them. For they teach the faithful that the Jews are rapacious and greedy, the same priests who come in secret to us for loans so that they may purchase houses, clothes and jewels for the women whom they keep hidden, or to furnish tutors for their children, or to pay their bishops for an office in which to grow fat in their old age. In such ways, and worse besides, they break their own sacred rules without a blush of shame, asking us for money in secret yet condemning us from their pulpits as lenders without faith or mercy.

'Likewise, the Christians say by their laws and ordinances that we may not employ them in our houses, or that we may not purchase land, or that we may not practise the crafts which we choose, or that we may not do other things. Yet which Jew does not know that all is permitted in return for payment to those who at the same time declare to others that their faith forbids them to receive it? Likewise, be the Christians ever so stern against the Jews, so great is the greed of those who blame us for the same vice that few there are among them who cannot be tempted to sell even their souls for gain.'

But at these words of mine there suddenly rose among them one shouting in the Frankish tongue that I was a perfidious Jew, he being a certain Christian priest of Zaitun by the name of Fra Bartolomeo, and whom I saw trembled with anger. Yet I continued without pause, knowing that I spoke the truth of God, the merchant Anlisciu graciously praying the said Bartolomeo, curses upon him, that I be permitted to speak so that all might learn the truth from my lips, as follows: 'The Torah forbids the pious Jew to buy and sell idols, or any other things that may serve the idolater in his worship. Yet who does not know that in all the lands of the Franks the priests of the Christians trade with us in the buying and selling of the rare and precious things of their churches, and that it is we who bring incense to them? This in their decrees they call simony[4] but which abbots are not guilty of it, as when their greed for spices and choice things conquers their hatred of us? Nor are the princes of their faith slow to take gifts from us, but such things are forbidden to a judge in Israel, of whom it is commanded that they shall take no gift, for a gift blinds those who have sight.

'O, how such blasphemers preach poverty but, like other men, covet wealth, railing against trade as a peril to the soul and naming the merchant to be minister of the devil, God forbid, yet for their own enrichment they lay out the money of their churches in the argosies of the Jews. Likewise, they declare that usury is an offence against the divine bounty, but their very prelates lend money for gages and profits beyond those permitted to the Jews, while yet other Christians lend to them, as the Salimbeni lent without shame to the abbey of Fiastra at 100 per cent when they fell into ruin. For everywhere Christians tell falsehoods about money, saying that their loans are free while ours are usurious, yet by false accounts of price and payment they hide their great profits. Thus, these pious citizens, who are themselves nothing but usurers, declare with a false document that they have sold goods to the taker of their money, who must pay for them on a later day at an increased price, and they use many similar stratagems besides.

'But if a man intends to borrow from another, giving the other a gift and saying, This gift is so that you may lend me money, this is usury paid beforehand. And if the said man should give the lender a gift for a loan that has already been made, this is usury after the fact, as Rabbi Gamaliel teaches.[5]

'Yet all these things the pious Christians practise, confusing by such stratagems the difference between that which to them is lawful and that which they declare to be sinful. But if their souls are put in peril by such tricks, they do not appear troubled. For so skilful are the Christians in false reasoning that they make even the most wicked of their deeds to appear without fault by permission of the canon law itself. Thus is wrong by trickery made right, so that they are even ready to condemn others and put them to the fire for the same sins that they freely commit themselves. And how much money do its legates and prelates borrow from us without return, to the honour of the Roman Church and its high priest,[6] as when my own father lent to the holy cardinal of my city, at the time when the Church sent him to squeeze the Jews in the name of their Cross?'[7]

---

'HIDE THEIR GREAT PROFITS'

*This is not fully explained by Jacob, but there is some evidence that under the guise of charging a penalty for 'delayed' repayment mediaeval lenders obtained interest in ways forbidden by the canon laws against usury. However, despite Jacob's implied disclaimer, Jewish bankers appear to have used the same devices. Thus, a debit note given to a borrower would be for a sum larger than the amount actually loaned, even 100 per cent larger, G. Luzzatto,* I Banchieri Ebrei in Urbino nell'Età Ducale, *Padova, 1902 (reprint 1983), p.37.*

At which words, which were the very words of truth,
Bartolomeo again shouted out with anger and derision in the
Frankish tongue, but I paid no heed to him, declaring that
such men were truly the fathers of the Church and its future
saints, may a curse be upon them for bringing us to our
plight.

For, knowing that I now stood in the sight of God, blessèd
be He, such was the strength in my soul and body, I
continued as follows, may God be thanked: 'Who but the
great bankers and usurers among the Christians, secretly
borrowing from us in their needs, manage the gains and
profits of the Pope of Rome? And who does not know that
when a pope is chosen, all his nearest think only of gain, their
minds being fixed not upon his virtue but on their own
provisioning, they themselves, whether men of holiness and
learning or not, becoming cardinals and legates as soon as one
among them ascends the impious throne of Peter?

'But must the brother of a saint also be a saint? For this
Church of theirs is no university of equals,[8] in which holiness
and goodness are rewarded, but a church of pride and riches
over which rule arrogance and evil-doing. Yet there is no limit
to the charity which my brothers show to their Christian
cities, just as we gave in the late earthquake that befell us, or
as my father showed to the priest Filippo when he took refuge
in the city. For in an earthquake who does not know that Jews
and Gentiles are buried together in the ruins, without regard
for their faith? Yet always the Christian, who preaches love for
his neighbour, halts in his step, may he be cursed, at the sight
of the Jew, peace be upon him, thinking him not to be a man
like others but that he should bear about him the mark of
Cain, so that those who follow the faith of love may take
guard against him.

'Indeed so unfaithful is the Christian that even those of
them who stand closest to us may not be found constant, as
when grief strikes us down. Nor do even the kindest shrink
from hurting us when they see that others do the same. At

our feasts and weddings they are our guests, and in our houses servants, just as we serve them in many things also, being wiser than they, while princes have us about them as counsellors and sages. Yet not even the wisest of such princes can forbear to treat us cruelly when the law of the prelates commands.[9]

'Likewise, learnèd Christian priests, for some there are, may study our sacred writings by our side,[10] yet at the same time who does not know that their Pope condemned our Torah, may God be thanked for His bounty to us? For such a Haman declared our wisdom to be a blasphemy against God, may God have cast him into Gehenna and destroyed his soul. Thus, they learn from us and study with us in the courts of princes, seeking the aid of our sages so that they may read the writings of the Greeks, of the Saracens, and of our prophets, may their souls endure. Yet at the same time these hypocrites among them are pleased to take our wisdom and to burn our books, so great is their wickedness and their hatred of us.

'Therefore, even when an entire realm or whole city depends upon the ingenuity of one of my brothers, those who do not possess his intelligence or his reason will still hold him in contempt. Indeed, such is their brotherly love that they rob us smiling and without shame, spurning our bodies but not our wisdom or our wealth, and seeking always to place the greater burdens upon our shoulders, and obstacles in our path, so that we may the sooner stumble and fall.'

---

'DECLARED OUR WISDOM TO BE A BLASPHEMY'

*In 1236, when Jacob was fifteen, Pope Gregory IX, at the persuasion of the Dominicans, condemned the Jewish Talmud as blasphemous and heretical; another papal bull of 1239, repeating that of 1232, ordered that all copies of it be destroyed. A burning of manuscripts of the Talmud 'by the wagon-load', as a contemporary described it, took place in Paris in 1240.*

At which words of mine, for which God be thanked, Fra
Bartolomeo cried out in his rage that I lied, God forbid, in
the Frankish tongue giving me warning that I, a Jew, should
suffer a great woe for those things which I had declared to the
harm of the Christian faith in the land of Sinim, and that
those who had killed *that man* should be forever condemned,
and other matters of this kind.

To whom I replied, God be praised, that the fathers of his
Church should then have no dealings with us, neither should
his abbots and prelates take money from us, nor sell us the
gold and silver of their altars, nor permit us to take their
pilgrims across the seas, albeit that such is also forbidden to us
by Torah Law, for which God be praised. But Bartolomeo, a
foolish man before whom I had no more fear, God be
thanked, would not be stilled, notwithstanding that the wise
Ociuscien and the merchant Anlisciu begged him to be silent
so that I might speak. Yet I had no need of their aid, for there
came to me from God, may the temple of Jerusalem be
rebuilt in our days, a great voice, in which I spoke as follows:
'Sires, even against the cruelty of the whole world, the Jew,
having greater knowledge, energy, and fear of God than other

---

'TAKE THEIR PILGRIMS ACROSS THE SEAS'

*Although unspecific, this suggests that Jacob had personal knowledge of, and may
even have participated in, the carrying of pilgrims from Italy to the Holy Land in
vessels belonging to or financed by Jewish merchant-traders; Ancona was a leading
port in such traffic. According to Henri Pirenne (*Economic and Social History of
Medieval Europe, *London, 1947, p.32), the 'demands of the crusaders' for
transportation by sea to Jerusalem 'galvanised' the Italian ports 'into incredible life
and vigour', until the defeat of Louis at Tunis in 1270, the year of Jacob's own
departure to the Orient. Nor was it merely a question of hiring out vessels: 'the
services of merchants who were second to none in their knowledge of the eastern
Mediterranean ... were rewarded generously' (N.J.G. Pounds, *An Economic
History of Medieval Europe, *London, 1994, p.365).

men, will, with God's aid, blessings be upon Him, vanquish every foe. Neither scorn nor hate, neither injury nor malice, will drive us from our chosen path, nor destroy our secret pride of heart.' Amen and Amen.

Whereupon, at these words of mine that the faithful Lifenli made known to the sages of the city, there was a great silence, as though they had truly heard the Word of the Lord, may blessings for evermore be upon Him, and I continued thus, this being a true account of all that I said: 'Sires, the man who stands before you, Jacob ben Salomone d'Israel, is without title of fame[11] in his own land. Nor, in my own land, may I move my finger or speak such words in my own defence as I speak here, lest the number of my foes multiply against me. For if a Jew of my land should complain against such a one as contemns him, that one will laugh at him and call him Jew by way of answer.

'Neither may the rich Jew show his wealth for fear of plunder, nor the poor Jew seem so blind and low as to invite distaste. Likewise, the wise Jew may not vaunt his wisdom lest others hate him from envy, nor the ignorant Jew show his ignorance for the greater contempt he will suffer. Hence, all of us must hide our true condition, in order not to give offence to other men. Thus for Israel to be poor, wretched, oppressed by grief and to live in the dust serves us no more than to be rich and proud, and to dwell in a royal palace no more than to live in a humble stall. For each condition has its own peril, since in each case the Jew, whether he be prince or beggar, foolish or learnèd, remains a Jew, may peace be with us. Thus, whichever we be, they place upon us the same badge, inviting the wicked to attack us as we go, yet when we seek protection among our brothers, they accuse us that we live apart.

'Likewise, when I have gone concealed, God forgive me, and was not thought to be a Jew, having taken off the sign, how many a friar, such as this one who is among you, showed himself kind and bestowed upon me the favours of his heart, and even gave me some holy relic? But how his face will

change, sires, and his brow grow dark when such a servant of
God, may the Lord forgive me the blasphemy of my words,
knows me to be a Jew, the very brother of *that man*,[12] which I
am in my own revealed person. Moreover, even when we wear
the sign so that it may be seen by them, like Janus they look
with one face to see that we wear it aright, and with the other
ask how much we will pay them to be exempt from the rule.
Likewise, if we show that we are bountiful, they accuse us of
seeking to corrupt them, but, if cautious, that we are miserly
Jews, and thus, if learnèd, that we are too wise, if proud, that
we are too proud, and if humble, that we creep like vermin.
So, also, if we refuse to become Christians at their command,
it is stubbornness which prevents us, but if we are
baptised, which God forbid, we remain Jews to those who
receive us.

'Thus it is that no Jew should betray the faith of his fathers,
preferring rather to be hated for that which he truly is than to
be hated for not being truly what he professes to be.
Moreover, the Christians themselves declare that the Jews
shall be preserved as witnesses to that which in their
blasphemy they name the truth of their faith, albeit that
friars, such as this one who has come among you, preach with
such hatred against us as though to wish us all dead, and that
we should be driven from the world. For such is the faith
which declares that men should love their foes. Yet the Jews,
peace be upon them, are not the enemies of the Christians,

---

'THE SIGN'

*The prohibition upon intermarriage and sexual relations between Christian and
Jew, first laid down in the Theodosian code of AD 438, was expressly repeated by the
Lateran Council; the 'badge of shame' which Jews were expected to carry on their
clothes under the decree of 1215 was allegedly designed above all to prevent
miscegenation in error. In fact the sexual taboo was widely ignored on both sides.
Hence, the frequent repetition of the prohibition by canon lawyers.*

being the fathers of *that man*, but rather it is the Christians who by calumny and the shedding of our blood, calling us a pestilence and a contagion, have made themselves our foes, may they be punished at the last day. But how, sires, may they speak the truth about us, who do not speak the truth about themselves?'

Whereupon, the priest, shouting in a loud voice to the sages Ociuscien and Lolichuan that I should speak no more, and with effort and blows against those who stood in his path, threw himself towards that place where I stood, declaring in the Frankish tongue that all my words were perfidious and false, being the words of a Jew.

But I, fearing neither the reproach nor the correction of any Christian, called upon Ociuscien that the priest be permitted to speak[13] and that my trusted Lifenli, peace upon him, make known the words which he should utter. Whereupon, Bartolomeo, drawing his cloak about him, with angry voice spoke all those things that are said by them against our people, as to our perfidy, heresy and usury, as also of our desire for the blood of the Christian, God forbid, and for the slaying of that thing which in their idolatry they call the host, and many such false things besides to do with their

---

'CALLING US A PESTILENCE AND A CONTAGION'

*This is not the full truth. The fifth-century Theodosian code used such terms as Jacob cites, but although it was never formally abrogated by the Church, it was tempered by the bull of Pope Gregory (AD 590–604),* Sicut Iudeis. *This bull was reissued, with various modifications, by no fewer than ten of the thirteenth-century popes, becoming a formal part of the canon law in 1234, when Jacob was thirteen.* Sicut Iudeis *opposed forced baptism, upheld the inviolability of Jewish synagogues and cemeteries and granted the Jews the right to practise their faith. Nevertheless, despite it, Pope Innocent III justified in 1205 the 'perpetual servitude' of the Jews, the Fourth Lateran Council of 1215 heaped further burdens and execrations upon them, and the 'Inquisition' was spreading in Jacob's time.*

idols, declaring also that the Law of our teacher Moses was of no worth, for which may the Holy One, blessèd be He, turn his face from him at the last day. Having spoken thus, the priest Bartolomeo did not return to his place but made as if to depart, believing that I, Jacob of Ancona, should have nothing to reply to him, and that, being a Jew and thus to him low and vile and full of fear, I should not dare to deny his words before such a great concourse of men.

But the strength of the Lord was in my heart and mind, and I feared nothing, answering as follows: 'You talk of God, blessèd be He, of the angels, peace upon them, of good and evil, of falsehood and truth, and of the idols whom you worship, God forbid. But what may you know of truth, when even your idols are those of Jews, such as the idols of *that man* which you set upon your altars and before whom you bend your knees, yet the Jew who stands before you, you deny and cast out?

'Sires, no Christian may know what is truth and what falsehood, nor give to them their just names, when the man whom he worships is a Jew whom he calls by the name of God, may He forgive me the blasphemy of my words. Likewise, their bloody killing in the name of their Cross they do not call by the word killing, but they say that it is the journey to the Holy Sepulchre or the pilgrimage to Jerusalem, speaking nothing of the cruel deeds they do along the way. He who truly worships God may worship Him in any place, in Aragon or Paris, but Christians must slaughter all in their path to the Holy City, in order that they themselves may become holy. Yet are not those who return thence the same wild beasts as those who set forth?

'But none of them may declare it, for the faith of the Christian stands upon great falsehoods of deeds as well as of words. Thus, in his pulpit such a one as he says that it is evil to shed human blood, yet the Christian takes the life of others without care either for his own soul or that of the slain. The foolish priest,[14] whose words come not from God but from

the deceits of men, speaks often of brotherhood, but the
Christians themselves live in hatred and schism one from
another. Nor are they able to choose a pope from among their
priests without great bitterness and division, so that even now
there is no pope among them.[15] Thus do they fight and
quarrel without end, also about who is superior in celestial
matters and who in matters worldly,[16] even to slaying one
another in the name of the idols which they adore.

'Therefore, is it not foolish and base that they should
declare to the Jews what is good and what is evil, and what is
falsehood and what truth? For in battle the Christians carry
the sign of the Cross on their banners, massacring one
another in the name of the brotherhood of men in the entire
world. Yet the Christians say that it is we ourselves, not they,
who are treacherous rebels against God, which is a false thing,
and that we hold in disrespect the Christian faith, which is
true and shall always be so, for which may God be praised.

'For to be a Christian assassin in the name of *that man* is
great villainy, and when they say that the Cross wishes to do
only that which is just, it is a simple lie.[17] Thus, was it not in
the name of the Cross and the Jewish idol which they place
upon it, God forbid, that brother slew brother in Byzantium,
carrying away gold and silver, precious stones, silks, furs and
rich clothing?[18] For so the Jews of the place gave report,
declaring also that Christian priests accompanied those who
drew the sword, sharing in the booty and giving blessing to
the slaughter. But what would the Christians have said of us,
if my brothers had carried out such bloody and impious
deeds?'

Thus my bitterness, alas, increased at the thought of our
griefs, may the Lord keep us in His hand, so that I was called
by Him to speak with His breath: 'O hypocrisy and
falsehood, O cruelty and folly, O blasphemous worship of
idols and the spilling of blood, your names are for ever
Christian. Even here your priests come and go as vagabonds,
preaching hatred against us so that there might be no place in

the world where we are safe. Truly the Dominicans are the
dogs of god,[19] for so they justly call themselves, being of that
species of rabid cur which bares its teeth and bites to kill the
stranger.

'For their priests, in the cause of love, give to us the signs of
fire, preaching that the peoples should kill all those who have
a beard and lend money. They say even that we are
circumcised as a sign, so that we may recognise one another
and enter into conspiracy one with the other without fear of
error. But never did it happen that a Jew showed another his
male member in order to persuade him of his faith. They
declare also that at our Passover we slay the Christian child,
which God forbid, drinking its blood at the Passover table, so
that each year we may remember with joy the death of *that
man*, may God curse them for such falsehood. For who does
not know that blood is forbidden us by our Laws, so that we
are even commanded to draw all blood from our meat before
we may eat it? Moreover, was it not at this same table that
*that man*, the Jew whom they worship in their idolatry, sat
with other Jews at the last days of his life, in order also to
remember our escape from bondage, may God be magnified
and lauded?

'Thus is one falsehood placed by them upon another, so
that truth is hidden by them in the name of truth. For is it
not they who at their altars make pretence to drink the blood
of the idol whom they worship and to consume his body,
wiping their mouths thereafter in indecent fashion upon
cloths proffered to them by their priests?'

At which words of mine the priest Bartolomeo with great
shouts of anger went out from the chamber of the sages,
together with those about him. But I, knowing that God held
me in His sight, continued as follows:

'Thus, in the way of the blasphemer, the Christian
worships him whom they call the crucified one, but who
cannot avail and cannot save. Yet, according to their
statements, the Christians say that he was the best man that

*301*

ever there was,[20] so good that he was indeed the Son of God, may God pardon me my words.

'But shall I, a Jew, believe that the Incorporeal One, may He be crowned in glory everlasting, entered, in Himself or through a spirit, the womb of a woman, O may God spare me for such utterance, and that He coupled with her in order that the words of our prophets might thus be fulfilled? But God, blessèd be He, is a foe to those who take His Holy Name in vain, for being incorporeal there could be no such congress, and if in spirit alone it could give rise to no corporeal effect.

'Moreover, if that Jew whom the Christians worship had both father and mother, why then did he himself have neither wife nor child? For if he might have the one, then why not the other? And what are they who speak of the trinity of God but deniers of God's unity, who have shut their eyes and cannot see?'

To which he who was named Cian, seeming to hold me in scorn, cried out that to such questions he did not seek the answer. Whereupon, being divided among themselves, some of the sages laughed and others besought the said Cian to hold his tongue, the wise Ociuscien reproaching him and begging me to continue, for which God be praised. Therefore I continued as follows, for the pious Jew who is beset by scoffers is not permitted to falter, nor to turn aside from that which God commands:

'Furthermore, the Christians wickedly say, in the manner of the priest Bartolomeo, that the Law given to our teacher Moses is lapsed and of no worth, and that *that man* is the Messiah who was promised by our prophets. They aver also that the Almighty One has made a new covenant with the Christians, who proclaim themselves with great foolishness to be the true Israel, and not the Jews, may God keep them.

'But when we deny such blasphemers, the Christians say with much scoffing that God has abandoned us, declaring that our sufferings are the proof of it. Yet it is they themselves who cause us such woes, they who worship graven images of a

Jew, and whose faith is not better than necromancy.
Nevertheless, they accuse us of blasphemy and sacrilege and
every other wicked thing, we who gave them their false
prophet, and whose prayers are the words of the Jews, and of
the anointed of the God of Jacob.[21]

'And how should we have slain our Ieshua,[22] who was put
to death by the Romans in a manner forbidden to the Jews?[23]
For our judges command that whoever among the sons of
Israel should prophesy falsely what he has not seen or what
has not been told to him, taking God's name in vain, contrary
to the Law of Moses our teacher, shall be strangled. But there
is no law among us which declares that such a one shall be
hanged upon the cross of a tree in the manner used by the
Romans. Yet the Christians wickedly and falsely proclaim that
such was our deed, and that it should be avenged to all
generations in the blood of my brothers, at the same time
declaring that it is not they but the Jews who give themselves
to revenge.

'Thus the Christians have sought to free themselves from
the holy commandments of the Torah, may God be praised
for His bounty to His people, to pull down our prophets from
their places, and to persuade the simple-minded with miracles
and wonders of the truth of their teaching. But in this way
one falsehood was placed upon another, so that they might
make princes of their prelates and deal cruelly with the Jews,
saying to all who would follow them that thus they might
gain eternal life. And upon this mountain of falsehood they
have set their saints and martyrs, of whom they make our
Ieshua the first. But the martyrs whom they have made
among the Jews in the name of a Jew may not be counted.'

To which words Cian, standing in a place among those
sages who were of the merchants' party,[24] answered that, for
all that the things which I spoke could be so, whoever was
neither Christian nor Jew should pay no heed to it. For each
worshipped the gods, or turned aside from them, as he
thought fit, so Cian declared.

Yet to this also I would not bow my head, for which God
be thanked, since He commanded me upon this day to speak
all these things to the assembly of the sages of the City of
Light. Moreover, although the travails of the city were great
and I knew that its fall was near, from the blindness and greed
of the people and the divisions among them, yet are the
divisions between the Jews and the Christians greater. For
they are divided in all the world according to their belief, and
the faith that the Christians profess being destined also to fall,
whenever God should will it, I know shall also bring down
many other lands and peoples in its ruin.

Nor can the faith of the Christian hold sway over Saracens
or Jews, when the most faithful of the Christians are those
who are most cruel to others, and the least faithful the most
mild and full of love. For the Jew has the most to fear from
those who are the most faithful in service of their idols, and
the least to fear from the others. When a Christian says to a
Jew, Why do you not become a Christian?,[25] he is therefore
offended by a demand so impious, as to submit himself to
idolatry, error and such bad faith.

Thus we do not despise the Christians for the words of
their faith, but reproach them for their deeds, which are
contrary to those things which they say. Moreover, since the
faith of the Christians rests upon that which the reason of
man may not believe, they themselves are much given to
secret doubt. Yet when they are given most to such doubt,
then do they become most ferocious towards my brothers, as
if we by our presence put them in mind of their false faith.
Thus, the Christian burns[26] the more when, with the sword
and flame, he pursues those whom he calls faithless, may the
wrath of God strike him down, than when he goes upon his
knees to pray before his idols.

But these things I say, may blessings be upon Him who
guides my hand, that, whereas we now stand in all lands at
others' mercy, prospering by the grace of others yet ready for
such turning of our fortunes as to make us flee or lay down

our very lives, the Jew will not be overcome by the malice of
others against him. Rather, we shall pass our days upon the
earth with our heads held high, for our sages are wiser than
others, and when we conduct ourselves badly, which God
forbid, it is because other men have made us so by their evil-
doing against us. But one day, for so our sages have said, there
will arise an evil and wicked people disposed to do such harm
to Israel as has been done by none since the beginning of the
world. Yet, at the last hour, when my brothers shall stand
upon the edge of life itself, the Ineffable One will surely pluck
us from the jaws of death and destroy our foes, their lands
and their possessions.

And thereafter the Jews shall rise again into the light of His
blessings, may God be exalted, for so it is promised, and they
will lead all peoples in the way of learning and of truth, until
the end of days and the coming of the Messiah. Of all those
prophecies I, Jacob of Ancona, am sure in my heart, for which
may God the Creator, blessèd be He, be magnified, cherished
and honoured, Amen, Amen and Amen. For, at the last, those
who oppress the sons of Israel will be as small as the dust
before the wind.

In this way I argued before Cian and all the sages to my
great honour, for there was much praise given to me by the
wise Ociuscien, whose words were approved by all. Therefore,
I went upon my way content, together with the faithful
Lifenli, having fulfilled my duty to God and to man. But as
we passed through the streets of the City of Light, in which
the great throng went up and down, hither and thither,
Lifenli sought to urge caution upon me, declaring that,
although my words had been learnèd and truly worthy of
praise, yet I had surely made a great enemy of the priest
Bartolomeo, and therefore of the other Christians of the city
also, having given them much offence, so that I should now
be suspected and hated among them. For so he declared.

Moreover, since all in the city were possessed by great fear
and bitterness, one against the other, as the merchants against

the party of the noble Pitaco, and the merchants one against
the other, and the sages and the people also,[27] he who should
now take a part in their assemblies, whether he be a citizen or
from another country, stood in peril, so that it were better to
keep watch than to be seen, and to listen rather than to speak.
Nor should I have faith in those who sent for me,[28] such as
the merchant Anlisciu, since, desiring to vanquish those who
stood against them and fearing that the people of the city
might take the side of Pitaco, those who commanded among
the merchants grew every day more bold and tenacious
against their foes, whether such be found among them or
outside. Hence, so said the faithful Lifenli, their words might
not be trusted, for they sought not the truth of things, nor the
good of the city, but their own ends. Therefore, it were better
that I attended more to my own affairs and departed the city
before my peril and the peril of my servants should grow
greater. He further declared that on all sides men spoke of the
approach of the Tartars, God forbid, so that each day the fate
of the city became more uncertain.

Thus the faithful Lifenli railed against me, yet seeking my
pardon for his counsel, whom I thanked for his concern but
reproached in turn for his fears, saying that it was not in this
fashion that a pious man might fulfil that which God
commands him to do. Yet the good Lifenli, peace upon him,
was by no means contented with my words, boldly saying that
I placed the things of God, may He be revered, before the
things of man, and that not the eye of God but the reason of
man must spy out the truth of things. For to believe that the
eye of God sees better than the eye of man that which is true
and that which is false, is not wiser than to give garlands to
wooden statues, painted and gilded, that have the semblances
of men. Thus the youth averred, may God spare me for what
I have written. At these words I laughed without anger, for
the boy was young, replying that to the true faith all such
things as he spoke of were an abomination, and that no Jew
gave garlands to idols in such a fashion, though Christians

and other idolaters might crawl on their knees before such images until their knees were broken, and with halters about their necks. But the bold youth was not satisfied with my answer, saying that all those who believed in God were of the same faith and that all were given to blind trust in marvels and that which has no true being, may God forgive these words.

To whom I replied as we went upon our way, amid the great crowd seeking ends without number: 'Among us also[29] are many who profess to see their future according to the natural course and disposition of the planets and their signs and points. But about those things I too have many doubts, seeing that the free will of man is also the gift of God, Creator of all things, by which good and evil may be done, and the Holy Law be observed or broken, not according to the stars but according to the wisdom and folly of each man.

'No doubt that there are marvels in the heavens and upon the earth, which no man may easily understand, and dreams by which the future may be discerned. But it is well to doubt, not trusting those who see spirits and demons on every side or those who go in fear of the enchantment of devils and witches, or those who believe that they can change the weather. For such things can turn the mind from the blessings of God and our duties to Him, may He be praised, as well as from the rational discourse of men. Moreover, forms exist only in matter and have no separate existence, so that that which has no corporeal substance should not frighten us, being the fruit only of our thoughts.[30]

'Furthermore, since the Christians are given to accuse the Jews of magical tricks and deeds of darkness, it is better for us to avoid hidden things, as divining and the excessive study of stars.[31] For our knowledge cannot grasp the future, and thus none may say that the Jews possess particular powers. For there is but One God who guides the sphere, Who created everything, and among all that exists there is no God beside Him. Moreover, He has created all the things that are other than Himself, may He be magnified and lauded, and neither shall these created things be themselves worshipped nor any form made of them, nor from them, Amen and Amen.'

Yet still Lifenli was dissatisfied with my answer, plying me with many questions both wise and impious about gods and idols, so that I was constrained to answer as follows as we went our way: 'Young man, our sages teach that the idol cannot know you, nor your thoughts and actions, nor can he hear your prayers, nor see your movements. Nor may the Ineffable Name take a human or any other form, nor is a Jew permitted even to think it. Nor shall the reason of the Jew admit that which a cunning man may create as if it were a marvel or prodigy against nature. Likewise, we are commanded to put away astrology, for the fate of Israel depends upon no star. Thus it may not be said by you, or by any other, that my brothers deny either the commandments of God, blessèd be He, or the reason of man.'

To which the faithful youth replied that there was never faith held in the gods in which there was not belief in such marvels as no man might explain, may God spare me for what I have written. Moreover, Lifenli declared that the Jews, since they had great faith in God, must surely also believe in that for which there is no proof.

I replied in turn that not all works of faith are equally worthy of respect or belief, some being tricks to deceive the foolish and others the acts of idolaters which have no value in the eye of God. True it is that God brought the sons of Israel out of Egypt by signs and miracles and took care of them in the wilderness, giving them the land of Canaan. But thereafter it was not given to man to act against the natural law, that is against nature,[32] these being the first and last things until the Messiah come.

But at my words, entering the house of Nathan and being greeted by my servant Buccazuppo, the young Lifenli laughed impiously so that I became angered, he declaring that the

Jews, although they had no idols among them, God forbid, also believe in that which is against nature and reason.

To whom I replied as follows: 'The followers of Aaron[33] were punished and justly slain, nor may any Jew take their idolatrous path. It is not appearance, nor the report of others, nor the beliefs and prophecies of idolaters which must be our guide, for such is the way to error, but reverence for the Divine Name together with the use of the reason and the intellect, which are the gifts of the Holy One. Thus we may not be deceived, neither believing that the spheres have souls, nor that the nature of things may be explained by letters or numbers, nor that it is unlucky to put on the left boot before the right, nor that trees may produce birds.'

Whereupon Lifenli, being more satisfied, God be thanked, demanded whether I believed in wonders. To whom I answered that I believed no more in the spirits of the air[34] than in the giant bird of which mariners speak, which they

---

'NOR THAT THE NATURE OF THINGS MAY BE EXPLAINED BY LETTERS OR NUMBERS'

*This aside seems to be a criticism of mediaeval cabbalistic learning. It is also a comment which would have been beyond Lifenli's understanding, and is clearly a product of Jacob's leisure. The cabbala (literally, 'tradition') was a system of philosophical mysticism, whose origin has been traced to the Jewish community of Gerona in Spain at the beginning of the thirteenth century. It taught that 'union with God' is attained by mystical speculation; that the world was not created by God but is (in a rather Blakean sense) an 'emanation' of God; and that 'the Eternal' is composed of ten radiating spheres, or Sefiroth, each of which is a source of grace and bounty. Cabbalistic learning and practice had bewildering aspects, presuming among other things to decipher the divine attributes by means of arcane scrutiny of the letters of the Hebrew alphabet, a practice to which Jacob appears to be referring. The followers of Maimonides were generally opposed to the cabbala, preferring Aristotle to the esoteric; while the cabbalists were opposed in turn to the rationalism associated with the thought of Maimonides.*

say has its habitation in the Moon. For it is not fitting for a Jew to admit that which may not be found in the Torah, nor that which his own reason denies. Thus it is not possible that there can be a bird which is taller than a man, with the feet and neck of a camel, and which, although it has wings, only runs, and as fast as a leopard, but cannot fly. Yet the mariners of Cormosa insisted that it was so and that they can run twenty leagues in a day,[35] but such a thing is not to be believed. For a bird with wings which yet cannot fly does not conform either with reason or with divine decree, while God has created nothing which offends the law of nature, which is itself the law of God.

But if objection were to be made that God in His power may create whatever He chooses, including such a bird, I should reply that He might do so, but not so that there should be confusion in the order of the created world. It is true that even our sages have spoken of a giant fowl whose wings darken the noonday sun, but we are not commanded to believe that which is against reason. Thus the Holy One would no more create a bird which cannot fly than a fish which cannot swim.

For each creature inhabits its own world according to the order which is in it, one the order of the waters and the other the order of the air. A fish, such as the great crocodile of Egypt,[36] or the frog, may live in the water and walk on the land also, according to God's bounty. A bird may likewise walk on land, swim in water, and fly in the air. But a fish that cannot go in the water cannot be conceived of, because it is against reason, no more than a bird that cannot fly.

I do not say that a bird must fly well or quickly, for, like the hen, it may fly badly. But that which has wings must fly in some manner, as a man with a soul must aspire to God.

In this way I argued, God be praised, but the youth Lifenli again laughed impiously so that I was constrained to reproach him, the girl Buccazuppo and the woman Bertoni remaining in our presence, although I had ordered them to leave us. For their manner had been so changed by the evil words of the woman Liciancie that I might no longer command them to go or stay according to my will, God forbid.

Whereupon, Bertoni lamented that dangers beset us on every side, and that from my tarrying in the city we should be lost, for the enemy advanced upon it. In addition, Buccazuppo made report that the faithful Armentuzio and Pizzecolli, seeing that the time for our departure from the land of Sinim drew near and being greatly angered at my absence, would next morning take their leave, in order to seek out in certain villages and hamlets[37] of the fiefdom of Zaitun such choice things for purchase as could not be found in the City of Light. But this I forbade, the next day being the eve of the Sabbath Terumah,[38] ordering Buccazuppo to go and tell them to await the due day.

At which Lifenli, with great boldness, declared that thus I showed myself to be given to the same magical arts as those I had accused before the sages of the city, saying that as the people of Manci think it to be a sin to step upon the threshold with the foot, so do the Jews fear to set forth upon the highway save upon an auspicious day. But I reproved him for his words, telling him of the gift of the Sabbath and of the Torah Law. But he was not stilled, saying that the Jews were not different from the Christians, who make the sign of the Cross upon their foreheads and breasts in order to ward off the evil eye.

To whom I replied that such things are truly found among my brothers also, as when a child upon the day that he first is brought to our holy letters[39] is covered lest he see a dog. For among our sages some hold that an unclean thing shall not come to the eye of a child when for the first time he learns the Ineffable Name. But such foolish things are not held to be just by all, nor may they darken the glory of our Sabbaths. For so I told him, God be praised.

Yet Lifenli, being stubborn, would not bow to my words, declaring that among the Mancini it is forbidden to bury a

dead person upon certain days which they call *tinsinci*, lest it
shortly bring death to another of the same family, and that all
such things, whether of the Jews or other peoples, are
contrary to reason.

To whom I replied as follows, may God be thanked for the
strength that came to me against my adversary,[40] for I was
greatly wearied: 'Some persons fear one thing and others
another, just as one people thinks that one thing is sacred and
another some other thing. Thus among those of Melibar it is
a virtue to be blacker than others and in the lands of the
Franks whiter. In the same way those of Melibar make their
idols black and their demons as white as white, for so I have
seen, while the Christians make the faces of their idols, God
forgive my words, white or pallid, and those of their demons
as black as night. Likewise the Indian accuses the Saracen and
Jew for eating the cow, the Saracen and the Jew accuse the
Christian for eating the pig, which God forbid, and the
Christian accuses the Jew and the Saracen for draining the
blood from their meat, while the stranger accuses the people
of Manci that they eat the dog and the snake, and he who will
eat no animal accuses all. Is there reason in this, or are all
wrong, reason having lost its power?[41]

'Likewise those of Greater India place their trust not in the
Holy One but in the ox, while among the Christians the more
contrary to reason the tales of their gods and saints, the
greater the hope and the faith they have in them. I have heard
tell that in the same way the Tartars seek to cast a spell on the
weather with fumigations of their idols, as the Christians
worship the skulls and bones of their saints so that they might
have good fortune from it. So in like fashion do other
idolaters not only pray before their effigies in the manner of
the Christians, but give them food to eat and do other such
foolish things.

'Thus in all the world where men make idols with a human
face, or permit fear to guide the mind and to set aside that
which reason and knowledge command, they act against the

Word and Law of God and are not better than the Christians,
but the same. For such idols and fears stand between man and
God, blessèd be He, as the idol of death of the Christians,
being the figure of a dead man upon a cross, stands between
the Christians and a knowledge of God, may He be magnified
and honoured. But a pious man must permit nothing, neither
idol nor false intercessor nor false rule, to come in the way of
his contemplation of the Holy One. Moreover, although he
who fears God must observe His laws, the ceremonies of faith
alone are not pleasing to God.'

Whereupon Lifenli wished to ask me further questions
about our laws, but I sent him away, for I wished not to be
angered by him but to be joyful in heart for the coming of the
Sabbath Terumah.

Having done my duty, for which God be praised, I set forth
from Zaitun on the fifth day of Adar[42] with my servants
Armentuzio and Pizzecolli, together with Nathan ben Dattalo
and his servant, one Cianta, so that we might purchase
cheaply those things that are more costly in the city. And
everywhere that we journeyed we found many inhabited
places, with towns and walled villages of trade and craft, with
much buying and selling, and fine districts with great
abundance of everything on which to live.

All the cities of the province and all the surrounding
provinces are in the seignory of Zaitun, and everywhere there
is lodging and habitation but a few *li* one from the other, each
*li* being two hundred and sixty Venetian paces,[43] and in every
house there is the making of silk to be seen, which is a wonder
to behold.

Thus many valuable wares are produced which are brought
for sale to the City of Light, but he who goes in the
countryside may have them more cheaply, as I have written.
Moreover, the villagers, both men and women, are friendly to
him who comes from another country, saying, May you find
wealth among us. For the land is temperate and fertile and

there is much wealth. There is also copious water running in canals among the fields which, notwithstanding the past drought, were as green as gardens. Beside the sea there grows bamboo in very great quantity, and in those districts they live also by fishing, by finding pearls which are brought from the nearby sea, and from the taking of salt. But in the towns of the land their wealth is greater, for here there is every kind of spice, herb and wood, as well as silks, satins and porcelains.

Everywhere there is a good strength in the land, so that it is like a vast and beautiful garden, with great mountains and valleys, and springs of purest waters, together with an abundance of trees which at no time lose their leaves but are always green, God be praised. There are also many lakes, pools and lagoons or marshes, and from those near the sea much salt is carried, yet there are also rocky hills on which are built the monasteries of the idolaters.

In the realm of Toutson, it is said that there are a thousand great cities, such as Iansu,[44] Pocien and Chiacien, as well as Chinscie, which realm comes as far as the southern banks of the river Chian,[45] where much grain and rice are harvested. In this region is also the Great River,[46] which causes much damage when it is full, as does the Po when it passes through our city of Ferrara. There are many messengers and runners who take messages and goods to all the cities of Manci, riding and running even at night, and crossing valleys or rivers. Thus the merchant may speedily conduct his trade to his great profit, as well as making payment with money or paper or by many other means of exchange.

But of all that may be had by the merchant in the seignory of Zaitun, the choicest and best is the silk-work of every colour, among which is also woven cloth of silk and gold, whose workmanship is of the highest that a man may find. Indeed, so well proven is the value of various silk-stuffs that it may be measured at a fixed sum against silver, yet in the country you may have one hundred *libbre* of the most costly for less than eight Venetian groats, God be thanked. Here you

may also find satins richer even than those which come to the
city of Zaitun, so that the like has never been seen, the richest
being sewn with small pearls, as well as Tartar stuffs woven
with such skill that not even a painter with a brush could
equal them, and of these I bought in abundance, God be
praised.

I found also porcelains of excellent quality with which they
make bowls as fine as glass flagons, of which I purchased six
hundred for two hundred groats, since they are the most
beautiful porcelains in the world. There is also in the province
so much fine sugar, which is in a black paste, as well as
saffron, ginger and galingale of the highest quality, of which I
therefore also bought greatly. They also have a certain kind of
saffron which they use against diseases of the kidneys and
stomach, and of this I bought also, as well as ointments for
the care of the teeth, and cassia[47] for the bowels.

Thus, guided by Nathan ben Dattalo and his faithful
servant, I purchased greatly to my profit, finding much good
indigo and alum[48] also, and saw so many spices that do not
come into our lands[49] and whose names I could not tell, as
well as paper, lacquer and choice herbs to drink.

Yet I feared greatly to be robbed, God forbid, so many are
the brigands on the way, fearing also the reports of the
countrymen that the Tartars drew always nearer, lest I should
die upon the road. But God, blessèd be He, kept me in His
hand, bringing me great profit without harm, even though I
did not fulfil all my duties to Him, for which may He spare
me at the last day. For as I was going on my way on the eve of
Sabbath Tetzaveh,[50] the night overtook me, may God forgive
me, nor did I entrust my purse to a Gentile, as Torah directs,
but kept it upon me in my fear. Nor did I even put it from
me in the hospice where I was obliged to pass the night, it
being more than a day's journey from the City of Light. But
all night long I prayed to God in His praise, thanking Him in
joy for the bounty of the Sabbath, as also for the grace of the
countrymen of Manci towards the stranger. For each

merchant who, making a journey, passes through these towns, whatever be his condition, it is ordained that he does not pay anything for his bed or for his sustenance, for which God be praised.

Thus, after an absence of seven days, I returned with my merchandise to the City of Light and rejoined my company of friends,[51] God be thanked, it being the eve of the fast of Esther and the beginning of Purim. Yet my thoughts were greatly troubled, for it was as though the towns and villages through which I had passed were awaiting their end at the Tartars' hands.

For the countrymen did not bestir themselves to defend their homes, may God keep them, but worked in peace according to their custom, awaiting slaughter as a lamb looks in innocence to the blade of the butcher. In this way they heard neither the steps of their Haman as he drew near throughout their lands, nor the words of those who might give them good counsel, but went to and fro like the people of the City of Light, thinking nothing of the morrow.

There also came to me in these same days the captain of the Saracens[52] together with my servant Armentuzio, our ships having been prepared, pleading that I now depart from

---

'HE DOES NOT PAY . . . FOR WHICH GOD BE PRAISED'

*The Sabbath had technically begun (p.315), and Jacob was in breach of the prohibition upon having money on one's person after Friday nightfall. Other Mishnaic prohibitions (there are fifty-nine categories) applying to the Sabbath day of rest – a day to be spent in joyful but restrictive abstention from the activities of the working week, in celebration of God's rest from the six days of creation – include not lighting a fire or lamp; not cooking; not travelling; not carrying a weight; not writing; and engaging in no activity involving trade, money, or the use and handling of money. Hence, Jacob's alarm for his breach of pious observance. It is also prohibited to fast or to mourn on the Sabbath, for it is a day set aside as a 'day of delight', on which freshly cleaned clothes should be worn.*

Zaitun lest we be put in danger by the weather, the mariners
being ready to depart.

But I was not yet willing to set sail, for a messenger had
come to me from the noble Pitaco, declaring that he would
address a great assembly of the city. For now it stood at its last
peril, such was the confusion of the citizens about every
matter which concerned them. He warned me also, peace
upon him, that although I should attend the said assembly,
since I had spoken words of great wisdom in every place to
which I had come, I should beware of the hatred for me of
the merchant Suninsciou, and many others of his party. For I
had counselled against them before the people, reproaching
for their greed those who sought only gain and wealth, and
praising those who preached the way of goodness, modesty
and truth, so that if I spoke further, I should assuredly be
driven from the city.

But after the messenger of Pitaco had departed, I sent away
the captain of the Saracens and my servant Armentuzio,
declaring that if Eliezer del Vecchio and Lazzaro, being
impatient to be gone, wished to set sail from the city of their
own accord, they should do as seemed fitting to them, but
that I should not depart until my duty had been done.

There then came to me also the evil woman Bertoni,
urging me with many words and Christian curses, for which
may the Adversary take her at the last day, that all should
forthwith depart, saying that the woman Liciancie held my
servant Buccazuppo in her power. For the said Liciancie had
come frequently to the house of Nathan while I was away
from the city, and also in the darkness of the night, which I
would by no means believe, God be thanked, hers being a
tongue of wickedness and not of truth.

Therefore I was greatly beset, but having laid my
phylacteries, thanking God for keeping the pious and learnèd
in His charge, I set out upon the sixteenth day of Adar, which
is to say the eighteenth day of February of the year 1272, to
the great assembly of the city, accompanied by the faithful

Lifenli, so that I might hear the speech of the noble Pitaco, may his memory be preserved.

When all were gathered together and they had made their customary devotions to their gods, bowing this way and that and laying a gift before the idol of the great hall, one among their number rose to his feet and uttered a hymn in a voice of lament for the woes of the City of Light, some among them weeping at their plight.

Whereupon there followed a great parley among the elders, merchants and sages of the city, in which the noble Pitaco was the first in honour and rectitude as in age, declaring with grave words that the Tartars had wasted the lands to the north, sacking the cities and destroying the treasures, so that their very books, in which the deeds of their fathers and of the present time were written, had been burned, and that such also would be the fate of the lands of Sinim to the south, unless the people aroused themselves to their peril.

He expressed himself in this way: 'The kingdom is without order and the city is surrounded by lures of which we in our idleness and pleasure take no account. Necessity induces us to pay heed to the defence of our city and to find new arms, for our weapons are old and unfitted for combat with the Tartars. Yet neither are we ready for resistance[53] nor do we possess the fortitude which the hour requires.

'But, as Menche teaches, just as when a man invites offence others will surely offend him, so when a city invites assault others will attack it. Nor can those be called sages who merely lead one another to fall. For, despising the ways of soldiers, we have given those who know nothing of the arts of war command over them, driving them from our presence and depriving them of their courage. At first this was justly from fear lest they should seek to usurp the power of the Son of Heaven, but now it is a custom that cannot be broken. Hence, our soldiers, many and skilled as they are, lack the means which they require at this moment when the enemy draws closer to our gates.

'Once also, there was a love of feats of arms among our nobles and their sons. But now they live at ease in the cities, showing contempt for strength of body and courage. Yet all the while the Tartars have ruined and done great damage to so many of our homes and fields, but still we do not stir. Now, even the cities of Sanian and Fancien, where the citizens are so famished that men say that their eyes have turned blue, are on the point of falling to the troops of the Tartars. Thus, the conquest of our own province draws nearer.[54]

'Shall we therefore do less than they, succumbing to the foe in shame, or shall we protect our honour? For we must dig deep ditches and raise our walls against the enemy, but what works have you done, sires, to defend the city? On three sides of the city we still have strong walls and turrets, but they are falling into ruin, being as they were in the times of our forefathers, while at the Gate of the Drovers the idle have taken away bricks from the very walls in order to repair the foundations of their houses.

'Therefore, the walls and gates of the city must be immediately made strong in order to protect it and to save it. Indeed, the circuit of the wall must be even enlarged and strengthened. For without an enclosing wall, well maintained and ten strides high and a deep ditch,[55] how can the Tartars be kept out? Moreover, without a high walkway, along which one goes on foot around the city, how can one see the parts beyond the city? Thus, we must make preparations with all speed, for within a strong place, no one need be feared.'

To the noble Pitaco, a certain rich and powerful merchant by name Lotacie, a man young in years and thin in body, now made reply as follows: 'Sires, even if our foresight had been the best in the world, the army of the Tartars and their people are on the point of conquest of Manci. Moreover, their troops are well trained to subdue cities and provinces, nor could we resist such a multitude without the same ardour as that of our

enemies, lacking which we cannot now stop the advance of
the foe.

'For when he fails to conquer at the first attempt, the Great
Cane persists until he has carried the day. Thus, how many
times has he tried to take Cipenchu and how many times
returned to the assault? Is this a king who can be dissuaded
from his purpose by a high wall and a deep ditch? Why
should we die in a battle which must at the last be lost? For
their armies are as a host of ants and their warriors are as
brave as lions, yet their cruelty is aroused only by those who
resist them, not by those who submit. Therefore, it would be
more pious and welcome to the gods that we bow to the
command of fate rather than disturb heaven with our vain
cries. We must accept our situation and not seek ends to
which we cannot attain. Men may think that the world
should be changed, but high providence thinks otherwise.
Sires, there is no escape from the decree of eternal fate.'

At which words the noble Pitaco, being greatly angered,
enquired thus of Lotacie: 'Do you know the will of
providence?' To whom Lotacie replied with contempt: 'With
the body of a sheep but clad in the skin of a lion, no victory
can be gained in battle. Or, like a fly on the tail of a noble
steed, will you, sire, travel ten thousand *li*? There is no need
for war, nor will any gain benefit from it. Moreover, as the
fortune of a realm rises under heaven so it also falls, while to
send the people to war when they are not trained is to bring
defeat upon them. And do we not know that if any city of his
realm rebels against the Great Cane, the neighbouring cities
are ordered to send their armies to destroy that city? But since
our city will be among the last to be conquered[56] by reason of
its position,[57] will we not therefore be at the mercy of our
neighbours, whatever we choose to do?'

To whom the noble Pitaco answered with all his strength:
'Then the greater is the necessity that our city should be
conjoined with the other cities of Manci, so that we may assist
one another against such fate.'

To whom the merchant Lotacie replied thus: 'The Tartars
have left many cities ruined and destroyed. But if we do not
resist them our own city may not suffer in such a fashion.
Whereas if we resist and fail, as we are sure to do, the City of
Light will be destroyed.'

To these words of Lotacie there was much assent, some
thinking him right in every way, while others remained in
silence, at which Pitaco cried out: 'Each one of us must be
ready and determined to bear himself well and bravely, for if
we act otherwise we shall bring shame upon the city. Let us
therefore prepare our defences, call our bravest generals
together, and show ourselves unafraid to meet the foe.'

Lotacie, laughing impiously in such manner that others
laughed also, replied as follows: 'And how will a man agèd as
you, so old that you have lost all your teeth, go valorously
into battle? Are you so courageous that the entire world must
fear us? When officials attain seventy years they should return
to their homes. But many there are, sires, who continue to
meddle in the affairs of the city. Yet since the age of a man is
what he affirms it to be, many of those who are very advanced
in years declare that they are younger than they are.'

At which the merchants in their places laughed in scorn at
the noble Pitaco, and many others also, God forbid, so that
Lotacie continued thus: 'To talk about virtue is not the same
as its practice. Old men who can talk are not equal to those
who are able to act. All that you say is oration only, and
whatever cannot move others to belief none will obey.
Moreover, not even the bravest men of the city are willing to
enter into misfortune, knowing also that the Great Cane has
done little harm and does not rob. Therefore it would be
better to follow willingly behind this people,[58] seeing his
bounty and lest our city suffer great harm from your false
counsel.'

To these words of the merchant Lotacie there was again
much assent, but the noble Pitaco, may his name be recorded,
appearing greatly troubled and with little strength to speak,

replied: 'Men such as you love gain but do not value the lives
of others. Instead of directing the greatest effort to the getting
and spending of wealth, it would be better if each one of you
directed such effort to the preservation of our honour. Then,
if you decided to conduct yourselves with valour, it would be
as it always used to be among us. For your forefathers held
that it was of greater worth to die on the field than to resign
oneself to the shame of defeat.

'You know well that our brothers in the north detest the
rule of the Great Cane because he has set over them in each of
their cities, as will assuredly happen in this city also, governors
who are Tartars, and more frequently Saracens, and these they
cannot endure since they are treated by them like slaves. Do
you wish such governors and ministers to rule over you also?
Moreover, has not the Cane sent his great barons with vast
troops of horse, even as many as eighty thousand, to watch
over the cities of the north at the expense of those who dwell
in them, to their great cost? Is that, sires, what you wish for
your own city? Did not the Great Cane declare to the other
cities, I have overcome you with weapons in hand and all that
you have is mine?'

To whom the merchant answered as follows: 'You are an
agèd scholar and it does not befit you to adopt the warlike
pose. Many of you too have been corrupted by greed, but
none of you has yet sought to ride without teeth into battle,
or to give instruction to others in the arts of war. Do not
the Tartars treat kindly with those of other faiths, calling
even the Christians by no term of reproach, but the fair
people? Are there not many from other lands among the
counsellors and servants of the Great Cane? And among the
wives of the brother of the Great Cane is not his most loved
a Christian woman, and does not the Great Cane rebuke all
those who cast gibes at the Christians and the followers of
other faiths?

'Therefore, may it not be said that the Tartars are a people
which honours the ways of others, and that if we conduct

ourselves in a fitting manner, we too shall not suffer but gain from their rule?'

Whereupon, Pitaco, peace upon him, again raised himself and with great anger spoke as follows: 'Your manner is base and cowardly. The Tartars are a savage people. Have you not heard tell of how the generals of the Great Cane treat their captives, even boiling them in great cauldrons? Have they not taken the officials of the cities of the north and slain them miserably, although they sought like you to be pleasing and acceptable to the Tartars? You in your cowardice trust that such men are meek, yet have we not heard tell how they eat the flesh of men executed with the sword?

'How long will you continue so vilely to declare that, even if we are conquered, you and your possessions will suffer no harm, and that we shall be treated justly and with moderation? For this is the counsel of cowards, who conceal their cowardice with the appearance of prudence. The Tartars are good fighters and do not fear death, while every breath you draw shows the desire to flee our foe,[59] rather than to leave for the field with courage and to fight with valour.'

But at these words of the noble Pitaco there was not praise but great derision, so that all clashed very bitterly, each merchant shouting in his place against Pitaco, may his

---

## 'MANY FROM OTHER LANDS (p.322)'

*It is true that in the Mongol court of Kublai Khan there were Arabs and Christians who served as chamberlains, doctors, astronomers and even as cooks. There was also at least one minister. As to Marco Polo – judging from his account of his seventeen years in China – he was employed by Kublai Khan, the Mongol ruler, as a court emissary, or legate, to various parts of China and, for three years, as an official in the city of Yangzhou. Chinese sources do not clearly confirm the latter but suggest that in 1277, at the age of twenty-three, he was nominated an agent of the Khan's Privy Council. Much of his work for the Mongol court appears to have involved travelling to distant provinces, including Yunnan, in order to report on conditions there.*

memory be preserved. So that he, again seeking to be heard, declared that the merchants spoke in a manner contrary to the order of heaven. Whereat one of their number, laughing impiously, cried out that the order of heaven should not protect them from the armies of the foe, but another among them declared that, even though they of the merchants' party had had the better of the argument, they should allow to speak even those who would bring the city to ruin. The noble Pitaco, being old and feeble, was not able to continue, so that a great silence now fell upon the assembly, those about him seeking to help him and to give him strength. At last, when he had more breath, he spoke in this way: 'You are like Lusou who talked much but lacked will. With such conduct as yours, you will be without refuge in the hour of danger, like the rat fallen in the flour and able only to roll your eyes.' Whereupon, some laughed and others shouted in anger, but the noble old man continued: 'The merchant Lotacie is weak and his wares are soft, for he is fearful and has a faint heart. You must therefore learn, sire, to control your cowardice and your desire for ease. Or will you wait until the savage Tartars are at our gates?

'Yet I think that not even then, so abject and fearful are you, and so ready to abandon everything for fear of the Tartar armies, would you show yourselves to be men. Instead, you prefer that by desolation our destroyers should teach us that we have for so long lost our way in greed, in pleasure and in lack of faith. How often were the kingdoms of the north brought down? Must we learn again the bitter truths that were taught to our forefathers by the Taniani, the Chitani and the Uceni,[60] who in our weakness laid waste our lands?

'Shall we suffer such loss and harm again from your ill counsel? Shall the hands of those who envy us our wealth, our trade, our skills, and the wisdom of our sages, be laid upon us? Would we not defend ourselves the better not only with strong walls and shining arms but with knowledge of the lost ways? And would we not prosper the more if our citizens

*Passover feast, taken from* Passover Haggadah, *Germany, c.1400* (AKG).

*Jewish school, taken from a German manuscript of Pentateuch, Megilloth and Haphtaroth, 1395* (British Library).

*Israelites in chains before Nebuchadnezzar ('Nabuccodonosor' in Jacob's text), from a thirteenth-century Italian manuscript* (E.T. Archive).

*Aaron of Colchester, caricature of a Jew dating to the late thirteenth century, with (bottom right) one of the forms of the 'Jewish badge'* (Hulton Getty).

*Caricature of a Jew*
(Public Record Office).

*Satire on the Jews of Norwich, drawn by Matthew Paris, thirteenth century*
(Public Record Office).

*Genghis Khan's march into China, from Berezin XV's*
The History of the Mongols (AKG).

*'The wise Menche', Mencius, Chinese sage of the fourth century BC* (Hulton Getty).

*Kublai Khan* (Hulton Getty).

*Marco Polo at the Court of Kublai Khan, detail taken from* Livre des Merveilles (AKG).

DETAILS FROM THE EARLY-TWELFTH-CENTURY SCROLL
'GOING UP THE RIVER AT THE SPRING FESTIVAL',
PAINTED BY ZHANG ZEDUAN
*(Werner Forman Archive Ltd)*

*River boat traffic near the city of Kaifeng*

*Crossing the bridge over the river*          *Market scene*

*Street scene*

*Shopkeepers and customers in the market*

*Street scene*

*The Divine Judgment on the Cities of the Plain, taken from a mediaeval Hebrew Bible* (British Library).

were united in their faith rather than divided by their vain desires?'

To whom the young merchant Lotacie, laughing, replied that a great army might not be defeated by virtue alone, and that there was never a foe which laid down its arms and fled at the sight of honest men.

To which the noble Pitaco, as if greatly wearied, answered as follows: 'The Tartars and their Cane will soon begin to advance against us. In such peril as this and knowing what has gone before, will you continue to lust for your riches and pleasures, while neglecting the defence of our ways and customs? Will you continue in vain to think yourselves better than others, while those who seek to destroy you gather up their strength? Again I say to you that you must be brave and valiant, and all should so comport themselves that the whole world will have to say of us, These were truly men of valour.'

But for the most part those who were present were not in accord with Pitaco, as if few desired to enter into battle for the city or to measure themselves against their enemies. Of these the merchant Lotacie was the chief among them, saying that it was better to be a people that never makes war upon others, and where all live in great peace with each other.

To whom Pitaco, who was pale with anguish, God forbid, declared in a soft voice as follows: 'But we do not live at peace with each other. Rather, each man, seeking his own ends and driven by desire and greed, is set against his brother. Nor does anyone gain rest or solace, however great his possessions. In ancient times, it was preached among us that we should love one another so that there might be no more discord among us, nor war.

'Yet now, such young men as you and your leader Suninsciou declare that only by the way of the lion and the wolf, and not by that of the dove, shall men prosper in the City of Light. But what manner of lion and wolf are you that you turn your backs upon the foe and seek the refuge of your lairs when danger threatens? Rather, if all stood firmly

together, the citizens would be content, the city be kept safe
from harm, and those who wished such a thing for themselves
might become richer.

'Instead, crowds of men day and night run through the
streets in search of prey, while each fears the next, so great is
the suspicion that one man has for the other. For this is the
City of Light which you, sires, have created, in which,
although the lanterns glitter in every place, there is only
darkness inside men's souls.'

But those about the merchant Lotacie, all being of the
party of Suninsciou, would not be moved by the words of the
noble Pitaco, the merchant Anlisciu rising to his feet and
asking as follows: 'Did not Chunfutsu reject those who
sought to wage war? Did he not say that death was too light a
suffering to visit upon those who showed the way, as Pitaco
shows, to devour the flesh of man? Did he not teach that even
those who are skilled in war should endure the severest pains
of justice? Yet you, Pitaco, an old man but without wisdom,
stand before us here counselling that we take up arms. Do
you then not merit death also?'

Upon these words of Anlisciu, there was a great silence in
the assembly, as though the Angel of Death, God forbid, had
come among them. But the noble Pitaco, may his memory be
preserved, showed no fear, asking only: 'Is then the Son of
Heaven to await death like a beast in a snare?'

Whereupon there were many cries from among the
people,[61] one uttering great curses against the Son of Heaven
himself and another declaring thus: 'What merits[62] the
thousand young women whom the Son of Heaven keeps in
his service, when the kingdom is in such peril? With this
dalliance of women what can he know, in his cowardice and
worthlessness, of arms?'

At which words some broke into laughter, but the noble
Pitaco told those assembled: 'You insult the Son of Heaven,
but you speak truly that the kingdom is in peril. Therefore
you should attend to what I say, and turn your faces from

those who counsel you to set greed before honour and fear before valour. The Tartars are not only excellent soldiers but serve as an example to us, not in their cruelty but because they can support hardship better than other men. Whereas we can support it least, so accustomed are we to think of our pleasures, without care for the morrow. Indeed, we are already subjugated, not by conquest but because we have set aside our customs and laws and thus lost our path.

'As for our men of riches, they think themselves clever merchants in every trade, and others esteem themselves to be good philosophers and learnèd. It is also true that among us there are many excellent doctors who know how to recognise illnesses and prescribe the proper remedies for them, as the doctors of other lands also declare.[63] But what have such knowledge of sickness, such philosophy and such cleverness in the matter of trade done to help us in our peril? Have not the Tartars without shame challenged the rule of our Son of Heaven, whom from our divisions some among us hold in contempt and others revere? Shall we now be put to the sword as Temucin[64] slew the people of Succiur?

'For if you do not heed my counsel the rivers of Cin and Manci will flow together, the skies will grow dark and the seas will burst their bounds in a great torrent, so that the City of Light will be swallowed up and all the people in it. For so the law of heaven will decree.'

Whereupon the noble Pitaco suddenly grew very pale and gave off a great sweat, so that I went to him in order to give him aid, yet there was much laughter at his words, he crying out in anguish as follows: 'Nothing gives more pleasure to the Cane than war and the conquest of lands. Yet you fools have no thought but for gain, ease and women. But unless you bestir yourselves, you will lose all.'

At which, turning to me, Jacob ben Salomone ben Israel, God be praised, Pitaco spoke these words: 'When they see the barons of the Great Cane with their host at the gates of the city, all of them will become fearful and tremulous, as those who have never seen combat, each in doubt for his own person. Such as they will not resist.'

Whereupon, although many were on the point of leaving, there was much shame among them that the noble Pitaco, God keep him, had spoken thus to a stranger. Yet although they gathered all about him with anger in their hearts, he paid no heed to it, saying: 'In the same way you have made no resistance to the ills and vices of your city, permitting the young to do what they will, closing your eyes to their wicked acts as well as to the greed of your merchants and the weakness of your army. Perhaps the stranger will tell you how to defend your city.'

Thus was I, Jacob ben Salomone, at last called upon by the noble Pitaco not only to listen but to speak before them. So that I declared as follows, some attending to the words I spoke and others going upon their way: 'I, being a stranger,[65] sires, cannot truly enter into the hearts of those who would defend this city and those who would surrender it to a foe. Yet some say that your brothers of Cataio cannot accept to live under the rule of those who come from other lands, whether they be Mongols, Saracens or other peoples. In the case of the Saracens who serve the Tartars as their counsellors, your brothers act rightly, since every crime is considered lawful by them, even the killing of whomever is not of their faith.

'Thus they are ready to kill all those who blaspheme against their Holy Scripture, to whatever people they belong and wherever they may be found. Moreover, when they occupy places of power, as at the court of the Great Cane, they are given to plotting against their masters. But my brothers do not do such things, it being forbidden by our Torah, for whose bounty may God be praised.

'As to the conduct of war, our sages teach that he who is without anger is greater than the mighty of the earth, and that he who rules his spirit is better than he who rules a city. Yet as our Rabbi Simeon ben Azzai also taught, we should run to fulfil the lightest duty even as we fulfil the weightiest. And what duty is weightier aside from our duty to God, may He be magnified, than that men should defend their own houses[66] and the houses of their neighbours?' Thus I spoke with great honour, God be thanked, giving comfort to the noble Pitaco, knowing that if a man shall not fulfil his duties to God, to his familiars[67] and his companions, as well as to his city, neither he nor his city will stand firm. And so I went away with the faithful Lifenli, seeing everywhere about me not light but darkness, which God forbid.

## CHAPTER NINE

# The Adversary

THE CHAPTER BEGINS WITH AN undertaking by Jacob, after tears have been shed by his illiterate young servant, Buccazuppo, to teach her her 'letters'. It ends with Jacob's judgment that the Chinese have gone 'too far to the depths' in seeking out knowledge; the latter passages contain remarkable material on the circulation of the blood, on a 'bursting powder', on paper-making and printing and other subjects. It brings into focus one of the manuscript's great themes: that of the necessity for pious enquiry into the nature of things, and of the bounds that piety itself may impose on such questioning. Nevertheless, there is some humbug in this on Jacob's part, whose questing mind and spirit, when he is fully engaged with the object of his interest, knows no bounds at all; as we have seen earlier. Again, the two-sidedness of his nature appears. We have already many times observed the merchant and the man of God in him; here the 'natural scientist' – to use an anachronism – who seeks explanations for everything under the sun, and the man of faith, whose reverence for the divinity of creation bids to stop him in his tracks, face one another.

But there is a still more important confrontation in these pages, as far as the modern reader is concerned. It is between Jacob and 'Anfenscian' (An Fengshan): the 'Adversary', or

'Satan', in the Hebrew which Jacob almost always uses as an epithet for him. Jacob had earlier used the Italian *avversaro*, adversary, for individuals with whom he was at odds; on one occasion it is 'the evil Bertoni' who is described in this fashion, and on another the usually 'faithful' Lifenli, turned thorn in Jacob's side on matters of religion. However, it is for Anfenscian that the specific designations of 'Satan' and 'the Evil One' are reserved (generally accompanied by the Hebraic expletive, 'God forbid', as if the mere mention of his name provoked in Jacob a shudder of righteous recoil).

Described as a 'philosopher of Zaitun', as 'reputed wise', and as 'young in years', Anfenscian's relation with Jacob has something forced about it. The former seems to seek Jacob out, to impose himself on him, even upon the Sabbath eve when Jacob should have been at his devotions. His ostensible, or real, purpose is to seek Jacob's answers to certain questions, especially on matters of pedagogy. What, Anfenscian wishes to know, do the Jews believe about the education of children? This and the succeeding questions draw great wisdom, at once humane and morally stern, from Jacob in his replies. But the dialogue between the two men, joined by 'Pitaco', in turn draws from Anfenscian positions and principles – or the lack of them – which appear truly 'satanic' to Jacob and which are radical even by the standards of today.

The struggle between them is heroic, or that of a Jacob wrestling with an 'evil and blasphemous' angel. We can still feel, across the barriers of time (and translation), the shock which the pious Talmudist registers at the young Anfenscian's opinions on the proper function and methods of the teacher, on the subjects a child should (and should not) be taught, and on the purposes of education itself. And in the further lament by the elderly sage Pitaco on the defects of the young, it is as though we were hearing the accents of a modern 'prophet of doom' upon the same topic.

❦

pon my return to the house of my brother Nathan, peace upon him, having spoken with Armentuzio about our merchandise, and of the great desire of the mariners to be gone, the evil Bertoni came to me in my chamber, declaring to me in the presence of Lifenli that Liciancie, his sister, had passed many hours with Buccazuppo, even though I had forbidden the woman to come to her for the harm she might bring to the young girl, from her contempt for the true and the good.

Therefore I reproached the faithful Lifenli, saying that none should come in the way of a master and his servant, unless the master by his grace permitted it, and that to me fell the duty of her care. For such I had undertaken upon my departure from Ancona. Whereupon, Lifenli replied that Liciancie, being one who might not be denied, such was the force of her will, would by no means obey an order to keep from a place that was forbidden to her, be he who commanded her the strongest in the realm, God forbid.

I therefore summoned Buccazuppo to me, in order to enquire of her the reasons for the presence of Liciancie. Whereupon, entering the room and observing Lifenli, she began to weep before him, lamenting her fate and speaking without truth of my hard treatment of her. To her the faithful Lifenli would then have given comfort, but I forbade him, declaring that Buccazuppo was in my care and the care of the woman Bertoni, and no other.

At which Buccazuppo wept further, may God have spared me such travail, saying that Liciancie had come to her in order to teach her to read, Liciancie having been angered that the servant of a sage, for so the said woman called me, may God be praised, should know no letters. At which I grew angry also, God forgive me, for I had undertaken that I should faithfully teach her upon the journey to our country, she having told me before of her desire to read.

But Buccazuppo, made impudent by the presence of

Lifenli, whom I therefore sent from my chamber, declared
that I could have no true wish to teach her, seeing that she
was but a simple young girl[1] and I a pious and learnèd man
much given to thoughts of God, and that therefore I would
not turn away from Him in order that she might know her
letters. Thus I had to counsel her to show patience, saying
that a pious man such as I should always do as he had
undertaken, and that if she should give herself to study, I
should be her teacher, so that she should have no more cause
to weep. She was well pleased at my words, and thereupon
went away.

Upon the next day, which is to say the seventeenth of Adar,[2] it
being the eve of the Sabbath Ki Tissa, such was the great
honour in which I was now held in the City of Light, by
reason of the words I had spoken, that many came to me at
the house of Nathan in order to converse with me and seek
my counsel further, for which God be praised. Thus, so many
were they[3] that I was constrained to send for help to the
faithful Lifenli, since among them was a certain Anfenscian, a
philosopher reputed wise albeit young in years, who wished to
know of me what was the doctrine of the Jews upon the office
of the teacher of the young.[4] This Anfenscian they call in
their language *sciofu*, which is to say a great teacher. But from
him I heard that which caused me much confusion and
distress in my soul, God forbid.

For I first asked that he, being young, declared his own
knowledge and opinion of those things that he sought to ask
me, as our sages themselves did,[5] and he replied as follows:
'Learnèd one, heaven has not sent us children whose
endowment[6] differs greatly one from the other. Things of the
same kind are alike in their essence.[7] As Menche teaches, all
shoes are alike because all feet are alike. It is the same also
with the ear, the eye and the other members. Should therefore
the brain and the heart not also be alike, possessing qualities
in common? The difference that arises between one child and

another is owed to that which attracts the inclination of each child, and to that which each child himself chooses to know.'

To whom I answered: 'Your opinions, young man, are feeble and from such a position no child may be instructed to be wise. Human beings are born with equal ignorance, but also with an equal desire to overcome such ignorance, save for those who suffer from a defect of mind. For the necessity to enquire and to know exists in all human persons, so that not even a young child is happy to be called stupid.

'But if he has been so poorly brought up and so badly nurtured in his mind and body from his beginning, that the inclinations of which you speak have suffered such harm that he seems little different from a wild animal, what will you, young man, say of him? Should we say, God forbid, that that is what a human being is really like, and that we must teach the child as we have found him? Is such a thing fair to him or to others? Or is it not to betray the duty of the teacher?'

Whereupon Anfenscian made this reply: 'We must discover that which is good in each child, for good there will be, keep hold of it and seek to nurture it, in the hope that it will remain. Thus each child must be taught not only according to his will but according to his virtues also.'

I answered as follows, God be praised: 'But what shall we say if the child is not similar to a child of reason and goodness, but seems to be lacking in both? For it is not a true principle that the teacher must teach only according to the will and virtues of the child, since, if it were so, few would be brought to excel. On the contrary, each child requires to be led beyond the limits of that which he might choose for himself. For only by such means may he be brought to an understanding of the soul which is within him, may God be praised for His bounty. Moreover, whenever a child wishes to choose one thing rather than another, he must be helped by those who are fitted[8] by their own wisdom to guide him in his choice.'

But to my words, which were the admirable fruit of my

learning, the young man paid no honour, but choosing the
way of excess declared as follows: 'If a teacher, guided by the
inclination of a child and knowing that which is good in him,
should observe that knowledge of a certain thing would
neither serve nor please such a child, as when he is set to learn
those things of which he can make no use in his life, then
such a teacher may justly teach him other things, in order that
the good in him may flower.

'For learning is not mere imitation, nor should it be
conducted within narrow confines, but as a means to awaken
the mind to the assumption of its freedom. Thus may a child
come to recognise that which is true for himself[9] and not
only that which is true for others.'

I replied: 'Your words, young man, are less wise than they
appear. For in the pursuit of that which is true for itself,
before that which is true for all men, the mind of the child
must become shrunk in the face of the world, rather than
expanding itself to its riches and glories, which are so for all
men.

'Moreover, the teacher may not permit the child to think or
to know first what is true for himself, and after that what is
true for all, for then he will not come to a secure knowledge
of what is right and what is wrong. Further, if such a child
should be so vitiated that he is not similar to a child possessed
of reason and ability, but even seems not to be endowed with
such qualities at all, knowing nothing of right and wrong, we
cannot permit such a child to choose that which is true and
good for himself before that which is true and good for
others.'

To which Anfenscian made this reply, God forbid: 'But
since children are greater in number in a school than are their
teachers, and are constrained to remain in their places often
against their wills, it is not just that they should be subject to
all those things which their sage teachers think to be good and
true. For there is no teacher who may not believe in error and
thus lead a child by a wrong path. Hence, the teacher should

be more humble, for there are many paths to the truth and to
that which is good, and not one, just as there are many gods
and many men, to each one of whom sometimes the same
thing and sometimes a different thing may seem the best
according to his judgment, and to which each in turn must
show respect.

'For only thus may the true and the good be found which
are also true and good for the many, and not only for the few.
You speak of the duty of the teacher, sire, but it is your words
that are less wise than they appear.'

In this manner of idolatry,[10] for which God spare me that I
should have written such things, Anfescian spoke, although a
young man, so that I fell silent. For before me I knew that I
beheld an evil man with whom I should be put in high peril
to converse, since his words would bring to travail the wisest
and most pious of men, which God forbid. Yet he, bowing
towards the ground and folding his hands in devotion,
awaited my reply, so that I was not able to remain silent, and
answered as follows: 'Whatever you may say, O young man, I
am wiser than you, having considered deeply the matters of
which you speak. Thus, there is no other way than for a child
to obtain, in each thing he studies, a true basis for his
learning, for to learn is not to guess, but to know. Therefore,
in order to read, a child must know the letters, and in order to
count he must be taught the order of numbers.[11] For without
such knowledge the child must remain in darkness, God
forbid, discovering only small parts of the truth by chance,
and not according to rule.'

To which Anfenscian, again bowing low, replied thus: 'The
master must be foolish to think that the things he says are not
known to me. But to memorise the laws of letter and number
is not to acquire true knowledge, but only the appearance of
knowledge, as a bird may be taught to speak. True knowledge
is a different thing. It is to think freely, and thus to find one's
own way by experience to the truths of life.'

But now I saw that I had before me the Adversary, and that

a wicked man stood over me, and that I must do battle with
him to the very end. For that which he spoke, although it
appeared to be wise, would at the last destroy the City of
Light.

Therefore, I argued as follows, may God be magnified and
honoured: 'We must go to the heart of the matter. Without
knowledge of the rules of learning, neither child nor man
shall think well, whether it be freely or no. For only with such
knowledge shall a child be raised to greater wisdom of word
and deed, while without it he must remain as a carpenter who
lacks his saw or the surgeon his knife. Thus a child cannot
become able to use his reason save by inducing him to attend
to the rules of speech and of logic. For without knowledge of
such rules, thought itself becomes obscure, with one thought
always at war with another, and with no means by which they
may be put in order so that they may be explained to others.

'But if a child is not able to explain his thoughts to others,
they will not be persuaded to judge him reasonable or
endowed with intellect. Rather, they will count him stupid,
but it is his teachers who will have been more greatly at fault.
But is it not unjust, young man, that a child should be judged
for defects which are not his own by nature, when teachers
err?'

Now Anfenscian himself fell silent as if he did not know
what to say, so wise and powerful were my words, in which
God, blessèd be He, was my Guide, for He teaches His
wisdom to those who have ears to hear Him. Moreover, that I
remained in His Hand was shown to me in that moment, it
being the eve of the Sabbath Ki Tissa,[12] for the woman
Bertoni came, declaring that even the noble Pitaco attended
upon me without a servant. For such was the honour in
which all men now held me, the fame of my wisdom having
spread throughout the city.

Then Pitaco himself entered my chamber, Anfenscian and
the faithful Lifenli bowing low before him, he giving me
thanks for my aid to him, and declaring that I, Jacob of

Ancona, was a truly wise man, both pious and learnèd, who, although I was a Jew from another land, yet knew such things as were fitting for all men to know.

Whereupon, since the Adversary, God forbid,[13] did not make to depart from my chamber, he being tenacious with all who come into his hands, I was now commanded by the Word of God, Who spoke to the very ear of His servant such was His trust in me, that I draw him by reason further into my power, so that the truth of all things might prevail over falsehood, and light over darkness.

Therefore, I enquired of Pitaco what was his judgment as to the nature and art of learning and the duty of the teacher. To which he replied: 'Alas, sire, the children of the city pursue their studies unwillingly or not at all. For they believe that in order to grow rich or to have the respect of others it is no longer necessary to be learnèd in either letters or numbers. Moreover, such learning, for so the *chuotsu* declare, is now held in less esteem than the free judgment of the young,[14] so that many do not go to school and even seek to drive others away from their studies. For now they are guided by an ignorance greater than their own, so that the rule of heaven falls, since few are now willing to submit themselves to the order of others.

'As our book of songs teaches, the hawk soars to the heavens, and the fish to the depths of the sea, and so the child in his learning seeks out the truth of the world in every place. Thus, our Chunfutsu declares that the man who is able to apprehend the truth is he who is accustomed to put his intelligence to work. But now our children do not value learning but rather despise it, while their teachers possess little knowledge by which to kindle a love of study among their pupils. Thus they are easily satisfied with the poor work they do, or are even without the will to judge its defects justly.

'Moreover, one teacher, feigning wisdom, will say that the old teaching was false or too narrow, another that each child must seek his own way, by his own will mastering those skills that life requires, and a third that only the ways of our ancestors are just. But, such is the confusion, the knowledge acquired by children in school grows less, and the knowledge and understanding of the teachers less also. Thus, one teacher can be heard to say that it is the fault of the officials and not their own defects that brings sorrow upon them. But another will say that a true judgment of the knowledge of a child may not be made, since each differs from the other. And a third will lament that it is those who hold teachers in greatest contempt who judge them most harshly.

'But in the meantime children grow less learnèd, even so that they can neither read nor write, while each blames the other[15] for such a result, none taking the blame upon himself. To all these things we have been brought by error and wrong principle, so that few now pay heed to the wisdom of the elders or to that which will bring damage to the city.

'Rather, the pen should be placed in the hands of the child not later than his fourth year and thus he should begin to learn the letters,[16] so that he may grow up a capable scribe, since to delay does great harm to a child. For at the age of six and seven he is already less adept to learn, especially if those about him are more instructed than he, at such an age being more easily diverted and prone to bad conduct if his mind has not already been directed to definite things.'

But hearing the noble Pitaco without courtesy, the Adversary could not stay his words, saying, 'It is not the purpose of the school only to teach letters and numbers but to secure the happiness of the child.'

To whom I replied as follows, God be thanked for giving me such strength that the Adversary might be vanquished: 'Such happiness comes from learning itself. If you neglect the learning of the child, how may the child be happy? Moreover, to secure the happiness of the child is neither the purpose nor the duty of the teacher. Rather, his first duty and purpose are to teach and make the moral principles[17] fixed and firm, to lead the child to a knowledge of the creation of the world and of the laws of nature, to teach him to understand the bonds of our human state, and thus to love God, blessèd be He, Who is the Creator of all things.'

Whereupon the Adversary asked with scorn, 'And how shall such things be taught to children?' To whom the noble Pitaco, may his memory be recorded, replied: 'By doing small things well. For great effects are produced by small causes in the life of a man. Thus by small steps a child is admitted to an understanding of right and wrong, and of other great things.'

To which I, Jacob ben Salomone, added as follows: 'We too believe this. Moreover, it was our sage, Rabbi Mose ben Maimon, peace upon him, who taught us in the Makala that the moral dispositions, which we call the *hilkotdeot* and by which the deeds of man are determined, must become fixed in the soul of a child by his parents and teachers, so that they are formed into a certain habit, God willing. For by nature man is neither good nor evil at the commencement of his life, but must become good and avoid evil by the actions of his parents and the instruction of his teachers. Thereafter, those who attain such a condition, for which God be praised, themselves acquire therefrom the duty of awakening those who have not yet attained it. This is the duty of the teacher.' At which words the noble Pitaco, peace upon him, declared: 'It is the teaching of our sages also.'

Whereupon I sought to continue my teaching, saying that if a child can be made bad by a bad example, he can be made good also by a good example. But the Adversary interposed, speaking thus: 'None can be compelled to follow the moral ideas of the teacher, for rarely are they fixed even for him himself. Neither should we permit this, nor place a prohibition upon that, but rather so instruct a child that he may be enabled to find his own path to truth and goodness. For the teacher cannot be the sole fount from which every truth derives.[18] Moreover, the child finds his own knowledge, as is right, to which the teacher must give respect and to which he must often cede.'

Pitaco, greatly angered by his impious words, replied thus:
'Then, when a farmer's chickens and hens go astray, does he
not have the sense to chase after them? And when the hearts
of your pupils stray from the true path, is it not your duty to
go after them in order to bring them back to safety?'

To which I in turn added as follows, praise be to the Holy
One: 'It is not possible for the mind of a child not to err,
since the minds of all men do so. Thus, the teacher who
permits his pupil to wander from his studies, or to sit idle
without a task, is failing in his duty.'

Whereupon, the noble Pitaco asked Anfenscian, 'Is it not
pleasant to learn with constancy and to persevere in duty?'

To whom the Adversary, may God overcome him at the last
day, replied: 'Shall we then be like the countryman who
pulled out his plants because they seemed to grow too slowly?
But when others went to look, the plants were all withered.
Those who cannot resist pulling at their plants not only fail to
help them but do them great harm. Thus, it is better to learn
by doing than to teach by telling. The craftsman may
demonstrate his craft to another but he cannot make him
skilful. For the other must work in his own way, and by this
means attain his ends.'

Pitaco replied briefly: 'Then you abandon your duty. For,
as Menche teaches, a craftsman does not put aside his plumb-
line for the benefit of the clumsy carpenter, as do you.'

Whereupon, as if in disdain for the said Anfenscian, Pitaco
himself asked me what the learnèd Jew taught of the task of
the teacher, to whom I answered: 'It is the task of a good and
wise teacher to help his pupils, by means of his own clear
understanding, to know the path they should follow for the
rest of their lives.' Pitaco in turn replied thus: 'Yet, in the City
of Light, it has come to such an end that the teacher must
help his pupils to see the way only by the dim light of his own
poor understanding. Indeed, some say that among us the
teacher without learning seeks only to share his dark condition
with others, in order to find some comfort for his blindness.'

Whereupon I continued: 'Sire, you ask me what the Jew
teaches. It is that which Moses our teacher has given us, that
it is our task to forbid the doing of wrong, one to the other.
Nor can such a task be accomplished save by those who
themselves fear God. As it is written by our sages, the others
neither know nor understand but go about in darkness, and
even when the light of truth shines in the skies, they do not
see it. But your teachers, who say that each child must go his
own way, are not among the sages. Thus, as I observed in the
island of Seilan, he who knows well how to swim brings up
pearls from the bottom of the sea, but he who does not know
drowns. So it is in all the affairs of men. Wherefore, children
must be taught not that which they choose to know but that
which it is required for them to know, in order not merely to
live, but in order to live as men among men.'

At which Pitaco enquired: 'But what do your sages require
that a child should know?' I answered in this way, God be
thanked: 'Our sages, peace be upon them, teach us that that
which it is required for a child to know is knowledge derived
from matter that has been perceived by the senses, knowledge
demonstrated with the aid of argument, experiment, analogy
and rule,[19] and knowledge contained in the wisdom of past
ages, and which it is the duty of present-day man to preserve.
To neglect any of these, God forbid, is to neglect the teaching
not only of the child but of all men. But above all other
things the child must be taught to distinguish good from ill,
that which is deserving of praise from that which is base, and
to act according to truth, and in justice and rectitude towards
all men. For he who has no knowledge of right conduct has
no part in the terrestrial world.'

Whereupon, the Adversary, God forbid, said as follows:
'But what is this good, this truth and this justice to which you
refer? Do you alone have a right understanding of them? The
teacher cannot command in every part or act so that that
which he teaches seems as a gift to the child, for which he
should receive its service and its duty. Nor should he teach the

child to be virtuous, for that is the task of the father, but how
to have courage to choose his own path, for which the greatest
virtue is to think and to act without fear.'

At which words of Anfenscian, the noble Pitaco declared
with anger that he wished to hear none of it, saying: 'All men,
being good by nature, are capable of acting well. But the ways
to act well must be taught. For without instruction the
springs of benevolence may by bad example run dry. But
when a teacher urges a child frequently to be good, and
teaches him the reasons for it, so that a motive pushes him
on, he will come to act well of his own accord.'

But the Adversary would by no means be stilled, denying
in a loud voice all that Pitaco had said, and uttering evil
thoughts such as none have uttered before, as follows:
'Neither a father nor a teacher may choose the way for a child,
neither determining what he must learn nor keeping secret
from him whatever he wishes to know. Nor, likewise, may
they impose upon him their own beliefs whether about the
gods or other men. Thus, they may not take such a child to
the temple against his will, nor forbid him to speak in
whatever way his own reason urges.

'For it may not be presumed that the happiness of a child
will be secured, in this way or that, because the father of the
child declares it to be so. Indeed, it is wrong that a child, who is
weak, should always do that which his father wishes him to do,
or to go wherever his father wishes him to go, or to say and
think whatever he wishes him to say and think. For a father may
no more impose his will upon his child than a child may impose
his will upon his father, since it is not just that either the father
or the child should be compelled to surrender to the other.'

Thus, never before in my life, for which God be thanked,
had I heard such things as were spoken by Anfenscian. But
the noble Pitaco, being in despair for the fate of the city and
as if unable to speak, and I, knowing well what I must say,
being in the Hand of God, declared as follows: 'These things
are evil and of the Adversary, whom God strike down. For by

such principles the bonds of nature,[20] those which tie fathers
to their children, shall be utterly broken, and the giving of the
knowledge of truth and goodness by the one to the other shall
be prevented. And thus shall the safety of the realm, the
sacred tie between the ages, and the life of humankind be
together put in great peril.'

But again the Adversary would not be stilled, speaking
wickedly and blasphemously in this fashion, so that the noble
Pitaco was constrained with great lamentation to place his
hands over his ears, in order that he might not hear his
words:[21] 'Sires, to seek that a child obey the faith or moral
rule of his father, thus passing it from one age to another
without doubt as to its fitness or truth, is a grave wrong.
Rather, to pose questions about all things is to find the light,
and is the duty of the teacher, but to question nothing is to
remain in darkness. Moreover, no one faith or moral rule
contains that which is true for all and for all times, nor can it
therefore serve as a guide for all persons. For no person,
however wise he be, can be assured in himself that that which
is true or good for him is also true and good for others.

'Thus, every child must surely be shown by his teacher what
it is possible to consider as the truth from among those things
which men have thought to be so, but without declaring that
one such truth is of greater wisdom than the others. For to do
so is to usurp the will of the child to choose his own way, and
thus not to teach him the difference between right and wrong,
but to take away from him his own moral judgment.'

But now my anger, God be praised, grew very great to hear
such things, so that I answered the youth Anfenscian as follows:
'This is the voice, God forbid, of the Evil One, who declares
that the worship of God, may He be exalted for ever more, and
the worship of idols are of equal worth, and that the law of our
teacher Moses, peace be upon him, is no better than the decrees
of Nabuccodonosor, may his memory be obliterated.

'You would further teach, O Satan,[22] that the will of a child
may prevail over the Will of God, and that that which is more

or less according to the desires and needs of man is the measure of eternal truth. But such teaching is an evil thing. For not every truth is of equal worth, just as an idol of wood or stone is not equal to the Ineffable Divine Name, nor every bumpkin fit to stand at the right hand of God. To give honour and respect equally to truth and falsehood, as to the wise man and the fool, is also to give respect to nothing and to no one. In the teaching of a child, God forbid, it is to lead him into the desert, but without a prophet to guide his steps. Indeed, it is better even that an idolater give respect more to his own faith than to that of another, than that he should give equal respect to all faiths or to none at all.

'For to accept everything without censure is the same as to accept nothing without censure, for it is to make no distinction between God and the Adversary, may he be struck down, and thus to have no staff on which to rest, but to be in confusion. For he who is taught to have respect for all things without regard to their value is as he who is taught to have respect for nothing. Moreover, he who teaches such things to others cannot become a light for others, but instead from generation to generation greater darkness must always descend, until the life of man, who was made in the image of God, is extinguished from the terrestrial world.'

But the Adversary, being strong, was not yet cast down and answered me thus: 'The child is not a soldier who must be trained, as by being compelled to learn that which the teacher demands that he should know, and who is prompt to punish him if he should fail.'

Hearing such false and cunning argument, I declared as follows, God be praised: 'The desire to excel, as by finding the answer to a question before others, is strong in every child, God be thanked, and this desire the teacher must nurture. For it is the will to learn which shows itself in the child's yearning, as our rabbis teach.'

To which the noble Pitaco, may he be remembered, added as follows: 'But now, among us, the desire to excel is held by many to be a vice, for it serves only to distinguish the more intelligent from the less. Rather, those who follow Anfenscian say that each child should have his own tasks set to him so that he does not vie with others and instead learns quietly whatever he requires to know, without causing others to feel at a loss should he be readier than they.'

Whereupon, Anfenscian, thinking that two wise old men had not yet the mastery of him, continued without shame as follows: 'It is true that the child should be urged, each in his own way and according to his own needs, to follow his own path to the truth and at such pace as is suitable to him.[23] Moreover, this should be according to the questions he asks and the knowledge he requires, nor should his teacher make him hurry. Neither is it just, if each child is thus following his own path, that any child should be judged to fail. Indeed, it is better by far that each child should hold himself to have succeeded according to his own measure, for thus a child is rendered happy and his soul remains free.'

To which Evil One I replied: 'In such a condition it is the teacher who has failed in his task, not the child. For if an ignorant child sets out upon his journey of life without the means to serve either himself or others, then his teacher has betrayed him in his duty, having given him not the will to persevere but only a taste for idleness, whose end is the denial of the Divine Presence, may God spare me for my words. Thus a child may also not be permitted by a teacher to make excuses for his failure to do the tasks he has been given. For this is the beginning of great failure and falsehood in life itself, when the child, grown to a man, finds reasons for not doing what is set before him, or for not aspiring to the good when it is presented to him. It is likewise the duty of the teacher to ensure that in school the time is not wasted. For the habit of study comes from being attentive to instruction, as from listening in silence to the teacher, and from being asked questions without warning.

'Indeed, you, young man, follow an evil path, not being disposed to say whether a thing is right or wrong, either because you yourself do not know, or because you do not wish to submit a child to be corrected, lest such a child be thought to be less intelligent than others. In this way you destroy study and knowledge themselves, while the child in your charge remains without the means to fulfil his duties to himself, to God, blessèd be He, or to other men. Moreover, the child who studies well deserves honour, while those who study badly merit censure. For if all receive equal reward whether they know much or little, or whether they do well or ill, none will aspire to the better.'

To which the Adversary, bowing, replied thus: 'Stranger, you speak like one of our ancients, who also judged the present as if it were the past.'[24]

Whereupon the noble Pitaco, being angered by the words of the youth, declared: 'You speak lightly, and without respect for the sage who has come among us. In former times, about which you jest, our children learned twenty separate letters

---

### 'TWENTY SEPARATE LETTERS'

*Plainly Jacob means Chinese pictograms, whose nature he seems to have understood very well (see p.358), despite his earlier mistaken reference (see p.339) to 'letters' of the alphabet. They are not 'letters' but an extremely complex system of signs, or 'characters', recognisable by the eye but not dependent for their meaning on the (various) sounds given them by different Chinese language or dialect sub-groups. That is, the same written text can be read aloud in different dialects, with one spoken version of the text being incomprehensible to the speakers of another dialect. Yet the same written script, when seen by the eye, means the same or similar thing to all Chinese readers. This has been the case since the standardisation of the script at the end of the third century BC. The written language has therefore functioned since then as a unifying instrument in Chinese literary culture and political rule. In 'six years', according to Pitaco's assertion, a child, given a school year of, say, 150 days, would have learned more than 15,000 characters. This could not have been so. Some 7,000 are estimated to have been in common literate use in China in the thirteenth century. (I have translated as 'twenty separate letters' Jacob's* lettere mozze xx, *which literally means twenty 'cut' or 'abbreviated' letters.)*

each day for six years, as well as the art of writing and the numbers of Manci.[25] They also knew from memory the words of the poets, learned well to be pious, and were taught to play musical instruments. But now young men such as you declare those things to be mere learning by the wheel, declaring that it is as the tethered ox that turns in a circle, with a cloth bound about its eyes, and never sees the light.

'No longer do our halls resound to the voices of children reading our poets together. Even the knowledge of Lipo and Toufu[26] is passing away. But when we plead that they must not be forgotten, and that we have a duty to teach their beauty to our children, we are received with scorn, as if such was the truth only of old men. No longer do they have knowledge of our sages, or of deeds of former ages. Yet, according to Chunfutsu, in acquiring knowledge of the past, we may better understand the present and how it may be ordered and governed. But now when we say that such study should be maintained according to the precepts, for without it our children have no models of virtue and honour by which to guide their steps, none hears us.

'Instead, as in the markets of the city, so in the schools there are many goods from which the child may choose, so that he chooses only the things which are most agreeable and sweet to him, and not those which are disagreeable and hard. Once, without learning, a man could have neither place nor money, but only the most bitter labour for small payment.[27] Now, he who is without education, provided only that he be a man of potency and force, may have an excess of all that he desires, until such excess destroys him. Indeed, to gain a hold upon the blessings of life neither modesty nor wisdom are now valued nor necessary, but rather to the contrary.

'So far is this the case that many who now command the city know little of past sages and kings, and even do not have the art of writing nor can they read with ease. But the young have suffered yet greater harm, being full of dishonest tricks by which they hope to conceal the defects of their knowledge. For they have not only neglected much through the fault of their teachers but have lost the shame that comes from awareness of their vices.

'Thus, one person talks in a loud voice so that none may approach closely and discover his lack of knowledge, while another uses wiles to obtain the complaisance of others so that they will not judge him harshly, and a third makes false accusations against others, denouncing them as fools, the better to hide his own folly. Therefore, now, not even the sages of the city are learnèd in the knowledge they profess, but instead trust to the greater lack of knowledge of those who come to them for instruction.

'Yet should any seek to point a finger at them for their defaults, they are prompt to defend themselves by means of calumny and falsehood against those who accuse them, declaring them to be men without worth or learning. In this way, one false thing is defended by another, in the manner of Anfenscian, so that none may discover the truth. Instead, all proceed upon the same path, flouting the law of heaven and bringing ruin to the city.'

Upon hearing these things, the Adversary departed, as if not wishing to hear more, the noble Pitaco seeking to be comforted by me, for which God be thanked. Therefore, since it is the duty of the pious and learnèd Jew to teach wisdom to such just men as may be willing to hear it from his lips, I spoke to Pitaco as follows: 'Sire, pious men must take counsel together in the face of the Adversary. Therefore, I pray you to listen to me, even though the hour of my Sabbath has come. We ourselves should know that all men desire to know,[28] may God be glorified and honoured. But the perfections of man exist only in a hidden state and require instruction in order to be seen. Thus, in every child there is the capacity to reason, and intelligence, that is to say potential intellect, which the teacher, by drawing it forth and rewarding him with praise, assists to become active intellect. But if the teacher fails in his duty, the child fails also, and, to the contrary, if the teacher fulfils his duty, the child is able to do so also. The child who is in a condition of not yet knowing what it is fitting for him to know has before his eyes a veil, which veil it is the task of the teacher to raise, so that he may little by little see the truths of the world and stand in the light of reason,[29] God willing. But the greatest virtue of man, as our sage Mose ben Maimon, peace upon him, teaches us, is to become rational in his actions. For through it man is man, while whoever has not been taught to be rational, nor is rational in his actions, God forbid, is not a man but an animal, having only the shape of a man.

'For God, blessèd be He, has made man only a little lower than the angels, as our King David, peace upon him, sang. Thus the child comes to school with an intelligence already given to him by God but one that is without polish, so that it is the duty of the teacher to make it shine, whereafter the child may walk the earth as a man in the image of Him by whom he was created, blessèd be He.

'Moreover, since men have by the gift of God dominion over all creatures, they should be well prepared in their understandings for their charge, learning to be worthy of their station and of its duties. For without such understanding, the child may become in manhood as a fierce wolf wandering at large in the city, or as a cur which trembles and cowers in its lair, barking at the whole world.

'Thus, as I have said, it is the task of the teacher to make shine the lights and lamps of the intellect of the child. Yet among you, so it seems, many teachers do not know how this may be done, whether because the child is resistant[30] and this the teacher does not know how to overcome, or because the teacher lacks the true art of his office, or for some other cause.

'Yet so long as the intellectual faculty has not passed from potential to action, which is to say the acquisition of knowledge, it cannot be part of the true providence of God,

blessèd be He. For by reason, which is the divine part of man's
being, a child begins with the help of his teacher to obtain a
true knowledge of God, of the natural laws and of man, by
means of which he himself draws closer to God, may He be
exalted.

'Moreover, not only is a soul without knowledge not
good, but he who does not seek knowledge in his lifetime is
one whose soul is lost. Therefore, honoured sire, especially
since it is held by us that a man cannot learn the laws of God
without reading that which was told to Moses our teacher,
namely the laws of right conduct towards God and man, and
since a man may not call himself a Jew without such
knowledge, there is none among my brothers who cannot
read the Holy Law, for which God be praised. For, as our
blessèd Salomone ben Judah taught, knowledge is the end of
human life and the reason for our being.[31] Hence a Jew who
lacks knowledge is a thing against nature and can nowhere be
found.'

Thus the noble Pitaco declared that a man such as I, if one
could be found among them, might save the city from
destruction with the aid of my wisdom, for which honour
God be thanked. Yet he declared also that it would be wise for
me to depart the city soon, since those who were of his party
stood in danger, and that I, being a stranger, had offended
many by the words which I had spoken.

Whereupon his servants came to attend upon him, saying
that he should accompany them in haste,[32] for it was reported
by some that the Tartars drew nearer the city, and that there
were many among the merchants who made ready to greet
them.

Thereafter, having sent the faithful Lifenli away with the
command to make all ready, page by page, of those things
which we had written, and putting on fresh clothes,[33] I
welcomed the Sabbath Ki Tissa with my brother Nathan,
praying that my iniquities be taken away and that my

days be increased in this world and in the world to come,
Amen.[34] Yet although a Jew is commanded to be joyful upon
the Sabbath, God be praised, I felt greatly afflicted in the
night, hearing voices of weeping all about me[35] and in my
dreams seeing again the body of my father, may peace be
upon his soul. Moreover, I was troubled in my heart by
many base things, seeing before me the hidden parts of
women, God spare me, so that I cried out in anguish,
lamenting also the death of my brother Vivo and that I
should be in such a dark place without my beloved Sara,
may God keep her.

Thus I wept greatly in the night, fearing that the
Tartars should come upon me and upon my possessions, or
that I should be drowned in the seas, may God spare me that
I should have been in such doubt. Therefore I arose in the
darkness, praying that with the light of the Sabbath morning I
might be restored, and that no evil had befallen the city. For
all about me was now a deep silence, and no sound might be
heard, as if all in their houses were in great fear.

But even on the morrow, none came out of their houses,
all doors remaining bolted,[36] so that the girl Buccazuppo and
the woman Bertoni were also greatly afraid. For it was as
though the Angel of Death, God forbid, had come upon the
City of Light, yet with few to render wise counsel or to point
the just way. Therefore, although my servant Armentuzio
came to me in great danger on this day while I was still at
prayer, urging me with many cries to depart, and declaring that
all the mariners, together with my brothers Eliezer and
Lazzaro, stood ready at their posts, I again would not, for
which God be praised.

Upon the day following, which is to say the nineteenth of
Adar[37], a messenger from the noble Pitaco again came to me,
accompanied by the faithful Lifenli, declaring that the voices
which had spoken of the approach of the Tartars were false,
but that there was much anger and hatred among the people
against the merchants who had made ready to receive them.

Of these, the merchant Anlisciu had met his death in the
night at the hands of a great mob, who had been angered at
his desire to surrender[38] the city to the Mongols. Others also
of the followers of the great merchant Suninsciou had been
put to the sword in the darkness, of whose number none
might say, God forbid. But now the city was still, for its
merchants, sages and officials had resolved that they must on
the morrow begin to seek greater concord among themselves,
lest the City of Light, by neglect of its duties to the citizens,
fall into yet greater travails.

Thus I too resolved to seek to give my counsel to the elders
of the city, so that it might govern itself wisely according to
the teaching of our sages, peace be upon them. Whereupon,
having sent all those about me from my chamber, I gave
thought to the tribulations[39] of the great city, so that it might
be saved.

Hence it came into my mind, for which God be thanked,
that, although the city had fallen into great confusion so that
none knew which was the just path or how the virtues of men
might get the better of their vices, among them not only were
there great riches and a plenteousness of all things, but they
had in wondrous fashion come to such great understanding of
the natural law[40] that many of the secrets of the material and
corporeal essences had been disclosed to them by the
experiments of their sages.

Thus, the said sages blasphemously declare that there is
known to them the nature of the prime mover, as well as of
the smallest matter of life.[41] But those they will disclose to no
stranger, for they hold them to be secret things. However,
certain of them who are practised in alchemy declare that they
know the vital principles both of the heavenly bodies and of
the bodies of men, and that such principles are alike.

Therefore it is said by them that the vital principle of the
body of man is in the heart, and that when the heart moves it
makes run the blood of the heart, which comes and goes, and
that the beating of the pulses[42] marks the flux and reflux of

the blood in the body. In the same way they say that the vital principle of the heavens, which lies in the sun, God forbid, makes the heavenly bodies move, whose flux and reflux corresponds to the motion of the blood.

In this fashion their sages set up their idols, making the prime mover not God, but the heart and the sun, or whatever other thing they may choose in the manner of idolaters. Yet it is God alone Who created and gives vital spirit to all things, may He be magnified and lauded. In addition, those who follow the ways of their sages have much belief in the magic arts, some seeking to know the secret of eternal life, may God strike them down, others to give back youth to the old, others to move themselves from one place to another in the twinkling of an eye, and many such magical things, which God forbid. Nor do they hold them to be blasphemies, but declare that they are the means by which men will become

---

### 'THE FLUX AND REFLUX OF THE BLOOD IN THE BODY'

*'When the heart moves it makes run the blood of the heart, which comes and goes' (p.353); in the Italian,* quando move 'l cor fa scorrer lo sangue del cor che ondeggia. *This is a rudimentary description of the circulation of the blood, some 350 years before William Harvey's essay on the subject published in 1628. Harvey (1578–1657), who studied for a time at Padua, described how blood enters the right auricle, passes to the right ventricle, and is pumped out to the lungs through the pulmonary artery, and hence by the pulmonary veins to the left ventricle, with valves preventing the blood flowing back. Thus the blood is circulated throughout the body by means of the cardio-vascular system, consisting of the heart, the arteries, the veins and the capillaries. Before Harvey it was generally believed that the arteries contained air, and that the blood passed from heart to veins in a simple to-and-fro movement. Jacob's account of Chinese beliefs on the matter suggests that the latter already stood mid-way between the simple ancient understanding and modern knowledge, the use of the word* ondeggia *– with its sense of a wave-like ebb and flow – seeming to suggest circulation of the blood, or at least the contraction and dilation of the heart's motion and the 'flux and reflux' of the blood which it pumps.*

blessèd, saying that those who are able to uncover the secret
laws of nature shall not only know the forces of the created
world but be united[43] with them.

But this I declare in turn to be a blasphemy against the
Divine Name, for man thus to consider himself equal to God.
Moreover, those among them who seek out the means to
eternal life dream that they may live for ever in this material
world, without need for the coming of the Messiah, may God
forgive me for writing these words. Thus may even the wisest
of men err who turn aside from God, seeking those things
which may not be found. Yet that some among them are wise,
even though the Adversary has turned them from their way,
may not be doubted, since I saw those whose hearts had failed
them returned to strength, the deaf enabled to hear, and even
the blind to see. In addition, many live to a great age, even to
seventy or eighty years, for they have certain secret medicines
by which they may remain in good health although greatly
advanced in age. But among our sages,[44] there are also many
who know how such an end may be reached, and other
wonderful things besides.

Thus, does not our master Mose ben Maimon wisely teach
that the ills of the body answer to the troubles and sadnesses of
the spirit,[45] so that when a man is in discord with his soul his
body also becomes sick and infirm? Hence, he who seeks to be
healthy should act justly also, and in accord with the will of
God, so that illness may enter neither into his soul nor his body.

Of the secrets of alchemy the sages of Manci also have great
knowledge, for they enquire into many things. So that,
although some are foolish and others practise tricks of magic,
others justly wonder at the bounty of God, knowing that in
the earth are hidden all those things by which men may find
good or harm, while upon its surface it carries great cities and
mountains without feeling their weight.

Thus the alchemists of Manci have made by experiment
many machines of war, albeit that the will to fight is lacking
among them, of which one is called by them a thunderbolt

that shakes the sky.[46] For, using a magical powder that bursts[47] and which they place in a tube of iron or copper, they can throw a swift and flying fire to a great distance, and to the great harm of the foe. Such a thing is the work of the most cunning alchemists among them, those who follow that which they call the way of Tao, and who have also made catapults that send forth stones of iron at such a speed that the eye of no one may follow them. When they hold feasts it is also their custom to fill sticks of bamboo[48] with their bursting powder, to which they put a flame and make merry with the sparks of light.

But a pious man should not hold such things in contempt, for the existent world is given to us in bounty, not only to marvel at but also to understand and use, for such is our duty to the Creator. But as our master,[49] who was the wisest among men, teaches, magical tricks and sorcery are uncleanness, as the recalling of a dead man to life, the transforming of one substance into another, the inducing of love and hatred by secret ways, or the inflicting of diseases on a man by speaking certain words in a certain way. For these are the works of God, not of man.

---

'A SWIFT AND FLYING FIRE'

*In the original Italian* foco veloce e volante, *this appears to be the first known description of the action of 'gunpowder' – which is made of coal, saltpetre and sulphur – and of what seems to be a form of flame-thrower! 'Catapults' (*balliste*) which 'send forth stones of iron' (*lapidi di ferro*) obviously describes some form of cannon. It is not, however, clear whether Jacob's knowledge is based on observation, but since he does not say that he had seen these things himself – as he does, for example, in the passage dealing with paper – it is unlikely. He may have had it from a fellow merchant among the Jews resident in Zaitun, or perhaps from Lifenli. The Tartars are also said by some scholars to have had cannon – the secret perhaps learned from the Sung Chinese – as early as 1232, and to have used such arms in Europe in 1241, at the battle of Sajo in Hungary.*

Thus, although things are given to us such as the magnet stone that attracts and moves iron without touching it, or herbs which when thrown in the water cause fish to leap upon the land, and many other things in the world which are even more subtle to find out, a pious man shall not go among the Chaldeans.[50] For although the reason and nature of man compel him to seek out the truth of all things, to know certain secrets of nature would cause men great ill and harm, as our sages teach.

Yet by discovery there are many wondrous things of which the Mancini have knowledge, as the best way of making paper and parchment, for which they make a pulp of the wood and bark of the mulberry. Moreover, the people of the land of Sinim speak many and diverse languages, and are not able to

---

### 'MAKING PAPER AND PARCHMENT'

*The means of manufacture of paper using mulberry (* Broussonetia papyrifera*) had been known to the Chinese since at least the first century AD, knowledge which reached Europe in the late twelfth century and early thirteenth centuries. It is notable that Jacob describes the Chinese as knowing the 'best way', suggesting he was familiar with other ways of producing it. 'The first (and for a long period, the only) paper manufactory was that established and maintained by the Jews at Jativa, near Valencia' in Spain, says C. Roth in* A Short History of the Jewish People *(London, 1948, p. 216), discussing thirteenth-century Europe.*

*Small 'forms of wood' (p.358, forme di legno) may be the first known reference to the already well-established Chinese use of wood-block printing employing (as Jacob tells us) 'a brown ink of their own', with which an impress was made upon mulberry-pulp paper. This in fact represented the use of what we would now call 'moveable type', antedating the similar Gutenberg process (mid-fifteenth century) by some five centuries. Jacob's reference to 'many different' books and pamphlets, some with the impress of 'carved images' upon them – is there a pious recoil from idolatry even here? – confirms the already known fact that there was large-scale printing of books in the Sung era. Printing itself is thought to have reached back in China to the early Tang period (AD 618 onwards).*

understand one another well, yet in writing they have only one form of letters which, although they have different sounds among them, have the same meaning for all, so that through that which is written they are able to understand one another.[51]

Wherefore it brings very great profits to those who make paper and books,[52] and these books may be bought for small sums and are numerous. Indeed, among them they use small forms of wood on which not only letters but images are cunningly carved, and with which, using a brown ink[53] of their own, they make an impression upon their paper. Thus, employing many such forms they are able to make many different books, such as the writing of their sages and poets, together with tales and fables that are pleasing to the common people. Of these, however, many are wicked and base, having images[54] of the act of love and of cruel misdeeds, in which there is a great trade. For they may be freely sold by the traders in books, who may make whatever books they wish. Thus, those who seek not instruction but to satisfy their wicked desires by seeing images, given form, of the coupling even of men with beasts and other abominations, may also do according to their will in the City of Light.

But to know such things, and other cruel and wicked things besides, is not to become wise. For a man must distinguish between that which he learns by reason and from fear of God and that which the Adversary places in his path. Therefore, although among the Mancini there are those who know a thousand things which are not known to us, for some of their sages say that they can see even that which has no form and may listen to the voices of the dead, God forbid, they also know such things as should lie hidden, and which it is impious for any man to know.

For when the understanding goes too far to the depths,[55] whether in the matter of the natural laws or the conduct of men, it may come to know too much, turning that which is a good into an evil, and destroying that which was venerated by men. Thus it is also as if to strike a thing with the blows of a stick, or as when the heart is cut from the body so that it may be the better studied, the anus and mouth of man becoming as if they were the same thing.[56] Nor is it true wisdom for the intellect to undo that which is whole, or by craft to make men doubt those things in which they trust.

For knowledge is not to be found in everything which man understands, as the false sages of all lands believe, nor is it always to be found in that which the sages themselves know. Moreover, just as there may be an excess of light which dazzles the eyes,[57] so there may be knowledge which enriches the understanding but which often robs the soul. Thus, thinking these things in my chamber, God be praised, I understood better that from excess of riches and knowledge, just as from their lack, men may come to the point of ruin.

## CHAPTER TEN

# Clouds of Mortality

THESE PASSAGES ARE SURELY THE crown of Jacob's account of his journey and of his adventure. In them he gives us the essence of his beliefs, moral and 'political', and describes the disastrous culmination of his efforts to 'give counsel to the sages and elders of the city'. He shows both a tenacity of purpose and an extraordinary presumption; it is as if we can see more clearly than he, yet from his own description, the wisdom and the folly of some of his words and actions – as far as he discloses them and can be trusted.

At the heart of the discourses here are ancient questions of governance, liberty, justice, order, punishment and the 'common good'. But the exchanges among those gathered in assembly and at the house of Nathan ben Dattalo, although there are aspects which are now almost beyond our grasp – and were often very difficult to translate – still have the most 'modern' of resonances. Even the assertion that 'all men are equal' is heard. Indeed, the brief discussion among the Chinese elders about equality and fortune is arresting by any measure.

But no less significant are Jacob's increasingly confident and magisterial pronouncements upon how a city should be governed. Delivered as if *ex cathedra*, they contain a mixture of sense, pride, meddlesomeness and the authority of a Talmudic thinker. He lectures (or claims to have lectured) his audiences

on reward and honour, on virtue and merit, and above all on
duty. The passages on the last have been a powerful influence on
me; I borrowed freely from Jacob d'Ancona in *The Principle of
Duty*, making the notion of the 'civic order' – which he unusually calls *'la civitate'* – my own. Moreover, for him, 'duty' was
more than a mere moral abstraction. He divides it into particulars, advising that every city should prescribe the duties of its
citizens in its charter.

For his 'political philosophy' in general, I earlier (pp.242–5)
tried to provide a context, indicating that I believed him to
hold views which, although relatively free-thinking, did not
reflect the more 'advanced' opinions and practices of his own
day, in particular in some of the increasingly independent
Italian communes. In the passages which follow, he suggests a
system of conciliar (and sub-conciliar) election from among
'the citizens', coupled with the 'summoning' to lead such
council of a 'loyal and brave' individual who would be 'put at
your head for two or three years in order to keep the city in
hand'.

Thus Jacob is no 'liberal', nor is there any reason for us to
hope or to expect him to be, save from the sympathy (or sentiment) he arouses in us. However, there is room for disagreement
about my judgment of him. For he comes closer to 'modern'
political sensibilities in stating (twice) that 'one rule is suitable
for one people and another for another', and that 'each city
may make its own civil law as it sees fit': arguably both the
most Aristotelian and the most 'advanced' – because freest – of
all Jacob's political nostrums. Such a position was plainly influenced by the impulses at work in the early Italian city-states, and
anticipates by half a century the view of, for example, Bartolus
of Sassoferrato (1314–57) who held as a juristic principle that
*'civitas sibi princeps'*: 'the city is sovereign to itself'.

Nevertheless, Jacob's views, as on punishment, are also often
'illiberal' and severe. There may be a few stray signs of what today
would be called 'relativism' in his opinions on the arts of government, but there is (in general) none on questions of ethical

principle, the doing of justice, or moral commitment. It is presumably this which dictated his unyieldingness in matters of faith; his resistance to the pleas of his servants to leave China (or, in Buccazuppo's case, to stay); his valiant struggles, almost to the death, with the 'Adversary'; and his refusal – which sometimes seems pig-headed in its intransigence – to back down in the face of the clearly growing hostility in Zaitun to his opinions.

It is also here that the great qualities, and puzzles, of Jacob's account emerge. Some of his testimony, as we have already seen, is highly coloured, even perhaps fantastical. But other parts we can judge to be deeply naive (or innocent?), providing us with evidence of Jacob's seeming lack of sensitivity to the implications of what he was doing and saying. (Or is he cleverer than us, and not unwitting but *knowing* in every sense?) Thus we, but it appears not he, can detect the moves of a faction, or cabal, against him. But who were the parties to it and who, indeed, was really in command of the city's affairs? How, and by whom, were the decisions that affected the fates of Jacob and Pitaco taken? Was there surveillance, and entrapment? Was Jacob a useful dupe, for all his wisdom, in a struggle about whose lineaments he gives us some evidence, but of which he himself was not fully aware, or aware at all?

All we have are tantalising glimpses of the possible answers to such questions. They suggest, among other things, the great but undisclosed authority of Jacob's 'Adversary'. They also suggest alignment and alliance between the merchant-leaders, with their entourages (or gangs), certain of the 'elders and sages', and hirelings among the common people, pressed to do the formers' bidding, including by the carrying out of acts of violence and counter-violence.

At one point, Jacob himself describes the rich merchant Anscinen as the 'messenger' of 'the Adversary', as if he understood that there was some kind of 'political' relation between individuals of different provenances and interests who were together rounding upon him. In the same fashion, the embattled Pitaco refers, when addressing himself to Jacob's 'Adversary', to 'those who are like you' (p.395) as being 'ready even to commit violence against us', that is his 'party' of tradition-bound elders and officials. This too suggests the presence of a threatening cabal in the city, whose existence aroused in 'the noble Pitaco' a perilous disdain and contempt.

There is also more than one passing reference in Jacob's man-uscript to 'rebels' in the city or its surrounding districts. It is not, however, clear who they might have been, or whether they were politically linked to – or even synonymous with – the opponents of the *ancien régime* of the Sung emperor with whom Jacob also found himself dangerously at odds. But judging by the egregious positions adopted by the well-born Uainsciu, as well as the free-thinking stands taken by Anfenscian – the Adversary – and the merchant Lotacie on a number of subjects, there seems to have been a group of young populists and 'ratio-nalists' in the city who, while divided among themselves on some topics, espoused a radical mixture of 'egalitarian' and 'lib-ertarian' opinions.

With these, Jacob, for all his evident intellectual and moral stamina, plainly found it taxing (and even *shocking*) to deal; not least, perhaps, because of the free-thinking, rationalistic, strain in his own beliefs. Jacob's personal conduct, both in the stews of the city and at the crux of the passages which follow, is not wholly creditable. And at the last, when his egotism and seem-ing unawareness show him at his worst – and Pitaco's nobility shines forth in contrast – he makes embarrassingly clear that he is concerned only for his own skin and his possessions.

But he is also anxious to ensure, in the way of the true his-torian (and the Jewish 'remembrancer'), that the tale of his vicissitudes should be told – and he is obviously generous in rewarding his faithful amanuensis for the services rendered to him, before setting sail 'towards the south-west' with his pre-cious cargoes and his pious lamentations upon the human condition.

❦

n the next day, it being the twentieth day of
Adar,[1] having dismissed in great anger the
woman Bertoni, who sought to speak evilly of
my servant Buccazuppo, and having also sent
away the clerk Armentuzio, who would by no
means stay longer in the land of Sinim, I set forth with the
faithful Lifenli to give counsel to the sages and elders of the
city.

But upon reaching the place of their assembly, I found my
way barred, for the guardians had received orders that I, Jacob
of Ancona, should not be admitted, the merchants of the city
fearing the force of my words against them. Moreover, I heard
tell that certain of the Jews among the Mancini,[2] being
faithless and disloyal brothers, had made complaint against
me, declaring to the elders that I should be made to keep
silent lest I bring harm upon the Jews of the city. For so
cowardly and base did those who professed themselves to be
Jews show themselves to be, that they declared even to
idolaters that the words of the pious one should not be heard,
seeking thus to put me in peril of my life, may God keep me
in His Hand.

But the faithful Lifenli, may his name be recorded,[3]
entering the assembly, where many hundreds of the people
were gathered in order that concord might be established in
the city, and praying to the noble Pitaco that I might be
admitted, I also entered among them, may God be praised
that I should be shown such honour. Whereupon I found the
elders and merchants arrayed one against the other,[4] the
merchants being greatly angered that the said Anlisciu had
been slain and that those about Pitaco accused them of being
traitors to the city.

Yet since they had determined to seek concord among
themselves, the better to defend the city from its foes, all at
first heard the noble Pitaco in silence, who spoke to them as
follows: 'There is a moral conformation both in heaven above
and in material nature below, and its laws are one. They

decree that to act justly and rightly is to act according to the same principle by which the seasons succeed one another and the sun and moon appear with the alternation of day and night.

'And as the operations of nature take their course without conflict or confusion, so must we strive for the same among ourselves. As Ciancienmin taught, with right principles even a corpse might govern the realm. But in order to maintain concord, men must set about tasks while they are still simple, and take precautions before evil appear. For it is better to regulate matters before discord has begun, just as it is better not to wait until the roof falls in order to repair its beams.

'Yet now in Chinscie, in such low esteem is public office held, and so fearful of the future have the people become, that the worthy no longer wish to burden themselves with such things. Thus only scoundrels and men without intelligence enter civic occupation, while the rest devote themselves to dress and adornment, to idleness and music, with no thought for the good of others. Or they go from one thing to another, counselling now one thing and now its opposite, as if their heads were turning on a spit.

'Those who hold office in this city, sires, are likewise men without wisdom, who have no care for the teachings of our ancestors or respect for the order of heaven. Thus, as in Chinscie, we live under a bad government, which does not know which path to take. But if the future life of the citizens is to be better than that of the present, we must take a different path.

'Therefore we must seek justice, which is the doing of those things which are due and right, of which the first is always to give honour to those who are worthier than ourselves. Yet among us many now refuse such a title of honour to others, whether they be older, wiser in the ways of men, more learnèd or in other fashion worthy of our respect. But in the denying of honour to those who are better than us, justice itself is fled and can no longer be done.'

To whom an old man[5] replied: 'I, in my years of toil, first collected wood-tax and then I guarded the floating bridge, but shall I be called a lowly person?' To whom a young man by name Uainsciu replied: 'No, for all men are equal.' At which words there was much laughter, the merchant Lotacie[6] declaring: 'No man is equal to another, neither can one man be made equal to another. We may only permit each to practise his skills as best he may, without placing many obstacles in his path. But life itself is not just and cannot be made just by the actions of men. Instead, each must take his own way and suffer the effects of his own deeds.'

To whom Uainsciu in turn now answered: 'We do not seek to make men equal to one another,[7] nor to make life wholly just, nor to permit men to be exempt from the effects of their deeds, but to find a remedy for such ills as may be cured for the benefit of all. Or shall the orphan[8] be left to wander the streets of the City of Light in order that it may follow its own will, and the maiden be left as a prey to the pander? Or shall not the city from its wealth provide shelter to both, so that we shall not be covered in shame for our hard dealing?'

The merchant Lotacie replied: 'It may, but you seek to change the course of fate, as though misfortune itself could be averted. But you do not possess the wisdom or the power of heaven.' To whom the young man cried out: 'Then we must call upon the Son of Heaven to help us.' To which Lotacie answered with scorn: 'How foolish it is to call upon the Son of Heaven, when his realm will soon be no more.'

But at these words great were the cries that resounded throughout the assembly, some sustaining the opinion of Lotacie and others shouting against him, so that nothing could be heard.

Wherefore I, Jacob di Salomone, resolved to take command and spoke as follows, for which God be praised: 'Sires, from those things which I have heard and seen, such a city as yours cannot remain united but must be conquered and fall, unless you begin to live in a different fashion and with a different ordering of communal duties, so that peace, justice and the common good may prevail over pride, greed, covetousness and strife.

'For to govern that body which is a city is like steering a ship, while in order to maintain the realm in tranquil peace it makes sense that in each city all reward shall be according to merit, which is to say, to each merit there is owed a just reward. By this I mean that reward ought to be proportional and demerit also,[9] so that honour be not shown to the wicked nor contempt to the good, but that the ranks and orders of the city be formed not according to riches or nobility but according to desert.

'Thus the principle of equality for those of equal merit comes before all other principles whatsoever, while only that city or realm which gives the rule to the wisest and most virtuous may prevail.'

But no sooner had I pronounced these words than many cried out against me with great hatred and anger, the young man declaring in a loud voice: 'From such principle of merit comes so much injustice that the whole realm must suffer from it. For only if all are considered equally, without regard to merit, can peace reign among men.' At whose words those who had cried out against me were divided among themselves, God be praised, so great were their passions.

Yet feeling no fear, for the Holy One stood once more at my side, I continued thus: 'Sires, without due reward for those actions which are worthy of a man, there can be no active virtue in any city or realm. Instead, true worth must always be justly rewarded, if you would keep the citizens from idleness and rebellion. Therefore, those who deserve well of the city, be they ever so humble, should be sure to receive the honour which is fitting for their conduct.

'For to do them honour is not only to reward them themselves but to strengthen in others their understanding of justice. Thus, recompense for acts which are done according to duty, or for worthy service to others, should not be neglected, for there must be a distinction between those who do their duty, whether to God or to man, and those who do not, which God forbid. For without such distinction it matters to none how a man conducts himself, when those who act evilly fare as well as those who are an ornament to the city.

'Thus the rectitude of the citizen should always be honoured, and at the same time he in turn will live better under the protection of those who feel a duty to him rather than under the rule of those who are only strong or cunning. Therefore, so that the citizens of Zaitun may live in peace with one another, there is need for an accord between you which prescribes the duties of the citizen to the city, so that the City of Light may mend and renew itself for the good of all. For the city, sires, exists for no other end than the common good, as our sages teach.'

To these words of mine the merchant Lotacie sought to reply, declaring that wherever a man might freely take his own way, becoming rich or remaining poor according to his own merit, such was also for the common good. But to him I would not yield, God be praised, continuing as follows: 'Sires, the common good is a moral end, and may not be attained when each does as seems fit to him alone. Therefore, each city, being a body or corporation,[10] should have its own charter, in which are also written the duties of each citizen to the whole. For if each city does not determine for itself what the duties of its citizens are, a tyrant, having conquered the city, may the more easily and by his own will determine what such duties should be, increasing them as he sees fit even to the point of servitude.

'Among us, Christian scholars declare that the civic order[11] is the fruit of human nature and of the wisdom of man, the source of justice and deserving of our love and duty. Yet, although it is an ill thing for a man if he is not a citizen, they exclude the Jew from the common good, but at the same time demand that we fulfil our duties to the city or to the prince.

'Therefore, it is better and more just that in each civic order all should be governed by the same rule, that all those who receive the protection of the city or the prince should fulfil the same duties, and that all who govern it are likewise bound by the same duties. For although men may differ among themselves about the true nature of the city, some saying that it is the work of God, and others of craft and reason, and some saying that it should be ruled by a prince and others by the people, there may be concord among the citizens only when there is a common will[12] which gives rule to all, thus protecting the civic order from being undone.

'True it is that all men have an inner liberty to think according to their will and whose thoughts are known only to God, for it is He, and no man, who rules over all, may He be magnified and exalted. Indeed, since the Holy One is King of the Universe, there is no need of other kings on earth,[13] while the tyrant who would rule for his own ends alone, and not for the common good, ought to be cast out. But when men speak out and act, their liberty becomes less and must be governed by law. For it is just, both in the eyes of God and of man, that that which affects others should be subject to a general rule, because without such a rule inner liberty may become an external harm.

'Indeed, in your city, sires, in which I have seen that many citizens are unfaithful and disloyal, it means that a wondrous number of men consider themselves to be bound to no one and nothing.[14] Therefore, you should elect three or four of every hundred or thousand, and one of these, loyal and brave, ought to be summoned[15] and put at your head for two or three years in order to keep the city in hand with justice and severity.

'For it is better for a city to be ruled by good laws without a prince than by a prince without good laws. Yet it is also better for judges and other officials of a city to put their trust in the goodwill of the citizens. But when such trust is betrayed by them, it serves none to await the time when the conduct of the people shall improve, while the condition of the city grows worse from day to day, as is the case among you. Rather, you must act with energy before it is too late to find a remedy for the city's ills. Therefore, citizens and officials alike must be taught their duties, and those who do not fulfil them must be punished, for it is better that they perform them unwillingly than not at all.

'Moreover, in order to govern the city better, so great is the confusion among you, you should have in each district a group which chooses a head and a statute of authority, and if anyone commits any act against it, he should be punished. And this same group ought to watch over all the affairs of the district, in order that there be concord among the citizens of each place.

'For in all cities, sires, be they large or small, there can be but one end, which is the good of the whole, and a harmony of the orders of men. But when the affairs of the city are given over to the free will of each,[16] it is the strongest will, not the most virtuous, which must prevail. Much different is it when the citizens choose someone from among them who is loyal and brave, or who is brought from another place, to rule over them for a certain time, for such was the way of government proposed by our prophet Samuel, may his name and memory be revered. But the rich merchants among you disturb the peace of the city with their vices, so that they must be taught to temper their desires and to use their riches for the good of others and not only for themselves.'

All these things I, Jacob, told them, and many more I would besides, for which God be praised. But they would no longer hear me, some shouting and others seeking to lay violent hands upon me, God forbid, so that I was not able to continue but had to depart, together with the faithful Lifenli.

Whereupon, having returned to the house of my brother Nathan, I found that my servants also were arrayed against me, God forbid, the clerk Armentuzio declaring that my brothers

Lazzaro and Eliezer, having been ready for many days and being unable to delay further, had set sail, and that we, being alone and having waited too long, should be in great danger of pirates and of bad weather. Thus, Armentuzio declared that now there was a great peril in sailing and that we should go towards our ruin or be obliged to turn back, for we should soon lose the north-west wind.

But I would pay no heed to him, for which God be praised, or to the laments and anger of the Saracens, who even cursed me that I was a Jew, may God punish them, saying that we should all be lost and my riches also. Nor could the cries of the evil woman Bertoni and the girl Buccazuppo alter my mind, God be thanked, the one seeking to go forthwith, and the other pleading with many tears that she might remain in the City of Light, at which I marvelled greatly.

Against all these, however, I stood firm and unyielding, for I had resolved that I should give my counsel to the elders of the city until the end, for so God had commanded me. For when a pious Jew does that which he is commanded to do and speaks Torah truth to the peoples, he may not be harmed, but God will keep him in His Hand and his memory will be recorded to all times.

Thus I sent my servants away, keeping only the faithful Lifenli about me, and commanding Buccazuppo to wait upon him. Later, when it was already night, there came to me Cianianmin, counsellor to the noble Pitaco and learnèd master of medicine, enquiring whether anyone had harmed me. I showed much courtesy to him, as befitting one who was greatly advanced in years and who had paid me such honour. Moreover, since he had come in darkness through the streets of the city, I declared that although none had done me harm, he stood in greater danger to pass through the streets in a chair when night had already fallen.

Cianianmin replied: 'In the past, the watchmen walked about the quarters of the city, but now it is true that it has become too perilous in many places. Once, if they found a person in the streets beyond the lawful hours it was customary to hold him and present him in the morning to the seigneurs. But even the watchmen are afraid of the violence of the young and have ceased to go about the city, leaving them to their crimes, so numerous have they become.

'Thus few inhabitants of the city have the courage to go out of their houses[17] in the night-time, save those who are given over to wicked pleasures. Moreover, in the past the day and night guards, of whom there were not less than two thousand, were prompt to go to the help of the people, and few dared to rob their neighbours when punishment was certain.

'But now, sire, some crimes are terrifying, so that young men stab old women with knives or by violence harm their honour, despite their white hair, or slowly kill others so that their bodies are pierced through in every part and thus they die in torment. Others go about the city seeking to do all the damage they can, and when they have achieved their end they return to their houses as from work well done, while others rob the citizens at midday as they go about.'

Whereupon, Cianianmin having spoken in this fashion, there entered unexpectedly into my chamber, although the hour was late, the Adversary, or he who went by the name of Anfenscian, declaring that he needed to listen further to my wisdom, for which God be praised. Therefore, having permitted him to take his place among us, for even the Adversary is one sent by God who commands all things, I besought Cianianmin to continue, he speaking as follows: 'How, sires, shall human life be lived except according to certain laws made under heaven? Yet now the judges of the city do not want to put anyone to death, deeming it to be unjust even if such a one should have cruelly killed another and deserves death. Indeed, some among them show horror, both at the punishment of death and of the torture, even holding in scorn those who urge that the assassin should pay a just price. Thus, even though a man may have killed many others, they do not condemn him to death, but say that he too should be treated with pity. Yet in the past our ancestors showed pity not to those who caused harm but to those who suffered it, so that peace might reign under heaven.'

To whom the Adversary, God forbid, replied: 'But Latsu declares that a man should do good to the wicked, in order to make them good.' I answered: 'To the wicked it is better to do some harm as just recompense according to measure. For to be good to the wicked seldom makes the wicked good, unless they have first been punished. Moreover, to be good to the wicked dissolves the difference between good and bad, so that the young may the more easily be led to do harm, thinking that to do harm is neither good nor bad. Therefore, sires, it is more just to all to punish the wicked and not to do them good.'

Whereupon the Evil One replied: 'You cannot act as if you were chasing a stray pig, for man is a different animal. Nor are you content to return this pig to its sty, but must also tie its feet together.' To whom the sage Cianianmin impiously answered: 'Yet, truly, slight is the difference between man and the beasts, as our Menche teaches.'

To whom I, Jacob, said as follows, may God be thanked: 'Then your Menche was mistaken. For God made man in His own image, which, though man betray it, is not shared by the other creatures of God. For, lacking the soul of man, as well as his reason and the acquiring of virtue, they are distinct from him.'

To which Cianianmin replied: 'But the acts of men are not better than those carried out by animals. Indeed, they may be deemed worse, for insofar as he possesses reason, as the pious stranger maintains, he is able, unlike the beast, to distinguish between right and wrong. Therefore, it is just to punish him for his misdeeds.'

Whereupon, the Adversary, he who went by the name Anfenscian, answered: 'Would you then have it, learnèd sire, that, as among the Tartars, we struck blows against those who

have committed a petty theft, or that those who have stolen a
horse should be cut in half with a sword, or that, as among
the Saracens, a man's ears or hands be severed for his crimes?
Or shall we break their necks, as was formerly done in this
city, or shall we kill them with poison or drown them in the
sea? In the past, they were beaten with the heavy stick and the
light stick and put to the question,[18] until their flesh was torn
and their blood flowed forth so that they shouted and
groaned as to rend the skies. But how shall such things serve
to make men good?'

The learnèd Cianianmin replied: 'Sire, the purpose of such
punishments is not to make wicked men good but to warn
those who observe them that they should not act as the
wicked act, or they too will suffer the just reward. Moreover,
among the Tartars they no longer have need of herdsmen or
others to watch over their cattle and their possessions, because
their law is truly severe. For not only may a malefactor himself
be punished, but his brothers and his children also, while the
wickedest among them is slaughtered like a sheep.'

To which Anfenscian, hot with anger, answered: 'That
which you speak of is truly the law of wild animals. Better
indeed that men should break the law than that punishment
should make us less than men.'

The sage Cianianmin replied: 'You err. In the past, before
men's knowledge of right and wrong came to be lost, he who
killed or robbed was held to transgress the rule of heaven.
Moreover, those whose habits went beyond the due measure
and who caused harm to others went in peril not of their lives
but of their freedom, or their pleasure, some for their wrongs
and misdeeds being kept close in prison, some remaining free
but being subject to interdict and prohibition, and some
being sent into exile.[19] But now not only are many wicked
men not castigated but they are often permitted to go free,
with the excuse of their poverty or other causes.'

To whom the Adversary replied: 'But even if a man is bad,
how can it be just to harm him?'

Cianianmin answered: 'You are too soft and your nostrils have no breath in them.' The Adversary replied: 'When the innocent are put to death in the name of the law, a noble man may justly leave his country, as Menche teaches.' Cianianmin replied in turn: 'But as Menche also teaches, whoever is without compassion is not truly human, whoever is without shame is not truly human, and whoever is without knowledge of right and wrong is not truly human.'

To whom I declared, 'Then Menche is in agreement with our sages, peace be upon them.'

But the Adversary and Evil One would by no means be stilled by our words, but spoke as follows: 'The prisoner[20] remains the human. Therefore, for the prisoner there must be respect, and his worthiness must be protected, however great his wrong. Neither should he be compelled to toil against his will, nor to abase himself before his guards, but, save in respect of his loss of liberty, he should be treated as if he were a free man.[21]

'But very often not even punishment or reproach is just, as when a violent deed has been done by such a man who is not in himself violent, but who suffers from a low and blind spirit. This is so above all among the young, who, although they may seek to do harm to others, are frequently angered not from their own fault but from the absence of care shown to them by others.

'Moreover, he who in prison shows remorse and is of good conduct, even if he has done the most wicked of acts, should be set free so that he may again pursue his ends, provided that they be according to law. Thus, instead of depriving such a one of his freedom, he may himself be brought to understand the folly of his actions and be returned to the brotherhood of other men. For a man may not be justly burdened all his life by the consequences of his deeds. On the contrary, we should seek as quickly as possible to excuse those who have caused harm and offence, so that their lives at the last may not be without fruit.'

But to the Adversary, who is sent by God in order to test the pious man, I replied: 'Young man, in this, as in all things, it is wise to avoid excess. Thus it is better that those who are imprisoned and put in chains should alone be those who are a peril to others, while the rest should be put to work under guard. Men who are full of vices we must not set free, nor give to them gardens of sweet flowers, virgins, God forbid, ease and delicious wines, but hard toil, strict rule and small provision. For he that is put in prison must be fed with the bread of adversity and the water of affliction.

'Your reasoning does not suffice for the doing of justice. For if you neither educate a child in that which is right and wrong, nor punish the malefactor in a way that is fitting and which gives honour to the law, you cannot expect the people of your city to be good.'

Whereupon, although the night was greatly advanced, the learnèd Cianianmin besought me to declare what was the teaching of the Jews, God keep them, upon justice and the just man. So that I spoke as follows, God being the guide of my words: 'Our sages teach that the knowledge of right and wrong lies in the heart of all men. Thus the good desire that the just shall rule over them and that the unjust shall be cast out, for the human soul flies towards justice as a bird flies to its nest, may God be praised.

'Likewise the vices of men are the creatures of the will, since men, being made in the image of God, may choose between good and ill. From such choice arises the guilt of man, and for his choice it is just that he pays the price, if his choice is to do ill. Moreover, to deny such truth is to add ill to ill,[22] serving neither him who does ill nor him to whom ill is done.

'Nor may those who are endowed with free will say that they are ill-born, as if that were an excuse for all things. Thus when God, blessèd be He, asked the wicked Cain why he had killed his brother, the evil one responded, I am wholly innocent, the fault is yours because you infused in me the

wicked instinct. Thus our wicked one spoke with great
cunning after he had slain his brother, just as among you in
the City of Light the wicked speak with the same tongue and
words.

'Hence, because all men may choose between the paths of
good and evil, humankind is an attested danger, each man for
the other. More perilous still, therefore, is it when the
difference between right and wrong becomes uncertain, so
that the memory of the just is no longer blessèd, God forbid,
nor do the names of the wicked perish. Therefore, that which
is unlawful must also be clearly distinguished from that which
is licit, so that the elders of your city must by no means be in
doubt about them. Rather, the young should be instructed
about the just limits of their actions and know their
consequences before they shall have cause to repent.

'Sires, the inclination to cause harm to others, which God
does not wish, arises from diverse causes, as the philosopher
Aristotle teaches. One is lack of restraint, or excess, another is
misuse of the reason or deceitfulness, and another is the
savagery of some men, who may be as pitiless as wild animals
even though they are not the same as them. Each must
therefore be considered differently, so that the cause of each
man's wickedness may be found out and due punishment
imposed, for such is the wisdom of our sages, peace upon
them.

'Never, also, should there be punishment which is not just
and which does not correspond to the ill which has been
done. Therefore, as our sages teach, only an eye may be given
for an eye, a tooth for a tooth, but not an eye for a tooth or a
life for a mere wound,[23] save where a son strikes his parent,
which God forbid.

'Yet also among those who act to the greatest harm of
others are men who are infirm in mind, or whose souls are
diseased. Of these our Rabbi Mose ben Maimon teaches that
they should go to the sages, or masters of the soul, who must
seek to cure their disease by the moral qualities which they

shall show them, until they return to the middle way. If they
do not, then they must cease to be counted among men of
reason, nor may they be permitted during their lives to go
among others, lest without warning they should strike a man
down, or do him other great harm.

'But, as our judges teach, peace upon them, when a man is
to be judged for his misdeeds let the balance first be in his
favour, but when it is determined with sound proof that he is
guilty, then let not the judgment be mild.'

Whereupon the Adversary, being put at a loss by my
wisdom, again denied the truth of my words, saying that
they who would be severe in judgment add only harm to
harm, bringing not peace and justice but hatred and fear to
the city.

To which I replied as follows, according to the wisdom of
our sages: 'Truly, it is better to save a life than to take it, if a
man show remorse. Truly, also, it is a wrong and a crime to
inflict cruel pains upon the body, as in whipping or torturing
the condemned, which God prevent. For this is to mistreat
those who are made in the image of God and shows disrespect
to the dignity of man.

'Especially this is so if such things be done, as has often
been suffered by my brothers, God keep them, for the
pleasure of the common people. But without rigour there can
be no true justice. Therefore, the sentences of the judges
should be severe, but just. For justice, even though a judge
may show mercy, requires always to be steadfast, since
without steadfastness it will be held in disrespect, and thus
invite the wicked to do yet greater harm.

'Nor, young sir,[24] should men be afraid of a harsh
judgment out of a false pity. For although the kind man seeks
always to avoid harm to others, punishment is the only
remedy that serves for many diseases. Thus, to be meek or to
show compassion is not the best remedy for the City of Light,
but the doing of true justice, by which the evil-doer is made
to pay in due measure for his misdeeds, whether he be

condemned to die or to be excluded from the company of
men, and from the privileges of the city.[25]

'Indeed, to spare the wicked is to cause more harm than to
punish the innocent in error. For in the first case the wicked
man is likely to do wickedness again and to bring grief to yet
others, while in the second case it is the judge who must make
peace with his soul for his wrongdoing. But above all things it
is against the rules of law that wicked acts should go without
punishment, which must always follow upon injuries and
wrongs. For if evil-doing has no price, then goodwill shall also
have no value.'

Upon these words of mine, the learned Cianianmin spoke
greatly to my honour, declaring that the sages of the Jews were
truly the wisest of men.

Thus I continued, even though the dawn drew near: 'Our
sages teach that a man should not cause the peace of the city
to be disturbed by his own greed, or by his other vices. Thus,
there is need in your city, sires, for a more attentive watch, so
that the people may no longer go in fear. For when the citizen
must always be on guard for himself and his possessions, the
wicked grow ever more impudent, knowing that others are
afraid, while fear gives no wise counsel, often delivering the
fearful into the hands of the wicked themselves.'

The Adversary, seeking to raise objection, yet also bowing
in honour to me, would by no means agree with my words.
For he declared that I used cunning in my argument, God
forbid, not in order that there might be justice in the city, but
so that its governors might rule the better over its citizens,
watching over them by day and by night as a father over his
children, and that thus neither the city nor its citizens might
remain in a free condition.

I replied as follows: 'The worst thing is dissension, as when
men act against each other without reason and when violence
dictates their deeds. Nor is it true that only those who obey
according to their own will, whether they be child or man, are
free.[26] For to obey even unwillingly permits the city to live in

peace, while to act only according to will is to destroy the city itself.[27] Moreover, only when justice is steadfast, as I have declared, may the person who is drawn to break the law be brought to greater virtue in his conduct, which gives to him a greater freedom in truth than is possessed by him who is bound to vice.

'Therefore, you must forbid many things that your law permits you.[28] For although men differ from animals, unleashed men are as mastiffs unleashed. Both, if they are not to become wild, require to be brought to order and taught how to live peacefully in human society. Wickedness must be combated, yet instead your city abandons itself to evil-doers, so that its wrongs go unpunished and it becomes accursèd in the eye of God, may He be exalted.

'But man must not deviate in this way from the path of justice, but feel the suffering which true justice brings, may God be praised.'

These words the learnèd master Cianianmin much approved, declaring that I should again speak before the assembly of ministers and elders, for when the day dawned they should once more seek concord in the confusion of the city.

But the Adversary, may God strike him down at the last, stood out against me, saying: 'You, stranger, speak evil. For in the name of justice you seek suffering, and in the name of truth you give only your own teaching. Thus, the citizens should not hear you, for in the name of wisdom you promise only fear and discord. Moreover, few will seek to take your way, which is the way of obedience and not of free judgment. Nor do you truly know the purpose for which men should be punished, since you believe that to be severe is to be just and to be merciful brings harm to the city. Therefore, it is right that you should be driven from our midst, lest your counsels bring us to greater confusion.'

To whom I replied as follows, the Holy One leading me by the path of Torah truth, for His Name's sake: 'The purpose of

punishing a man is to cause him to feel shame.[29] For if he is
not brought to shame he will have no desire to change his
conduct, but remain always in his darkness of soul, upon
which only the light of justice may shine. Moreover, he who is
brought to shame is often brought also to repent for his
misdeeds, so that the citizens may the more easily call him
back to his duty, God willing. For as the light of the eye
comes forth from the black of the eye, so if a man has been
justly punished may good come forth from evil. But in order
to secure this end, justice must be active, so that the vices of
men, to which all are drawn, may be tamed.

'Therefore, the Holy One in His righteousness magnified
the Law and clothed it in honour, for the Law is that which
binds man to God, blessèd be He, and permits him to attain
to the supreme good. Moreover, he who honours the Law
should himself be honoured by all men, while he who brings
shame to it should himself be brought to shame.

'This, sires, is the teaching of the Jews upon the Law.'

It being now the twenty-second day of Adar[30] and the first
light of the sun being in the heavens, for which God be
praised, the learnèd Cianianmin and the said Anfenscian went
away so that I might fulfil my duties and take my rest.[31]
Whereupon certain guardians came to me, ordering that I
leave the city and the realm before the setting of the sun. For
thus was my wisdom rewarded. Yet I resolved, God be
praised, that notwithstanding such a decree, I should again go
before the ministers and the elders of the City of Light in
accordance with the will of the noble Pitaco, may his name be
recorded, and of master Cianianmin, peace be upon him.

Thereafter, while the faithful Lifenli took his rest, I
summoned my clerk Armentuzio, telling him that I would
attend the assembly of the elders and ministers of the city, but
that my fleet should be made ready to depart.

For one party and the other among the elders were now
arrayed against each other, each swearing to do ill to the other,

as well as to all whom they believed had brought harm to their city. Wherefore Armentuzio, accompanied by my brother Nathan, went away in haste to the harbour in accordance with my orders, so that the necessary things might be done and that all the provisions might be made ready.

Whereupon there came to me my servant, Bertoni, who had a great desire to depart without delay, declaring in fear that all spoke of the great portents of evil that the soothsayers of the city proclaimed, and which even a pious man might believe. For such was the confusion of the city and the dark things which were about to befall it. But I would not hear her pleas, God be praised for my valour, since first I would bring my last counsels to the city so that it might be saved from its foes, God willing.

There also came to me my servant Buccazuppo, who with many tears besought me that she should remain in the City of Light and there find her path, for whom I felt great compassion at her lamentations, she being young, yet as if without hope. Therefore I reproached her with tender words, declaring that she might not remain, for great was the danger in which the city stood, and that she would be lost upon the coming of the Tartars. Moreover, I declared that my promise to bring her safely to her native land bound me to my duty, and that therefore she should make herself ready to depart.

Thus, having determined all things in the house of my brother Nathan ben Dattalo and having roused the faithful Lifenli, peace upon him, I set forth to the grand hall of the prefect, to which others proceeded in a great throng, many of the common people also being attentive to hear what was spoken.[32] Yet they were as sheep scattered by the neglect of their shepherds, who had sought not the good of all but their own diverse ends. All now feared what each might do according to his own will and desire, there being so little concord among them, so that a man might say that the City of Light, albeit not yet taken by the Tartars, God forbid, had already fallen.

Thus, I, Jacob of Ancona, God be praised, entered for the last time the assembly in which were gathered all the elders, counsellors, merchants and sages of the great city, together with other high officials,[33] in order that I might help the noble Pitaco[34] and give wise counsel by which the city might yet be saved.

Before them the prefect first spoke as follows: 'Sires, let the vicious remain outside and only the virtuous enter, let thieves and vagabonds keep away, and only the lovers of good doctrine who care for the safety of the city, come! And let those who speak speak in a manner brief and courteous, as is fitting, without ill-temper or harmful words! And let there be among us neither red mouths nor white tongues!',[35] which is to say neither anger nor falsehood according to their language.

Whereupon, having made their devotions to their idols, God forbid, many spoke with bitter feeling of the travails of the city, some being of one opinion and some of another, so that among them there was none who commanded the opinion of all, nor any who might govern the city with the agreement of another. Moreover, their sages quarrelled without wisdom in order only that each might get the better of the other in ignoble fashion, while some among them, being without the will to act for the good of others, denied that their city stood in peril.

Yet such was the hatred also of one man for another, the merchants of the city being filled with pride and strength, and the elders being in great despair at the vices of the people and borne down by their lack of faith, that there now came into my heart a great thought, and my courage began to swell.[36] Thus, notwithstanding that many among them had shown me hatred, but others great honour, I humbly besought the prefect, peace upon him, that I be permitted to speak with the help of the faithful Lifenli. Yet the guardians would by no means allow it, declaring that I had received a decree to depart from the city and the realm, while many among the ranks of the merchants and the sages cried me down for a stranger and a man without wisdom, for which may God at the last day strike them down.

But the noble Pitaco and the learnèd Cianianmin, together with the great sage Ociuscien, pleaded that I be heard, so that I was able to speak as follows, praise be to God: 'Sires, it is our duties in the eyes of God and of man which stand at the centre of all things upon the earth. It is therefore the task of the wise to enquire and to answer what such duties are, teaching them to others for the benefit of the generations to follow.' These words I said with my soul alive and with the inspiration of God, blessèd be He, and continued: 'For how shall men prosper if all take from the city and one another, and none give? And how shall your City of Light defend itself from its enemies unless the body of citizens[37] learns that their city is the source of right and must therefore be defended by their duties? Thus it is necessary to make each person aware of his duty, so that the city may be saved.[38]

'For duty is the heart of the being and essence of a man, our very duty lying in the doing of our duty, which is the sole thing a man may always do, for which God be praised. Moreover, every citizen must be taught the difference between that which he has the power to do and that which he is permitted to do, so that discord and seeking too much may be avoided.

'In addition, the ordinances of the city must be observed and strengthened, and the people must be obliged by pact[39] to fulfil their duties, not for the sake of obedience itself but in order to defend the city. Furthermore, the rulers of the city must learn to distinguish without fear the bad citizen from the good, and if such a one is neither willing to add to the well-being of others nor even to cease causing harm to them, you must punish him in just fashion or drive him from the city.

'In the same way, those who hold public office or discharge civic business[40] have a duty above all others to do good for

the city. Therefore, only he who is free of corruption should
be entrusted with rule over the city, so that those among you
who are not worthy of such great trust should be sent away.
Nor should a citizen seek or accept money when he has
discharged his duties honestly and well, for such is an ignoble
thing. Rather, it is honour which you must show him, doing
right for those who are worthy, and harm to those among you
who betray your city.'

Whereupon, my speech was overwhelmed with shouts of
praise from one side and of condemnation from another, so
that Pitaco, although weak from age, was constrained to
declare as follows: 'It is our duty to set the world of men in
order, as the wise Jew has said. Even when we reach that end
where there is neither form nor substance, and neither place
nor sound, we should still seek order under heaven, as
Chunfutsu taught us. For where many of the inhabitants of a
city pay no heed to their duties in the relations[41] of life, it is
not possible that such a city should be permitted by heaven to
subsist for long. Therefore, as the learnèd Jew instructs us, it
should be our aim to educate both children and men in their
duties, and to call forth in each a will to fulfil them. But such
a will may not arise throughout a city or a realm without a
balance among men. Hence, the imbalance which the rich
have brought to the City of Light by reason of their cupidity
and wealth must be corrected, and greater duties be imposed
upon them in proportion to their riches.

'For there will be a just order under heaven only when the
rich have more duties than the poor, and those who
command have more duties than those who are subjected to
them.'

But these words of the noble Pitaco greatly stirred the
wrath of those who were of the party of the merchants, for
they would by no means accept that the rich owed more
duties than others. Wherefore the merchant Lotacie rose in
anger, declaring that by such means it was sought to drive
from the city the merchants who alone brought it good, and

that some of them had already been shamefully put to the sword. Moreover, with great calumny the said Lotacie proclaimed that I, Jacob of Ancona, spoke only so that I might create discord among the people, giving my counsel to those who sought to do harm to the most powerful of the city, which God forbid.

Thus with great wickedness he pointed his finger to me so that I was brought to tremble in my place, may God forgive me for my cowardice, declaring that all knew of the decree of the guardians and that at the setting of the sun I should be gone.

But I once more feared nothing, God be praised, being turned by His guidance from cowardice to courage, and spoke as follows: 'My counsel, sires, is not that of a wretch but of a wise man who has seen and understood many things, God be thanked. And although, as I believe, one rule is suitable for one people and another for another, and cities may make their own civil law as each sees fit, that which is virtuous and just in one people is virtuous and just in all.

'For we are all made in the image of God, Jew and Gentile alike, and therefore have the same duty to obey the moral law. Moreover, in the heart of each human being is the image of duty,[42] to which each of us is summoned by God, blessèd be He, in order not only that He may be praised but in order that men may live with their neighbours in concord.

'This duty of which I speak is to take account of others and to express it in action, so that the duties of men are of two kinds, although they are often mingled, these being the duties of the heart, which have to do with the thoughts and are of the inward part, and the worldly duties, which concern conduct towards others.

'Of these duties the greatest are to praise and to fear God, may He be exalted, and to sustain and to revere life in other men and in the rest of divine creation, the duty to live with dignity and according to reason, as being created in the image of God, and the duty to study and to toil. In this way honour

may be done to God, to ourselves and to others, and thus we
may be able to add our gifts, God willing, to the common
good. Nor is it sufficient only to generate children, but we
must take care of them, give them just nourishment, and
ensure that they are instructed in matters of right and wrong.
Moreover, in reverence to God, we should show reverence
towards the animals and the plants which the earth brings
forth upon the command of God, for to them also men bear a
duty lest, albeit that such are themselves without soul or
reason, they be harmed without cause.

'Thus, by means of such care, each man in fulfilling his
duties may give that which is owed by him to God and to
other men, and thus also protect the city by taking account of
others, acting in all things not as do the citizens of your city
but as a good man should.'

At these words of mine, for which God be praised, the said
Uainsciu now asked as follows, the leaders of the merchants
speaking in great anger among themselves: 'But what of the
duties of the city towards the citizen? Does the city have none?
Or must the people go on their knees before the rich in search of
favour?'

I replied: 'Young man, your questions are wiser than those
of the merchants of your city, who understand nothing of its
sufferings. For you cannot expect that a citizen will perform
his duty if you do not perform your duty to him. Rather,
duty which is mutual, being just, serves as a bond among
men. Moreover, if I fulfil my duty, my neighbour must fulfil
his also, just as when those who govern us demand that we
fulfil our duties, they must themselves fulfil their duties to
us.'

Whereupon the noble Pitaco declared: 'The pious Jew
teaches us great wisdom, for our city has truly forgotten its
duties under heaven. So without care have we become that
heaven itself has turned its care from us, while men below
have hatred in their hearts for those who seek to recall them
to their duties. In consequence our city must be destroyed,

unless it be again led in the way of wisdom such as the Jew teaches.'

I replied before the great assembly as follows: 'May God be praised for the honour the noble Pitaco shows me. For indeed, sires, you have failed in many things, so that you must listen in shame and with hatred in your hearts to one who is wiser than you.'

At which words there resounded great shouts and screams[43] against me, but God, blessèd be He, urged me to feel no fear. Thus one among the merchants impiously cried out that to show obedience to our forebears, and to consider only the good of others, was the work of slaves, and not of men of will and pride.

To whom I said: 'Sires, only certain men take it upon themselves to sustain and serve the good of others. They are those who with effort and will seek that others, and not only themselves, shall live in security and be contented. For in their souls, which are given to them by God, there is a thing of greater preciousness than the finest ruby, which is the desire to serve the common good.

'But especially when a city is in great confusion and peril, all must be brought to the desire to act well and justly.[44] Yet in the City of Light your peril is the greater, for many among you believe that each has a right to all things that his will may crave, and that such desire has the first place above others. In this you are the greatest fools of the whole world, for no city or realm may stand upon the desires of men alone.

'Rather, in order to save your city, it must be freed from the fist of greed, and the hand of benevolence be laid upon it, God willing.[45] Moreover, that a citizen ought to do that which is his due, and neither withdraw nor turn from the way of duty,[46] must become the rule for all, and better that such duty be discharged freely than that it be done under constraint.

'But not to impose duty, whenever it is necessary, is itself to commit injury against those who willingly do what they

should. Likewise, the faith of men in the law of their city is
the less when some are constrained to do what others freely
neglect. Therefore, all must be made accustomed[47] to do their
duty, at the last all doing voluntarily what some were first
brought to do only by fear, so that all may lead a quiet life.'

Yet despite the wisdom of my words, the number of my
foes seemed to increase about me, the merchant Lotacie
declaring that mine were principles that would take away the
wealth and splendour of the city, and extinguish its light. But
my arguments were in fine order, praise be to God, and there
was neither merchant nor sage among them who could get
the better of me.

For few, save those about the noble Pitaco, felt a duty
towards the city as a whole, each being occupied only with
that for which he himself had care. Hence they could by no
means free themselves from their own confusion, but
struggled like fish upon dry land or were driven off course like
ships without anchor, so that a wise man might pity them
their travails.

Thus, first one and then another spoke angrily in the cause
of his own desires, while none could persuade another of the
truth of his words, so great was the suspicion each bore of the
other. Therefore, seeing that such blindness ruled the hearts of
even the wisest among them, I knew the greater wisdom of
the Torah, for whose bounty may God be exalted, and that
the learnèd Jew must for ever serve as a light to the Gentiles,[48]
who cannot see their way.

Thus I, Jacob ben Salomone of Ancona, spoke to them as
follows: 'When you have no true God, blessèd be He, and no
faith save that of the merchant, you must live without counsel
or precept, and become forgetful even of life and death, and
of the passing of time, which God forbid.

'But men cannot live only for low ends, most being made
unhappy by their own vice and folly. Therefore, you would
the better serve the city and yourselves also, if you sought to
arouse the desire for good which is to be found in all men of

reason. For just as there are few who do not yearn to love another more than they love themselves, so there are few who do not desire to serve by their good deeds the needs of others, and to have received the praise of the city for what they have done.

'Moreover, if you wish to live in peace and plenty, you cannot permit that others, as well as yourselves, should be released from every duty, and that others as well as you have care for nothing but their own desires. For a man without duty is at the last like a dog that has lost its master, and runs up and down with eyes that do not see, barking at every passer-by and seeking only that his master take him back in his hands, so that he may know again what he should do.[49] Likewise, to recall men to their duties is not to make them servile and weak but to teach them what they are, while to fulfil these duties is the only way of salvation for your city.

'In your peril you must turn back from your course in order to conserve the peace, and to make justice and reason rise again in your realm. If you do not, then you will not only find no firm place in which to stand in this turmoil, but you will lose both your liberty and your realm together. And if this fair City of Light should fall to the Tartars from the avarice of its merchants, the foolishness of its sages, and the vices of its people it would be enough to make the whole world speak of, to your everlasting shame.'[50]

After I had spoken in this way, a certain Cian,[51] curses be upon him, came to me greatly angry, and struck me with his fist upon the mouth, God forbid, shouting that I should be brought down for my presumption, while many others cried out that I should be straightaway driven from the city. But several among the guardians came to my aid, may God be magnified and exalted for His loving-kindness, one of them declaring to the assembly that at the setting of the sun I should be gone. At which words the ranks of the merchants and the sages rejoiced and laughed greatly, so that I felt much bitterness in my soul.

Whereupon, the noble Pitaco, may his memory be blessèd,[52] rose and spoke as follows: 'The Jew has taught us wisely, but you gravely offend heaven in deed and word. In striking our honoured guest you have forgotten the moral law in every way. For that which we do not wish others to do to us, we should not do to them, as Chunfutsu teaches.[53] We must also do to others that which we wish others to do to us, serving our fathers as we wish that our sons will serve us, and acting towards our elder brothers as we wish our younger brothers to act towards us. Moreover, that act which is correct and just it is a duty to do, for right conduct and duty are one.

'Thus, we must give honour to worthy men, as the wise Jew has said, as well as do duty to our kindred, give aid to the weak and show courtesy to strangers from far countries,[54] by welcoming them when they come, helping them when they remain, and giving protection to them when they go. For to do otherwise is to disturb the harmony of heaven.'

Whereupon one among the merchants asked: 'And what should we do to the stranger who seeks to meddle in the affairs of the city?' One of the sages also declared: 'Just as help cannot be given to all, so not every stranger is a sage,' at which many laughed without shame.

But to them the noble Pitaco replied in this fashion: 'If a man wishes to be a ruler he must fulfil the duties proper to a ruler, and if a man wishes to be a citizen he must fulfil the duties proper to a citizen, as Menche teaches. And when those who govern are dutiful, the citizens are more ready to be dutiful also. But when the ruler neglects his duties, the citizen neglects his also.'

Whereupon, the young man Uainsciu, bowing low before the noble Pitaco, asked which duty of the citizen stood above all others, to whom Pitaco replied: 'There are many duties, young man, which one should discharge,[55] but that of a son to his ancestors is the highest.'

To which the young man answered: 'How many of the

poor will be fed by such observance, and how many find the
means to cover their heads?'

Upon hearing which, being unable to keep silent, God be
thanked, I spoke as follows: 'Insofar as I know and can speak
of it, the rich of this city truly have great abundance, but most
of the poor among you also have much to eat and drink,[56]
God be praised, and many other things besides. Yet such as
you complain of injustice, as though every poor man ought to
be a prince and live at ease, and none should work save at his
own time and according to his own will. If it were to be so,
what should become of a man's duties?'

To which the merchant Lotacie replied impiously: 'This is
not the time to speak of duties, for we have duties enough. It
is time, rather, to speak of those things that a man must be
able to do freely, and of how he may be protected in the
seeking of his own ends.'

To whom Pitaco said: 'He who opens his mouth so easily
does so because he has never known the duties of great office,'
at which words many among the merchants gave themselves
to mock him, God forbid, for all that he had white hair and
was deserving of honour.

But the young Uainsciu silenced them and spoke as
follows: 'You mock him, but what is it to be rich? Is it not
that you yourselves are free from the duty to work if you do
not choose, while the poor can do no other? Is it not unjust
that you should be permitted to lie on a soft couch,[57] with
servants about you, while others have to carry the heavy pole
upon their shoulders?' For all that he spoke in this hot
fashion, Uainsciu, being himself the son of a lord, for so the
faithful Lifenli informed me, knew nothing of such toil,
making pretence of his knowledge for the sake of his fame as a
young man of the people.[58]

To him Pitaco replied with anger: 'You have the head and
eyes of a lion for the poor,[59] but not for the realm itself.'

But the young man answered immediately: 'You speak of
duty, but intend by it only that men should be obedient to

their rulers. You speak of service, but only in order to make
the people offer up money and fealty to the Son of Heaven.
And you seek a bond between men, but only that they be
bound together in chains.'

To whom I spoke thus, God guiding my words: 'You
believe, young man, that your opinions are good and well-
founded, and that he who holds them must also be a good
and worthy man. But there is no greater servitude than that of
the mind to false ideas, such as that, in order for the city to
prosper, there is no need for a man to fulfil his duties, or that
between him who fulfils such duties and him who does not
we should make no distinction.

'For it is thraldom to think that lack of virtue gives no less
entitlement to reward than virtue and goodness, since in
order to believe such a thing, the soul of a man must subject
itself to falsehood. You make mock of duty, but he who does
so must therefore think it without importance whether a
citizen be good or bad, and whether he acts wickedly or well.'

When he had understood what I had said, the young man
did not know what to say, so skilful was my argument, and
fell silent.

But there rose in his place the Adversary, the said
Anfenscian, who, commanding all to silence and bowing to
me, for which God be praised, spoke as follows: 'But who is
to decide such matters, sires, as whether a citizen is good or
bad? Do you, stranger, lay claim to know who among your
neighbours is a good man and who is bad, and who has
performed his duty and who has not? Is not the greatest truth,
you who speak so much of truth and falsehood, that no man
is virtuous enough to judge the virtue of others, each being in
himself an admixture of good and bad, and at times better
than others and at times worse, however pious?

'And is it not also the case that you, in a city to which you
have come as a stranger, hold a special faith, which in your
pride you would thrust upon others as the sole truth of the
world? I care nothing for your God or your sages, but I have

my own understanding of what is right conduct and what
wrong, yet I have not read your scriptures,[60] wise though they
may be.'

The Adversary I shut from my heart, may God be thanked
for my strength, declaring before them that the words of
Anfenscian were against reason, and that if none might judge
the virtue of others then there might be neither justice nor
law in the realm. But the Adversary would not be stilled, God
forbid, but rather grew in strength, seeming in his face to
exult, and answering as follows: 'Sires, on the contrary, we
defend reason, while he who is against us goes against reason
itself, for we seek to find out the true causes and effects of all
things.

'Thus we think that it would be contrary to reason,
considering the good of the city, if those who did not desire
that all citizens should live well were to exercise rule and
supremacy over us. Yet those who speak on behalf of the rich
alone cannot defend the city. For it is only those who urge
that all, whether rich or poor, should be free to pursue their
own ends in whatever way they choose who can command the
fidelity and obedience of all.'[61]

To whom I replied, God guiding my path: 'You declare
that none is worthy to judge the virtue of others, yet you
yourself judge what is in accord with reason and what is
against it. Likewise, you complain against the pious man who
claims that right is all on his side and all wrong is on the side
of others, but do you not do the same?

'For to you, O Adversary, your foes are without any virtue
and wrong in all their judgments. Yet it is you who at the
same time say that everything is an admixture of good and
bad, and that none can determine what is right and what is
wrong, but that to everyone equally should come honour and
good. Therefore there is no meaning in your opinions, which
are neither logical nor true, being without cause and reason,[62]
and thus can serve as a guide to none.'

Whereupon, those who were about the noble Pitaco, and

some of the sages also, laughed at Anfenscian, for which God be praised. But the Adversary was greatly angered, replying with fists clenched: 'Jew, you do a great ill in making mock of me, so that I pray you not to make jest of me further. We have received you well and with mildness, but now we shall treat the matter as reason demands.[63] For we would rather die at the hands of the Tartars than permit those who stand in the way of another man's will and his right desires to remain in the City of Light.' In such a fashion did the Adversary speak, while the sages in their cowardice remained silent, fearing to answer.

But the noble Pitaco, albeit that he was infirm and weak, alone stood to reply to Anfenscian: 'Once, each rank of officials wore the colour for their cloaks that was fitting, black and white for the most lowly, above the third degree purple, above the sixth vermilion, above the seventh green, and above the ninth the colour of heaven.[64] But now all wear purple without distinction, and all is confusion among us.'

At which there was such great laughter that none might be heard, so that the prefect and the guardians were obliged to call all to silence.

Whereupon the Adversary without shame addressed the following words to the noble Pitaco: 'Shall we revere you then, old man, merely for your old age and the colour of your garments? Or in what does your merit consist, you who condemn everyone but yourself?'

Pitaco replied: 'I condemn myself also, Anfenscian, but only that I did not resist you, and urge others to resist you, when there was yet time. For you and those who are like you are men who, having wished to become officials yourselves, now profess contempt for your elders, and are ready even to commit violence against us, whether by word or deed.

'Once, not only was there no man among us who did not know his duty, as the learnèd Jew preaches, but all who bore the same title were bound by obligation the one to the other, and each was devoted to his superior according to the law of heaven. But now so many are divided from their homes, their parents and their children, that all come to the City of Light in search of bodily pleasure and riches, and thus no order can be preserved.'

To whom the merchant Lotacie answered: 'You are a foolish old man. The city you seek in your dreams would be a place of death, or fit only for gods, not men, to inhabit. For men are bound to substance and to time, and it is their fate to die, while the world you seek is one in which they cannot live, and where none will dwell in times to come.'

But when I heard such impious words by the mouth of the faithful Lifenli, I wept with grief for the lot of men, seeing which many pointed their fingers at me and laughed greatly at my dolour.

So that I, Jacob ben Salomone ben Israel, spoke to them as follows: 'Yet, sires, a city in which everything is permitted must make all who live in it the unhappiest of men. For there can be no happiness without rule and no rule without prohibition, the powers of God alone, blessèd be He, being without bound. But in the world of men there can be neither order, nor justice, nor faith, without interdict[65] and limit.'

Whereupon Lotacie replied with words never before heard in the world, may the Holy One forgive me for what I have written, as follows: 'We may be sure, sires, only of the base passions of men. For upon those things that are bound up with his low desires others may always depend. But the high virtues of which you speak are found in only a few and change as the wind, so that none may place his faith in them without being deceived. Therefore, not only is the truth with us and not with you, but all must protect themselves from the falsehoods which you speak.'

Thus, with the aid of Lotacie, the Adversary, may God strike him down, continued in the seeking of his own wicked ends and could not be denied, so strong was his faith, at last declaring to us: 'Your principles, sires, are full of deceit, for you have but one belief, secretly holding that only where men

are obedient from fear may peace be preserved. So Anfesu
taught and you believe also, but you lack the courage to say
it.'[66]

Now it was as though I heard above me the wings of the
Angel of Death, God forbid, for the very sky began to darken
and the thunder to sound, the noble Pitaco, albeit greatly
troubled in his heart, seeking to sustain to the last the honour
of all men, may God redeem his soul.

Thus he said to Lotacie and Anfenscian as follows: 'You are
both like Cienciunsu, who wished to be thought a man of
truth but neglected all his duties. Thus, you too, Lotacie,
because you have great wealth, consider that you may do
whatever you choose, while the poor man thinks that, being
poor, he is exempt from all duty save to himself. Therefore,
both rich and poor now deem themselves, each in their own
way, to be beyond the bounds of law and subject to their own
wills alone. But neither is a true citizen, for the one is subject
to his wealth and the other to his needs. Yet you, Lotacie, are
worse, for you wish to betray your city to the Tartars, there
being none among you who would not prefer riches to
combat.'

To which Lotacie replied briefly: 'Old man, these words of
yours do not concern me. For you are lost and we will no
longer hear you.'

Hearing which, and since none had the valour to stand
against the messengers of the Evil One, I therefore declared as
follows: 'Sires, these principles of which we have spoken are
just, and so will be to the end of the ages, may God be
praised. For unless a man fulfil his duties to all, his city shall
not stand. Moreover, those things which the noble Pitaco has
spoken, as of the rich and poor who show no care for any but
themselves, were wisely said.

'Nor is it of any account to a learnèd man that his
proposals should be welcome to some but not to others. For
although they be the wisest that man has made since the
creation of the world, as those of Solomon among us, others

will always have great envy of him who has made them, and for this they will come to be rejected.'

To which one of their sages, the said Cian who had earlier struck me, may God strike him down, replied as follows: 'Sire, we feel no envy of you, for everything you have taught was already known to us. Indeed, we long ago held opinions such as those which you have uttered in our city, so that nothing that has been said by you may teach us what we do not know. Yet there are some weak men among us, whom Pitaco strives to lead against the city, who covet the fruit from the garden of another, for in their baseness they find such fruit sweeter than their own.

'Thus, Jew, he who is a stranger is treated by them with greater honour than one who is our own. Likewise, he who comes from a foreign land and declares himself to be a sage is received as a sage, whether he be truly wise or no.'

Whereupon another sage added: 'The learnèd Cian, he who is the wisest of men, has spoken rightly. What the Jew has said did we not already know, and are not those things which we do not know empty and without worth? Have we not always believed that a man should be pious and do that which he is bound to do? Then why does the noble Pitaco prostrate himself before the stranger, when all his principles we have long followed, as our fathers before us?'

And a third sage declared: 'There is an ordinance of the Son of Heaven that has been sent to the city, and in which it is written that a stranger shall not give us counsel in our peril.'

Thus the sages of the City of Light spoke with hatred in their hearts, for the Angel of Death, God forbid, had entered into the assembly, and stood among us.

Whereupon, the noble Pitaco, may his name be recorded, as if understanding that his death was at hand, spoke thus: 'Sires, since the times of our most distant ancestors, the years of order among us have been few and the years of confusion many. Yet in each age the people wish to live in peace amid the zephyrs, and hope that no storm will come upon their

heads. In times of peril in the past we turned to our emperors
and great ministers to restore peace to the realm, but now
such emperors and ministers are no more. Even Chunfutsu
passed many years of wandering from court to court, seeking
a ruler who might observe his precepts, but found none.

'So much the greater therefore, sires, is the need that each
man should think now of his duty, so that the order of heaven
may once more be cherished, and that when a pious stranger
comes among us who knows the right way he should be
treated benignly and with honour.'

Thereupon, the noble Pitaco, taking me by the hand, for
which God be praised, also declared as follows: 'Sire, seeing
that you are held in great account and esteem, since your
judgment on many matters is sound,[67] we desire you to
remain among us. Moreover, in every city and among every
people, men seek out and wish to follow the superior person,
who among us is called *ciuntsu*. As our teacher Chunfutsu
instructed, such a man must be upright, loyal, pious and wise,
and only such as he is worthy to rule.

'Therefore, if you agree to be a counsellor[68] to us in matters
of law, we shall follow your judgment as if it were sovereign,[69]
so that men may once more find the true way and the city be
restored.'

Thus, the noble Pitaco, may peace be upon his soul,
declared that I, Jacob of Ancona, should be entrusted with the
office of a judge,[70] and that I should give wise counsel to the
elders of the city, for which honour shown to me may God be
magnified and exalted.

Yet there were many who shouted in anger against Pitaco
and gave themselves to deride and disparage me, while some
wished me to be lord[71] over the city. Others declared that for
their part they were ready to make me one of their judges,
and to obey my decisions with the same respect and homage
as they gave to the other judges of the city. But yet others
cried out against them, declaring them to be traitors.
Whereupon the prefect, ordering them to be silent, called

upon the noble Pitaco to renounce his proposal, but he would not be moved.

Therefore, hearing once more the sound of thunder, may God be magnified and exalted, I spoke as follows, with God as my guide: 'Sires, I cannot be considered as a man of wisdom and of worth beyond measure, but a pious and learnèd Jew who has studied the Torah and the ways of men. Nor is there any true reward from rule.[72] Men should rather place their trust in God, may He be lauded, Who alone can make us blessèd. Yet for the honour you have shown me I am grateful, although I am not worthy of it.

'But it is clear that among you many others lacking in true worth rule also. Moreover in our lands, too, masters learnèd in civil and moral law, who are noble in wisdom as others are noble by birth[73] or by the sword, are often summoned as counsellors in the courts of princes, among whom are many of my brothers, may God keep them in His hand. For they possess practical wisdom[74] and political prudence,[75] these being virtues which come from an understanding of men. Indeed, some among us say that a profound mind better fits a man to rule than noble blood.

'Further, our preacher teaches that that which is lacking is without end, there being always more fools than wise and many rulers who are without the wisdom which their realms require. Yet others hold that it is better for the wise man to continue in his studies, living the life that he has known, rather than to change a simple dress for the royal purple.[76]

'But here in your city, so great are the greed and violence of the citizens, and so strong the belief of each that he alone is the best judge of right and wrong, that not even Solomon, our sage of sages, peace be upon him, could have found the way to establish concord among you. Moreover, in your city the learnèd fools who should guide you, and who make pretence before you to be wise, have themselves lost the desire for virtue, and no longer know the difference between good and evil.'

At these words of mine, for which God be thanked, all in
the assembly fell into a great silence, none giving a sign of
their judgment, so that once more the sound of thunder
could be heard in the heavens.

Therefore I continued: 'But although a pious man should
by no means leave his studies, yet my ancestors, peace upon
them, served as counsellors to the princes of our lands. Thus
my father, may his soul rest in Eden, being consulted in the
concord with Venice, went many times to our brother
Alleuccio in order to lift the heavy weights from our city.

'Moreover, as our sages teach, he who out of humility does
not fulfil his duty falls into error. For when a man has the
power to exercise right and justice among others, he shall not
turn aside, lest he who withdraws himself play a part in the
ruin of the land. Wherefore, sires, so that I may give aid to the
noble Pitaco and in order to save your city, I accept his
proposal, for it would surely be the greatest honour in the
world.'

Whereupon all those who were gathered made so great a
noise, with shouts so ugly to the hearing, that my heart was
saddened and my eyes could no longer see what was before

---

'LIFT THE HEAVY WEIGHTS FROM OUR CITY'

*This lifting of 'heavy weights' from the city of Ancona after the reaching of agreement
with its rival Venice, in which negotiations Jacob states that his father took part,
may refer to the commercial treaty concluded between the cities (under threat by
Venice of war) on 29 July 1264, six years before Jacob's voyage began. The treaty
terms, however, were themselves oppressive – and not as Jacob implies, if this is the
'concord' in question – seeking to restrict the merchants of Ancona in their commerce
with the Islamic and Byzantine worlds by imposing a special import tax on Ancona
of 20 per cent on goods brought from outside the Adriatic area. But it appears that
Ancona merchants ignored the treaty terms and continued defiantly to trade
wherever they chose – as the manuscript confirms – including in partnership with
Venetian merchants themselves.*

them, God forbid. For I, having sought to bring truth and
wisdom to the City of Light, which now stood in darkness,
had come to be spurned before the people.

In which tumult, Anfenscian and the great merchant
Anscinen, being the messengers of the Adversary,
accompanied by Cian and certain others, came forward to
address the assembly, with such falsehoods as have never been
heard by man, the said Anscinen speaking as follows: 'One
among us, who is not worthy to live, has for long been in
rebellion against the laws, seeking to pull down those who
rule over it, to drive out those who bring riches to the city,
and to arouse discord among the people, as well as speaking
ill, even before a stranger, of all who serve the common good.
Moreover, he has presumed to invite those, as this Jew, who
are not worthy to be honoured, in order to make judgment
upon our ways, as if there were not many learnèd men among
us who know better than the stranger what is good and what
ill in our city and in the realm.'

At which words Anfenscian, God forbid, pointed his finger
at me and declared thus: 'Sires, this one who is among us is
not such as he appears. He declares himself to be pious, yet
holds the faith of others, as that of the Christians, in such
contempt that the Christians of our city have brought forth
an accusation before the judges, so that he might be
condemned for his words against them. For he would teach us
duty who himself holds in scorn the piety of others, teach us
wisdom who contemns the wisdom of all men but himself,
and teach us faith who denies all gods but his own.

'Moreover, this foolish Jew, who seeks to teach us virtue,
thinks all men base save himself. Yet, this same one, who
passes judgment upon the greed of others, has come to our
city not in search of wisdom but of wealth, purchasing in
every part the richest things upon which he might lay his
hand, such as jewels, silks, spices and many other things
besides.

'He judges us also for our vices, as our vices of the flesh, yet he himself has frequented the lowest places of the city, lying with women in lust, which a certain Uaiciu[77] has reported. Likewise, it is said that this Jew, who speaks much of the duty that is owed by one man to others, cruelly treats the women servants who are about him, imposing upon them his base desires,[78] so report is made.

'Nor do the Jews of the city speak well of this man, declaring him to be one of those who, sowing discord among the people with so much skill, gains thereby.[79] Moreover, they say that such as he are not truly Jews who do not pray among their brothers, but remain aloof from the society of others.

'Yet it is this man whom Pitaco sought to name as a judge among us, so that his wicked plot might be advanced against the city, and this is the man whom the judges have decreed should depart from our land before the setting of the sun.'

Thus, never was such wickedness uttered by one man against another as was uttered against me by the Adversary, my faithful servant Lifenli whispering that he wished to speak before them on my behalf. But I forbade it lest great harm should befall him, at the same time thanking God that by the falsehoods of the Adversary He had given me protection from my own weakness and pride.

For had I not also falsely declared before the assembly that to be a judge among them was the greatest honour in the world, when such honour belongs only to Torah study, may God be lauded for His bounty? Nor should I have returned again to my land and my beloved Sara, whom God keep in health, but have been lost in the furthest ends of the earth and slain, which God forbid.

Therefore, while all raised their voices against me, and the guardians stood close about the noble Pitaco, I gave thanks to God that thus had He spared me for my pride and for the folly of my heart, which may lead a man, however pious and learnèd, into the greatest error.

Yet a man may also not permit those who seek to deprive him of his repute to speak ill of him without any reply, for a

good name is better than the sweetest perfume. So that I was
constrained to answer as follows, God be praised: 'Sires,
everything which has been said against me is falsehood, but so
base that no wise man can lower himself in order to deny it.
Moreover, all that I have declared among you of your duties,
in order that your city may be saved, is true, as you yourselves
know.

'You also say that I am but a stranger, but we should hear
the truth from whomever declares it, be he Mancino, Frank,
Saracen or Jew. Yet since you will not hear me, but instead
wish to drive me away, may God keep me for what I do. For I
do not seek gratitude from other men, since the best deeds
and the noblest ends are often the least rewarded.'

Whereupon, the sky growing darker and the Angel of
Death being among us, there entered into the assembly the
great Suninsciou, the leader[80] of all the merchants of the city,
accompanied by his guardians, who spoke in a loud voice so
that all could hear, as follows: 'We do not doubt that there is
treachery and a plot against us, that there are those who seek
to commit great harms against our free condition, and that
even a stranger is taking part in such crime.'

At which words my heart became as though frozen, and
each person for a moment remained quiet and mute. For
Suninsciou did not appear as a man but rather as a storm,[81]
his whole body being convulsed with hatred and his eyes
swollen with rage. The same Suninsciou, God forbid, now
shouted at the noble Pitaco, may God keep his soul, as
follows: 'Old man, what do you know of combat who urge it
so idly upon others? How much rest does the merchant take
in search of gain?[82] You have persisted too long with these
insults against us of which the whole city speaks, and for
which many have already shed their blood. But now the time
has come to cause you and your companions every harm
possible in your persons and possessions.'

These things he said with great ferocity, God forbid, yet
Pitaco did not tremble.

Suninsciou, with his followers gathered about him and
attended also by the guardians of the city, continued thus,
pointing his finger at the noble Pitaco: 'Old man, it is such as
you who counsel that we be pure of person, and who instruct
us to permit nothing which is contrary to just measure. Yet all
know that you yourself do not live by such a rule but are a
man of great riches, which you conceal by simple dress. You
tell others to hold in low esteem the possession of worldly
goods, but you yourself are engaged in the market. Likewise,
you enjoin others to keep from the society of low women, but
you yourself are given over to the vices of lust.

'You speak also, old man, against those who seek their own
ends, but none may excel you in pride, and you charge others
with cowardice but would yourself destroy the city in order to
have the better of other men. Lastly, you praise the faith of
our ancestors and the law of heaven but are a friend to the
enemies of the city, going at night to their houses, as to the
houses of the Jews, in order to advance your ends.

'Old man, you have betrayed our city and your last hour
has come.'

Whereupon there was a great silence in which none spoke
or stirred, the noble Pitaco standing upright before the great
merchant Suninsciou without fear of death, but with a
courage which was a wonder to behold, may God be praised.

Then Pitaco spoke as follows: 'The false cannot at the last
overcome the true, although it may have a long life spent to
the sound of others' praise.[83] Those things you have declared
of me and of the pious Jew would draw even a dumb man to
speak, for you kindle the fire without name. But summer flies
such as you should not speak of the mortal cold, nor the frog
which stands at the bottom of the well[84] talk of the sun or of
the heavens.

'You complain, brother Suninsciou, that I have sought to
teach that nothing should be done beyond measure, and you
complain justly. For the universe is composed not of
contradictions but is a balance, which balance must be found

by the sages in every realm. For the place where the balance should rest is not plain to all.

'One part consists in showing respect for that which was done before and the other part in accepting with a good heart that which is new. Likewise, one part is composed of a casting out of the evil things of the past and the other part in casting out the evil things of the present. To hold a just balance, O Suninsciou, is a difficult art. But such art cannot be learned without a knowledge of the principle of duty, as the Jew has also told.'

But at the words of the noble Pitaco, the Evil One stood before him and declared: 'You speak of a just balance, old man, but you have betrayed the city. For you have conspired with a stranger, as every man makes report, in order to sow discord among us. Thus, in such an hour of danger it is our duty to seek out and put to death the forsworn traitors, and in the name of the City of Light to attack you and all who speak as you, so that we may do our best to break you in pieces.'

Whereupon, great were the cries and shouts against the noble Pitaco, may his soul rest in peace, one crying out that in a free condition each man was able by his own will thus to overcome another, while those about the merchant Suninsciou launched themselves immediately against him.[85] They ran at Pitaco with great fury,[86] one being armed with a knife, God forbid, which was plunged into his left side so that he fell to the ground, the blood running from his body, which was painful to behold. Thus he who had wished the best for the city had the worst fortune.

---

'HAD THE WORST FORTUNE'

*This presumably signifies that Pitaco was killed, but it is noteworthy that Jacob does not say so in terms. The last reference to Pitaco in the manuscript also speaks only of the 'misadventure' (sventura) which had befallen him (p.409).*

At which, fearing for my life, the sun having already set, I made my escape in the tumult, God be praised and exalted, for they ran one against the other so that there was a great turmoil,[87] but the faithful Lifenli remained always at my side, for which God be thanked.

Thus I took to flight, running as fast as possible. For those things I had taught them counted nothing for them, I crying out that they should do as seemed better to them and that I did not wish to cause them further grievance, some seeking to rain blows on my head, God forbid, and some tearing at my clothes, while others sought to shield me from the anger of the people.

But it was the will of God, blessèd be He, that I should escape them. I, albeit weak in body, ran alone to the house of Nathan ben Dattalo, having first ordered the faithful Lifenli to go and bring thither all that he had written.[88] I ordered my servants Bertoni and Buccazuppo to make ready, sending also for Micheli and Fultrono, declaring to them that the hour had come to leave the land of Sinim, for I saw that it was not possible to remain longer.

When Lifenli returned to me in haste with those things I had sought, I made rich payment to him for his aid with many besants of gold, bestowing on him, in such way as none might see, a precious jewel of Seilan, and gathering up those things that had remained hidden in the house of my brother Nathan.[89] Towards Lifenli, even though he had spoken lightly of my faith, I felt much love, he having at all times served me well in the city of Zaitun.

But now, while I was speaking with him, my servant Buccazuppo began to lament greatly, declaring that she would not depart, and holding Lifenli by the arm, so that she might not be taken from him. At this I was greatly astonished, the woman Bertoni seeking to draw her away, while Lifenli was in much travail, for it seemed that his heart had been given to the girl.

Therefore I ordered her to be brought by force to the ships,

Micheli and Fultrono having to carry her thither, for the sun was long set and I feared lest I should be killed, may God for ever shield me. Yet on the way there came the woman Liciancie, who sought also to hold the arm of Buccazuppo, crying out falsely that I was a man of evil will, and that my servant had but one desire, which was to remain in the City of Light. Wherefore I was obliged to strike her down, God forbid, lest we be all taken by the guardians of the city, the faithful Lifenli, albeit much moved by the cries of those about him, giving aid to Micheli and Fultrono.

Thus we came to the port, for which God be thanked, where my fleet stood at the ready, the guardians bowing low at my coming, God be praised. There, with many tears, I bade farewell to my brother Nathan and to the faithful Lifenli, casting anchor upon the twenty-second day of Adar[90] with my wealth safe and my body without wound, for which God be praised, honoured and exalted, Amen, Amen and Amen.

For, as I have written, the vessels were already prepared and furnished with all necessary provisions. The ship of my brother Isaia of Basra, which was of great capacity,[91] carrying more than eight thousand cantars,[92] was fully loaded at prow and stern[93] with all my wares, God be thanked, and thus we parted from the City of Light, the two galleys going ahead.

Thus I bore away, together with my great stores of merchandise from Greater and Lesser India, no fewer than one hundred cantars[94] of silk, twenty-five cantars[95] of the finest satins, as well as a great quantity of porcelains, ginger, galingale of Sinim, saffron and camphor, as well as four hundred[96] cantars of sugar, together with many types of incense, medicines, herbs and other spices, as well as paper, precious stones and the choicest pearls, and so many other things besides that never before was such a treasure borne upon the sea, for which God be magnified and exalted.

Moreover, the wind from the north-east was fair, albeit that there was thunder in the heavens, and the moon full,[97] so that

the mariners might make their way with ease towards the
sea.[98] Thus we departed from the city, which became smaller
the further we sailed, so that at the last its lamps and lanterns
became very small points until it was gone from our sight. Yet
this was not the City of Light, but of clouds of mortality,[99]
God forbid, nor were those who dwelled there the sons and
daughters of light but of blindness and darkness.

For such a city merited that fire and stone should cover its
misdeeds, as a Sodom. The day grows dark at evening and in
the dawn the light returns, for which God be praised. But
darkness had fallen upon this city of Zaitun, upon which the
light will not shine hereafter, unless it be changed. Rather, it
will be entirely destroyed, with all that is in it, its men, its
animals, its possessions and its spoils, and it shall be a heap
for ever, and not be built again. For when men with the faces
of dogs and of loud tongue prevail, when the son dishonours
his father and when duty is held in scorn, when wisdom fails
and presumption reigns in its stead, then the city becomes
desolate and no truth can be found.

Thus in the City of Light, which was no light, the
merchants disturbed the city's peace with their vices, nor did
they seek to temper their desires so that the just measure
might be found. Here, rather, I saw the ill which may afflict
all men when avarice governs the city, and when those things
which give men pleasure make them blind to the perils of the
morrow.

Thus our fleet made its way beneath the moon, for which
God be thanked, towards the south-west,[100] my servant
Buccazuppo, having wept greatly at our departure, now
becoming quieter yet speaking no word to any, albeit that I
had declared to her that I should teach her according to my
promise.

Whereupon, having carried out my duties, God forgive me,
I gave much thought to the sad memories of the city and the
misadventures that had befallen my servant Turiglioni and the
noble Pitaco, at the same time thanking God, may His

Unspoken Name be praised, that He had spared my life and my possessions.

For although upon first entering the city I had been truly confounded by its riches, and had thereafter seen many wonders, for which God be praised, I now looked upon it as a free man upon a captive, or as a man bathed afresh in pure water looks upon one who is smeared with mud. Yet I had also sinned greatly, God forbid, setting my eyes upon such things as a pious man might not see, for which in the night I prayed to God that I might be forgiven, since no man is exempt from the desires of the flesh, for which God be praised.[101]

But the punishments God had given me for my transgressions had surely been great also, since many were the travails I had suffered in that city. Thus, even though I had found many rich things by which a man's heart might be gladdened, much injustice was done to me as though to a traitor, so that I was constrained to act as I did, and to flee without taking counsel of any. For, had I not, then surely they would have slain me and thrown my body where it would not have been possible to find it, which God forbid. But with the aid of the Holy One, none recognised me as I ran through the city, nor took account that I fled, for which God be thanked.

Yet at the same time I lamented in my heart, for I might have been a prince[102] in Sinim, but my counsel was all in vain. Indeed, had they learned from my wisdom, I would surely have merited the praise of the whole world. But I thanked God that I had thus learned so much of the ways of men, and that in the City of Light the blind life of the Zaituni had been revealed to me.

For I saw that free men in a free condition of life had brought themselves to ruin in the sight of God. True it is that the laws of men differ, because each city may decree such laws as it sees fit for itself, and those laws which are fitting for one may not be fitting for another. But the law of God is eternal

and cannot be changed, albeit that our sages show us how we
may the better do God's will, or instruct us in those matters
upon which He remained silent when He gave the Law to our
prophets, may He be praised for His bounty to Israel.

Thus I saw also that the inhabitants of the City of Light,
revoking all the commandments among men, and being
always prompt to bestir themselves with others, ran hither
and thither in vain, seeking what might bring them pleasure,
yet without comfort for their desires. For their souls were
without rest, God forbid, that which they desired giving them
no pleasure and in that which they possessed finding no
peace, their merchants teaching them that each man should
pursue his own ends and their sages being unable to
distinguish between good and ill. For in such a way did the
Adversary and his messengers strive to mock the blindness of
those wretched people.

Indeed, there is no glory of God so bright that a veil of
darkness may not be drawn over it for a time. Thus men put
aside their very lives in order to attend to their gain or desire,
not knowing that thus they live in vain and as though they
went unseen by God. But shall a man live for ever in his shop
or at his counter, and God enter only at the last day?

Hence, I lamented greatly for the lost people of the City of
Light, yet was inwardly glad that it would go hard for them
and that the judgment of God according to the decrees of
eternal justice should not permit it to stand for long. For
having taken the wrong path, and all their affairs going from
bad to worse, the city stood close to its end.

Yet from the great abundance of its goods, and the greed,
vanity and faithlessness of the greater part of the inhabitants
of the said city, few could see the fate which drew near. Thus,
the greater part were heedless of the advance of the Tartars,
who wish to subjugate the entire world, which may God
forbid. But those who live under the rule of folly cannot
know by what means the Adversary may be vanquished, nor,
however strong their arms, may they overthrow his evil will

without the aid of God, since the Adversary has more sharpness and cunning than they.

Thus there is no thought of which the Evil One does not know how to make use. For his cunning can move in all directions and is able to wear all the garments of truth, whereas both wisdom and folly have only one garment each, and each goes by only one road, and is thus at a disadvantage.

With many tears did such thoughts come upon me as I lay without sleep in the night, together with a strong desire fixed in my mind to return as fast as we could to my land, if God should spare me. For I bore with me great riches that fortune had brought me from my trade, so that I thereupon rose from my bed the better to give thanks to God, and since the seas were high. For the Angel of Death, God forbid, has no power over a pious man who is engaged with the Torah, so that I gave myself over to study until the first light, while my servants, peace upon them,[103] slept.

And thus we voyaged by sail and oar until we were far from the port, making our passage towards the south-west.

## CHAPTER ELEVEN

# The End was Good

I HAVE CHOSEN FOR REASONS of length to cut most of Jacob d'Ancona's account of his homeward journey, which occupies twenty-three leaves (forty-five pages, the last being blank) of the manuscript. Having left Zaitun on the night of 24 February 1272 with a favourable north-west wind, but much later in the month than his impatient mariners and servants had wished, his small argosy of three vessels was forced to sail without the security of being part of a larger fleet; his fellow Italian-Jewish merchants, Eliezer of Venice and Lazzaro del Vecchio, had sailed ahead.

However, in what Jacob calls 'the sea of Ciamba', off today's Vietnam, his vessels rejoined those of his fellows 'two days after Passover' – that is on 26 March 1272 – a festival which found him on board and doing what he could to practise his devotions, or 'duties'. His account contains the following observation:

> Being at sea on Passover and the ship bearing much
> *hametz*,[1] yet it not being possible to observe the ordinances,
> I made to clean the place reserved to me by the light of my
> lamp, searching for the traces of that which is forbidden
> also in the cracked beams, as it is ordered, thus allowing
> nothing of leavened bread to pass my lips, may God be

praised. Whereafter, I delivered thanksgiving to the Divine Presence for the redemption of our forefathers from their servitude in Mitzraim, regarding it as if I myself had in these days come forth from captivity, as Rabban Gamaliel instructs.

A month later, on 26 April, with the south-west monsoon weather turning against them – bringing with it 'very strong contrary winds, a tempest' and heavy rains – they had once again to shelter in 'Java the Less', rather than Ceylon, as Jacob tells us that he had intended. Here they remained until 29 May 1272 in almost continuous rain, although it did not deter Jacob from making further purchases and observations.

In this period of enforced shelter in Sumatra, during which he started his teaching of his servant Buccazuppo – of whom he speaks kindly – he laments, as he will do again, that he 'might have been a prince in Sinim', fantasising about the lost opportunity of rule which he believes was offered to him, and which was snatched away by his calumniators. Despite the continuing bad weather, and in order to catch the monsoon winds which from June to September helped mediaeval sailors up the Indian coast to Arabia, his argosy then risked the journey to the Nicobar islands and Ceylon, 'not wishing we should be further delayed', as he puts it. The winds were strong, the seas turbulent, and the rains heavy, but they reached Ceylon – Jacob praising God in his customary fashion – in mid-June.

Among the interesting remarks Jacob makes about Ceylon he says this:

So great were my profits in the land of Sinim that I made more purchases of jewels, of which one ruby, shining as a flame of fire, and one sapphire of the purest quality that could be found, together with a necklace of coral and gold most delicately worked, I chose for my beloved Sara, who adorns herself with so much effect. Thereafter, I also

purchased a necklace of pearls of great value and a bracelet
of amethysts[2] so that I might have them as dowry for my
daughters. Here I also bought long cinnamon, which is
more prized than the cassia of Malabar …

Although there were great rains, my soul was refreshed
to see so many coloured birds in the trees, but of wild
animals there are also large numbers in the shaded places,
where it is a peril for any man to go.

After a stay in Ceylon of only five days, from 18 to 22 June –
including the Sabbath called 'Pinchas', as Jacob carefully
informs us – the vessels of the three merchants proceeded, often
in rough seas, up the Malabar coast of western India, calling at
Colam (Quilon), Callicote (Calicut), Marrabia and Tana (near
Cannanore). In the lines that refer to Quilon, Jacob's manuscript contains the following, a combination of the commercial
and the elegiac so characteristic of him:

Here there was fine ginger which I bought for Alexandria
and Ancona, together with indigo for the house of my
brother Abramo of Foligno, dyers, as well as secret things
in order to remove the pain which anyone might have in
the body, and for this reason everyone wants some of
it …[3]

Here I was sheltered as before by my cousin Levi, who,
being astonished at the riches which I had brought from
the land of Sinim, God be praised, and that I had come in
peril of my life among the Mancini for my love of wisdom
and justice, showed me much love, so that upon parting
from him I shed many tears, knowing that we should meet
no more.

It was at Tana that Jacob spent the Jewish New Year, which
fell on 23 August 1272, giving us an account of Jewish customs
in the place, but also alluding again to premonitions of his
father's death:

It being the last day of Ellul and the day of the new moon
towards the autumnal equinox and the eve of the New Year,
which is to say the twenty-sixth day of August in the year
1272, God be praised that he should have kept me thus in
safety, all the Jews of the place betook themselves to the
synagogue and spoke the due prayers, one saying to the
other in Arabic and in our tongue, In this year may you be
in good fortune and may everything that you do have a
prosperous outcome.[4]

Thereafter, each one ate of honey, praying that the year
might be sweet, whereupon I strove that I might not weep,
knowing in my heart that my father was no more. And
upon the next day, when the horn of the ram[5] had given its
sound, may God be magnified, praised and exalted, I
prayed that injustice might close its mouth, and that every
evil should be scattered like clouds of smoke when the
Holy One shall secure that the rule of pride abandons the
earth, Amen and Amen.

But, despite Jacob's angry religious protests, and under the
mariners' pressure to reach Aden with the help of the favourable
monsoon winds, the Day of Atonement, 5 September 1272,
was spent at sea. It evokes from Jacob a memorable passage of
prose:

Thus at dawn of the sacred day, the rains having ceased, so
great was the heat that a man could have thought it noon,
so that my body suffered much from the dryness,[6] my
servant Buccazuppo pleading with me that I should take
water, which God forbid.

Rather, as the sun rose in the heavens upon this day of
dismay and repentance, for which God be praised and
honoured, I heard in my heart the sound of the ram's horn,
which made my body tremble. For there is none whose
soul may be still when in his ears there come the *terua* and
the *tekia*,[7] blessèd and exalted be He. So loud was the

sound which I heard that it seemed to echo in the sky, yet
there was none about me who might hear it, so that I cried
out to God to forgive the sins which I had committed in
the land of Sinim, praying also for the soul of my beloved
father, peace upon him, and for my forefathers, peace be
upon their souls.

For the Holy One records and numbers all things, and
remembers even that which has been forgotten. And when
the great trumpet sounds,[8] and the angels cry out, Listen
upon this Day of Judgment, then the Holy One opens the
registers of accusation and proclaims that which is written
there, as who will live and who shall die, God forbid, who
will become poor and who will raise himself up to riches,
God willing, who will be brought low and who raised up,
and who will perish by fire and who by water,[9] which God
also forbid.

For a man is like the flower that wilts or a shadow that
passes,[10] like the dust that blows here and there, or a dream
that flies far away.[11] But God lives for ever, may He keep
me always in His hand, Amen and Amen.

Thereafter the rains ended, and in a sudden heat that
brought some of the mariners 'almost to death' the little fleet
made the port of Aden – which Jacob locates in 'middle India'
– in the first days of October. He calls the port variously
'Edente', 'Ahaden' and 'Edena', and has left the following
description of it, together with (commercialised) judgments on
the old question of 'idolatry':

[Aden] stands upon an island close to the lands of the
Saracens and contains more than three thousand Jews, God
keep them, among whom are the richest of the place, they
being under their own law and having synagogues, courts
and great possessions. There are also some who have great
ships and warehouses, among whom is my cousin Efraim
of Ceneda, and others who command the levying of

customs. Here reside many merchants of Malabar from
Cambaetta, Tana, Calam and other places, as well as of
Seilan and Java the Less, who have trading-houses and
factors.

In this place the Saracens have a great hatred of the
Christians and are of violent behaviour, but they are well
disposed towards the Jews, whom they call their elder
brothers and common sons with them of Abraam our
father, peace be upon him.

Here I bought greatly of the finest balsams and incenses,
since many are the kinds which may be found, as red
dragon,[12] myrrh[13] and storax.[14] The choicest of them they
put in little boxes and small jars, as among us, and others
in pots, which all being placed together are a beautiful
thing to behold, being the bounty of God, may He be
praised.

Of all things, however, the most prized is the
frankincense,[15] of which I purchased a great store of that
which is called *zaffaro*[16] for the idolatrous brothers of the
monastery of Santa Croce close by Mount Catria,[17] since
they will have nothing for their devotions but that which is
of the purest, refusing mixed incense, that which is dark
brown. For they say that it is not fit for the incense-
burners[18] with which they incense their altars and other
things, when they go about singing their orations. Thus
they have greater care for such matters than for the true
love of their fellows, choosing only the finest spices for
their ceremonies before their idols.

Yet it is also written by our sages that it is forbidden for a
Jew to sell such things to Gentiles, since with them they
make reverence to their idols. But others teach that it is
permitted to sell on all days save those which come before
the greater festivals at which they celebrate their gods.
Thus, since great profits may be made from the Christians
and their offices, for sixty besants I purchased through my
brother Abramo of Baudas two cantars of the said *zaffaro*.

Before setting sail from Aden, with 'the heat remaining great and the wind hot as before', Jacob tells us that he sent ahead to 'Ciusar' or Quseir, a port on the Red Sea, a request that 'four hundred camels, fresh and rested' be prepared for his coming, 'as well as donkeys and horses'. He then paid off the 'mariners of Basra', who had joined him when his large vessel was hired there on the outward journey, as well as others who had been 'taken on' in western India and China. Some of them, he laconically adds, had 'died upon the way', some elected to accompany him further, and others returned to Basra, probably in the vessel which he had undertaken to return to his son's father-in-law, Isaia of Basra. He then appears to have hired another vessel, or vessels, into which he loaded his cargoes; and, as he puts it, having 'secured our advantage by means of gifts' – presumably bribes to the harbour officials in Aden – he departed for the Red Sea and Egypt.

En route, he made an early landfall at the 'island of Carnoran', which I have not been able to identify with certainty,[19] and about which he makes some highly entertaining observations upon a community of 'Jews' he claims to have found there.

On the island of Carnoran, which is near the land of Habescia[20] but before the traveller passes through the Sea of Zede,[21] there is a strange people who call themselves by the name Christians but who seem to be Jews. For they know nothing of *that man*, yet, making the sign and abhorring the pig, have the appearance of Jews although their skins are black.

These also assemble in their temple four times a day, crying out together *alleluja*, and upon one day in the year, although it be not the Day of Atonement,[22] make penance for their sins, beating their chests. In addition, they do not eat meat and take milk together, and also marry in the manner of the Jews.

Among them are the names Isaco and Iachba, which is to say Jacob, and Zion also, for which God be praised. Yet they scatter incense as do the idolaters, although they have no great liking for wine, in which they are as the Jews. Moreover, they use among them not an altar but an ark, in which they keep their scripture, but it is written in a language which is not known to others. Yet they also carry the cross, God forbid, in their worship, although they may seem to be Jews. For all those who have male children, as soon as they are thirteen years of age,[23] are considered to be of the covenant, may God be magnified and honoured.

But if a man should ask of them as to the Law under which they live and from whom they received it, they reply that they had it from their ancestors. And if a man should further ask them when these ancestors lived, and for how long they have followed their faith, they reply seven hundred years, but that for a long time they have remained without any teaching. Yet of their laws they also reply as follows: 'As we received them from our ancestors, so accordingly we celebrate and revere our law and rule.'

Therefore a man might say they are of the lost people of Israel, God be praised, yet who live in darkness, which God forbid. For the Christians have brought idols to them, whose shadows hide the face of God.

On 26 October 1272 Jacob, with his companions and servants, reached the port of Quseir in Egypt, where his goods, as he had arranged in Aden, were loaded on to the backs of 'four hundred' camels and many horses and donkeys. He describes this, and the (for him) grievous event which took place thereafter, as follows:

Then they loaded my merchandise on to camels, each of them bearing ten cantars weight, and carried it nine days over land to the great river of Mitzraim,[24] where we came upon the tenth day of Kislev.[25] Of camels there were more than four hundred, so that none before had seen such a great number, together with ninety-five donkeys, each bearing four cantars,[26] and thirty horses also, so that it was a wonder to see, we being attended by our bowmen.[27] For here the Saracens go about robbing whatever they can find.

Thus we travelled in a great column, feeding upon dates, milk and water, as well as sweet bread, but attentive to keep watch about us. For especially at night when there is no moon, the Saracen robbers approach the caravans in order to steal and the watchmen are not able to see where they have gone.

Thus we came to Cius and the great river, where my goods were placed in boats. Yet here there was also found a great villainy, for of the camels which had set forth from Ciusar, there was one which was lacking, together with the goods it bore. Whereupon, the faithful Armentuzio and Pizzecolli having made report of it, I became so angry that my heart almost stopped beating in my body, God forbid. For the Saracens rob merchants with a will, while the craft of the driver of camels is that of a thief, as our sages teach.

Wherefore at Cius I suffered a grave loss, for which may God punish the evil-doer, yet, since the greater part of my wealth was safe, in my heart I gave thanks to God that He had brought me from the land of Sinim to the great river of Mitzraim with my body whole. Here, as I have written, they placed my goods in the boats, carrying even the saddles of the camels[28] upon their shoulders, as is forbidden to us by our sages, may peace be upon them.

From this place all my goods and servants, together with those of my brothers Eliezer and Lazzaro, were now borne upon the river, so that we came after ten days to Fustat, entering the city upon the twenty-second day of Kislev.[29]

Jacob remained only a few days – the first days of the Festival of Hanukah, he tells us – in Fustat (Cairo), disappointingly leaving no account of the city. Instead, and presumably after further unloading and loading of his merchandise, he departed for Alexandria. A journey of 'two hundred Venetian miles', it took him ten days, and during it he was accompanied by his 'brothers', or co-religionists, who, he says interestingly, 'act as escorts' between the cities. During this journey, he adds piously, he lit 'the candles of the sixth to the eighth days' (of Hanukah), simultaneously seeking God's forgiveness for the unspecified neglect of his duties.

In Alexandria he spent the winter of 1272–3 with his brother Baruch, his son Isaac, his daughter-in-law Rebecca – whose wedding he had attended in Basra – and grandson. Here he also learned of the death in Ancona of his father Salomone on 19 February 1272, a few days before his own departure from Zaitun; his first anxious visualisations of his father's death had been premature. But we must let him speak movingly for himself:

> The city of Alessandria is a market for the whole world, the harbour being always filled with the fleets of merchants from all the kingdoms and lands, there being many merchants of Ancona also who dwell in the city. Here I found my beloved brother Haim, my son Isaac, my daughter Rebecca, and my grandson Mose David, may he be blessed with happiness and a long life. But here I learned also, with such grief of which no man has known the equal, of the death of my father, may his soul rest in Eden, upon the tenth of Adar, being the eve of the Sabbath Tetzaveh in the year 5032.[30]
>
> Upon hearing which I wept for many days together, for the world is bitter without end, praying that his dear soul be kept safe, at the same time thanking God that as one Jew passes from the world so another is born. Thus I held in my arms him who, bearing the names of our teacher and our king,[31] should keep the ways of our faith all the days of his long life.
>
> Wherefore, although I spoke the Kaddish with my heart broken and my eyes filled with tears, for I was the unhappiest man in the world, yet each day I rejoiced to see

my child,[32] so that my travail was measured by my joy, one thing corresponding with the other. Moreover, the Holy One makes in all things a great recurrence[33] so that life follows upon death, as the spring upon the winter, for which may God be magnified and honoured.

Despite his griefs, Jacob was not idle during this winter in Alexandria. It appears from the last phases of his manuscript that he may also have made his journey to the far Orient specifically to discover the more general state of trade there, as Tartar rule spread across China. (We have already detected covert hints that, despite his fulminations against the Church, he might have had some kind of diplomatic mission on its behalf.) In the next passage, he seeks to counsel his fellow-Jewish traders in Alexandria. More accurately, it appears as if he was formally summoned by the Jewish merchant community (? or guild) of Alexandria to give an account of his voyage, only to find his warnings – as in Zaitun – rejected. This is what he writes:

To the great Efraim Ha-Levi and Salomone Hasdai[34] I was also called to give report of my journey to the land of Sinim and of my ventures there. Thus I advised my brothers that they should instruct those of Alessandria who had trade with Manci to look to their safety, for the Tartars of the north would soon take Chinscie and the city of Zaitun, as others also declared.

But the said Efraim showed trust in the Cane, saying that, although he might cause harm to the people of Manci, the merchants of other lands would surely find favour among the Tartars, as also in Cataio and other parts of Tattaria, for the wealth that they brought to their realms. Thus I was not able to bring them to believe that, such was the confusion of the said city, all should be destroyed by its ills, as the city of Sodom also was destroyed. Rather, they laughed at my fears, for they knew nothing of those things which I had seen and heard, saying that money is the master of all things on earth, God forbid, and would vanquish the Tartars as it vanquishes other men.

But it being the eve of Sabbath Vaera,[35] and I feeling great sadness in my heart that my counsel should be regarded by my brothers with such contempt, I prayed to God that He might teach them greater wisdom, and that under their rule the light of His Torah might not be extinguished from the whole world, may God forgive me my words.

This rebuff, the extraordinary regret which he expresses as to what *might have been* if he had donned the princely purple in Zaitun, and the grief he plainly felt for his father's death, show Jacob to us in disconsolate mood. But, apart from the joyful presence of his grandson, Mose David, in Alexandria, it was the success of his merchant life that buoyed up his spirits, and, seemingly, the spirits of those around him:

Here [in Alexandria] I sold for a great profit a part of my store of spices, as also of silks and other things, so that I had from the sale of six hundred cantars[36] a greater price than that for which the whole of my merchandise had been purchased. Thus I had much profit from my (?) honey-incense and aloe wood which I sold for their weight in gold,[37] so that the hearts of the faithful Armentuzio and Pizzecolli were made glad, as of my other servants also. Therefore I gave them wines and sweetmeats with which to make their feast, my servant Buccazuppo now showing herself to be of virtuous and quiet conduct, for which God be thanked. For thus she had learned virtue from study, as all men may do.

Whereafter I purchased a great quantity of cotton of Alessandria for Ancona, as well as fine dates and sesame, together with yellow copper, vessels of silver and choice medicines for dropsy and consumption, against the tertian and quartan fevers, and for the heart and kidneys also.

Indeed, during his homeward journey his purchases seem to have exceeded those of the outward journey. In 'Ciamba' he bought aloes – which he calls *'tarum'* – and cardamom; in Java the Less 'twenty cantars' – roughly one ton – of 'pepper, both black and white', as well as nutmeg, cloves and cubebs. These goods he describes as being 'for Alessandria and Ancona' and were all purchased 'at a low price'. (An unknown proportion of his spice purchase made in the East Indies on the outward journey had been sold in China, as he tells us.) Jacob also bought substantial quantities of East Indies sandalwood, lac, brazil-wood and cochineal, the last two items presumably for sale as dyestuffs.

On the homeward journey he devoted much effort, too, to the purchase of the best quality incenses – 'frankincense for the idolaters', as he calls it – especially benzoin and camphor, the latter of which he again bought in Sumatra. He declares that he did so 'for the abbot of the monastery of San Lorenzo in Campo and for the bishop of Fano', from whom he must have had a commission. In Sumatra, and also at Quilon in southern India, he purchased spikenard ('*spigo*'), as well as cassia, more galingale and ginger, and 'many other most rare spices'.

In western India he continued to buy 'pepper' – both a generic and a particular term – which, he tells us, 'they harvest in May and June'. In Marrabia, he bought 'large cinnamon' as well as apothecary items, some of which can no longer be translated, but including mirobalans and '*turpetto*', or *Radex turpethi*, both of which he had also bought on the outward journey and doubtless sold, or bartered, in China.

At the port of Tana, in Gujarat, he bought more 'indigo of Cambaetta', buckrams and 'embroidered mats of leather', which he says are 'much prized by the Saracens of Alessandria'. And in Aden he bought further kinds of incense for his Italian clerical clients, sold some of his spices and other wares in Alexandria and Ragusa, while purchasing cotton, copper-bars, dates and medicines in Alexandria, presumably for the Italian market.

Together with Eliezer of Venice and other merchants, he left

Alexandria in convoy on 3 March 1273, his own 'fleet' of 'five vessels' sailing under the colours of Venice, as he informs us, although three of the vessels were of Ancona. He also tells us that he put 'the richest' of his cargoes in 'two swift galleys with oars', in each of which were 'eighty men-in-arms', and the rest in two ships 'with two hundred mariners' – nothing is said of the fifth vessel – all of them being 'the ships of my brother Jacob of Sinigaglia',[38] and which were presumably let out to our Jacob on hire.

He again called at Ragusa, where he conducted business in apparently leisurely fashion, and Zara, where he spent the Passover from 4 to 11 April 1273, remaining in port – for reasons he does not explain, but perhaps for repairs to a vessel – for a further three weeks. Jacob arrived in Ancona on 5 May 1273, or 'the sixteenth of Iyar in the year 5033' as he puts it, 'in my fifty-second year, God be praised'. While he might have failed to become a 'prince in Sinim', it would seem from his powerful account of his return home – set out here in full – that his material fortunes had been made; at least in the short term.

On the eve of the Sabbath Behar, it being the sixteenth day of Iyar in the year 5033[39] since the creation of the world and in the fifty-second year of my life, we came at last to Cònero,[40] for which I gave praise to God that I had returned safe to my home with my wealth and all my servants about me, except for the brave Turiglioni and the boy Berletto. For when I had departed I had feared that my voyage would end in misadventure, but on this day I returned with a fair wind, in good health and with my ships laden with riches, for little was spoiled or lost, save those things which had been stolen by the Saracens.

Therefore, I thanked God for His mercy that I should have returned in good order, for so I had prayed upon each day of my journey, both in the morning and the evening, at rising and upon laying myself down to rest. Thus I came to Ancona with so much pepper of Greater and Lesser India, both round and long, ginger of Sinim and Melibar, long cinnamon and thick cinnamon, stem cassia, saffron, nutmeg, cardamoms, cloves, sugar of Manci, sandal of Sumoltra, aloes, camphor of Fansura and olibanum of Edente for the brothers, together with ten thousand pods of musk, of which a little brings a great profit, that any man might wonder at my good fortune, for which God be magnified and praised.

Of cinnamon I had one hundred and twenty cantars, of cubebs sixty cantars, of cloves one hundred and fifty cantars and of ginger forty cantars,[41] together with great quantities of other things, as of amber, pearls and coral.

Great also was my store of choice silks, as great and small cloths of silk and gold, gold brocades[42] for my brother Samuel of Lucca and damasks, as well as cotton from Alessandria, together with the best lac, of which I purchased two hundred and fifty cantars, as well as much brazil-wood, indigo and mirobalans for the house of my brother Abramo of Foligno.

Of medicines I had the best cubebs for Isaac d'Arezzo and many other medicines besides, as fine rhubarb,[43] pearls for pounding up,[44] *squinanti*,[45] shells for the eyes,[46] celandine,[47] galingale from Sumoltra and lesser galingale, and turpeth,[48] together with *succus lycii*[49] for the eyes and other secret things.

With such great store and with God's blessing I was restored to my loved one, having been absent from her for three years and twenty-four days from the day of my departure to the day of my return. My Sara, O my light, had passed grievous years without me, having been greatly troubled by many things. So that she wept bitterly to speak of my father, yet being greatly comforted by other things also, as the birth of our son Mose, upon whom the sign was made before the eighth day, for which God be praised.[50] At the jewels which I had brought to her she also felt much joy, so that at last with heart secure she became calmed.

Thus I came to Ancona with my treasure, for in Melibar and the land of Sinim I had made great profits, so that my partners received a good return, may God be thanked. Moreover I had hidden about me many choice jewels and pearls of Seilan and Manci, as well as having much coral and beads of amber for the idolaters,[51] together with golden besants in number [...], to serve me and my children should tribulation fall upon us, which God forbid.

For with such benefits as I bore at my return shall the pious and steadfast Jew always be rewarded, who is sustained by his own deeds and the fulfilment of his duties, as well as by the goodness of his brothers, peace upon them. Thus I praised God that, after having seen and heard so much, the end was good, for the Lord will guard your going out and coming in for ever.

Whereupon, we disembarked from the ship,[52] I having given to the faithful Armentuzio a rich gift, and to my servants Pizzecolli, Bertoni and Buccazuppo each a purse of gold, with to Buccazuppo two fine pearls also for her ears, may God forgive me my sin.[53] But it being already the hour of the Sabbath Behar, I gave over my merchandise into the guard of the servants of our house, while each went to his own house and to his family in order to praise God, each in his own fashion. For He had brought us safe by His hand to harbour, may He be magnified and lauded.

Thus I blessed my children, thanking God, who is the Light of the World, that He had kept them and guided me home to my native place, for all is in the hand of God, praying with my beloved Sara that He might send the Messiah to deliver us in our days, Amen and Amen.

And even though there is no escape from death, for it comes to all, I gave thanks to God for sparing me upon the sea and in distant lands. For although we have no certain place or last abode save Jerusalem, may the Temple be rebuilt in our times, this march of Ancona is shelter and home to me.[54]

Moreover, to this place God surely gives His care, for here there is never a generation without learnèd men among the Jews, who teach others what might be forgotten, and men of wealth who by their compassion bring help to their brothers. May God continue therefore to keep us as His treasure and in the shadow of His strength, looking not to our sins but to our dolours, Amen.

That which appears in this volume is a correct record of all that I, Jacob ben Salomone of Ancona, observed, heard and myself did and spoke in my travels, in which I might have been a prince in Sinim. Yet in great doubt have I revealed such things, for it is better to say little and do much, while a name made great is a name destroyed. Nor does anything go unseen by God, blessèd be He, so that a man may spend his time in vain in setting forth that which is already known to Him.

Yet in the ordering and narration of the fortunes and misfortunes that befell me, and of the perils I have undergone, I have been made content, for which God be praised. For each man has a duty to cast up the account of his life, so that he may measure it well and make a true reckoning of it, learning from the errors which he has committed. Thus I have sought also to make my writing plain,[55] thanking God that he has enabled me to reach this time and to complete my tale.[56]

For although I have been in relation with the truly wise since the days of my youth, God having opened my understanding at an early age, never before had I known or heard such things as those which I learned in Zaitun, which is called the City of Light. Yet I fear that if all that I have seen and written were now to be made known to others, no faith would be placed in me, God forbid, because of the wonders I have observed and narrated, and other parts would be held a serious wrong.

But even the follies which I have suffered and the sins which I have committed, may God spare me, have instructed me in the correct and just way in which all men should live. Therefore, O God, blessèd One, number me among those who are counted wise in Israel, and may the light of Your countenance shine upon me for ever, Amen, Amen and Amen.[57]

# Epilogue

A LITTLE OVER A YEAR after Jacob's departure from Zaitun in February 1272, the Tartar military campaign against 'Manci', or the Southern Sung empire, began in earnest under the Mongol general Bayan (1236–94). The besieged city of Xiangyang and fort of Fanzheng, to which Pitaco refers in one of his speeches to the elders of Zaitun, fell in March 1273. In the years 1273 and 1274 more of Southern Sung gradually came under Tartar sway; in January 1275 Bayan had advanced to Jacob's 'Chinscie' (Kinsai), seat of the Sung imperial court, where the then emperor, successor to the 'Toutson' of the manuscript, accepted vassaldom under the Tartars in March 1276. Zaitun, the City of Light, fell in 1277 to a Tartar army officered by Uighurs, Persians, Arabs and others.

The Sung emperor of the d'Ancona manuscript, Du Zong, had died in 1274, leaving (it seems) only minor children, one of whom succeeded him, with his grandmother acting as regent. Within two years, their capital Kinsai having fallen to the Tartars, most of the imperial family were taken into captivity, the princesses of the household being sent to Khanbalik (Beijing), where they are said to have been well treated by Kublai Khan. At least two others of the young sons of Du Zong had escaped capture, one of whom was proclaimed emperor by the Sung dynasty's last supporters; he is said to have died in

1278 on an island in the South China Sea. A second young son
took his place, but a year later, after a final sea-battle between
the remaining loyalists of the Sung dynasty and the Tartars, the
Sung chief minister leapt into the sea with the child-emperor in
his arms and both were drowned.

Most of the great families of the Southern Sung aristocracy –
its nobles, its landowners, its 'mandarins' – had thrown in their
lot with the invaders before the Sung empire's final fall in 1279,
six years after Jacob's return to Ancona. Kublai Khan thus
became emperor of all China, with Mongol rule turning out to
be as oppressive as the 'noble Pitaco' had warned in his impas-
sioned arguments with the defeatists of Zaitun. Indeed, the
Chinese of 'Manci', and thus of the 'City of Light' also, are said
by historians to have suffered particularly harsh discrimination.
They were largely ousted from government and administration, forbidden to possess arms, and subordinated everywhere
to Mongol and Turkic officials, who came to constitute a new
military and civilian ruling caste.

The Mongol rulers of southern China permitted the chief
governing posts to be held only by Mongols, describing the
Chinese in official documents as 'subjects'. (Murder of a
Mongol by a Chinese was punished with the death penalty;
murder of a Chinese by a Mongol, with a fine.) Press-gang
labour was introduced for public works, other unpaid periods of
compulsory service were demanded of the Chinese by their
new rulers, and lands were confiscated. According to Gernet,[1]
leading craftsmen, among them perhaps those whose porcelains and other artefacts were purchased by Jacob, were taken
prisoner and 'kept well guarded in special buildings', where
they were prevented from changing their occupations: another
form of forced labour.

However, not all was acquiescence with Tartar rule.
Zhangzhou, for instance, was recovered by the Chinese two
months after its conquest by the Tartars in 1275, even if (after
further resistance) it was finally overrun and most of its inhabitants slaughtered for their defiance of the invader – precisely

the kind of outcome of which the 'peace party' in Zaitun had warned during the debates which Jacob records.

The economic effects of the Tartar conquest of southern China are in general held to have been negative,[2] and 'in some respects disastrous'. The Mongol administration, it seems, was corrupt, nepotistical and negligent, causing great damage, for example, to the sophisticated canal and water-conservancy systems of the Chinese, which had cost the labour of generations. Yet such was the rigour in other respects of Mongol rule that there was also greater security; merchants travelling across country, whose earlier fears Jacob expresses in his manuscript, were safer. Moreover, foreign trade flourished under Mongol rule, contrary to the warnings Jacob delivered to his brother-merchants in Alexandria.

It is even argued by some modern historians that, under Mongol repression of the Chinese, foreign trade came to be almost entirely conducted by foreigners; that is, the Chinese merchant, immemorially trading out of Chinese ports with the East Indies, India and Arabia, was displaced under the Mongols by foreigners who took the trade from him. Certainly, it was not until *after* the death of Kublai Khan in 1294 that many European merchants seem to have left China, as disintegrating Mongol rule began to make trade, and trade routes within China, unsafe.

But in the more immediate aftermath of the Tartar conquest of Zaitun and the other mercantile cities of southern China, foreign merchants – and even foreigners in general, as Marco Polo's experiences with Kublai Khan attest – were favoured by the Mongols. This was especially so (it seems) with Muslim, or 'Saracen', merchants, and it was probably true of Jewish merchants also, since both had knowledge of the banking practices of the Western world and a formidable reach in their trade. It is an irony that the self-interest of a merchant like Jacob d'Ancona, who took the part of the traditionalist Pitaco in urging resistance to Tartar conquest, might have been more served than harmed by such conquest.

At the same time it is known that Mongol rule over southern China not only brought down the prevailing social order – already undermined by the mercantilist values described in Jacob's account – but led to the ransacking of much of its wealth. The property-owning classes, such as the nobility and the rich merchants, had hoped to maintain their status and preserve their personal wealth by accepting Tartar rule, as so many of the voices in the Zaitun debates urged. Instead, they suffered greatly. (The peasants, and the poor of the cities, were less supine, as the historians show.)

The Mongol Khan imposed onerous taxes and tributes on 'Manci'. In Zaitun, the previously annulled dues and taxes of the 'free trade' port – according to Jacob's account – were replaced, as Marco Polo tells us, by swingeing imposts. 'The Great Khan,' writes Polo, 'derives a very large revenue from the duties paid in this city ["Zayton"] and haven. For you must know that on all the merchandise imported, including precious stones and pearls, he levies a duty of 10 per cent, or in other words takes tithe of everything. Then again the ship's charge for freight on small wares is 30 per cent, on pepper 44 per cent, and on lignaloes, sandalwood and other bulky goods, 40 per cent, so that between freight and the Khan's dues the merchant has to pay a good half of his investment, though on the other half he makes such a profit that he is always glad to come back with a new supply of merchandise. But you may well believe from what I have said that the Khan has a vast revenue from this city.'[3]

The ideal of 'free trade', so ardently espoused by the pre-conquest merchants of Zaitun, was over, at least until our own times. But foreign traders continued under the Tartars to trade profitably – according to their apologist Polo – despite the oppressive conditions. On balance, however, the forebodings of the (apparently) assassinated Pitaco were closer to the truth of what was to occur than the enthusiastic report of Tartar rule provided for us by the Khan's retainer, Marco Polo.

In the event, the Tartar dominion, riven by corruption and

internal plot, and clumsy as well as harsh in its authoritarianism, lasted less than a century. It was opposed by large-scale rebellions of the poor, in particular those organised by the secret society of the 'Red Turbans' (1351–66) a half-century or more after Jacob's time. In a society habituated to unbridled consumption, as the manuscript so vividly illustrates, and living beyond its means – with a consequent deficit in the balance of trade, only partially covered by the export of its precious metals – inflation and the social conflicts which it generated also helped to bring down the Mongol regime.

It was succeeded by what we now know as the Ming dynasty, whose first emperor was a former Buddhist monk. Under its efficient rule, stability and many of the old ways, whose passing 'the noble Pitaco' had so bitterly lamented, were restored, China becoming settled and prosperous once more. As for the Tartars, they returned, after their final expulsion from China, to their original homelands, re-establishing their court at Karakorum, on the river Orkhon in Mongolia.

After the Tartar conquest in 1276 of the Sung dynasty's capital, Kinsai, a new 'Office of Religious Affairs' was created there. The following year it was put in the charge of a notorious Tibetan monk, a certain Yang Lian Zhen Jia, whose shamanistic Buddhist faith was in favour among the Mongols. Among the many crimes this monk committed against the sensibilities of the vanquished Chinese was the sacrilegious violation in 1278 – six years after Jacob's departure from Zaitun – of the tombs of the Southern Sung emperors (the 'Sons of Heaven') near Shaoxing, and the rifling of their treasures.

But it was Islam which can be said to have benefited most from Mongol rule over China, not least because many of the Mongol armies were recruited from among the Muslim Central Asian, and especially Turkic, peoples. The construction of the Khan's great court at Khanbalik (Beijing) was entrusted to a Muslim architect; Muslim governors were appointed to conquered Chinese provinces such as Yunnan; new mosques were built in south China, including in Zaitun and Guangzhou;

and there are said by historians to have been large-scale conversions of the Chinese to the Islamic faith. Thus, the long-standing hope of the mediaeval Western papacy that the Mongols could be converted to Christianity and assist the Church in its own struggle with Islam bore few fruits. One, however, was the conversion in 1294 by Giovanni de Monte Corvino,[4] later archbishop of Beijing, of Öngut Körguz, a Mongol prince.

In general, historians hold that the 'progress of thought' in China suffered considerably under Tartar rule, although less in the remarkable development of Chinese mathematics, science and technology – some scholars argue that they did not suffer at all – than in philosophy and ethics. For Mongol rule encouraged the marked predisposition of its learnèd men, of whom the contemptuous Jacob has left us an excoriating description, to follow the transitory biddings of power, doubtless in the name of preserving 'order under heaven'. The Mongols are also said to have had a weakness for magic and superstition, which doubtless appealed to those whom Jacob himself identified as 'magicians and soothsayers' among the 'wise men' of the city.

During Jacob's three-year absence in the Orient, relations between Venice and Ancona worsened.[5] Indeed, from 1277, four years after his return, battle between the fleets of the two cities was joined several times, until a peace treaty was signed in 1281, in Jacob's sixtieth year (presuming him to have been still alive). Although it does not refer specifically to commercial matters, the treaty confirmed Venice's supremacy in the Adriatic; it was on this basis that peace was established after a conflict which had lasted some 150 years. Relations with Venice improved further during the fourteenth century, in particular after a new treaty of 1345 – long after Jacob's death – in which Ancona's trade with Ragusa (Dubrovnik) and with the markets of the Byzantine empire was put on a more secure and agreed footing.

But in the wider economic and political context Italy was torn by civic struggles in the fourteenth century and afflicted by the Black Death (1347–50), while in the upheavals leading economic interests suffered severe reverses. Some of the largest Italian merchant-financiers (non-Jews) of the middle ages, especially those of Florence, were bankrupted in the period, the Bonnaccorci and the Corsini in 1341, the Bardi, Peruzzi and Acciajuoli in 1343. Nevertheless, as Pirenne describes it, 'the supremacy of Italy in banking and luxury industries was ... successfully maintained over the rest of Europe, in spite of the political disunion, until the discovery of new routes to the Indies [in the fifteenth century] turned the main current of navigation and commerce from the Mediterranean to the Atlantic.'[6]

During the upheavals of the fourteenth century Ancona itself fell briefly under the dominion of the Malatestas of Rimini from 1348 to 1355, after which it returned to the papal sovereignty. It is pleasingly glimpsed in a document of 1392 as a '*notabilissima, potentissima et ditissima civitas*' (a very noteworthy, powerful and rich city), with an 'infinite' number of ships and three-masted galleys in its harbour; exactly as Zaitun had appeared to Jacob a century earlier.

We can only speculate over whether Jacob's descendants were among those who sailed in these vessels *ultra mare*, beyond the seas, but it is unlikely.[7] For the increasing restrictions which were imposed upon Jewish commercial activity in the fourteenth century would probably have driven his family successors out of Italian international trade. It is also possible that Jacob himself, hopefully protected by the wealth he had accumulated in the Orient – although he would have had to share some of it with his partners – would have turned to domestic banking in his own lifetime.

A glimpse of the particular lot of the Jews in Ancona can be gained at a time when Jacob was doubtless still alive: in 1279, when he would have been fifty-eight, and six years after his return from southern China, the Jews of the city were accused of having provoked the earthquake which struck Ancona in that year![8] Much worse, of course, was to befall the Jews after Jacob's time, not least under the influence of the Franciscan preachers of the age. Most notoriously, Bernardino da Siena (1380–1440), Giacomo della Marca (1391–1476), Giovanni da Capistrana (1386–1456) and Bernardino da Feltre (1439–94) sowed fear among the Jews, provoking the lower classes against them by regular resort to the depiction of the Jews as guilty of ritual murder and 'profanation of the host'.[9]

Nevertheless, in many mediaeval and renaissance Italian dukedoms and other independent cities – Mantua, Parma, Ferrara and Urbino among them – as well as within the Papal State itself, the Jews survived and even prospered despite intermittent physical attacks, restrictions and expulsions. In 1554, during the papacy of Julius III, there were 115 synagogues in those parts of Italy where the Jews were permitted to settle,[10] thirty-four of them being in Jacob's region of the Marche. But although Ancona appears to have had a long history of (relative) amiability towards the Jews – after 1569 the Jews of the Papal State were (officially) allowed to live only in Rome and Ancona – an undercurrent of hostility might always surface, as Jacob's anxiety in an earlier period makes plain.

The worst event known of this kind in Ancona occurred during the papacy of Cardinal Gian Pietro Carafa (1476–1559), who took the name of Paul IV when he became pope in 1555. In the city there were some one hundred families of Portuguese Marranos, enforced Jewish converts to Christianity, who had taken refuge in Ancona in the 1540s and who had returned to the open profession of their original faith. In the name of accelerating the 'conversion of the Jews', Pope Paul IV fell upon the Anconetan Marranos with inquisitional zeal, ordering that their possessions be confiscated and demanding of them a resumed and true practice of the Christian faith.

Twenty-four men and one woman, who resisted torture and refused to the end, were strangled and burnt at the stake between April and June 1556, some three years after the books of Urbino's Jews had also been publicly burned.[11] Whether any of Jacob's descendants were still in Ancona to witness these sanguinary events cannot be known. But his anxious spirit must have been alive in many hearts.

Having painstakingly translated Jacob's extraordinary work, and so reflected upon his persona that I came to sense his presence all about me, it is a tantalising thing to know no more 'facts' about him than I do, not least about his end. But then there is the same feeling of loss and inadequacy in many historians who at the last draw back from the elusive figures of their studies, knowing that for all their efforts they can draw no nearer to them.

Such frustration of purpose is communicated in the words of the great scholar of mediaeval China, Henry Yule, who, writing of the Mongol conquest which Jacob so feared, declares: 'Missions and merchants alike disappear from the field soon after the middle of the fourteenth century, as the Mongol dynasty totters and comes down. We hear ... of friars and bishops dispatched from Avignon; but they go forth into the darkness and are heard of no more ... A dark mist has descended upon the farther east, covering Mangi and Cathay [and] those cities of which the old travellers told such wonders, Cambalic and Cansay and Zaytun and Chinkalan. And when the veil rises ... a century and a half later, those names are heard of no more ... Not only are the old names forgotten, but the fact that those places had been known before is utterly forgotten also.'[12]

As for Jacob ben Salomone d'Ancona, scholar, traveller, merchant, and perhaps rabbi and doctor, he is more helpful (and fortunate) than most, having left his manuscript behind him for our instruction and pleasure. But whether he died and was buried in Ancona none can now say. If his bones were laid to rest in the old and abandoned cliff-top Jewish cemetery of Ancona, it would have been a fitting place. For it looks out

upon the Adriatic and the route he took, while its tombstones
– some of them have long ago fallen into the sea below – are
turned to Jerusalem, the city which on the penultimate page of
his manuscript Jacob calls his 'last abode'. Wherever he ended
his days, 'may peace be upon him', as he would have said.

# Afterword for the Paperback Edition

MY TRANSLATION OF JACOB OF Ancona's manuscript raised wide general interest on the one hand – leading to its retranslation from my version into more than a dozen languages, from Catalan to Chinese – and academic incredulity on the other. The latter was expressed in much speculation (and some aspersion) about the provenance and authenticity of the Ancona text. Many of the 'objections' to the work, however, were frequently inconsistent and contradictory among themselves: what one scholar asserted to be true of, say, life in Sung China, or mediaeval routes to the Orient, or the provenance and date of certain words and terms which Jacob uses, was flatly denied by another.

I was therefore driven to suggest, perhaps with misplaced irony, that 'a Committee of Scholars (Hebraists, Arabists, Italianists, Sinologists and others) be formed ... in order to arrive at a common critique of the text' (*Times Literary Supplement*, 20 November 1997). For to me, knowing the truth about the manuscript and bound by an undertaking – to the legitimate frustration of academics – that I would guard the anonymity of the owner, most of this kerfuffle was unhelpful. Nor was there anything new in the kinds of argument about authenticity which broke out.

Thus, there are some 150 variant manuscripts of Marco Polo's travels, none of which can be identified as the 'original', nor is it clear, even, in what language this 'original' might have been written. Moreover, just as doubts have been cast, at one time or another, upon the veracity of almost every other ancient traveller, so some modern scholars doubt whether Polo went to the Orient at all. Yet this has not prevented the continuing acknowledgment of his book as one of the most intriguing of all travellers' tales – fanciful or not as may be – nor can it impede our sense of Marco Polo as a real persona of the Italian past, as author, adventurer and courtier of the Khans.

And what of the 'Old Testament', a disputed palimpsest of manifold sources, authors, redactors, languages and purposes? Or the texts of the Gospels, with their challenged provenance, authenticity, authorship and dating, and their fundamental factual contradictions? In all these cases, as with the works of Homer or Virgil or Shakespeare, the absence of an 'original manuscript' may frustrate our curiosity but, for the most part, does not trouble our judgment as to the virtue or truth of that which we read and ponder.

In the introduction to the first edition of my translation of *The City of Light*, published in October 1997, I was myself cautious about who actually wrote the Ancona manuscript, allowing for the possibility that it was a copyist's work. I allowed, too, that it could have been an Italian translation from a Hebrew original, and that it cannot be securely dated. I roughly placed it, in the first instance, in the period of the 'last years of the thirteenth century or the first years of the fourteenth', before hazarding a date (perhaps wrongly) between the 'early 1280s' and 1290, on the speculative and hopeful ground that the manuscript was written in Jacob's lifetime and is in Jacob's hand. Professor Chun-shu Chang of the Department of History at the University of Michigan – who 'found no conclusive evidence to support the theory that the book was a forgery' – believes it to have been written in the late 1290s (written communication, 26 May 1998). I myself showed that no date *before* the 1280s was possible, from the presence of words not current until then. (Thus certain alleged 'anachronisms' – such as the name 'Toutson' which Jacob gives to the Sung emperor – could only be anachronisms if an earlier date *than the earliest I proposed myself* is attributed to the manuscript; and some critics did precisely that.)

My own caution did not, alas, deter the scholars who rushed to judgment about *The City of Light*, in some cases even before its publication and when only proofs were in circulation. Fancy knew no bounds in immediately proclaiming the text a 'hoax', even the 'literary hoax of the nineties'; or a 'clever way of getting attention'; or a political satire written by me in the manner of a Swift or a Montesquieu, a considerable compliment to my wit and erudition; or a novel. On several occasions, in broadcast interviews and articles, I declared myself flattered by the last suggestion, for, if it were true, Jacob of Ancona would be my Don Quixote and I his Cervantes.

But, oddly, in the dozens of reviews and comments, the fact that Jacob's manuscript is, among other things, a Jewish work of considerable piety, containing an account of historic Jewish tribulation and defiance, as well as excoriations of Christian 'idolatry', was barely mentioned. This aspect of the text led me to say that 'if there were still a Vatican Index it would surely be placed on it' (*The Times*, 23 December 1997). My analysis of the language of the manuscript was also ignored, as were the many footnotes highlighting some of the more interesting or unusual passages and terms used in the original.

I was also able to observe how some critics rode roughshod over complex historical facts. Thus I was told by one scholar that Jacob could not have set sail from Ancona in 1270, since at that time the Venetians had 'suppressed voyages from Ancona to the rich ports of the East'. On the contrary, as J.F. Leonhard shows in his book *Ancona nel Medio Evo* (Ancona, 1992, pp.106–9, 252, 268–9), the Venetian effort to blockade Ancona in the late 1220s, and thereafter, failed, and Ancona in 1270 was an independent and flourishing mercantile city. It possessed its own currency, was the principal port for the wares of Tuscany and central Italy, and the Vatican's main point of egress to Byzantium and beyond (*op. cit.*, pp.112, 116–17, 249ff.)

It was declared, likewise, that wood-block printing, about which Jacob writes, had 'not caught on' in southern Sung. Yet the opposite is true (Jacques Gernet, *A History of Chinese Civilization, op. cit.*, pp.333–5), printing being widespread in the southern provinces at the time of Jacob's visit. It was insisted, too, by critics that the port of Zaitun could not have been in any sense a 'free port', as Jacob declares that it was, yet it is known that some, and perhaps many, merchants trading in southern China at the time were exempt from the payment of taxes on trade (see S. Yoshinobu, *Commerce and Society in Southern China*, Michigan, 1970, pp.26–7). Then it was said that public debates in Zaitun of the kind which Jacob describes – descriptions which I myself suggest, several times, in my commentary were likely to have been elaborated by Jacob on his return to Italy – could not have taken place at all, since the Chinese 'had great difficulty in communicating verbally with one another' – and this in a period known for its turmoil and open controversy on public issues! (R.P. Hymes and C. Schirokauer, *Ordering the World: Approaches to State and Society in Sung Dynasty China*, Berkeley, 1993, p.1 and *passim*.) It was in addition argued that a foreign merchant would not have been treated with the degree of respect that Jacob claims was (at first) shown him. But Laurence Ma's *Commercial Development and Urban Change in Sung China* (Michigan, 1971) shows the opposite in Chinese attitudes to foreign traders.

Or, descending to particulars, it was asserted that saffron could not have been purchased by Jacob, as he claims, since it was 'unknown in China at that time'. But this assertion is untrue, saffron being mentioned, for instance, in official dynastic annals from the time of the Sui dynasty (AD 581–618), as well as being one of the items of a flourishing but illegal trade with the Tartars in the period of Jacob's visit (S. Yoshinobu, *Commerce and Society in Southern China*).

Again, Jacob's magnificent account of the noise of the streets of Zaitun, in part caused by 'carriages', was equally pronounced inauthentic. It was said that this was 'not an area of carriages', the citizenry instead allegedly going about in sedan-chairs. Yet the scroll-artist, Zhang Zeduan, whose depictions of street-scenes in twelfth-century Kaifeng embellish the first edition and appear in the plate section of this edition, shows all manner of wheeled vehicles, while Marco Polo refers to an 'infinite succession of carriages' in the streets of Hangzhou (*The Travels of Marco Polo*, eds., H. Yule and H. Cordier, New York, 1993 [reprint of 1903 edition], vol. 2, p.234).

The Sung Chinese, I was also told, would not have referred to themselves as 'Mancini', a word with disparaging connotations. But they do not refer to themselves as 'Mancini'; Jacob does. The name of 'Pitaco', I was likewise informed, does not appear in the lists of 'prefects of Zaitun'. But he is not referred to as a 'prefect of Zaitun', but only as a 'former prefect', of a place unnamed. Another alleged inauthenticity was discovered in the fact that silver was not used as a currency in China until a century after Jacob's time. But Jacob does not say that silver *was* used as a currency in China. Similarly, I was told that quotations from the Bible would not have been made by a pious Jew in Italian. But such quotations are nearly all in Hebrew, as my commentary and the footnotes clearly disclose; there were, I think, only two exceptions to this in the entire manuscript.

And so it went on: hasty judgments being arrived at without due care or attention, and on the part of those who were simultaneously making a virtue of their superior scruple. Indeed, these scholars' slapdash criticisms were to me as odd as my account of the provenance of the manuscript evidently was to them.

Then there was the supposedly decisive 'smoking gun' in Jacob of Ancona's text: his use of the Arabic word *mellah* for the Jewish quarter of Cormosa (Hormuz, or Bandar Abbas) in the Persian Gulf. This word, it was declared, was first used in 1438, 'when a specific area of salt marsh in the city of Fez [in Morocco] was set aside for use as a Jewish quarter'. For *mellah*, it was implied, has an exclusive association with the Arabic word for 'salt', and Jacob's use of it was a crashing anachronism.

There are no salt marshes in Fez. Moreover, the word *mellah*, employed by Jacob some 140 years before our critics would allow it, is more likely to be derived not from the word for 'salt' but to be a variant of *mahalla*, or 'encampment', a common and ancient term in Arab lands for 'Jewish quarter', with the associated meaning of 'place of refuge'. Moreover, as Dr Tudor Parfitt of London University's School of Oriental and African Studies has informed me, the word was in use with this meaning at the time of Jacob's journey in Iraq and in Persia; that is, precisely where it occurs in his account.

A more serious point, which some critics laboured, was that Jacob of Ancona's text 'would have been' or 'ought to have been' written in *Hebrew*. There can be no such certitude or rule, quite apart from the fact that, as I have already pointed out, I myself suggested the possibility of a 'Hebrew original' of the manuscript from which I worked, a manuscript which contains a substantial amount of Biblical Hebrew but which is for the most part written in the Italian *volgare*, or common speech. It has been pointed out that Italian Jews of the mediaeval period also had their own form of 'Judeo-Italian' – an Hebraised 'dialect' of Italian, as Yiddish is an Hebraised 'dialect' of High German – which they wrote in Hebrew characters.

This might therefore have been the form of a (missing) 'original' of the text from which I worked. But it is unlikely, since the use of 'Judeo-Italian' transliterated into Hebrew characters seems to have been confined to *religious* texts (see, e.g., G. Jochnowitz, *Romance Philology*, vol. XLVIII, no. 3, February 1995, pp. 297–300).

*The City of Light*, although written by a pietist (of incomplete orthodoxy), is most definitely not a 'religious text', for all its religious elements and the frequent recourse to Hebrew citations from the Bible and the Talmud amid the Italian. Jacob's own learning, as I wrote in my original commentary, had much of the secular in it, and there are Christian philosophical influences upon it too, as I noted. The text is essentially this-worldly and *profane*, at least from an orthodox point of view.

More important, the Jews of mediaeval Italy, being indigenous rather than birds-of-passage, were as much Italian, or settled inhabitants of the Italian peninsula, as they were Jews; their first presence in Rome predates the Christian era. Whatever Hebraised Italian dialect they may have spoken among themselves, or used in liturgical writing, their language of everyday discourse with their friends and neighbours – and, in Jacob's case, with his Christian fellow-merchants and the leading citizens of Ancona – was, and could only have been, Italian.

Indeed, mediaeval and Renaissance churchmen intermittently repeated prohibitions against Christian parents sending their children to Jewish teachers, as was established practice in some places in order for them to learn to read and write. And they surely did not attend such teachers in order to learn Hebrew or 'Judeo-Italian'. Moreover, Jacob's own studies in Naples would plainly have required knowledge not of Hebrew, but of Latin, Arabic or Italian, or all three; and all three, together with Hebrew, are found in his manuscript.

It is therefore not difficult to posit an original text *in Italian*, the cultivated Italian of Jacob's work. The notion that he, as a Jew, 'ought to have written in Hebrew' is not much less absurd than the suggestion that I ought to do so too. It is, not to mince words, a ghettoised concept, which excludes *a priori* the choice by an educated thirteenth-century Jewish merchant of Ancona of an erudite literary Italian as a mode of written expression, on the grounds alone that he was a Jew. The implication is unacceptable. Moreover, even the great rabbinical commentator, Solomon ben Isaac of Troyes (1040–1105), otherwise known as Rashi, introduced vernacular French terms into his Hebrew text when he wished to make his meaning clearer.

It was also privately put to me, this time by an Italian Hebraist, that a *buon ebreo*, or 'good Jew' – a criterion I dislike – would not have made use of the 'Christian calendar' in the dating of the passage of events which he was describing. Again, it is clear that the merchant-traveller Jacob, whose life was clearly not lived exclusively among his co-religionists but whose contacts and experiences ranged literally to the confines of the known world, was not intellectually constrained in the conventional ways that such (Jewish) critics might prefer. It could of course be that the use of 'Christian' dates in the Ancona manuscript entered via a copyist-translator. But it is also notable that the manuscript shows a variety of usages in dating: sometimes the 'Christian' date is put first, sometimes the 'Jewish', sometimes the 'Jewish' date only is used, and sometimes – but very rarely – the 'Christian' version alone is employed.

As with the majority of the observations on the Ancona manuscript, nothing can be made of this in arguments as to authenticity. And if Jacob is in some particulars *sui generis*, as he is in his foibles as a man as well as in his moral opinions, his religious practices and his philosophical positions, why not? Or is a modern scholarly schema which dictates what a man-of-the-past 'ought' to have been, and what he 'ought' to have known or done, preferable to what he was and knew, and says himself that he did?

The arrogance of (often underinformed) academics tends to dictate the former, lest received knowledge, however incomplete – as it is bound to be – is disturbed. Life dictates the latter. Thus it was insisted by a critic that 'medieval people' did not wear earrings, so that Jacob could not, on their return to Ancona, have presented his long-suffering young servant, Buccazuppo, with 'two fine pearls for her ears', as he describes it. But Jewish practice – to say nothing of the emulation of what the travellers had seen in the East – protests against such 'knowledge'.* More particularly, the reference to the wearing of

---

* cf. 'And Aaron said unto them, Break off the golden earrings, which are in the ears of your wives, of your sons, and of your daughters, and bring them unto me.' Exodus 32:2.

earrings – '. . . *Et met en ses deus oreilletes / Deus verges d'or pendans greletes* . . .' – in the late thirteenth-century *Roman de la Rose* (ed. D. Poiron, Paris, 1974, p.553, lines 20977–8) supports Jacob's account of his gift. Similarly underinformed was another critic's assertion – without the adducing of any authoritative evidence or proof – that Jacob 'could not have had' two female servants as washerwomen in the entourage which accompanied him to the Orient.

There was also a particularly interesting, if prudish, series of objections to Jacob's vivid account of the sexual mores of Zaitun: that the behaviour he describes was unknown among the Sung Chinese (or among the Chinese at all), or that the account by Jacob was 'too explicit' for the times, or that Jacob, as a pious Jew, 'would not have written' in such fashion.

As to the first, Jacques Gernet in his *Daily Life in China on the Eve of the Mongol Invasion, 1250–1276* (London, 1962) describes how an 'uncouth, warlike, rather stiff and hieratical society' had given place to one that was 'lively, mercantile, pleasure-seeking and corrupt' (p.14). In Hangzhou – and what of a great port-city like Zaitun? – 'there was hardly a single public place, tavern, restaurant, hotel, market, "pleasure ground", square or bridge where one did not encounter dozens of ladies of the town' (p.96). There were also male prostitutes, Gernet tells us, in Kaifeng in the twelfth century, who 'simpered, used cosmetics, decked themselves up, sang and danced just as their feminine counterparts did' (p.99), and of which Jacob gives his own disapproving report. In addition the Taoist pharmacopoeia contains many potions and devices to enhance virility and erection.

As for Jacob expressing himself in this vein at all, one has only to know a little of thirteenth-century Jewish literature, especially poetry – including the poetry of Italian-Jewish writers contemporary with Jacob – to know that the boldness of his writing, declared 'impossible' by certain critics, is, on the contrary, authentic of its provenance and time. (*The Penguin Book of Hebrew Verse*, ed. T. Carmi, Harmondsworth, 1981, is the most accessible source for the general reader.) Moreover, the Jews, including, and even above all, *pious* Jews, have rarely shared Christian pruderies about the body, seeing sexuality as a 'gift of God', rather than as a wickedness to be lashed with scorpions.

Thus Moses ibn Ezra of Granada (c. 1055–post 1135), a writer both of erotic poetry and synagogue meditations, sings, 'These are the delights of the world ... do not stop sipping the moist lips until you hold your rightful portion – the breast and the thigh' (*op. cit.*, p.325). Todros Abulafia of Toledo (1247–post 1295), a contemporary of Jacob of Ancona, in his poem *Behava Chalta* ('Oh, to be a woman!'), exclaims, 'How very beautiful were your feet when they twined and climbed my neck' (*op. cit.*, p.411), sexual acrobatics of whose description Jacob was equally unshy. And then there is the anonymous mediaeval Jewish poet who describes 'The Ideal Woman' in explicit anatomical terms from the mouth to the feet, adding that 'during intercourse . . . on her bed'. The manuscript, declares T. Carmi (*op. cit.*, p.361), explaining the break in the poem, is 'defective at this point', while Jacob's account of such matters is marvellously entire.

Hence, as with so many of the misdirected judgments upon the Ancona manuscript, this arrow also misses its target; Jacob's combination of piety and 'eroticism' is no aberration.*

Other matters I have referred to in a very small number of amendments or additions to the footnotes. There has been one correction to a significant typographical error in which the 'Fast of Gedaliah' appeared as the 'Feast of Gedaliah'; a correction of

---

* An amusing modern parallel to the pious Jacob's behaviour in exploring the underworld of Zaitun is furnished by a case involving the principal of a Jewish seminary in Jerusalem caught in a 'nude bar'. Accused of 'moral corruption', he argued – almost exactly as does Jacob of Ancona in his Talmudic dialogue with himself – that he had 'made a supreme sacrifice in going to the abominable place', in this case 'to see if any of his students frequented it' (*Daily Telegraph*, 30 January 1998).

a spelling error in the map; and two corrections of fact in the introduction to Chapter 2.

In every respect, Jacob of Ancona's splendid text stands. As I write this, the cudgels are being taken up by others in defence of the manuscript's authenticity – after a period of shock at the destructiveness of the efforts, some of them concerted, to discredit it – while translations are under way in many places. Moreover, despite the present difficulties of furnishing final proofs, the authenticity of the manuscript is coming *prima facie* to be accepted. For example, *Corriere della Sera* of Milan on 23 December 1997, in describing the antiquity of Italy's link with China, cited without further comment three forerunners in this contact, 'Marco Polo, Giacobbe d'Ancona and Matteo Ricci', the Jesuit missionary.

Of course, I had originally hoped, while I was at work on the translation, that, once completed – but not before – other scholars might be given access to the manuscript in order to assists in its authentication. But although the Ancona manuscript remains unavailable to scholars (and 'scholars') – just as, worse still, the 'original manuscript' of Marco Polo's travels, if there ever was one, is lost entirely – Jacob, like Marco Polo, lives, and his book, like Polo's, will surely endure.

*David Selbourne, Urbino, 1998*

# Glossary

**Alessandria**  Alexandria, in Egypt
**amotzi**  (Hebrew) prayer of sanctification over bread
**Baudas**  Baghdad
**cahanim**  (Hebrew) men of priestly family
**Cambaetta**  Cambay, in the Indian state of Gujarat
**Cane**  Khan
**cantar**  from Arabic *quintar*, equivalent to about 50kg/110lb; 100
    cantars is therefore equivalent to about 500kg or 5 tons
**Cascaro**  possibly Kashgar
**Cataio**  Cathay, or northern China
**Cataini**  inhabitants of Cathay
**Chaifen**  Kaifeng, in China
**Chesimur**  Kashmir
**Chinscie**  Kinsai (Hangzhou), capital of Southern Sung
**Cin**  China
**Cius**  Qus on the River Nile
**Ciusar**  Quseir on the Red Sea
**Colam**  Quilon, in the Indian state of Kerala
**Corchira**  Corfu (Kerkira in Greek)
**Cormosa**  Hormuz
**cubeb**  spicy berry used in medicine and in cooking
**Edente**  Aden
**Eraclione**  Heraklion, in Crete
**fóndaco**  warehouse, trading-post, also serving as hostel for travelling
    merchants
**Frank**  Western Christian
**Fuciu**  Fuzhou, in southern China

**Fustat**  Cairo

**Gazurat**  Gujarat, state of India

**Gehenna**  the Jewish hell

**Haman**  high official of King Ahasuerus of Persia (486–465 BC); planned massacre of the Jews, but was thwarted by Queen Esther and hanged

**hametz**  forbidden food at Passover

**Hanukah**  Jewish festival of 'Dedication' or 'Lights', instituted in 165 BC by Judas Maccabeus

**Java the Less**  Sumatra

**Kaddish**  (Hebrew) lit. 'holy', the mourner's prayer for the dead

**kiddush**  (Hebrew) lit. 'sanctification', the blessing of the Sabbath wine

**lac**  lacquer, used in dyeing

**li**  Chinese measure of distance, roughly equivalent to quarter of a mile

**libbra**  Italian measure of weight, equivalent to about 180gm; 100 *libbre* is therefore equivalent to 18kg, or about 40lb

**luban javi**  (Arabic) frankincense of Java

**Manci**  southern China

**Mancini**  inhabitants of south China

**Mancino**  used by Jacob in the sense of the Chinese language

**Marsiglia**  Marseilles

**Melibar**  western coast of India

**mellah**  (Arabic) Jewish quarter of a town

**menorah**  (Hebrew) seven-branched candlestick used at Hanukah

**mirobalan**  'plum-like' fruit from India used as a medicine and in dyeing

**Mishnah**  oral law of the Talmud

**Mitzraim**  (Hebrew) land of Egypt

**Nabuccodonosor**  Nebuchadnezzar

**nacchi, nacchini**  (Italian) types of brocade

**Nicoverano**  Nicobar (isles)

**olibanum**  (Latin) frankincense

**Ragusa**  Dubrovnik

**Sacchia**  Buddha

**Sacchiani**  Buddhists

**Sandu**  Shangdu ('Xanadu'), place of the court of the Tartar ruler Kublai Khan

**Saracen**  Arab, but also a synonym for Muslim

**Schandu**  *see* Sandu

**Seilan**  Ceylon (Sri Lanka)

**Ser**  (Italian) sire, or sir, abbreviated from *signore*

**Shavuot**  Jewish Festival of Weeks, or Pentecost

**Shema** Jewish prayer, 'Hear, O Israel'

**shofar** (Hebrew) ram's horn

**Simhat Torah** Jewish festival of the Rejoicing of the Law

**Sincepura** Singapore

**Sinim** China

**Sinimiani** inhabitants of China

**Succoth** Jewish festival of Tabernacles

**Suciu** Suzhou, in southern China

**Sumoltra** Sumatra

**Tattari** Tartars, or Mongols

**Tattaria** Tartary

**Tauris** Tabriz, in Azerbaijan

**tekia** (Hebrew) note blown on the shofar (q.v.) in certain Jewish religious services

**Tentsu** (Chinese: Tian Zi) 'Son of Heaven', honorific title for Sung emperor

**terua** (Hebrew) note blown on the shofar (q.v.) in certain Jewish religious services

**Vinegia** Venice

**yehaz** (Arabic) probably a frail boat for local traffic

**zaffaro** variety of frankincense

**Zara** the port of Zadar, now in Croatia

**Zaituno** inhabitant of Zaitun, south China

# Jewish Calendar of Months

Since the Jewish year is basically lunar the months go from new moon to new moon and thus generally straddle the months of the solar Julian calendar, as the table shows. The names of the months themselves are of Babylonian origin.

| | |
|---|---|
| **Tishri** | *September–October* |
| **Heshvan** | *October–November* |
| **Kislev** | *November–December* |
| **Tevet** | *December–January* |
| **Shevat** | *January–February* |
| **Adar** | *February–March* |
| **Nisan** | *March–April* |
| **Iyar** | *April–May* |
| **Sivan** | *May–June* |
| **Tammuz** | *June–July* |
| **Av** | *July–August* |
| **Elul** | *August–September* |

# Names

More than 175 names of persons, Italian, Jewish and Chinese,
are referred to by Jacob d'Ancona in his manuscript. I have
arranged most of these names in three sections, in alphabetical
order in each section, and I have given whatever brief description of each is possible.

*Italian*

**Andrea**  priest of Famagusta
**Angeli, Matteo**  captain of the people, Ancona
**Antonio**  called '*ser*', customer for sword-blades
**Armentuzio, Pietro**  clerk, servant
**Bartolomeo**  called '*ser*', customer for medicines, probably apothecary
**Bartolomeo, Fra**  Christian priest of Zaitun
**Berletto**  cooks' 'servitor'
**Bertoni**  clothes-washer, servant
**Bladioni, Giacomo**  captain of the people, Ancona
**Buccazuppo**  clothes-washer, servant
**Capocci**  called '*ser*'
**Confaloniere, Giovanni**  *podestà* ('mayor') of Ancona
**Filippo**  priest of Ancona
**Fultrono**  'bodyguard', servant
**Gualdi, Domenico**  partner/investor in voyage, of Florence
**Guglielmo of Pisa**  Italian merchant of Zaitun
**Micheli**  'bodyguard', servant
**Pecte**  cook, servant

**Pietro** 'friar of Sant'Angelo'
**Pietro di Todini** merchant of Ancona
**Pizzecolli, Simone** clerk, servant
**Raniero** called '*ser*', cardinal-legate in Ancona from *c.* 1244 to 1249
**Rustici** cook, servant
**Simone** called '*rettore*', legate in Ancona
**Tarabotti, Alberto de'** and
**Tarabotti, Benvenuto de'** partners/investors in voyage, of Ancona
**Turiglioni, Atto** ship's helmsman, navigator
**Vioni** Italian merchant of Zaitun, formerly of Genoa

*Jewish*

All these names are listed in alphabetical order of their first names. Jacob writes many of these names in Hebrew, including (sometimes) his own. Where he transliterates them, he does so without consistency. Thus 'David' is Davit and Davide; 'Jacob' is Iacob, Iacobbe, Giacobbe and Iacopo (once), and so on. I have myself been inconsistent; in a few cases – as for 'Jacob', 'Aaron', 'Isaac', 'Nathan' – I have chosen a single, 'anglicised' (or familiar) version, but left the others as they are given in the manuscript; except where I have used 'J's for his 'I's and added final 'H's as when his 'Iuda' becomes 'Judah'.

**Aaron of Barcelona in Aragon** the 'great merchant'
**Aaron Ebreo of Eraclione** merchant/factor, Crete
**Abraam of Baudas** merchant, Aden
**Abraam of Foligno** (probably) dyer
**Abraam Hagiz** doctor and apothecary, Basra
**Abraam ben Leo of Mestre** merchant trading with China
**Akiba** rabbinical sage
**Alleuccio** a Jew of Venice, involved in negotiations with Ancona
**Asher ben Jehiel** rabbi, Hormuz
**Baruch Bonaiuto** brother-in-law of Jacob d'Ancona
**Baruch Ebreo** merchant, Cochin
**Beniamino** factor, Cambay, cousin of Menahem Vivo (q.v.)
**Dattalo Porat of Fano** guardian of Jacob's wife and children
**David** brother of the philosopher, Mose ben Maimon (q.v.)
**Efraim of Ceneda** merchant of Aden, and Jacob's cousin
**Efraim ben Judah Greco** factor, Sumatra
**Efraim Ha-Levi** 'great merchant', Alexandria
**Eleazar** rabbinical sage
**Elia of Famagusta** merchant (?), Cyprus, and Jacob's uncle
**Eliahu ben Elhanan of Colam** rabbi, Quilon

**Eliezer** rabbinical sage

**Eliezer ben Isaac** rabbinical sage

**Eliezer ben Nathan of Venice** merchant, Jacob's companion in voyage

**Ezra** merchant, Aden

**Gaio Bonaiuti** signatory on last page of manuscript

**Gamaliel** rabbinical sage

**Gershon ben Judah of Venice** merchant

**Haim** merchant (?), Alexandria, and Jacob's brother

**Haim ben Abraam Ha-Levi of Sinigaglia** merchant

**Haim ben Joel of Baudas** rabbi, officiant at marriage of Jacob's son and daughter-in-law

**Hillel** rabbinical sage

**Hillel ben Samuel** rabbi (?), friend of Jacob

**Isaac** son of Jacob d'Ancona

**Isaac of Arezzo** (probably) apothecary

**Isaac Bekhor** factor, Cambay

**Isaac ben Isaac of Ceneda** rabbi and merchant

**Isaia of Ascoli** merchant, Basra, father-in-law of Jacob d'Ancona's son, Isaac

**Isaia ben Simone of Curzola** merchant

**Isaia Sullam Hagiz** guardian of Jacob's wife and children

**Israel of Florence** rabbi, grandfather of Jacob d'Ancona

**Jacob ben Salomone ben Israel** (Jacob d'Ancona), merchant

**Jacob of Sinigaglia** merchant/ship-owner, Alexandria

**Jose** rabbinical sage

**Josef the Nagid** Spanish-Jewish vizier

**Joshuah** rabbinical sage

**Judah** rabbinical sage

**Lazzaro Ha-coen** elder of Ancona community

**Lazzaro del Vecchio of Ancona** merchant, Jacob's companion in voyage

**Leo ben Benedetto** factor, Ragusa (Dubrovnik)

**Levi** banker of Ancona

**Levi di Abraam of Camerino** partner/investor in voyage

**Levi d'Ancona** merchant, Quilon and Jacob's cousin

**Meir** rabbinical sage

**Meir ben Joel** rabbi, Cormosa (Hormuz)

**Menahem** rabbi, Ancona

**Menahem ben David (Vivo) of Mestre** merchant, Jacob's companion in voyage

**Mose David** grandson of Jacob d'Ancona, son of Isaac and Rebecca

**Mose ben Maimon (Maimonides)** (AD 1135–1204) Jewish

philosopher, doctor and rabbi

**Nathan ben Dattalo of Sinigaglia** factor, Zaitun

**Rebecca** daughter of Isaia of Ascoli, daughter-in-law of Jacob d'Ancona

**Sabbato ben Menahem** elder of Ancona community

**Salomone of Ancona** merchant, father of Jacob d'Ancona

**Salomone Hasdai** 'great merchant', Alexandria

**Salomone ben Judah** Solomon ben Judah ibn Gabirol (*c*.1021–*c*.1058), grammarian, philosopher and poet

**Salomone ben Judah of Basra** rabbi, officiant at marriage of son and daughter-in-law of Jacob d'Ancona

**Salomone ben Moise of Colam** rabbi, Cochin

**Samuel Ha-Nagid** (AD 993–1056), Spanish-Jewish vizier of Granada

**Samuel di Nathan of Lucca** partner/investor in voyage

**Sanson Ebreo ben Mose** broker, Cormosa (Hormuz)

**Sara Bonaiuta of Jesi** wife of Jacob d'Ancona

**Sheshet Ha-Levi** merchant, Zara (Zadar)

**Simeon** rabbinical sage

**Simeon ben Azzai** rabbinical sage

**Simeon ben Zoma** rabbinical sage

**Yannai** rabbinical sage

*Chinese*

This list is of Jacob's transliterations of Chinese names into (presumably) their nearest Italian sounds, as they appear in the manuscript, and as he must have heard them. Where they are followed by names in brackets, these are my suggestions in modern spelling (pinyin) as to what they might have been. Where names appear without bracketed alternatives I give the names established from other sources.

**Anfenscian (An Fengshan)** philosopher of Zaitun, 'reputed wise', 'young in years', and identified by Jacob as the 'Adversary' or the 'Evil One' (i.e. Satan)

**Anfesu** ?Han Feizi (*c*. 280–233 BC), a 'legalist' philosopher

**Angati** The 'yellow emperor', probably Huang Di

**Anlisciu (An Lishou)** 'great merchant' of Zaitun, described by Jacob as 'coarse and rough', and also as 'wicked' and 'foolish'

**Anscinen (An Shinian)** 'great merchant' of Zaitun, identified by Jacob as 'messenger of the Adversary'

**Cauiau (Kao Yao)** 'a judge of the City of Light'

**Chun/Chunfutsu** Confucius, Chinese philosopher (551–479 BC)

**Cian (Zhang)** 'sage' of Zaitun, also called by Jacob a 'sophist', consistently hostile to the latter

**Ciancienmin** unidentified

**Cianianmin (Zhang Yanming)** elderly 'sage' of Zaitun, 'master in medicine' and 'counsellor to the noble Pitaco' (q.v.)

**Cianta (Zhang Da)** servant of Nathan ben Dattalo, factor of Zaitun

**Cienciunsu** unidentified

**Cienlian** almost certainly Chen Liang (AD 1147–1194), a political thinker considered by modern scholars to have been a 'pragmatist'

**Cingis Cane** Genghis Khan, Mongol emperor

**Ciumin (Zhou Min)** 'sage' and adviser to Sung emperor, Du Zong

**Ciusi** Zhu Xi (AD 1130–1200), Confucian philosopher

**Gaiudincia (?)** 'sage' and adviser to Sung emperor, Du Zong

**Ianciu** probably Yang Zhu, a figure of Chinese legend

**Iunien (Yun Yan)** 'abbot' of the temple of the Stone Phoenix, near Zaitun

**Latsu** Lao Zi, philosopher, contemporary of Confucius

**Liciancie (Li Zhanqie)** sister of Lifenli (q.v.)

**Lifenli (Li Fenli)** Jacob's guide in Zaitun, son of Guglielmo of Pisa (q.v.)

**Lipo** Li Bai, poet (AD 701–62)

**Lo Hoan (Lou Hean)** Chinese-Jewish rabbi, Zaitun

**Lolichuan (Lou Laiguang)** 'sage' of Zaitun, 'much revered in his learning' and a 'master of great lineage'

**Lotacie (Lo Dadie)** 'a rich and powerful merchant' of Zaitun, 'young in years' and of the defeatist camp

**Luscu** unidentified

**Man** perhaps the emperor Wang Mang (ruled AD 9–23)

**Menche** Mencius, Chinese philosopher of fourth century BC

**Migti** probably Ming Di (ruled AD 58–75), Han emperor

**Oantatte (Huang Dadie)** a 'man of the people' of Zaitun

**Oaou** perhaps the Han emperor Wu Di (140–87 BC)

**Ociuscien (He Zhushen)** a 'great sage' of Zaitun, 'learnèd in various faiths and teachings', and appearing well disposed to Jacob

**Ouaninsci** perhaps Wang Anshih (AD 1021–88), Sung ruler

**Pitaco (Bai Daogu)** elderly former prefect, of whom Jacob generally uses the description 'noble'

**Scipi (Shi Bi)** 'sage' of Zaitun, 'grand master of astronomy'

**Sengsu** probably Zeng Zu, disciple of Confucius

**Sumacien** Sima Qian, Han dynasty historian

**Suninsciou (Sun Yingshou)** 'a great merchant' of Zaitun, 'leader of all the merchants of the city' and 'much feared by reason of his wealth'

**Temucin** Temujin, original name of Genghis Khan, Mongol emperor

**Toufu** Du Fu, poet (AD 712–70)

**Toutson** Du Zong, emperor of Southern Sung dynasty (d. AD 1274)
**Uaiciu (Huai Zhu)** tavern-keeper (?), Zaitun
**Uainsciu (Hua Yingshou)** a 'young man' of Zaitun, described by
Jacob as the 'son of a lord', of egalitarian and other radical views

# Jacob's Language

THE MANUSCRIPT OF JACOB D'ANCONA, as I soon became aware, is a complex amalgam of many linguistic influences and even languages. It is, first, Italian: largely, it seems, Tuscan, but probably with some Venetian usages, especially in the case of proper nouns and word-endings, together with many educated Latinisms. It also has turns of phrase, verbs and other forms which are almost French, or French-Italian. In addition, there is a modest amount of pure Latin, and much Hebrew, as well as a scattering of Arabic and Greek words written in their own scripts. To these must be added curious, and sometimes incomprehensible, transliterated Chinese personal names, place-names and officials' designations, most of the last of which are still unidentified.

In Italian, quite apart from the Latinisms and the 'Franco-Italian' vocabulary, there is a host of arcane terms. Among those which particularly caught my (at first untutored) attention are relative commonplaces, which I choose at random: *duolo*, *doglio*, *duol* – variants of a single word, as I shall show, are themselves a constant feature of the manuscript – for 'grief', *doglioso* for 'grievous', *contrada* (country, region), *loggia* (house), *signoria* (rule), *periglio* (danger), *mastro* (master), *reame* (realm, kingdom), *ospizio* (lodging), *cupidigia* (greed), *piove* (rain), *fe* (faith), *matera* (matter), and *reo* (wicked), the last a word very frequently used by Jacob, sometimes in the sense of 'tainted'. Others are more recondite or unfamiliar: *speglio* for mirror, *negghente* for neglectful, *presto* for priest, *labbia* for face, *corsalo* for pirate, *palagio* for palace, *veneno* for poison, *ariento* for silver, and *naula* for hire. There is *inveggia* for *invidia*; *soprano* for *sovrano*; *manciar* for *mangiare*, *loico* for *logico*, *aitar* for *aiutare*, *archimia* for *alchimia*; and, remoter still from modern usages, *mai* for *mali* (ills, evils), *augelli* for *uccelli* (birds), *lai* for *lagni* (complaints), *fi* for *figli* (sons) and the homely *fazzioli* for beans and *tegghia* for plate. I also became accustomed to *anco* (*anche*) for 'also', *fori* (*fuori*) for 'outside' and *niuno* (*nessuno*) for 'no one'.

Many of the words used by Jacob – including some of those I have mentioned – are recognisable as merely archaic spellings of modern terms; in fact, compared with the differences between, say, Chaucerian and contemporary English, there has, it seems to me, been much less change in vocabulary and even grammar in Italian. Thus Jacob uses *dimando* (for *domando*), *calamaro* (for *calamaio*), *feruta* (for *ferita*), *posta* (for *posto*), *dificio* (for *edificio*), *intrando* (for *entrando*), *cultello* (for *coltello*), *forastieri* (for *forestieri*), *lagrime* (for *lacrime*) and *giudicio* (for *giudizio*), and there are many other similarly modest differences with modern Italian.

Indeed, with certain kinds of words, more analysis discloses patterns of difference. For example, there may be an extra 'i' which distinguishes Jacob's vocabulary from modern usage: *sentenzie* for *sentenze* (sentences), *lievar* for *levare* (to lift), *brieve* for *breve* (brief), *leggiero* for *leggero* (light), *sustanzia* for *sustanza* (substance), *niegar* for *negar* (to deny), *cimiterio* for *cimitero* (cemetery) and others. Conversely, a word may be without an expected 'i': *spirto* for *spirito*, *dritto* for *diritto*, *queto* for *quieto*, *merto* for *merito*, *sentero* for *sentiero*, *pensero* for *pensiero* and others.

Or, there may be an 'i' for an 'e', as in *quistioni* for *questioni*, *discriver* for *descrivere*, *nimico* for *nemico*, *dimoni* for *demoni*, *diserto* for *deserto* and others; or, conversely, an 'e' for an 'i', as in *devoto* for *divoto*, *trestizia* for *tristizia*, *uomeni* for *uomini* or *pre-gioni* for *prigioni*. Or there may be an 'e' for an 'a', as in *greve* for *grave*, *assessino* for *assassino*; or, conversely, *maraviglia* for *mer-aviglia*. There may be a 'u' for an 'o', as in *vagabundo*; or a 'g' for a 'c', as in *dugento* for *duecento*, *lagrima* for *lacrima*, *aguto* for *acuto* and *gastigar* for *castigare*; or, conversely, a 'c' for a 'g', as in *macro* for *magro* and *navicando* for *navigando*.

Clumsily, to our ears, there may also be an extra 'u', as in *pruova* for *prova* (proof), *cuoprono* for *coprono* (they cover), *truovano* for *trovano* (they find); or the familiar 'u' may be absent, as in *mover* for *muovere* (to move), *scola* for *scuola* (school), *rote* for *ruote* (wheels), *cocer* for *cuocere* (to cook), *sonar* for *suonare* (to sound), as well as in *bono, novo, foco* and *voto* for the modern *buono, nuovo, fuoco* and *vuoto*. Confusingly, Jacob also uses inconsistent forms and spellings of the same word at different places in the manuscript, making it clear to us that, as in mediaeval English, spellings were unfixed and therefore inconstant; we have, for example, *cor* and *cuor* (heart), *giovanetta* and *giovinetta* (young woman), *periglio* and *pericolo* (danger), *esempio* and *esemplo* (example), *imprenta* and *impronta* (an impress), and *giudei* and *zudei* (Jews); sometimes these variants of the same word occur within a few lines of one another.

In addition there are numerous unfamiliar inversions of con-sonants in the middle of words, in particular in verbs: Jacob uses *vegnono* for *vengono* (they come), *stringer* for *strignere* (to compress) and *ritegno* for *ritengo* (I maintain). There are also unexpected – and, here and there, incomprehensible – past par-ticiples: *ecceso* (exceeded), *ragunato* (brought together), *onrato* (honoured), *ascoso* (hidden), *soprato* (overcome) and *miso* (sent) were among the oddities I noted. Peculiar, too – so peculiar that I at first thought that they were a quirk of the manuscript hand – were the 'i's which *preceded* certain words, whether nouns, verbs, or adjectives: *isperanza* for *speranza* (hope) – but Jacob also uses *speme* – *istrade* for *strade* (paths), *ignude* for *nude* (naked), *ispezerie* for *spezierie* (spices), *ispirti* for *spiriti* (spirits) and even *ispada* for sword. There are other examples in the manuscript besides.

But of more substantial interest to the historian of Italian etymology and grammar is Jacob's continuous use of the verbal infinitive form, with definite article, in the place of nouns, as in *il voler, l'ordir, il narrar, il cangiar,* and even *il dar,* respectively, the will, the ordering (of), the narration, the change, and the giving (or gift). Thus, 'comprehension' is (sometimes) *il comprender,* 'the search' *il cherer,* 'speech' *il parlar,* 'cure' *il guarir,* 'food' *il mangiar* or *il manicar,* 'life' or 'livelihood' *il viver* and 'selling' *il vender.* Indeed, 'my speech' in Jacob's manuscript is (several times) *il mio parlar,* his choice *suo sceglier* and (more than once) 'their pronouncements' *loro dire.* At the same time, however, Jacob employs an unusually wide range, for mediaeval Italian, of abstract nouns, whether ending in *-ezza* (*pienezza, debilezza, durezza, secchezza,* even *amichezza*), or in *-anza* and *-enza* (*simiglianza, sembianza, conoscenza, parvenza, doglianza*), or in *-mento* (*pensamento, parlamento, nascimento*).

There are also many abstract nouns ending in *-ion* (without the final 'e') – almost three dozen of which I made particular note – which appeared to me to correspond to the Venetian usage. These included *orazion, ragion, cagion, perfezion, profession, oblivion, diluvion, derision, estimazion* and even *proporzion;* there were also dropped 'e's', in the Venetian style, in *baston* (stick), *ordin* (order), *pregion* (prison) and *religion* (bond, tie).

There is a large category in Jacob's writing, too, of Latinised abstract nouns and concepts – the language of the educated man – such as *felicitate* (happiness), *salutate* (safety, health), *bontate* (goodness, bounty), *etate* (generation, era), *pietate* (piety), *civitate* (civic society, as we would say), and *autoritate* (authority). But there are also other Latinisms, among them *turpo* (wicked) – a word much liked by Jacob – *sueti* (accustomed), *patre* (father), *stulto* (stupid), *magno* (large), *nigre* (black), *pulcro* (beautiful), *festino* (rapid, hasty), *milite* (soldier), *delicti* (crimes), *labore* (work), *arbore* (tree), *peregrino* (stranger), *templi* (temples), *apti* (fitted) and *civi* (citizens).

In addition, there are pure Latin words and phrases in the manuscript – as distinct from Latinised Italian terms such as those I have listed – some of which I have identified in the footnotes. Of these there are *contra naturam* (used several times), *rerum natura* (used twice), *res publica, in actu, proprium, prudentia politica*, and *spelunca latronum* (lair of thieves); together with a recourse to Latin (*inter crura, mentula, labra* and other words) in the libertine passages of sexual description.

Yet, typical of Jacob's style and remote from such learning, are rather raffish Italian abbreviations, *'n* for *un, 'na* for *una, 'l* for *il, de'* for *dei* and *degli*, and others. There are in addition many phrases – *suso e giuso* (up and down), *quinci e quindi* (here and there), *di 'verno e di state* (in winter and summer), *al merigge* (at noon) immediately come to mind – which sound to an inexpert like the 'common' usages of everyday speech. There are also many elisions of word-endings, apart from the 'Venetian' ones already mentioned, which give a vernacular kind of speed, that of spoken rather than written speech, to Jacob's prose. Instead of *il bene e il male* (the good and the ill) – that standard couplet of Italian manichaean thought, ancient and modern – we have *'l ben e 'l mal; il cuore buono*, the good heart, is *'l cor bon*. In the same way, with Jacob's grander nouns, there are *poder, amor, piacer, dover, valor, splendor, favor, error, onor, romor* (for *rumore*) and *mar* (for *mare*), and many others.

These are words which 'should' end in 'e', but whose elision is easy and was certainly common in his time. But Jacob often also removes 'o' endings, to give *fren, titol, vincol, cammin, piccol, uom, vassel, ver* (for *vero*), *ciel*; there is *lor* for *loro*, and in the same spirit of abbreviation, *gran* for *grande, vergogn'* for *vergogna* (shame), *vicin* (for *vicino*), *son* (for *sono*) and even *han* for *hanno*.

It is here that one sometimes feels that one is reading French, or a Franco-Italian dialect, as I indicated above, in which the modern boundary between the languages barely seems to exist. Jacob's habit of elision carries us part of the way: *gentile* becoming *gentil, male* being *mal*, or *bestiale* becoming *bestial* in the manuscript, also turn into, or may be read as, 'French'. *Sanza*, in Jacob's frequent usage for 'without', is close to the French *'sans'*; *secreto* (rather than *segreto*) to French *'secret'*; *sovente* (often) to *'souvent'*; *om* to *'homme'*; *la dimane* (tomorrow) to *'demain'*; *pien* (full) to *'plein'*. Jacob's *tien*, rather than *tiene*, seems more 'French' than 'Italian'; so, too, do *egale* and *egal* (equal), used by Jacob for *uguale*, or *sol* (sun) for *sole*, or *pan* (bread) for *pane*, or *pie* (feet) for *piedi*. Indeed, there are very many of these usages in which the abbreviations and contractions employed by Jacob point up the commonality of the two languages in his time. He writes *al fin* (at the end); while *ver* and *inver* (towards) sound like, and are, the French *vers* and *envers*. When Jacob abbreviates *mani* (hands) to *man*, we can hear the French *mains*; when, for *regine* (queens), Jacob uses *reine* the languages are almost one.

As to Jacob's technical vocabulary, as I would call it – the languages of the sea, of the merchant, of the (?) medical collector of simples – there is a great deal to interest the scholar. He was no mariner himself (some of his terms and descriptions are plainly those of a landlubber), but he is precise about wind-directions and the geographical or compass direction taken by his vessels. Winds are, for example, *al maestro* (from the north-west), *alla tramontana* (from the north), *al ponente* (from the west), *al mezzodi* (from the south) and *al gherbino* (from the south-west). The north-east wind he calls *'l vento greco*, and the north-west wind *vento maestro*; he speaks, almost colloquially, and briefly as if to the nautical manner born, of voyaging *per gorbi* (towards the south-west), as well as, a little more formally, *verso isciroc* (towards the south-east). He is also generally careful: his vessel travels *verso levante e sciroc* (east-south-east), or *verso greco e levante* (east-north-east), and in most, but not all, cases, these directions can be squared with the map and the routes he tells us he was taking.

He seems, however, much less expert and is less detailed about the nature and parts of his vessels, although there are numerous enough words which relate to them. He refers to decks as *ponti*, to *prora e poppa* (prow and stern), and to *orza e poggia* (leeward and windward). His vessel makes its 'way' (*passaggio*) 'by sail and oar' (*a vela e a remi*), it is carrying a *buxida* (compass), he calls his captain both *mastro* and *ammiralio*; the ballast (*zavorra*) shifts in a storm. Yet there are other terms which are those of the landsman: 'calm water' Jacob timidly calls *acqua piccola*, and a heavy swell is *acqua grande*. He fears the *rottura*, or breach, of his vessel; to embark is, for Jacob, awkwardly, to 'enter' (*entrare*) the vessel, and to disembark from it merely to 'leave' (*uscire*).

In matters of commerce, his vocabulary is generally reticent as to profits and accounting methods but (characteristically) more detailed on taxes, percentages and imposts, although some of the words here are obscure or untranslatable. He variously pays *il quarantenum* (?2.5 per cent), *il decimo*, *il quindecimo* and *il ventesimo*. He weighs his purchases ounce by ounce (*oncia a oncia*); he purchases for an object's weight in gold or silver (*a peso d'oro, a peso d'ariento*); he pays cheaply (*a denari piccoli*); he makes large profits (*grandi guadagni* or *avanzi*). He also gives and gets discounts (*sconti*); gold besants (*bisanti d'oro*) are carried in purses (*borse* and *tasche*); he visits his trading-posts (*fondachi*) and treats, or quarrels, with agent (*commisso*) and factor (*fattor*). There are references to taxes and dues, to gains and losses, to revenues and net income, as well as to the keeping of accounts 'in a large volume' by his chief clerk Armentuzio; but Jacob is, frustratingly, too secretive (it seems) to go into business detail.

However, in the matter of his actual purchases – the cloths (*nacchi, cammucche, maramate, zituni, bucherame* and others), the spices, the medicaments, the incenses – there is a wealth of words, some obscure, others familiar, many of which are detailed in the footnotes and glossary. His medical terms, which interestingly include *parlassia* (paralysis), *tisi* (?tuberculosis), *idropsesi* (dropsy), *livore* (?anaemia), *la terzana* and *la quartana* (?malaria), contain a variety of terms for different parts of the anatomy, from the gums to the genitalia, some in Latin, as well as a rich array of words for herbs and simples bought en route.

The Hebrew words, epithets and (usually brief) Biblical and Talmudic passages are very numerous. Indeed, some of the epithets, such as 'God be praised', 'peace upon them' and so on, are continuously repeated. Most of these have been cut, but still many remain, since the translation would in my judgment have lost some of its particular character without them. A considerable number of the Biblical and rabbinical references remain unidentified; where, with help, they have been located, as for example in the Pentateuch or the Mishnah, I have tried to use existing authorised translations.

Jacob very consistently uses Hebrew terms (in Hebrew script) for the names of the Sabbaths, the Jewish Festivals and the names of Jewish prayers, for the names of the months according to the Jewish calendar (see Glossary), for the names of Jewish sages and rabbis, and for the names of relatives and fellow Jewish merchants – some of these latter being in part, as with their places of belonging or origin in Italy, transliterated from Italian into Hebrew script. But he also almost invariably uses Hebrew and Hebrew script for particular words: as for all appellations of God (save in one place), as well as for Torah, Messiah, Gehenna, synagogue, Ark, king – an oddity, but it is almost always *melech* – Moses, Covenant, gentile, chaos, Egypt, scoffers, marriage (and the wedding canopy), circumcision, divorce, phylacteries, the ram's horn and (more obviously) Amen, which appears frequently. When the generic words 'sage' and 'sages' refer to Jews, he uses (in Hebrew script) *haham* and *hahamim*; but for non-Jews he uses the words *savio* or *saggio*, and *savi* or *saggi*.

Many repeated phrases of Jewish significance are also almost invariably written in Hebrew in the manuscript. They include those which refer to God (God's wrath, the bounty of God, the truth of God, the glory of God, the word of God, the law of God) and to the Torah (Torah truth, Torah law, Torah wisdom, the lamp of the Torah). In addition, the phrases 'the Holy Land', 'a Haman', the Book of Forgiveness, the Angel of Death, 'our Exile', the Children (or Sons) of Israel, the Evil One (or Adversary), 'at the End of Days', and (twice) the City of Light are in Hebrew.

Invocations and imprecations, some of them elaborate, are also almost always in Hebrew. The simplest invocations, such as 'God willing' and 'God forbid', 'peace upon him/them' and 'blessèd be He', 'God rest his soul' and 'may God forgive me', are ubiquitous, always in Hebrew, and sometimes (disconcertingly) abbreviated to one or two Hebrew letters. God (most frequently termed 'the Holy One') is blessed, praised, thanked, honoured, cherished, magnified, revered and exalted, sometimes 'for evermore': often without mention of the grounds, but sometimes for His bounty, for the 'gift of the Torah' and even, declares Jacob, speaking of himself, 'for my valour' and 'for my strength'! God is also asked to aid, to forgive, to have mercy, to have pity, to 'keep us', or to 'keep His people' and to 'spare us ... trial'. For himself, Jacob asks (always in Hebrew) that God should shield him, spare him for his faults, keep him in His hand, and (several times) forgive him for the writing of certain passages in his manuscript. For others, he prays to God that they be kept in health, that their lives be protected, that their memories and names be blessed, 'known', or recorded, that they rest in Heaven or Eden, and that their souls endure or are redeemed. For the Jews as a whole, he prays, again in Hebrew, that 'the Temple of Jerusalem be rebuilt in our days'.

Conversely, his imprecations – or curses – are equally energetic and sometimes terrifying; 'may God punish them' is the mildest. Sometimes, the mere mention of a foe, or other object of odium, earns the epithet '... whom God strike down'. 'May God's curses fall upon them', 'may God shorten his life', 'may his name be erased', 'may his memory be cancelled', 'may God strike him down at the last day', and (of the wicked Haman) 'may God have cast him into Gehinnom and have destroyed his soul' are cries which still have the force to reach us. But, sometimes, words fail even Jacob: in recall of grief or in despair, he writes 'oh', 'ohime', 'oh me', 'ahime', 'ahme' and 'ahi', and cancels the distance between us.

# Notes and References

CHAPTER 1

1. For example, F. Wood, *Did Marco Polo go to China?*, London, 1995.

2. There is also a reference, dating from 1254, in the city archives of Dubrovnik (Ragusa) to a certain 'Antonio Bonaiunte', described as a 'merchant of Ancona', J.F. Leonhard, *Ancona nel basso Medio Evo*, Ancona, 1992, p.288 fn.

3. G. Luzzatto, *I Banchieri Ebrei in Urbino nell'Età Ducale*, Padova, 1902 (reprint 1983), p.59. I am grateful to Dr Lauro Guidi of Urbino for this reference.

4. Averroes, or Ibn Roschd, was born in Cordoba in 1126 and died in Morocco in 1198. An Arab philosopher and physician, his commentaries on Aristotle had a great influence on Western Christian thought. He was also accused of having abandoned Islam.

5. Avicenna (980–1037), of Ibn Sina, Persian in origin, was born in Bokhara and was a philosopher and physician. He is known for his works on medicine and for his philosophical encyclopaedia. He combined Aristotelianism with a version of neo-Platonic thought.

6. See M. and L. Moranti, *Il Trasferimento dei 'Codices Urbinates' alla biblioteca Vaticana*, Urbino, 1981, in which the whole tale of the inventory and the disappearances of books is told. I am grateful to Maria Luisa Moscati Benigni of Urbino for this reference.

7. *La Vita di Alessandro VII*, Prato, 1839, vol.2, p.185.

8. Other mediaeval travellers to China who left accounts of their journeys include the Japanese monk Jojun (1011–81); Rubruquis, who reached the Karakoram mountains in 1253; the Armenian Hetoum (or Hayton), who was in China in 1307; and the German knight, William of Boldensele, who was in the Orient in 1336.

CHAPTER 2

1. See S.D. Goitein, *Letters of Medieval Jewish Traders*, Princeton, 1973, p.270; the hoard was discovered in the 1890s.

2. See S.D. Goitein, on both Jewish and Muslim merchants in mediaeval Cairo: 'The learnèd middle-class merchant' was a 'rather common phenomenon', *op.cit.*, p.9, and 'some were scholars', *ibid.*

3. J.F. Leonhard, *op.cit.*, p.15.

4. *Ibid.*, p.193.

5. From the tenth century, the Holy Roman Empire was formally in the hands of the ruling dynasties of Germany. As titular rulers of their Italian kingdoms (and crowned as emperors by successive popes), they claimed rights – expressly granted them in 1153 – over the increasingly independent-minded Italian city-states, periodically going to war in Italy, including against the papal armies, in order to assert them.

6. Such 'colonies' of foreign citizens generally had their own quarter, church, shops and warehouses.

7. J.F. Leonhard, *op.cit.*, p.72 fn.

8. 'Since Jews were in fact better educated, more cultivated and more skilful than their Christian counterparts, legend must reduce them below the level of common humanity, filthy in their persons and debased in their passions, menacing Christian society from below, requiring the help of the powers of darkness to work evil far beyond their own contemptible capacities', R.I. Moore, *The Formation of a Persecuting Society, 950–1250*, Oxford, 1987, pp.151–2.

9. There were known to have been Jews in Rome in 160 BC, over 200 years before the fall of Jerusalem to Titus in AD 70. Jewish 'elders in Rome' are also cited as authoritative interpreters of Jewish law in the Mishnah, a compilation of decisions on legal and ritual questions dating back to a period between the second century BC and second century AD, Abodah Zerah, 4:7.

10. Some modern scholars, such as Noël Coulet, argue that the Jews of mediaeval Provence – whose position and long settlement made their condition analogous to that of the Jews of Italy – held genuine citizenship, seemingly with the same privileges and liberties as Christians (*Minorités et Marginaux en Espagne et dans le Midi de la France, VIIe–XVIIIe siècles*, Paris, 1986, pp.203–19). But so far as I am aware there is no direct evidence for Jewish citizenship under law in mediaeval Italy. Of the Jews of Ancona, Jacob in his manuscript says that some are 'both noble and rich'. This surely cannot mean noble by birth – but rather noble in dignity and style, or in learning – for he also distinguishes between 'the nobles of the city' and 'my brothers', or co-religionists. He also declares specifically that the Jews are not among 'the principal citizens', who in the thirteenth century would have chosen the city's consuls; whether the Jews were, nevertheless, *full citizens*, albeit of lesser

rank, he unfortunately does not say. It is most unlikely that they were.

11. Rabbi Benjamin of Tudela in the twelfth century found Jews even in the papal entourage. A certain Jehiel, whom he describes as 'a handsome young man, wise and prudent', was the pope's domestic administrator, *Travels*, London, 1783, p.44.

12. A. Milano, *Storia degli Ebrei in Italia*, Torino, 1963, p.127.

13. The name is still found scattered throughout the Mediterranean – colonies of Ancona merchants were widely settled in the middle ages – and it is probable that most of those who carry such a surname of provenance were originally Jews.

14. J.F. Leonhard, *op.cit.*, p.219 fn.

15. Described in the papal correspondence as 'goods useful to the infidels', Leonhard, *ibid.*, p.277.

16. Mediaeval Lucca was an important centre of the cloth and silk trades, and Camerino, a hill-top town in the southern Marches, had notable trade relations in the middle ages with Ancona, which served Camerino as the port of embarkation for the export of its wares to southern Italy and the Levant. There were significant communities of Jews in both Lucca and Camerino in the mediaeval period. Samuele di Nathan and Levi di Abramo would doubtless have been wealthy merchants who financed expensive overseas undertakings such as Jacob's, not only in return for a share in the profits, but probably also to obtain particular goods at a favourable price.

17. 'Gualdi' is not a Jewish name. Although such Jewish-Christian collaborations in sea-going ventures do not appear to be recorded, there are records of banks and loan-companies in which Tuscans (especially Florentines) and Jews were partners. For central Italy at the end of the thirteenth century they have been identified at Montegiorgio in 1295 and Ascoli Piceno in 1297.

18. H. Pirenne, *Economic and Social History of Medieval Europe*, London, 1947, p.11.

19. R. Lopez, *The Commercial Revolution of the Middle Ages, 950–1350*, Cambridge, 1976, p.60.

20. H. Pirenne, *op.cit.*, pp.47, 50, 94, 166.

21. *Ibid.*, p.214.

22. S.D. Goitein, *op.cit.*, p.184.

23. See, for example, C. Roth, *A Short History of the Jewish People*, where he asserts that 'obstacles were everywhere put in the way' of the Jewish merchant, pp.203–4.

24. J. Gernet, *A History of Chinese Civilization*, Cambridge, 1985, p.327.

25. i.e. by the Jewish calendar.

26. See p.455 for this and other months of the Jewish calendar.

27. Jacob refers several times in the manuscript to his *legnaggio rabbinico nobile*, which can only mean that he was descended from a distinguished

line of rabbinical sages and takes pride in it.

28. These 'misdeeds' might have included the failure to repay loans made to the Church by the d'Ancona family. Cardinal Simone was legate in Ancona from 1266 under the papacy of Clement IV; Cardinals Raniero (or Rainer) and Capocci di San Giorgio in Velabro were previous legates. The 'recompense' appears from the manuscript to have involved a (possibly secret) church partnership in Jacob's voyage; see also pp.48, 129.

29. The monastery of Santa Croce di Fonte Avellana is some fifty miles from Ancona.

30. 'Sinim' is written in Hebrew characters throughout the manuscript.

31. This can only mean 'un-kosher' food.

32. This is presumably a reference to a local contemporary rabbi who evidently practised the superstitious Jewish tradition of giving Jacob a coin as a kind of talisman, or protection, against misfortune; a tradition that continues among Jews to the present day.

33. Slaves appear to have been mostly employed in mediaeval times in domestic service and in galleys; economic historians have described the trade as having been prevalent in Venice in Jacob's period. The manuscript employs the female plural, *schiave*.

34. A port on the Sea of Azov.

35. A factor buys and sells for another; see p.73.

36. Such agents, *commissi* in the original Italian, acted on a commission basis as representatives for the overseas merchant; see pp.72–4.

37. Zadar, now in Croatia. In an agreement of March 1258, signed in Ancona, it was provided that the merchants of Ancona and Zara (Zadar) should be reciprocally exempted from dues and taxes. Ties between the two ports were therefore close. Zara was also united with Ancona in hostility to Venice.

38. MS. *nostro filo d'oro*; probably used in embroidery.

39. See p.34; it is noteworthy that Jacob affixes the honorific *Ser* (sire) to the Gentile names only.

40. Probably a Jewish shipowner, who would have hired out vessels, including armed vessels, for the dangerous journey to San Giovanni d'Acri (Acre); chartering appears to have cost less in Zadar, whose shipbuilders were known for their skills, than in Ancona.

41. The island of Korcula.

42. This passage, with many others which make reference to Talmudic texts, is persuasive (although not final) evidence of Jacob being a rabbi by training. It is close to Erubin, 4:1 of the Mishnah, or Oral Law; a passage particularly notable for the proof it contains of a pre-Christian Jewish presence in Italy.

43. 26 April 1270.

44. 'Brother' appears to signify co-religionist.

45. Presumably Leo ben Benedetto of Ragusa.

46. A particular honour in the Sabbath service.

47. 18 May 1270. 'The day of Lag Ba-Omer' (Hebrew in original) is the day of the Scholars' Feast, observed in memory of the ending of an attack of plague among the students of the sage Akiba (c. AD 50–132).

48. The islands of Karpathos and Rhodes.

49. Perhaps the Samuel di Nathan of Lucca referred to on p.40 as a shareholder in the voyage; Lucca was an important mediaeval centre for high-quality cloth.

50. A Christian possession in the eastern Mediterranean from 1104, Acre (San Giovanni d'Acri) was reconquered by Saladin in 1187, and retaken by Crusaders under Richard Coeur de Lion in 1191.

51. This is probably a reference to a quarrel which had broken out in 1255 between the Venetian and Genoese colonies in Acre, over the ownership of a church which stood on the boundary between the two communities. In the ensuing fighting, which drew in others, a large part of Acre was destroyed.

52. MS. *maomettani*; Jacob appears to use 'Saracen' and 'Mahometan' (Muslim) interchangeably, although when he uses the latter term he is plainly thinking of them less as a people, or constellation of peoples, than as a religious community.

53. 'Lesser India' (*India minore*) broadly seems to have covered the area of Sumatra, Malaya, Thailand and Indo-China, or Vietnam and Cambodia.

54. MS. *volume magno*; presumably an account-book, or ledger, kept by his clerk.

55. Arabic in MS.; a letter of credit issued by one party – in this case Jacob – to be used by the bearer, here his uncle Elia, in order to collect payment from a party, or parties, elsewhere, in this case Ragusa and Ancona, who would have held funds belonging to the issuer.

56. Here the word *arabi* in the manuscript seems to signify Bedouins.

57. Equivalent to some 125 kg, which was the weight of, say, two adult persons.

58. A Venetian palm measured ten inches.

59. This would have been out of respect for the Sabbath prohibition.

60. In fact, the Tartars invaded northern Syria in the following year, the Mameluke Sultan Bundukdar, who ruled from 1259 to 1276, arriving in Damascus in September 1271. The information given to Jacob was exact enough, since the Sultan's policy was indeed to drive the Christians, as well as the Tartars, out of Syria.

61. Baghdad.

62. I take this to be the river or *wadi* Hauran, a little over halfway to Baghdad and approaching the eastern edge of the Syrian desert.

63. The name of a Babylonian deity; given to the day on which the Jews commemorate the breaking down of the wall of Jerusalem by Nebuchadnezzar.

64. The Fall of the First and Second Temples is mourned on the ninth day of Av; in his description of his own mourning, Jacob uses phrases, written in Hebrew in the manuscript, which are taken from Jeremiah 1:1,3,6 and 12. Readings from Jeremiah are made in the synagogue on this day.

65. That is in thirty-seven days from Damascus, giving a rate of some twenty miles per day.

66. Basra, which Jacob variously calls Bastra, Bassora and al-Basra – when the word is written in Arabic in the manuscript – was founded in AD 638 by the caliph Omar. It reached its greatest splendour under the Abassids. Although it went into decline following Bedouin incursions, it remained an important port of access in mediaeval times to the Persian Gulf, India and the Far East.

67. I cannot translate these terms, which presumably refer to varieties of brocade.

68. Originating from Ascoli Piceno in the Marche, he is likely to have been personally known to Jacob, and may have been a relative.

69. This is a title of honour.

70. As distinct from arbitrary and variable.

71. MS. *quarantenum*; 2.5 per cent of the value of imported merchandise was a low rate, since merchants could pay up to 10 per cent, and even beyond, on selected items. It is probable that the items which Jacob says he secreted about his person would not have been declared.

72. This phrase perhaps furnishes evidence that Jacob had had some form of medical training, although the precise ingredients of a salve for mosquito bites might well have been known to many.

73. MS. *il novilunio verso l'equinozio d'autumno*.

74. i.e. daughter-in-law.

75. In memory of the destruction of the Temple, as well as to signify the frailty of all things, happiness included.

76. Isaia of Ascoli thus joined the partnership already established, but the proportion of his share is not specified.

77. Diminutive of Iacobbe.

## CHAPTER 3

1. The equivalent of between 400 and 500 tons.

2. This (together with the other details) may be an exaggeration but Friar Odoric (see pp.9, 11) claimed that the vessel in which he sailed to China had '700' persons on board.

3. Perhaps the rarer spices.

4. These dates can be precisely fixed at 2–11 October 1270; also see Glossary.

5. This is probably a reference to the Talmudic injunction that a husband must have sexual intercourse with his wife at least once every six months.

6. MS. *nell'agonia mortale della quartana.* This is generally regarded as malaria, but the term was also used by mediaeval doctors for unspecific fevers; *quartana* merely means that the fever returned every four days. The trembling of Berletto's legs, which Jacob notes, suggests that it may have been malaria, while the speed of his death suggests some other cause.

7. MS. *perdei li polsi.* The taking of the pulses and the examining of Berletto's eyes and tongue by Jacob are the clearest evidence furnished by the manuscript of his medical knowledge.

8. This indicates that Jacob himself spoke Persian, a *lingua franca* among merchants trading in the East.

9. Haman, an official at the court of King Ahasuerus of Persia, sought to massacre the local Jews from motives of injured pride, but was thwarted by the (Jewish) queen, Esther.

10. There is no philological ground for relating *corano* in this place-name to the Koran, as Jacob appears to be doing here ('Kesmacoran' is now the area of Makran, which straddles Iran and Pakistan, and reaches to the Indus delta and modern Karachi).

11. Probably the port which stood near the mediaeval city of Kij in Makran.

12. This is an exaggeration by Jacob, since, judging from the chronological information, it could not have been more than four or five days at most.

13. Musk, extracted from the musk deer of the Himalayas, and used in mediaeval times as a medicine both in the Orient and in Italy, must have been brought to these ports of Persia through Afghanistan.

14. That is, from Kashmir, and clearly a reference to sables.

15. Kashmir, which Jacob calls variously Chesimur and Chesimuro, was held by the Tartars under Kajjala from 1259 to 1287.

16. 8 November 1270.

17. This wish for death, written in Hebrew, but a blasphemy for the pious Jew, has been partially scratched out in the manuscript, but remains legible.

18. Simone Pizzecolli, second clerk.

19. This is an interesting allusion to what appears to have been a Jewish merchant guild in Cambay, which would have had rules and sanctions against mercantile misconduct.

20. That is, 5 feet or 1.5 metres wide.

21. I cannot trace the meanings of *custo* and *kino*. Mirobalans are astringent plum-like fruits once used in dried form both as a medicine for intestinal troubles, and in dyeing, tanning and ink-making. They were much prized in mediaeval times. Jacob later administers a concoction of it to his servant Buccazuppo.

22. MS. *lo indo*; I have translated this as 'Indian', but it may be intended by Jacob in the sense of Hindu.

23. The cubeb is a spicy berry that was used in mediaeval times among other

things as an antiseptic, especially for infections of the genito-urinary tract – including venereal infections – and for other intestinal troubles. It was also used as a spice in mediaeval cooking, being called 'cubeb pepper'.

24. I cannot identify this.

25. It is not clear what this means, but Jacob must surely have made landfall at other places between Cambay and Mangalore.

26. This is likely to have been Mount Delly, north of today's Cannanore in the Indian state of Karnataka.

27. The name has been changed and over-written in the manuscript so that it is barely legible. It is however identifiable from the content of the passage as being Cranganore, or Cochin, in the state of Kerala, which from the most ancient times was a place of substantial Jewish settlement. The Sabbath Vayeshev can be precisely dated to 6 December 1270.

28. From other indications in the manuscript, this may refer to differences upon matters of Jewish observance.

29. The Festival of Dedication, instituted in 165 BC, commemorates the purification of the Jewish sanctuary after it had been defiled by Antiochus Epiphanes.

30. This is almost (but not quite) decisive evidence that Jacob was a rabbi, since it is highly unlikely that his guidance on difficult Torah questions would have been sought if he was *not* a rabbi, especially in circumstances where the local congregation had a rabbi of its own. Nevertheless, nowhere does Jacob declare himself in terms to be such, referring only, as here, to his 'lineage'.

31. Presumably so that he does not have to carry its weight in his hands, which would fall foul of the prohibition upon Sabbath work.

32. This is equivalent to 500 kg, or half a ton, a very substantial amount which gives a good indication of the scale of Jacob's buying.

33. Quilon, or Kollam, 100 km north-west of Cape Comorin, the southern tip of India, was one of the great ports and markets of Asia in the middle ages.

34. Men of priestly descent.

35. This word (for Ceylon) has been over-written in the manuscript by a seemingly different hand; the word beneath cannot be deciphered.

36. The word here is either *pere* (pears) or *perle* (pearls), and is almost illegible. I chose 'pears', since Jacob is speaking of songbirds and trees.

37. MS. *vanno tutti ignudi*; although these are masculine plurals, it is unclear whether Jacob is referring to men alone.

38. 'Paccambou' is an accurate enough version of Prakrama Bahu who ruled Ceylon from 1267 to 1301; Sundara is plainly the Hindu name of a princeling engaged in war with the Buddhist 'Seilani' of the south of the island.

39. Oil of turpeth was an emetic used in mediaeval medicine, and made from a plant found in Ceylon and elsewhere. Ser Bartolomeo was probably an apothecary.

40. Jacob draws a veil over the details of the transaction.

41. Batticaloa, on the east coast of Ceylon.

42. That is, Sakya-muni, or the Buddha.

43. This is arguably one of the grandest, and most succinct, mediaeval expressions of Aristotelianism, and shows (among other things) the influence upon Jacob of the teachings of Maimonides and his followers.

44. This can be dated to 24 January 1271.

45. That is about three feet, or 90 cm.

46. There is the unusual suggestion here that Jacob thinks it is the 'Jewish God' who will save her.

47. It will be recalled that the vessel had, according to Jacob, four masts and twelve sails, together with two other masts 'which they raise and place in position'.

48. Presumably the two smaller vessels accompanying the main boat.

49. The Jewish mourner's prayer, which is basically a prayer for the speedy coming of the Messianic era and the recognition of God's supremacy throughout the world.

50. The thinly disguised implication is that the 'great Aaron', who had earlier shown lack of complete fidelity, by Jacob's standards, to Torah rule, was 'wicked', an 'evil-doer'.

51. The name of a province in north-west Sumatra, although Jacob seems to think it the name of the port; Jacob gives no identifiable name to the port that offered shelter from the north-east winds, and, it seems, the means for ship-repair. It might have been Daya.

52. Sarha was on the north-east coast of Sumatra, since Jacob says that it is close to 'Sumantala', or Samarlanga, the capital. However, to move from Daya round the headland of north-west Sumatra in order to moor at Sumantala must have been a dangerous undertaking, but was presumably necessary for the re-fitting and re-victualling of the vessels.

53. This fell on 28 March 1271.

54. A region of Sumatra, south of Lambri.

55. Equivalent to 60 kg.

56. Equivalent to 500 kg, or half a ton, of cloves and 1000 kg, or a ton, of pepper, which seem very large quantities.

57. Hebrew in MS.; Efraim, who perhaps spoke to Jacob in Hebrew (for concealment) on the occasion which Jacob describes, has quoted from Psalms 38:13.

58. This suggests that Jacob had given him an *extra* 5 per cent on a standard agent's commission, a rate which was perhaps controlled by a local merchants' confraternity.

59. MS. *del gherbino*; the south-west monsoon had come, giving the fleet a

favourable but turbulent wind at their backs for the run to southern China.

60. These would probably be the islands of the archipelago at the southern end of the Malacca strait, off Sumatra and Singapore. But Jacob's remark may also refer to the Celebes and Moluccas, of which the sailors might have spoken.

61. This may refer to a port in today's Malaysia, or was perhaps further north in Thailand.

62. This is the island of Poulo Condore, off the southern coast of today's Vietnam.

63. MS. *fini*; this word is ambiguous, meaning both 'limits' and 'purposes'.

64. Religious duty, or bounds commanded by the word of God.

65. 20 June and 27 June 1271, respectively.

66. 'Zabai' cannot be identified, but Ciamba (or Chamba) – which is related to the modern word for Cambodia – appears to have been part of today's Vietnam. 'Comari' is perhaps the Khmers.

67. 15 August 1271.

## CHAPTER 4

1. H. Yule and H. Cordier (eds), *The Travels of Marco Polo*, New York, 1993 (reprint of 1903 edition), vol. 2, p.234.

2. This is *double* the figure for the estimated population of China in the eighth century, the outcome of growths in food production, economic expansion and urban agglomeration.

3. J. Gernet, *Daily Life in China on the Eve of the Mongol Invasion 1250–76*, London, 1962, p.17.

4. Cf. Bishop Andrea di Perugia, the Franciscan bishop of Zaitun from 1322, who in 1326 commented on the multiplicity of 'cults and sects' in the city in letters home to his superiors, *Sinica Franciscana*, ed. A. van den Wyngaert, Florence, 1929, vol. 1, p.376.

5. Also see J. Gernet, *A History of Chinese Civilization*, p.376.

6. 'The Chinese cities, unlike cities in medieval Europe, were centers of bureaucratic administration under the firm control of the [sc. Sung] emperor, not autonomous centers of power for the burghers,' W.W. Lo, *An Introduction to the Civil Service of Sung China*, University of Hawaii Press, Honolulu, 1987, p.1. Similarly, Gernet declares that 'in spite of the gigantic scale of development, nothing more happened than that merchants became wealthy', *op.cit.*, p.61, and that 'social relations imposed by custom, moral code and laws' made 'all emancipation of individuals and of social groups radically impossible', *ibid.*, p.62. The d'Ancona manuscript shows that this was not so.

7. R.P. Hymes and C. Schirokauer, *Ordering the World: Approaches to State and Society in Sung Dynasty China*, Berkeley, 1993, p.1.

8. *Ibid.*, p.19.

9. *Ibid.*, p.20.

10. J. Gernet, *Daily Life in China, op. cit.,* pp.16–17.

11. Gernet writes that 'under the Sung, desperate battles were waged between the partisans of armed intervention against the Barbarians and the partisans of the policy of paying for peace by offering tribute ... the violence of the conflicts which occurred within government circles was one of the novelties of the period', *A History of Chinese Civilization*, p.63; a view amply confirmed by the d'Ancona manuscript.

12. For contemporary descriptions of the city of Zaitun, see H. Yule and H. Cordier (eds), *The Travels of Marco Polo,* New York, 1993 (reprint of 1903 edition, with additions), vol. 2, pp. 237 ff., which also contains a discussion of the location of Zaitun.

13. Hebrew in MS.; literally 'of the light'.

14. This word is almost illegible and is scored over in the manuscript; with the help of Shu-ching Naughton, of the Bodleian Library, Oxford, to whom I am grateful, I have hazarded the version I give, which would be near to *guangmang zhi cheng*, the 'City of Light'.

15. Huang He, the Yellow River.

16. I presume that this again signifies 'co-religionist' rather than blood-relation. However, his provenance from Sinigaglia (Senigallia), which is on the Adriatic coast north of Ancona, makes familial relationship a distinct possibility; that Jacob should have been given lodging by him for so many months, together with his two servants, perhaps strengthens the possibility.

17. Probably today's Guangzhou.

18. Perhaps today's Siberia or Russia.

19. MS. *una città e un porto in stato franco.*

20. I take this to mean the regions of northern China, also called 'Cathay' by foreign travellers, which had already fallen under Tartar rule.

21. MS. *inghilesi.*

22. Or, 'great China'.

23. That is, Kublai Khan, who ruled northern China from 1260; he was about fifty-five in 1271.

24. Du Zong (d. 1274), the Sung emperor of southern China at the time of Jacob's visit.

25. That is, Shangdu ('upper court'), more familiarly transliterated as Xanadu, where Kublai Khan had his court until the completion of the building of Khanbalik (Beijing).

26. Jacob's version of Kinshe, or Kinsai, the modern Hangzhou, capital of the Southern Sung empire at the time of his visit.

27. That is, the more familiar Genghis Khan. Jacob calls him a blacksmith, but I cannot trace the origin of this assertion.

28. If, as I presume, this is the *'rettore* Simone' referred to on the first page of the manuscript, the use of the name here without title or honorific

suggests considerable familiarity between them. There is also a remote indication in this passage that Jacob may have had an undisclosed diplomatic mission.

29. There is, however, no evidence in the manuscript that Jacob had personal contact with the Tartars while in China.

30. The Tartar invasion of Bohemia occurred *c.* 1241–2.

31. MS. *non avendo addosso pelo niuno salvo che nel capo e nella natura.*

32. I have found no reference to the existence of a Jewish synagogue in Zaitun. It is known, however, that Zaitun possessed a mosque – to which Jacob later refers – built in 1009, and is considered to have been one of the major centres of Islam in China, F. Wood, *Did Marco Polo go to China?*, London, 1995, p.94.

33. This must mean Hebrew.

34. Presumably other *Italian* Jews, although that there could have been 'many hundreds in the city' is entirely unlikely.

35. This must mean the type of Chinese Jews mentioned earlier as having their own synagogue and rite in Zaitun.

36. The whole of this sentence is in Hebrew in the manuscript. The texts of the four *Books of the Maccabees* which we now have are in Greek, the Semitic originals having been lost. They are an historical account of the period from Alexander's conquest of Asia (332 BC) to the death of the Hasmonean ruler Simon (135 BC) and chronicle the wars and other struggles of the Jews. The passage cannot be credited; indeed it is credulous in the extreme for Jacob to have believed it. *The Wisdom of Jesus the son of Sirach* (or *Ecclesiasticus*), whose author was known to the Talmud as Ben Sira (fl. 200 BC), was extant in its Hebrew original until the tenth century, but was then lost until the end of the nineteenth century, when about two-thirds of it was rediscovered in the Cairo Genizah hoard. It is not wholly out of the question that a copy of the Hebrew manuscript of this work might have found its way to China in the middle ages, or earlier, but it is very hard to credit, despite Jacob's assertion.

37. This is accurate; the rebel Bae-choo carried out a massacre of settlers and those of minority religions in Guangzhou in AD 877. See J. Finn, *The Jews in China*, London, 1843, pp.61–2, which confirms the accuracy of Jacob's reference to 'one Baiciu'. The full passage in Finn's work reads: 'A solitary glimpse into their [i.e. the Jews'] middle-age history is found in an account of India and China, *by two Mohammedan travellers of our ninth century* [my emphasis], who describe a rebel, named Bae-choo, taking Canton by storm, in AD 877, and slaughtering 120,000 of Mohammedans, Jews, Christians and Parsees'; the ninth-century source is not given by Finn. It is thus possible, or even probable, that Jacob was drawing on an Islamic text known to him, or on an Islamic tradition, in the writing of his own account of earlier Chinese history. There also

appear to be Islamic sources elsewhere in Jacob's narrative, as in his
account of the Jews of 'the island of Carnoran', p. 419–20.

38. MS. *gran mastri della medicina*; *mastri* has the sense of teachers, or
    guides.

39. So far as I know, there is no confirmation of Chinese scruples on such
    matters.

40. Presumably Jacob is referring to a vessel like a Chinese junk.

41. Although Jacob declares that he was 'not able to find the truth' about
    'Alofeno', more usually known as Olopan, this is a reasonably accurate
    account of the Roman missionary who is said to have come to China in
    the seventh century. He obtained an edict in AD 638 from the then
    emperor Tai Zong, permitting him to build a church at Chang'an.

42. This is surely an exaggeration; the subsequent reference to 'a thousand
    people' even more so.

43. The suggestion here seems to be that porcelain was being produced in
    Zaitun. However, it is more likely to have been the decoration of such
    wares to which Jacob refers.

44. This suggests that there was in Zaitun something akin to a daily press,
    which in addition to publishing decrees also contained the 'acts of the
    citizens' and was distributed free.

45. MS. *in francesco*.

46. MS. *delle nostre contrade*; this almost certainly signifies the regions, or
    cities, of what is now Italy.

47. An early, if unspecific, sense of Italy as a single entity is surely present
    here. Dante uses *Italico* to signify that which pertains to 'Italy' in
    *Paradiso*, IX, 25–6.

48. 'Cremation, which was certainly less costly than burial, had become
    widespread, especially among the lower and middle classes. This prac-
    tice, so contrary to traditional ways, had been increasing since the end
    of the tenth century in several regions of China (Hopei, Shansi and the
    maritime provinces of the south-east) in spite of opposition from the
    government,' J. Gernet, *Daily Life in China, op. cit.*, p.173.

49. 22 August 1271.

50. This must refer to the fair at the time of Ascension.

51. Written in Greek in the manuscript, the word 'chaos', which is followed
    by a classic imprecation written in Hebrew, once signified the shapeless
    mass from which the universe had been formed at Creation. (It has
    now lost such resonance entirely.) The prospect of a return to such a
    condition clearly represented to a pious Jew the most fearsome that
    might be imagined. It is therefore an extravagant simile for Jacob to have
    used here, and would probably not have been employed by an orthodox
    Talmudist.

52. There must be some doubt about Jacob's observation here; mutton is not
    commonly eaten in southern China.

53. I think that 'us' is intended to refer to the Jews. However, I do not know of other evidence that there were *female* Jewish merchants and brokers in the middle ages, but it is very probable.

54. 'Unclean' fish would have included crustaceans and eels.

55. Presumably water-clocks.

56. Plainly a gong.

57. MS. *mingendo ver la strada*.

58. The Sabbath Netzavim fell upon 5 September 1271, and the Jewish New Year on 7 September 1271.

59. The Day of Atonement, 16 September 1271. Although Jacob tells us that he 'abstains from all food' on this day, it is noticeable that he appears to spend much of it considering the variety of foodstuffs available in Zaitun.

60. MS. *daini della cà*.

61. Milk and cheese have always been avoided and disliked by most Chinese, especially in the south, but not on religious or hygienic grounds. Jacob's observation that garlic was regarded as an 'abomination' seems unusual, although as J. Gernet notes in *Daily Life in China, op. cit.*, p.135, 'fervent Buddhists … abstained … from eating vegetables with a strong smell (onions or garlic), meat and eggs'.

62. This alludes to former 'state monopolies'; see also pp.258, 264.

63. Between 1265 and 1274, the government of Southern Sung did indeed put notes into circulation, backed by gold and silver, in consequence of which cash coins (mainly of copper) lost much of their value.

64. I have translated *signori delegati dal re* as 'lords-official of the king', the anachronistic word 'mandarin', to which it might be said to correspond, not being used in English until the sixteenth century.

65. MS. *mastro del colto*; presumably master of the Confucian rituals.

66. 30 September 1271.

67. MS. *maligna*; the word means 'disposed to evil'.

68. The continuous equation which Jacob makes between Christianity and idol-worship, magnificently defended and even justified as it is in Jacob's later arguments, nevertheless offends the Talmudic teaching of the great mediaeval rabbi, Salomone ben Isaac of Troyes ('Rashi'), 1040–1105, who ruled that Christianity was *not* to be classed as idolatry.

69. MS. *ordine*; the word has the meaning of spiritual system or organisation.

70. Jewish orthodoxy would condemn all effigies and refuse to make Jacob's distinction.

71. MS. *lignee e dorate*.

72. MS. *immagine*; we would now say 'an illusion', but the word Jacob uses is more complex, meaning 'image', 'representation', 'figuration', and, as I have translated it, 'impression'.

73. MS. *la natura stessa di Dio*. There is more of deism than Hebraism in

this – and Jacob's blunt use of *'Dio'* is uncharacteristic, since he generally prefers the elusive Judaic terms, written in Hebrew abbreviations, which avoid such naming of the godhead. Jacob here shows himself to be a true follower of Maimonides, and outside the bounds of mediaeval rabbinical orthodoxy, in suggesting that the form and substance of the created world *is* God.

## CHAPTER 5

1. These histories are all works which, as far as I know, have not been translated. They include the *Du Cheng Ji Sheng* (1253), the *Men Lianglu* (1275) and the *Wu Liu Jiu Shi* (1280).

2. The word is said to be derived from the Khitan, a nomadic people of the Chinese borders, whose earlier conquests had given the name Kitai to northern China.

3. J. Gernet, *A History of Chinese Civilization*, Cambridge, 1985, p.287.

4. On a wider scale, the fortunes of many Italian trading cities were in part bound up with China's fate; cf. Gernet, who argues that the Italian cities that prospered most in the mediaeval period were those 'at the terminus of the great commercial routes of Asia', *ibid.*, p.347.

5. The manuscript has *'l'umile'* ('the humble one'), *'al sapiente'* ('to the learnèd one'), and *'in questa poverella dimora'* ('in this poor abode'). These terms of self-deprecation by the speaker, and of aggrandisement of the addressee, are sharply observed.

6. Identifiable as a reference to the legendary sovereign Huang-ti, whose period of rule was regarded by the Chinese as a golden age.

7. Clearly Confucius.

8. MS. *reame celeste in terra.*

9. MS. *barattieri*, meaning those men holding public office who take bribes, or who otherwise profit from office.

10. Presumably officials' medals or other tokens of honour were hung at the waist in this period.

11. A polite reference to Jacob himself.

12. 'At the beginning of the twelfth century the custom of cremation, which had grown considerably, was still frowned upon by the government and in various circles: everywhere, in fact, where Confucian traditions were most clung to,' J. Gernet, *Daily Life in China, op. cit.*, p.173.

13. Roughly 8 kg or 18lb weight; that is 2¼lb or 1kg for a Venetian groat.

14. MS. *zittani*; Jacob derives satins from the name of Zaitun, or Zitun as he often calls it. The OED however gives 'satin' as a derivation from the Italian *setino*, from *seta* or silk.

15. MS. *galanga*; a plant of the ginger family, much used as a spice in mediaeval times; a capon might be cooked in ginger, cloves, cinnamon and galingale. It was also used as an aphrodisiac and a narcotic.

16. MS. *allume*; a bulky cargo used in the preliminary processes of the

dyeing and starching of cloth. Before 1275, when it began to be produced in quantity from the mines of Phocaea in Greece, it had to be
brought to Europe from the East, especially China.

17. MS. *il ben e 'l mal d'opre e de' fatti vengono dal fattor stesso e 'l suo voler.*

18. Here Jacob has sought to reconcile the moral law with the rule of reason,
in a way characteristic of the Maimonidean school.

19. Clearly identifiable as Mencius, the Chinese philosopher of the fourth
century BC.

20. 10 October 1271.

21. It is not clear to me what is meant by 'the four punishments'. The
Southern Sung dynasty punishments included the death penalty (in
various forms), exile, forced labour, beating and fines. Nor is there – it
seems – any other source to confirm that such punishments were in
abeyance, or considered 'a wicked act against the malefactor'.

22. To mark the formal coming of age.

23. MS. *cui la cura strigne.*

24. This must mean that 'the faithful Lifenli' had taken down, presumably
in Chinese, what he had heard, and that Jacob obtained some form of
translation from him, which (as I have surmised) must have been greatly
elaborated in the writing.

25. The words 'May God forgive what is written here' are added in Hebrew
in the margin.

26. MS. *alcuni beono oppio e dormono dopo ben iii di.*

27. From this description of 'priests' in hats of black silk with a border of
gold (*al vivagno d'oro*) and dressed in black gowns (*cappe nere*), they
would seem to have been Taoists, although why they should have been
in the stews of Zaitun Jacob does not suggest.

28. Latin in MS: *aut in postico aut in porta feminea aut inter crura.* Here, as
in another such passage which follows, Jacob resorts to Latin, perhaps
for purposes of concealment from less educated co-religionists (including his family members ?), perhaps from some kind of personal
reticence. The former seems the more likely.

29. It is notable that Jacob has made no reference to the passage of the
Sabbaths in this period, as if he had lost sense of time while searching in
the 'underworld' of the city for his lost helmsman.

30. MS. *come lo stelo di fioretto che s'inclina al vento.*

31. It is not clear what this means, but it presumably refers to her dancing.

## CHAPTER 6

1. i.e. 26 November 1271. There is a puzzle about this, forty-five days
having elapsed since a date (12 October 1271) was last given by Jacob,
on p.180. This suggests either that Jacob spent longer in the 'underworld' of Zaitun than he is ready to admit, or (more likely) that he was
engaged in business transactions – such as the ordering of porcelains –

and did not choose to record what had occurred. However, the given chronology of the search for, and discovery of, Turiglioni is thrown into some doubt.

2. Presumably the vision of his father's death, p.203.

3. 29 November 1271.

4. 5 December 1271.

5. MS. *cocer 'l drago e uccider la fenice*.

6. Jacob here seems to be claiming (importantly) that the magicians and seers among the Chinese lacked the learning of their Italian counterparts.

7. I think this must mean 'among the Jews', rather than among the 'Italians', but it was true of both.

8. 'Doctrine' *(dottrina)* contains the sense of 'teaching', 'knowledge', 'theory' and even 'science'.

9. MS. *sembiano savi a loro che li odono*.

10. MS. *l'oblivion*; an educated Latinism. See appendix on Jacob's Language, p.462.

11. MS. *volti*. There is an untranslatable pun in this: *volto* means both 'face' and 'turned'.

12. MS. *a rivelar e rinovarlo*. The whole of this passage is intensely Hebraic in its formulation, the obligation to 'review the world' being at the heart of the Talmudic concept of *Tikkun*, the redemption or the *repair* of the world's ills.

13. MS. *ipocrisia*; seemingly in the same sense as our usage of the word.

14. Literally, those who 'place themselves apart' *(parteggiano)*, and, by extension, form themselves into factions or parties of particular interest. A few lines above, the word *parte* is used by Jacob in a phrase I have translated somewhat loosely as 'of the party of'. A closer translation might have been 'on the side of'.

15. 12 December 1271.

16. This must mean tigers, since there is no record of lions in these parts.

17. This can only mean that Jacob feared the disorder of an interregnum and the breakdown of law until a successor's writ had been established, during which time the travelling merchant would be particularly vulnerable.

18. MS. *della mia terra e fe*; that is, of Italy and his Jewish beliefs.

19. This is inexact on Jacob's part; it is usury among Jews which is expressly forbidden.

20. Jacob here echoes the (dubious) position of Maimonides and his followers; cf. M. Cohen, *Under Crescent and Cross: The Jews in the Middle Ages*, Princeton, 1994, who argues, *passim*, that in the thirteenth century the Jews of the Islamic world on the contrary experienced much less persecution and hardship than the Jews of Western Christendom. Moreover, this hostile remark of Jacob's is at odds with the earlier sense

of his judgments upon Jewish-Muslim relations. Scholars have traced the view which it reflects to Maimonides' 'Epistle to Yemen' in which he refers to Muslims 'debasing and humiliating us', A. Kalkin and D. Hartman, *Crisis and Leadership: Epistles of Maimonides*, Philadelphia, 1985, p.126.

21. Although Jacob does not refer to any specific incident, the Dominican Order had condemned the Torah in 1234 as being 'prejudicial to the faith'.

22. This is clearly a reference to the sacking of Ancona by Saracen forces in AD 840 and 850; 'may they rest in peace,' written in Hebrew in the manuscript, is an unusual imprecation if the victims were all Gentiles, but it may imply a local tradition that there were Jews among them.

23. Arabic in MS.; Al-Hakim (996–1021) was the Fatimid Caliph of Egypt who indiscriminately destroyed Jerusalem's synagogues and churches, including the Church of the Holy Sepulchre. By 'princes of the Berbers' Jacob must mean the Berber Almohads, whose conquests in Yemen, North Africa and Spain from the mid-1140s brought death and terror to both Christians and Jews. Although the references are brief, they are (here) specific and accurate.

24. This event, evidently a matter of common knowledge to Jews two centuries later, took place in Granada on 31 December 1066, when a mob killed Joseph Ha-Nagid, also called Joseph ibn Nagrela, who was the royal vizier of Spain.

25. MS. *il minore*; that is, the speaker. 'The greater' is of course Jacob.

26. The dates of the Zhou dynasty (1122–255 BC) make such antiquity of Jewish settlement in China very unlikely, but not wholly impossible.

27. This is exact, corresponding to the prohibition of Genesis 32: 32.

28. That is, the Jewish people as a whole.

29. Presumably outside the Jewish 'house of study', and thus outside the community itself.

30. MS. *strazio*. This is a very harsh word, meaning 'suffering', 'pain' and 'torture'.

31. Hebrew in MS.; in the margin the words 'Amen and Amen' (in Hebrew) have been added.

32. 29 and 30 December 1271.

## CHAPTER 7

1. Sir Thomas Browne refers to this tradition, declaring that Aristotle 'acknowledged all that was written in the Law of Moses, and became at last a Proselyte', *Pseudodoxia Epidemica*, 4th ed., 1658, p.445. Browne cites as his sources 'Rabbi ben Joseph' and 'Abraham ben Mordecai Farissol', an Italian rabbi, who, Browne declares vaguely, had it in turn from 'an Egyptian book'.

2. However, the writings of Marsiglio (*c.*1275–1342), with their early

notions of popular sovereignty, and of William of Ockham (*c*.1280–1349), with his equally 'modern' ideas that 'all mortals are born free', and that it is the duty of rulers to maintain the rights and liberties of citizens, were still to come.

3. 1 January 1272.

4. MS. *grande popolano*. This could mean, simply, a 'great commoner', or 'great man of the people'. But from consideration of what Jacob conveys of Suninsciou's authority, and of the seeming disposition of powers in the city, I have preferred the suggestion (which I believe to be contained in the word *popolano*) that he possessed some kind of formal status as a leader of the mercantile interest. 'Burgess', although an alien word, is the nearest I can get to this sense.

5. MS. *gente nova*; a phrase which seems to correspond almost exactly to that of *nouveaux riches*, or *arrivistes*.

6. MS. *maladetto*; this expletive plainly points forward to his role in the conflicts of the city, as Jacob reports them.

7. Suninsciou was presumably referring to 'the way' of the Taoists, but it is not specified as such.

8. MS. *chi vien piu vicin' al foco vien piu presto caldo*.

9. MS. *libero arbitrio*; I have generally preferred 'free judgment' rather than 'free will' as a translation of this phrase.

10. As far as I know, there is no evidence that the Southern Sung emperor had a monopoly in such trade, although it seems to have been the case in Northern Sung under the Tartars.

11. MS. *il dritto della libertate*.

12. January 1272.

13. 5 and 6 January 1272.

14. MS. *a tener gran parlamento*.

15. MS. *uom libero in stato franco*.

16. This must refer to orphans.

17. MS. *aitorio*; this is a payment of aid, alms or subsidy.

18. Presumably this means that the king cannot keep the realm within bounds, or maintain it in order.

19. MS. *piu mercantanzie vi si vendono piu si comperano*.

20. MS. *come si coce lo pesce piccol*; perhaps, as we would say, 'don't overdo it'.

21. MS. *sanza comune incarco e 'l negozio civil*.

22. Salt and iron had traditionally been imperial monopolies; here Pitaco is suggesting that the merchants of Zaitun were now exercising some form of control even over these commodities.

23. This is a tantalising reference to what may have been an organised rebel movement, but we learn no more of it.

24. This is one of the few references in the manuscript to the common internal problems of order in the other Southern Sung cities.

25. MS. *torna cosi la rota della mercatanzia*.

26. MS. *sulle punte.*
27. MS. *una tegghia di fazioli caldi.*
28. This indicates Jacob's strong sympathy, but it is not clear whether it is both for the earthiness of the merchant's sentiments and for the redeeming laughter of other men, or for the latter only.
29. This suggests that the merchants of Zaitun were also local landowners.
30. MS. *a sospigner Anscinen con le mani.*
31. That is, according to the physical laws of the material world. As water flows downwards, so, presumably, will wealth.
32. MS. *disfar*; literally 'to unmake', it also has the sense of 'to decompose', as of a corpse.
33. Latin in MS.; *res tantum valet quantum vendi potest.* It is perhaps clearest in these exchanges between Jacob and the merchant Anlisciu that the manuscript was written at some leisure, containing arguments which could not have been put forward at the time. Also see appendix on Jacob's Language, p.462.
34. MS. *nostro grande Aquina*; these are extraordinary epithets for a 'pious Jew' to use of Aquinas, and point to the breadth of the former's sympathies and learning. They also reveal how far Jacob stood from rabbinic orthodoxy.
35. The 'first' presumably being that 'a thing is worth as much as it can be sold for'.
36. The Italian word, *grado*, has the meaning of 'rank', or 'social position' as well as of 'steps', as in a ladder. Here I think it could refer to the places in the assembly where the merchants were ranged, presumably together.
37. Some twenty words written in Hebrew in the manuscript; the passage has something of a Christian ring, but is traceable to the Mishnaic Sanhedrin 10:3. (The erring figure is there described as 'the Epicurean'.)
38. 9 January 1272.
39. It appears that Jacob's fellow merchants went by land to Chinscie (Kinsay), but returned by sea.
40. MS. *novecentomillia fumanti.* This seems an impossible figure; at, say, four persons per 'hearth', it would give a total population of over 3.5 million. The preceding and following figures appear greatly exaggerated also.
41. 20 and 27 January 1272.
42. MS. *promessa*; this perhaps indicates a formal undertaking by Jacob to the girl's parents, before departure from Ancona, that he would be responsible for her safety.
43. MS. *oppinioni*: this word seems to have had a weightier sense than our 'opinions', meaning 'judgments', 'thoughts' or 'beliefs'.
44. MS. *gigli d'oro.*
45. MS. *bozzi.*
46. This can be precisely dated; it was the early evening of 29 January 1272.

1. 4 February 1272. This date does not, however, square with Jacob's earlier assertion (see p.209) that the sages met 'every twentieth day', if his earlier appearance is dated as 8 or 9 December 1271.

2. Presumably for his earlier intervention in their quarrels, as well as for his contribution to the first assembly debate.

3. The speech, or diatribe, which ensues – to which I have made substantial cuts – shows the most obvious signs of having been elaborated *ex post facto*.

4. MS. *simonia*; this was the ecclesiastical offence of trafficking in sacred objects or profiting in other ways from church office.

5. The manuscript has *'usura anteriore'* and *'usura posteriore'* for these two forms of usury. Jacob's use of Latinised terms suggests familiarity with Church discourses on the subject, but I have been unable to identify the origin of the terms. The citation of Rabbi Gamaliel is traceable to the Mishnaic text Baba Metzia 5:10.

6. Latin in MS.; *ad honorem dei et ecclesie Romane et summi pontificis*. This was obviously an expression of savage irony for Jacob, but discloses some knowledge of Church Latin rubrics. The daring use of such invective by a Jew plainly made dissemination of the manuscript impossible beyond a small circle of trusted friends; see pp.2–3.

7. MS. *a succiar i giudei nel nome della croce*. The 'holy cardinal of my city' is almost certainly a further reference to Cardinal Rainer, or Raniero di Viterbo, papal legate in Ancona from *c.*1244 to 1249.

8. MS. *università degli iguali*; i.e., a corporate body of equals.

9. This may be an allusion to Jacob's experiences in Naples.

10. The picture of scholarly collaboration which Jacob briefly draws here may well be based on first-hand experience of it in Naples at the court of Frederick II, see pp.16–19. As to particular collaborations of this kind in Italy, it is known for example that Moses ben Solomon of Salerno (d. 1279) collaborated with a Dominican monk, Nicholas of Giovinazzo, in writing a commentary on Maimonides' *Guide to the Perplexed*. (See C. Sirat, *A History of Jewish Philosophy in the Middle Ages*, Cambridge, 1985, p.266.)

11. MS. *sanza titol di fama*.

12. MS. *fratello stesso di quel om*.

13. What seems to have happened here (in Jacob's account!) is that while Bartolomeo attempted to prevent Jacob speaking further, Jacob himself wished the priest to continue, and for his words to be translated by 'my trusted Lifenli'. However Jacob, unusually, gives no more than a brief summary of the priest's diatribe, but there is a strong sense of authenticity in the passage.

14. It is not clear whether the epithet refers to Fra Bartolomeo or to priests in general.

15. This is the first clear evidence that these words at least might have been spoken by Jacob at the time he claims, even though, by February 1272, Jacob's assertion was false. Pope Clement IV had died in November 1268, but because of political conflicts among the cardinals no successor was elected until September 1271, nearly three years later, when Theobald of Piacenza was chosen. Thus, at the time when Jacob left Italy, it was true that there was no pope; and it seems that Jacob (and presumably Fra Bartolomeo) still did not know the true facts in February 1272.

16. This is plainly an allusion to the continuous conflicts between the Church and the Holy Roman Empire. Thus, Frederick II, whom the pope had crowned as 'Emperor of Rome', was deposed in 1245 by Innocent IV.

17. MS. *esser cristiano assessino nel nom di quel uomo è gran villania e quando dicono che la croce non vole far altro che diritto è menzogna.*

18. In the spring of 1204, seventeen years before Jacob's birth, Crusaders sacked Constantinople, heart of the Eastern Church, wreaking immense damage. 'Crusaders though they were, sailing to a Christian city, they made no attempt at a peaceful approach. When some fishing boats got in the way, they instantly attacked them; and when the fleet sailed... close under the walls of the city, the soldiers on deck were already cleaning their weapons for battle... It was Holy Week, but this did not deter the warriors of Christ. In three days of half-crazed rape, looting and destruction the soldiers sacked Byzantium once and for all... The greatest treasures of classical times were wantonly destroyed... Constantinople was left stripped of its glories,' J. Morris, *The Venetian Empire*, Harmondsworth, 1990, pp.28, 39, 41.

19. Latin in MS.; *domini canes*, a play on words of great mordancy.

20. MS. *fue il miglior uom che mai fosse.*

21. Hebrew in MS.; an epithet often reserved in the Jewish tradition to King David, and probably therefore a reference to the Psalms. Jacob appears to be objecting to the 'appropriation' of the Psalter in Christian prayer.

22. This is the Hebrew form for 'Jesus'; the first time he is referred to as other than 'that man'.

23. That is, by crucifixion.

24. It clearly seems from this that the 'sages (*savi*)' were divided into factions which reflected those in the city as a whole, some being of the merchants' 'party' and others supporters of the elderly Pitaco, and that they had grouped themselves together physically during this meeting.

25. MS. *poiche non fassi cristiano.*

26. MS. *arde*; another fierce pun.

27. This appears to mean that the sages and the people, as well as the merchants, were divided among themselves. This is the first specific reference to division in the merchants' ranks.

28. If the merchant Anlisciu was really among those who 'sent for' Jacob in order that he might again address the *concilio*, this suggests two things: first, that the merchants' 'party' was increasingly dictating events in the city, and, second, more speculatively, that Jacob was perhaps being unwittingly drawn by the merchant interest into some kind of trap, in which he would discredit himself (and Pitaco) by an intemperate display of animus, or by excessive intrusiveness into the city's affairs, to the benefit of the merchants' party. Could Lifenli have been warning Jacob against this?

29. I take 'us' to refer to the Jews, but it could as easily refer to common Italian beliefs at the time.

30. No doubt God and the angels were exempt from this statement of rule! The assertion is clear evidence of the influence of contemporary Aristotelianism on Jacob's thought.

31. In 1254, less than two decades earlier, a papal decree had ordered the Jews to 'cease from their magical practices', presumably having to do with astrology and divination, as Jacob indicates.

32. Latin in MS.: *id est contra naturam*. Jacob's general assertion here is not in accord with orthodox Jewish belief, since it would also appear to exclude further acts of divine intercession, or miracles, in human affairs – those of the escape from Egypt and its aftermath being the last. (However, it would serve as an answer to the modern question 'Where was God at Auschwitz?')

33. That is, those who worshipped the 'Golden Calf'.

34. MS. *ispirti in aere*.

35. Roughly equivalent to eighty miles. If this was the ostrich, as it sounds, Jacob's rationalism has betrayed him.

36. MS. *lo gran colubro di Mitzraim* (the last word is written in Hebrew).

37. MS. *castella*; this must mean not 'castles' but hamlets surrounded by a high clay or mud wall, such as are still seen throughout rural China.

38. 5 February 1272.

39. Presumably the letters of the Hebrew alphabet which he is being taught to read.

40. MS. *avversaro*; Jacob gives this name to several individuals – including the 'faithful Lifenli' – when he is at odds with them.

41. Jacob does not answer his own questions in the passage which follows, and thus does not say, or avoids saying, that the Jews are categorically right or wrong. His piety would not have permitted an openly sceptical answer as to Jewish dietary prescriptions. But that he should ask such questions at all in a considered passage, undoubtedly written after the event it records, brings him close enough to a sceptical position.

42. 7 February 1272.

43. MS. *dugentosesanta passi vinegiani*; a Chinese *li* is roughly a quarter of a mile.

44. This sounds somewhat like Yangzhou, but the other names are unidentifiable; the 'thousand great cities' is clearly an exaggeration.

45. Or 'Jiang'; that is, the Yangtze-Jiang.

46. Plainly the Huang He, or Yellow River.

47. This must have been the type of cassia that produced senna leaves, dried for use as a laxative.

48. For dyeing and textile-processing.

49. MS. *tante ispezie che nonne vegnono in nostre contrade*.

50. 12 February 1272.

51. MS. *mia masnada*; *masnada* means a group of intimates, doubtless Jacob's co-religionists.

52. Plainly the Saracen (or Arab) captain of Jacob's argosy, hired in Basra.

53. MS. *difensione*. I have translated this as 'resistance', rather than the more obvious 'defence', since the word had the connotation of stalwart opposition.

54. This is accurately reported by Jacob: Xiangyang and Fanzheng were under siege by the Tartars first in 1257 and then from 1268 onwards. They fell in March 1273, a year after this speech was given.

55. That is, a wall about 50 feet, or 15 metres, high.

56. This turned out to be true. Zaitun did not fall to the Mongols until 1277.

57. That is, in the south-east of Southern Sung.

58. MS. *dietro a questa gente*; presumably this means the Tartars, or at least the Tartar invaders.

59. MS. *'l voler di fuggir nostro nimico*.

60. Two of these names are clearly identifiable: the nomadic and tribal Tangut, who conquered parts of western China in the tenth century; and the Khitan, with whom a peace treaty was signed in AD 1004, but at the price of a vast annual tribute in silver and silk. The 'Uceni' may signify the Jürchen, whose armies took Nanjing and Kinsai in 1129–30, and who reached as far south as Ningbo in Zhejiang province, some 600 miles north of Zaitun.

61. MS. *'l popolo*. It is not, of course, clear exactly to whom this word refers, nor in what numbers 'the people' were present, nor whether they had places assigned to them, perhaps in some form of enclosure or gallery. A further puzzle is that the words attributed to the questioner among them are couched – at least in the Italian – rather formally, and suggest that the interlocutor is an educated person. However, this may also be a product of Jacob's elaboration after the event.

62. MS. *merta*. That is, 'what is the merit of...?'

63. Might this be an oblique allusion to Jacob, supposing him to have been a doctor of medicine?

64. Identifiable as Temujin, original name of Genghis Khan.

65. MS. *peregrino*, also containing the sense of 'wanderer', or 'traveller'.

66. MS. *case*; this can also mean 'households', 'families' and even 'lineages'.
67. MS. *famigliari*; literally, 'family-members'.

## CHAPTER 9

1. MS. *giovinetta simplice*; the instability of the spelling in Jacob's manuscript, is well characterised here, *'giovanetta'* and *'giovinetta'* both being
   employed within the space of some two dozen lines. There are many
   examples of a similar kind, with variant spellings sometimes occurring in
   successive lines; see appendix on Jacob's Language.
2. 20 February 1272. Jacob's specifying of the date on almost every day
   suggests that he is marking the final, historic phase of his experience of
   Zaitun with particular care.
3. There is surely a 'Baron Munchausen' element of self-aggrandisement in
   this.
4. MS. *del pedagogo*. I have translated literally as 'teacher of the young',
   rather than the now less specific 'pedagogue', because it is plain from the
   discussion that this is what is intended.
5. Presumably according to the dialectic method of Talmudic discourse.
6. MS. *dota*, a learnèd word.
7. MS. *son simiglianti in essenza loro*.
8. MS. *apti*, a pure Latinism; see appendix on Jacob's Language. The entire
   passage shows an Aristotelian cast of mind, or at least Aristotelian influence.
9. MS. *lo ver per se*. It was a temptation to translate this as 'truth *in itself*'
   – that is, a transcendent truth – but it is plain from the context that
   Anfenscian did not mean this. Jacob has devoted some care, recognisable
   from the elaborate and scholarly language he employs, to Anfenscian's
   arguments, either because the latter truly spoke in this way at the time;
   or because Jacob saw merit and interest in his views despite the former's
   protests against them; or because it makes the account of his exchanges
   more weighty and therefore creditable to him. It could also have been a
   mixture of the three.
10. Presumably because of Anfenscian's reference earlier to 'many gods'.
11. MS. *l'ordin de' numeri*.
12. 20 February 1272; but it is not clear why Jacob should interject this
    here.
13. This epithet, written in Hebrew in the manuscript, now accompanies
    each reference to the 'Adversary', or 'Satan', whom Jacob sees, or thinks
    he sees, in Anfenscian.
14. MS. *posposta al libero arbitrio del giovane*.
15. It is not clear to whom this refers; perhaps it signifies that there was a
    general conflict among those engaged in education in the city.
16. MS. *lettere*. However Pitaco would not have referred to 'letters' of the
    alphabet but to Chinese characters; Jacob imposes the same word on

Anfenscian a few lines later. But that Jacob understood the function of Chinese characters, at least in part, is plain below (see p.358).

17. MS. *a far fissi e fermi i principi morali.*

18. MS. *fonte unico ond' ogni vero vene.*

19. MS. *ragionamento ... esperienza ... analogia e ... regola.*

20. MS. *li vincoli naturali.*

21. The detail, even the relish, of Jacob's account suggests that he is giving full weight (and consideration) to the positions, however abhorrent to him, of 'the Adversary'. Was he, at least in part, beguiled by them?

22. Hebrew in MS.; we are invited by Jacob to believe that he addressed Anfenscian directly with this epithet, and in Hebrew!

23. MS. *al passo che lo convien.*

24. That is, who judged *their own* times as if they were in the past.

25. MS. *i numeri di Manci.* This suggests the use of particular mathematic rules, or perhaps tables, adopted in Southern Sung China.

26. The foremost poets of the Tang dynasty.

27. MS. *il labore piue aspro a denari piccoli.*

28. This is not 'Torah truth', but clearly derived from the famous first sentence of Aristotle's *Metaphysics.* It was a text which stood at the heart of mediaeval philosophical education (and which Jacob probably studied at Naples). That he should have asserted it here as a cardinal moral principle of his own demonstrates how Aristotelian ideas were assimilated into Judaic thought, including among the pious.

29. MS. *alla luce della ragion.*

30. MS. *ostante.*

31. This is almost certainly a reference to Solomon ben Judah ibn Gabirol (*c.*1021–*c.*1058), grammarian, philosopher and poet, and one of the first teachers of neo-Platonism.

32. MS. *a fretta.*

33. MS. *vesti novi.* This must have the sense of 'clean' or 'fresh' clothes, as enjoined for the Sabbath.

34. It is believed by pious Jews that he who atones for his sins on the eve of the Sabbath receives the blessing of the ministering angels.

35. Did Jacob hear Buccazuppo weeping?

36. MS. *alla spranga.*

37. 21 February 1272.

38. MS. *lassar.*

39. MS. *doglie.*

40. MS. *della legge naturale.* By 'natural law' Jacob (once more) plainly does not mean the moral law but the law governing the natural, or material, world.

41. MS. *della matera vital la piue piccola.*

42. MS. *'l batter de' polsi.*

43. MS. *uniti.* This word appears to mean that the Chinese believed that

they would come to share the powers of 'the Creator', and thus be able to rule nature itself.

44. It is (again) not wholly clear whether Jacob means specifically Jewish sages, or the sages of 'the West' as a whole, or of Italy. His immediate citation of Maimonides – in his capacity as physician – suggests the first.

45. MS. *i mali corporali respondono alle travaglia e duoli animali.*

46. MS. *folgor che scote lo ciel.*

47. MS. *magico polve che scoppia*; plainly an 'explosive' powder.

48. MS. *riempir stecchi di bambagio.*

49. Certainly a reference to Maimonides.

50. The Chaldeans were regarded by the biblical Jews as magicians, a perception reflected throughout the Talmud.

51. It is a measure of Jacob's *intellectual* grasp and persistence that he is able to explain all this accurately, doubtless as the result of thorough questioning of interlocutors. But the *merchant* in him is also quick to grasp its 'market' aspect.

52. MS. *quaderni.* I have translated this as 'books', which is allowable, but it possibly meant to Jacob something flimsier, our 'pamphlets'. The word is also used by Dante, *Purgatorio*, XII, 105, where it is said to have the meaning of an 'issue' of documents, perhaps of a single sheet.

53. MS. *incostro bruno.*

54. MS. *impressi*; literally, images *impressed* (on paper).

55. MS. *va troppo al profondo.*

56. MS. *come se fossero medesma cosa.* It is not finally clear what Jacob means here, but he seems to be suggesting that certain kinds of enquiry, gratuitously undertaken, dissolve moral distinctions between good and bad – or perhaps, 'useful' and 'useless' – knowledge. If so, this is a very early ethical criticism of the empirical scientific method, although elsewhere he appears to approve it.

57. MS. *eccesso di lume che abbaglia li occhi.*

## CHAPTER 10

1. 22 February 1272.

2. This suggests that they were from the community of 'Chinese Jews' in Zaitun; see pp.130–31.

3. Hebrew in MS. This is the first time that Jacob has extended this protective epithet, generally reserved to co-religionists, to his faithful servant.

4. MS. *disposti uno contra al altro.* This is the first time that the elders and merchants are described as being 'arrayed' against one another *en bloc*, in consequence of the disturbances. It is tempting, but doubtless wrong, to see them as embryonic 'estates of the realm'.

5. Unusually, Jacob does not give his name. He appears from the description

to have been a humble individual who may have called out from his place, as appears to have occurred in earlier debates.

6. Lotacie, earlier described as 'a man young in years and thin in body', had previously spoken forcibly against resistance to the Tartars; see pp.319 ff.

7. The use of the first person plural clearly suggests that Uainsciu was speaking, or claiming to speak, for others than himself, perhaps for a 'radical' or 'rebel' group earlier alluded to in the text; see p.265. But since he later invokes the Sung emperor in aid of his arguments, he cannot be equated (anachronistically) with a 'leftist' or a 'democrat', tempting as this might be in view of his professed belief in the equality of man. It is noteworthy that he also disclaims the effort to 'make men equal', but not the assertion that men *are* equal.

8. MS. *orbo*. This could also mean 'blind', but here it seems to have its older Latin meaning of 'bereft', 'destitute', 'orphaned'.

9. MS. *il remunerar de' esser altretanto e biasimo anco.*

10. Latin in MS. *corpus sive universitas.* Jacob's use of Latin terms here points once more to the speech not having been made in this form at the time, or certainly not with this technical vocabulary.

11. MS. *la civitate.*

12. MS. *voler comun.*

13. This is a trenchant expression of the Judaic recoil from kingship and absolutism; see p.244.

14. MS. *obbligati a niuno e neente.*

15. MS. *de' esser chiamato.* The word 'summoned' is again vague, but does not of itself suggest election – as we would understand it – by the constituent body. However, what Jacob is recommending may have been the method of creating civic bodies in mediaeval Italian city-states.

16. MS. *al libero arbitrio di ciascheduno.*

17. MS. *avrebbero ardimento d'uscir di casa.*

18. MS. *messi alla quistion.* This also signifies 'put to the rack', but suggests a projection by Jacob upon the Chinese of the methods of the Inquisition.

19. MS. *posti in bando.*

20. MS. *lo cattivo*; literally, 'the captive'. (The word *'cattivo'* has come to mean 'wicked' in modern Italian.)

21. MS. *come se fosse om libero.*

22. MS. *mal al mal.*

23. MS. *feruta.* The qualification as to a son striking his parent is traceable to the Mishnaic Baba Kamma, 8:5, where the punishment for such an assault in which 'a wound is caused' is death.

24. An odd politeness for someone identified by Jacob as the embodiment of Satan.

25. The whole of this passage exerted a strong influence upon me in the writing of *The Principle of Duty.*

26. Jacob seems to be alluding here to the Adversary's earlier views on education; see pp.333 ff.

27. Jacob's argument is not logically complete, since he presumably also means to say that to live in peace is a form of liberty, while to destroy the city is to lose one's freedom also.

28. MS. *dovete vietar anco molte cose che vostra legge vi permette.*

29. MS. *a sentir la vergogn'.*

30. 24 February 1272.

31. MS. *riposo.* 'Duties' would refer to the morning religious observances, but a truly pious Jew is not expected to 'rest', or to sleep, thereafter.

32. MS. *essendo attenti ad ascoltar le cose parlate.*

33. MS. *altri ufficiali maggiori.*

34. This is the only point at which Jacob openly declares his partisanship in this way.

35. MS. *ne bocche rosse ne lingue bianche*; Jacob's interpretation of the meaning of these terms seems plausible.

36. MS. *che venne gran pensero al cor mio e l'animo mio cominciò a gonfiar.* It is not clear what Jacob's 'great thought' was; the passages that follow contain a gathering-up of ideas which he has already expressed elsewhere in fragmentary form, ideas which were themselves rooted in his learning, both Hebraic and secular.

37. MS. *la cittadinanza.*

38. MS. *farlo ciascheduno accorto del suo dover.* This entire passage, from which I drew freely, had great influence upon me in the writing of *The Prinicple of Duty.*

39. MS. *la gente dev' esser obligata per patto.*

40. MS. *negozio civil.*

41. MS. *vincoli.*

42. MS. *nel cor d'ogni esser uman sussiste l'imago del dover.*

43. MS. *strida.*

44. MS. *al disderio d'agir bene e rettamente.*

45. MS. *se Dio v'aiuta*; one of the very few places in the manuscript where this is not written in Hebrew.

46. MS. *ne ritrarsi ne torcersi dal cammin del dover.*

47. MS. *sueti*, a pure Latinism; see appendix on Jacob's Language, p.462.

48. Written in a mixture of Italian and Hebrew in the manuscript, with *'lume'* for 'light'; cf. Isaiah 49:6.

49. This comparison by Jacob of man with beast contradicts his earlier recoil from the notion that there is a fine line between man and animal, see p.373.

50. MS. *la farne parlar il mondo intiero alla vostra vergogna eterna.*

51. Could this have been the same 'Cian' (Chang), earlier described as a 'sage', and with whom Jacob was in dispute about the Jews?

52. A very strong epithet for Jacob to use of a non-Jew.

53. This Confucian version of the 'Golden Rule' in the form stated by Pitaco is almost identical to the Hebraic version.

54. MS. *alli peregrini dalle terre che son di lontano.*

55. MS. *che si de' far.*

56. Jacob seems to have changed his ground on the condition of the poor, having earlier remarked on their indigence, e.g. pp.127, 159, 250.

57. MS. *iacer sul dolce lettolo.*

58. MS. *come giovine popolano.*

59. This clearly means 'you adopt a fierce demeanour on behalf of the poor'.

60. MS. *vostre scritture.*

61. This seems to be a more radical, or 'egalitarian', position than the 'Adversary' had previously adopted.

62. MS. *senza cagion e ragion.*

63. MS. *tratteremo cosi come ragion esige.*

64. MS. *sor lo terzo grado di porpora ... vermiglio ... color del ciel*; the last presumably means 'sky-blue' or 'turquoise'.

65. MS. *senza interdetto e fine.*

66. MS. *a voi manca 'l valor a dirlo.*

67. MS. *sano*; the word carries the connotations of 'healthy', 'normal', hence 'sound'.

68. MS. *consiglier.*

69. MS. *quale sovrano.*

70. MS. *incarcato come giudice.*

71. MS. *signoreggiar*; literally, to 'act as *signore*'. It is not clear precisely what this word means in terms of actual civic function – magistrate? governor? – nor can we detect, behind the account which Jacob gives, what was being offered to him. Pitaco appears to have wished him to be a 'counsellor', a suggestion that Jacob in turn evidently considers to be synonymous with 'judge'; which may itself have been presumption on his part. Once more, that aspect of Jacob's character which is quick to vaunt itself for its prowess seems to be at work here.

72. MS. *nel imperar*; literally, in 'dominating', 'governing', 'taking charge'. (This again seems to be well beyond what Jacob himself claimed – at first – to have been offered to him!)

73. MS. *dal nascimento.*

74. Greek in MS.; *phronesis*; Jacob here uses the original Aristotelian term.

75. Latin in MS.; *prudentia politica.*

76. MS. *cangiar vesta semplice per la porpora real.*

77. See p.201, where Jacob curses Uaiciu presumably for his later calumny, if calumny it was. The citing of Uaiciu by Anfenscian also suggests that some form of surveillance of foreigners, or collection of information, was in operation in Zaitun, as do the other allegations made against Jacob.

78. MS. *appetiti turpi.* We can only speculate on the source of such allegations but, given that Jacob repeatedly uses the epithet 'evil (*maligna*)' of

her, did he himself believe it to be his servant Bertoni?

79. MS. *seminando discordie tra le genti con cotanto acume per cio hanno guadagni.*

80. MS. *duce.*

81. MS. *non pareva om anzi una tempesta.*

82. This seems to be a reply to an earlier criticism of the 'ease' sought, and gained, by the rich merchant.

83. MS. *passata al son de' lodi altrui.*

84. MS. *la rana che sta ad imo del pozzo.*

85. MS. *si lanciarano contro a lui;* plainly *lui* refers to Pitaco.

86. MS. *si corsero a dosso con gran furia.*

87. MS. *gran mischio.*

88. I take it that this refers to notes or summaries made by Lifenli of Jacob's discussions; the son of Pisa seems to have been handsomely rewarded for his service.

89. Given Jacob's earlier references to his hiding of precious merchandise, those were presumably the most valuable of his purchases.

90. 24 February 1272.

91. MS. *di gran portar;* this was the vessel hired in Basra.

92. More than 400 tons.

93. MS. *caricata a pien a prora e poppa.*

94. Equivalent to almost 5 tons; this is surely exaggerated.

95. Equivalent to more than a ton, which also seems an impossible figure.

96. Equivalent to almost 20 tons.

97. MS. *tonda.* But Jacob was mistaken if, as he says, this was the 'twenty-second day of Adar'; the moon would by then have waned considerably.

98. Down-river towards the open sea.

99. MS. *delle nubi di mortalità;* a strange phrase suggesting a cabbalistic influence on Jacob's thought.

100. MS. *per gorbi.*

101. It is unexpected – given Jacob's earlier self-reproach – that God should be praised for the 'desires of the flesh'. But it can doubtless be attributed to the pious Hebraic preference for the celebration, rather than the mortification, of God-given human desire.

102. MS. *principe;* this is a further and clearly fantastical extension of the original proposal which Jacob alleges was put to him by Pitaco.

103. This is the only occasion where such an epithet is used by Jacob in reference to his servants.

## CHAPTER 11

1. Hebrew in MS. This means anything made from grain or flour, which is forbidden at Passover. As the following lines indicate, all traces of it must be ritually removed by Jews from their houses.

2. MS. *un cordone di perle di gran valuta e bracciale di amatisti.*

3. MS. *cose segrete a remover il dolor ch' alcun avesse nel corpo e per questo ognuno ne vuole*; it is notable that Jacob conceals the names of these medicaments, suggesting – as with the entire exclusion of the detail of his profits – that he had at least some kind of 'readership' in mind, from which he wished to keep these particular things private.

4. MS. *v'intravenga ben ogni cosa che farete*.

5. Hebrew in MS.; *shofar*, the 'next day', signifying 'Rosh Hashana', the Jewish New Year.

6. Jacob was of course fasting, so that the prohibition of water on a blazing August day at sea must have been trying in the extreme.

7. Hebrew in MS.; the *terua* is a quavering blast of sound, the *tekia* a sustained blast, calling a congregation to spiritual attention.

8. MS. *risona la gran tromba*.

9. MS. *chi perira di foco e chi d'acqua*.

10. MS. *com il fior che langue o l'ombra che trapassa*.

11. MS. *come la polve che volita o sogno che vola lontan*.

12. MS. *draco rosso*; a red gum-resin, used in dyeing.

13. MS. *murra*; a gum-resin used for perfumes and incense.

14. MS. *stirace*; a fragrant gum-resin, also apparently used as a medicine.

15. Hebrew in MS., *lebonah*. This is equivalent to *olibanum*, an aromatic gum-resin used as incense.

16. I cannot translate this.

17. A spur of the Apennines in the Marche region; the monastery is identifiable as that of Fonte Avellana, and is still active.

18. MS. *incensieri*.

19. It may have been among the large number of islands in the Dahlak archipelago, in the Red Sea off the coast of Ethiopia.

20. 'Hebescia' is almost certainly Ethiopia.

21. Identifiable as Jedda, on the Saudi Arabian coast.

22. Since Jacob makes no claim to have been present on this day, he must have had at least this 'fact' – and perhaps his account of 'Carnoran' in its entirety – at second-hand, most probably from the Jews of Aden.

23. MS. *subito che sono in età d'anni xiii*.

24. Hebrew in MS.; plainly the Nile.

25. 3 November 1272.

26. If Jacob's figures are to be believed, the camel-train was transporting about 200 tons in weight, and the other pack-animals a further 20 tons. (The ten-cantar weight carried by each camel was perhaps equivalent to some 20 bales of silk.) It is not, however, clear whether the merchandise of Lazzaro del Vecchio and Eliezer of Venice was part of this huge quantity.

27. It is not clear who these 'bowmen' were, but it is unlikely that they were the same 'armed men' who had originally sailed with Jacob from Ancona in order to protect his property from pirates, and who are not mentioned again.

28. MS. *selle de' camelli*; I cannot trace this peculiar taboo, but it must have to do with the sense of man's dignity being offended by bearing an animal's saddle on his back.

29. 15 November 1272.

30. The date was 12 February 1272, twelve days before Jacob's departure from Zaitun.

31. That is, Moses and David.

32. MS. *mio fi*; that is, his grandson.

33. MS. *una gran ricorrenza*, a rather heterodox conception for a pious Jew, and more 'oriental' than Talmudic.

34. Jacob does not say who these men were. But they may have been either the heads of an Alexandrian guild of Jewish overseas traders – the more likely surmise – or synagogue elders. (The latter seems less probable since their opinions suggest only a narrow mercantile interest.) It is thought that there were some 4,000 Jews in Alexandria at this time; Jacob gives no figure.

35. 23 December 1272.

36. About 30 tons, or 30,000 kg. This may have been no more than one-fifth or even one-sixth of Jacob's cargo, if his earlier indications as to its volume are to be believed.

37. MS. *dal mio (?) melincenso e legno aloe li quali vendevo a peso d'or*. I cannot identify the first, but it may have been a fragrant incense that smelled of honey; the second was used in the preparation of incense.

38. 'Jacob of Sinigaglia' – now Senigallia, on the Adriatic in central Italy – was perhaps an owner and hirer of ships which plied the Mediterranean ports; or possibly of vessels which served the particular needs of merchants travelling between the Levant and the Adriatic. There was a numerous Jewish community in Senigallia in mediaeval times, and a few families remain.

39. 5 May 1273.

40. The name of a hill standing above Ancona; this therefore has the sense of 'in sight of Cònero'.

41. All these seem very large quantities indeed and can hardly be believed. (Jacob makes no mention of the porcelain he bought in China.)

42. MS. *maramati d'oro*; this might also mean some kind of gold velours.

43. MS. *rabarbaro bono*; used as a purgative and tonic.

44. MS. *perle da pestar*; presumably used as a medicine.

45. Untranslatable; medicinal herbs?

46. Powdered shells were used as an eye-salve.

47. MS. *chelidonia*; a plant of the poppy family, used as a tonic.

48. MS. *turpetto*; used as an emetic.

49. Unidentified: '(?)juice of Lycius'.

50. That is, the 'sign' of circumcision, which is required to be carried out within eight days of birth.

51. For use as rosaries?

52. MS. *uscimmo di nave*.

53. I take the 'sin' to be the giving of such a personal gift to his young female servant.

54. MS. *questa marca di Ancona è loggia mia e mia ca'*.

55. MS. *a far piana mia scrittura; 'piana'* has the sense here of 'easy to understand'. It is a phrase which again suggests that Jacob had a circle of readers, however restricted, in mind.

56. MS. *compier la mia narrazion*.

57. The signature 'Gaio Bonaiuti' (see pp.7–8) is placed 7 cm below the last words of the manuscript.

EPILOGUE

1. J. Gernet, *A History of Chinese Civilization*, Cambridge, 1985, p.370.

2. A typical assessment is contained in W. Rowicki, *The Walled Kingdom*, London, 1991, pp.138–40.

3. H. Yule and H. Cordier (eds), *The Travels of Marco Polo*, New York, 1993 (reprint of 1903 edition), vol. 2, p.235.

4. See also p.11.

5. See also pp.20–21, 401.

6. H. Pirenne, *Economic and Social History of Medieval Europe*, London, 1947, p.223.

7. See also pp.27–9, 31–2.

8. A. Milano, *Storia degli Ebrei in Italia*, Torino, 1963, p.73. (I am grateful to Maria Luisa Moscati Benigni for this reference.)

9. For example in 1475, Bernardino da Feltre, preaching at Trento – where there were a mere thirty Jews – provoked the cruel deaths of some, and the expulsion of the remainder, with the allegation that they had murdered a child called Simone, aged two, in the course of the Passover ritual. Simone was beatified, but the accusation of his ritual murder by the Jews of Trento was withdrawn only in 1965.

10. The Jews were driven from Sicily and the southern regions of Italy – and from Milan too – during the course of the fifteenth and sixteenth centuries; they returned to Milan and Naples only in the mid-nineteenth century.

11. See also pp.3, 8.

12. H. Yule, *Cathay and the Way Thither*, London, 1866, vol. 1, p.172.

# Index